AMERICAN AFRICANS IN GHANA

The John Hope Franklin Series
in African American History and
Culture
Waldo E. Martin Jr. and
Patricia Sullivan,
editors

KEVIN K. GAINES

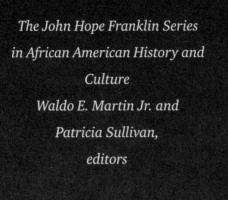

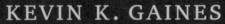

The University of
North Carolina Press
Chapel Hill

American Africans in Ghana

Black Expatriates and the Civil Rights Era

© 2006 The University of North Carolina Press
Manufactured in the United States of America

Designed by Jacquline Johnson
Set in Charter
by Keystone Typesetting, Inc.

This book was published with the assistance of the John Hope
Franklin Fund of the University of North Carolina Press.

Frontispiece: Time Life Pictures/Getty Images.

The paper in this book meets the guidelines for permanence
and durability of the Committee on Production Guidelines for
Book Longevity of the Council on Library Resources.

Library of Congress Cataloging-in-Publication Data
Gaines, Kevin Kelly.
American Africans in Ghana : Black expatriates and the civil
rights era / Kevin K. Gaines.
p. cm. — (The John Hope Franklin series in African American
history and culture)
Includes bibliographical references and index.
ISBN-13: 978-0-8078-3008-6 (cloth: alk. paper)
ISBN-13: 978-0-8078-5893-6 (pbk.: alk. paper)
1. African Americans—Ghana. 2. Ghana—History—1957–
3. Civil rights movements—United States—History—20th
century. I. Title. II. Series.
DT510.43.A37G35 2006
324.089'960730667—dc22   2005031382

10 09 08 07 06   5 4 3 2 1
11 10 09 08 07   5 4 3 2 1

For Penny

CONTENTS

8

ILLUSTRATIONS

ACKNOWLEDGMENTS

Although it is a bit sobering to note that this project has traveled with me to several institutions over the course of more than a decade, it is a singular pleasure to acknowledge the many individuals who have contributed to its completion. Throughout this period, I have had the enormous benefit of the insights of those who lived in or visited Ghana before and during the turbulent years of that nation's first republic. Jan Carew, Martin and Marion Kilson, Robert Lee, Bill Sutherland, Archie Lang, Conor Cruise O'Brien, Bob Fleming, Preston King, Frank and Dona Irvin, Adelaide Cromwell, Tom Feelings, Max and Jean Bond, George Houser, Jim Lacy, Victoria Garvin, Cecile McHardy, Christine Johnson, Hodee Edwards, Curtis Morrow, Ann and Bob Seidman, Russell Warren Howe, Frank Robertson, Cameron Duodu, Manu Herbstein, Vusumsi Make, David Levering Lewis, William Branch, June Milne, Maryse Condé, Pete Seeger, Grace Lee Boggs, George Lamming, Nell Irvin Painter, and Priscilla Stevens Kruize provided important information. Milton Henry, Rudolf Aggrey, and Fred Hadsel provided useful advice. Vera Wells, Joan Cambridge, Richard Gibson, Amowi Sutherland-Addy, and Abdullah H. Abdur-Razzaq provided invaluable assistance.

In Ghana, E. M. Bamfo was a generous and understanding host. Robert Lee, Emanuel Gawuga, Mike Eghan, Kwame Ninsin, Kwame Arhin, and Vibert Cambridge were generous with their time, patiently helping me get my bearings at the start of the project.

The archivists in the manuscripts division at the Schomburg Center for Research in Black Culture deserve special mention for their extraordinary contribution to the preservation and writing of the history of the African diaspora. Over the span of several years and numerous visits, Diana Lachatenere and Andre Elizee were unfailingly helpful and gracious. My scholarship has been immeasurably enriched by their extraordinary work. Thanks also to Jo Ellen Bashir of the Moorland-Spingarn Collection at Howard University and to Karen Jefferson for her fine work with the Kwame Nkrumah Papers at Howard. Patricia Wells facilitated my many visits to the Beinecke

xii Rare Book Library at Yale. Thanks also to Joan Krizack at Northeastern University, Special Collections, and to Nancy Shader at the Seely Mudd Manuscripts Library at Princeton.

Near the start of the project I spent a fruitful year at the National Humanities Center thanks to the transitory but unforgettable community forged by staff members Kent Mulliken, Corbett Capps, and Crystal Waters; librarians Alan Tuttle, Jean Houston, and Eliza Robertson; and fellows and friends, including T. J. and Lois Anderson, Genevieve and Michel Fabre, Wayne and Mary Donna Pond, Samuel Floyd, Jacquelyn Hall, Robert Korstad, George Chauncey, Ronald Gregg, Fitz Brundage, Trudier Harris, Stephen Vlastos, Gerald Horne, Mae Henderson, Ken Wissoker, Cathy Davidson, Don Lopez, Jane Gaines, Mark Tucker, Chris Waters, Pamela Simpson, Kenneth Janken, and Paula Giddings. John Hope Franklin shared his recollections of the American Society for African Culture and the heady early days of African independence.

At Princeton University, friends and colleagues helped me in formulating the early stages of the project. I am grateful to Nell Painter, Howard Taylor, Albert Raboteau, Wahneema Lubiano, Arno Mayer, Arnold Rampersad, Barbara Browning, Jeremy Adelman, Steve Aron, Dirk Hartog, Jeffrey Tucker, Belinda Redden, Laura Doyle, Nick Bromell, Susan Kent, Kathryn Burns, Sonya Michel, Teofilo Ruiz, Rick Sobel, Cheryl Hicks, Crystal Feimster, Ken Mack, and Clyde Spillinger. It was a pleasure to have Bob Vitalis as a semester-long guest in my upper-level undergraduate seminar on black expatriate writing. Special thanks are due to Christine Stansell and Judith Jackson Fossett.

At the beginning of the project, I was fortunate to have the support of Wilson Moses, Robert Tignor, Nell Painter, and Daniel Rodgers. Nell has been a considerate colleague and trenchant critic. Over the years, Wilson Moses has been a steadfast mentor and colleague whose peerless scholarship has been a model of rigor and integrity. At various stages I have benefited vastly from the advice, suggestions, and encouragement of numerous colleagues throughout the academy: Jean-Christophe Agnew, Abdul Alkalimat, Jean Allman, Beth Bates, Martha Biondi, Hazel Carby, Russ Castronovo, Ken Cmiel, Nancy Cott, John Dittmer, Mary Dudziak, Cary Fraser, Jim Giblin, Robert Hill, Martha Hodes, Jim and Lois Horton, Gordon Hutner, Abiola Irele, Matthew Jacobson, Amy Kaplan, Robin Kelley, Linda Kerber, Martin and Marion Kilson, Obiagele Lake, David Levering Lewis, George Lipsitz, Winston James, Joanne Meyerowitz, Jim Miller, Patrick Miller, Sidney Mintz, Dana Nelson, Donald Pease, Warren Perry, Barbara Ransby, Adolph

Reed, Barry Shank, Robert Stepto, Sterling Stuckey, Susan Pennybacker,
Janice Radway, Philip Richards, Cedric Robinson, David Roediger, Roy Ro-
senzweig, Stephanie Shaw, Joe W. Trotter, Timothy Tyson, Leti Volpp, Mary
Helen Washington, Jerry Watts, Harry Williams, Komozi Woodard, John
Wright, and Rafia Zafar.

I am grateful to John Stoner for his generosity in sharing his research.
Marika Sherwood was a fount of helpful information. Michael Hanchard
graciously shared information about contacts in Ghana. Thanks to Nancy
Kates for sharing her research on Bayard Rustin and for her friendship. I am
grateful to Janet Higbie for our conversations on history, African Americans,
and Africans. Bill Schwartz found the recording of Lord Kitchener's calypso
tribute to Ghana's independence, ending my quest of many years. Tom Feelings welcomed me with a stack of photocopied documents and unforgettable
warmth and hospitality. Lewis Bateman and Joe Wood were enthusiastic
early supporters of the project.

At the University of Texas, which generously supported my research with
a grant from the Office of Faculty of the Arts and Sciences, the collegiality of
our fellow occupants of Garrison Hall helped make Austin a wonderful place
to live, work, and begin a family. We are grateful to have been embraced
by our friends and colleagues there: Robin Kilson, Toyin Falola, Jim Sid-
bury, Judith Coffin, William Forbath, David Montejano, David Bowman, Neil
Foley, Angela Hinz, Gunther Peck, Kevin Kenny, Michael Stoff, Carolyn Boyd,
Howard Miller, Janet Davis, Martha Newman, Robert Abzug, Shelley Fisher
Fishkin, Aline Helg, Elizabeth McHenry, Sheila Walker, Mark Smith, Gail
Minault, Barbara Harlow, Jonathan Brown, Susan Deans-Smith, Ted Gordon, Saheed Adejumobi, and Robert Crunden. Ben Lindfors generously
shared his work on Ayi Kwei Armah's early career. A special thanks goes to
my mother, Marilyn Gaines, for coming to Texas to share childcare duties
with us.

At the University of Michigan, among colleagues working at the intersection
of the history department and the Center for Afroamerican and African
Studies, I productively engaged the challenges of writing a transnational
narrative linking postwar U.S., African American, and African history. At the
Center for Afroamerican and African Studies, the collegiality of Julius Scott,
Michele Mitchell, Mamadou Diouf, and Ifeoma Nwankwo helped me con-
ceptualize the lines of influence linking Harlem, the Caribbean, and West
Africa. In innumerable ways, colleagues at the Center contributed greatly
to this book: James Jackson, Lester Monts, Lemuel Johnson, Jon Lockard,

xiv   Jim Chaffers, Nesha Haniff, Coleman Jordan, Yaw Twumasi, Xiomara Santamarina, Al Young, Kelly Askew, Frieda Ekotto, Elisha Renne, Marlon Ross, Sandra Gunning, Arlene Keizer, Mbala Nkanga, Martha Jones, Paul Anderson, Tiya Miles, Richard Turits, Paul Johnson, Magdalena Zaborowska, Amal Fadlalla, Beth James, Robin Grice, Donald Sims, and Stephen Ward. I am grateful for the generous publication subvention award from the Office of the Vice President for Research and the College of Literature, Science and Arts at the University of Michigan.

In the history department, many thanks go to Earl Lewis, Rebecca Scott, Frederick Cooper, Sonya Rose, Maris Vinovskis, Terrence McDonald, Carroll Smith-Rosenberg, Juan Cole, Diane Hughes, Mary Kelley, Dena Goodman, Tom Trautmann, Kathleen Canning, Geoff Eley, Mills Thornton, Nancy Hunt, Phil Deloria, Carol Karlson, Maria Montoya, Matthew Countryman, Helmut Puff, Michael Wintroub, Gina Morantz-Sanchez, Jay Cook, Matt Lassiter, and Sueann Caulfield. Julia Adams, Susan Douglas, Catherine Benamou, Michael Kennedy, Jonathan Freedman, Alan Wald, and Derek Vaillant all provided a shot in the arm with good cheer and conversation.

Mamadou Diouf, David Cohen, Sonya Rose, Ray Silverman, Greg Dowd, Maris Vinovskis, Martin Pernick, Charles Bright, Barbara Metcalf, Tandiwe Moyo, and Doris Essah read the manuscript in its entirety. Cecile McHardy, Abdullah H. Abdur-Razzaq, Richard Gibson, Marika Sherwood, Brent Edwards, William Branch, Michael Hanchard, Frieda Ekotto, Mary Kelley, Françoise Hamlin, Geoff Eley, James Campbell, Sara Blair, Wilson Moses, Matthew Guterl, Robert Lee, and the members of the Brown University Race and Ethnicity workshop read portions of the manuscript and provided valuable criticism. James Campbell and Nikhil Singh enriched the work through their generous and incisive readings. A special thanks to Zach Mabee for his diligent research assistance. Maceo Gaines's humor, curiosity, and antics kept me focused during the long homestretch of the project.

My greatest debt is to Penny Von Eschen, whose companionship sustained me during moments when it seemed the journey had no end. Since our initial discussion of the project during a leisurely outdoor lunch one brilliant autumn afternoon in Princeton, her support, devotion, and intellectual engagement have been a gift. Through her scholarship, our innumerable conversations, her keen eye for narrative structure, and her passion for the project, she has indelibly shaped this book. I dedicate it to her with profound gratitude and joy.

AMERICAN AFRICANS IN GHANA

INTRODUCTION

Watching the World from Ghana

This is not just a change in attitude which denotes an increase
in privileges. It is a fundamental change in attitude even to
privileges which could have been claimed five years before. It
permeates everything Ghanaians do or say. And here one saw the
psychological significance of freedom. It does something to a man's
way of seeing the world. It is an experience that is not gained by
education or money, but by an instinctive re-evaluation of your
place in the world, an attitude that is the logical by-product of
political action. And again one felt . . . the full desecration of
human personality which is contained in the word: colonial.
One felt that the West Indian of my generation was truly
backward. . . . For he was not only without this experience
of freedom won; it was not even a vital force or need in his
way of seeing himself and the world which imprisoned him.
—George Lamming,
The Pleasures of Exile (1960)

The truth of the matter is that for most Negro intellectuals, the
integration of the Negro means . . . the emptying of his life of
meaningful content and ridding him of all Negro identification.
For them, integration and eventual assimilation means the
annihilation of the Negro—physically, culturally and spiritually.
—E. Franklin Frazier,
"The Failure of the Negro Intellectual" (1962)

Near midnight on March 5, 1957, Kwame Nkrumah and his senior
ministers mounted the platform at the Old Polo Grounds in Accra,
greeting along with the thousands assembled the end of British
colonial rule and the birth of the new nation of Ghana, its name taken from
an ancient West African kingdom. "Everybody was happy," recalled Komla

Gbedemah, who had held the nationalist movement together while the British jailed Nkrumah and others. Many years later, Gbedemah imagined the "cheering probably still resounding though we can't hear it." As the Union Jack that had flown over the Gold Coast colony was brought down and the flag of Ghana raised—a black star at the center of a red, green, and yellow tricolor—a visibly moved Nkrumah addressed the crowd with his associates, including Gbedemah, at his side. "At long last the battle has ended," Nkrumah declared, his remarks punctuated by cheers. "At last, Ghana, your beloved country, is free forever." Nkrumah proclaimed that "[f]rom now on there is a new African in the world. . . . That new African is beginning to fight his own battles, and show that after all, the black man is capable of managing his own affairs." Reminding Ghanaians that they were no longer part of a colonial society "but a free independent people," Nkrumah contended that the responsibilities ahead surpassed those of nation building. "We are going to . . . create our own African personality and identity; . . . We again rededicate ourselves in the struggle to emancipate other countries in Africa, for our independence is meaningless unless it is linked up with the total liberation of the African continent." Before the first playing of Ghana's national anthem, Nkrumah and his associates took off their white hats, initialed PG for prison graduates, a reminder of their sacrifice during the nationalist struggle. As the anthem's strains rose into the night, Nkrumah wept openly under the floodlights.[1]

For people of African descent the world over, Ghana's independence lent momentum to rising demands for freedom and self-determination and heralded the impending demise of the systems of racial and colonial domination instituted in the late nineteenth century in the U.S. South and on the African continent. Occurring as African Americans accelerated their demands for an end to segregation, Ghana's triumph over British rule was widely celebrated by people of African descent in and beyond the new nation. As Nkrumah declared, the birth of Ghana signaled the emergence not just of a new African but of a new world, fashioned in the image of black modernity and freedom. Ghanaians celebrated their independence and its leader with a song, "Freedom Highlife," by popular bandleader E. T. Mensah, that praised "Ghana, land of freedom" and "Nkrumah, son of Ghana."

Black peoples in Britain also reveled in Ghana's independence, as evident in the musical tribute by Lord Kitchener, a Trinidad-born calypsonian (ironically named after the British field marshal and colonial official) who had migrated to London, as had thousands of other West Indians, during the 1950s. "This day will not be forgotten / the 6th of March 1957 / When the

Ghanaian independence, Old Polo Grounds, Accra, March 6, 1957. *Left to right*: Archie Casely-Hayford, Komla Gbedemah, Kwame Nkrumah, Kojo Botsio, and Krobo Edusei. (Time Life Pictures/Getty Images)

Gold Coast successfully / get her independence officially," Kitchener sang over a lilting arrangement that evoked the hybrid rhythms of Caribbean calypso, West African highlife, and African American jazz. Kitchener proudly situated Ghana and Nkrumah within a history of pan-Africanism, referencing the mass movement led by Marcus Garvey as well as Ethiopia's Haile Selassie, legendary among peoples of African descent for his resistance to fascist Italy's 1935 invasion and conquest of his nation. A male background chorus sang the name of the new nation in unison as Kitchener supplied the rest of the refrain: "Ghana! Ghana is the name—Ghana! We wish to proclaim—we'll be jolly, merry and gay, on the 6th of March, Independence Day!"

Nkrumah would have approved of the song's evocation of a diasporic community of celebration. With his constant references to Ghana's leadership in the struggle to rid the entire African continent of colonialism, he encouraged the view that Ghana's triumph was to be shared throughout Africa and among peoples of African descent. A year before independence, Nkrumah wrote, "We believe that the constitutional advance of the Gold Coast has a significance far beyond the borders of our own country. It pro-

Record sleeve for Lord Kitchener, "Birth of Ghana." (Preston family)

vides a symbol of hope and inspiration to the people of Africa still seeking their national liberty."[2]

Another manifestation of the global significance of Ghana's independence was the large number of African, West Indian, and African American dignitaries in attendance, invited by Nkrumah as a gesture of solidarity for their support of Gold Coast nationalism or for their leadership of freedom movements throughout Africa and the Americas. These PMGs—the prime minister's guests—held almost as prominent a place in the independence festivities as the Duchess of York, who represented the British royal family. They certainly shared the limelight with Vice President Richard Nixon, the head of the official U.S. delegation. Over the several days of ceremonies, official cars cruised through the capitol city of Accra bearing such figures as George Pad-

more and C. L. R. James, both London-based, Trinidad-born pan-Africanist
intellectuals; Norman Manley, the future prime minister of Jamaica; Harlem
Congressman Adam Clayton Powell; United Nations official and Nobel laureate Ralph Bunche; and Lucille Armstrong, representing her husband, jazz
trumpeter and vocalist Louis Armstrong, beloved in Ghana since his visit to
the Gold Coast the year before but unable to attend the independence festivities. The list of African American PMGs also included labor leaders A. Philip
Randolph and Maida Springer, educators Mordecai Johnson of Howard University and Horace Mann Bond of Lincoln University (the alma mater of
Nkrumah and other African leaders), and Martin Luther King Jr., leader of
the recent successful bus boycott in Montgomery, Alabama. There was, however, a noteworthy absence among the list of black dignitaries from the New
World. Widely considered the doyen of pan-Africanism through his long
association with the movement, eighty-nine-year-old W. E. B. Du Bois had
been denied a visa by U.S. authorities on the presumption that his leftist
views posed a national security risk.[3]

Nkrumah was not the only person overcome by emotion at the raising of
the Ghana colors. But while similarly moved by the occasion, the African
Americans present, particularly King, also saw in Ghana's victory reminders
of the long, perilous struggle African Americans were waging back in the
United States. The poignancy of the moment for African Americans is suggested by a perhaps apocryphal story. During the official festivities, Nixon
reportedly asked several bystanders, "How does it feel to be free?," only to be
taken aback at their response: "We wouldn't know. We're from Alabama."
While the story of Nixon's faux pas captures the bittersweet meaning of the
occasion for African Americans, it also suggests the impossibility of confining
the problem of racial oppression to the United States. On Ghanaian soil,
Nixon was compelled to meet with King, who had vainly sought to engage an
apathetic Eisenhower administration on the issue of civil rights.[4] The story of
Nixon's failed attempt at small talk with African Americans he had mistaken
for Ghanaians points to the transformative significance Ghana's independence held for black Americans. The fulfillment of Ghanaian and African
demands for national independence informed many African Americans'
struggles for equal citizenship. The simultaneous upheavals touched off by
decolonization in Africa and civil rights demonstrations in the U.S. South
shaped the political outlook of black intellectuals and activists in northern
cities. While supportive of black struggles for equality in the Jim Crow South,
many northern African Americans remote from the southern desegregation

6   campaigns also championed the cause of African freedom and called themselves "Afro-American," challenging dominant injunctions that the Negro
was primarily, if not exclusively, an American.

For all its euphoria, the moment of independence itself did not constitute
unalloyed triumph, and African Americans were not the only people to experience something less than unqualified joy at Ghana's achievement. For Barbadian writer George Lamming, Ghana's achievement provided a barometer
by which the prospects for West Indian freedom—or the lack thereof—could
be assessed. As the epigraph to this introduction suggests, Lamming hailed
the transformation of Gold Coast colonials to self-determining Ghanaian
citizens as a way of articulating his sense of what was lacking in a Caribbean
culture defined by dependency. For Lamming and many others, Ghana's
independence was not simply a cause for celebration. In Lamming's eyes, the
Ghanaians' self-determination and confidence contrasted painfully with the
parochialism of a West Indian culture still enthralled by colonial models and
mentalities.

At the height of the civil rights movement, from the late 1950s to 1966,
scores of African Americans, including intellectuals, technicians, teachers,
artists, professionals, entrepreneurs, and trade unionists, left the United
States for Ghana. Ghana was a haven for a range of activists working at the
intersection of anticolonial, civil rights, leftist, and pacifist movements. Expatriates and visitors of African and indeed non-African descent were attracted to Ghana by the vision of freedom that Nkrumah voiced incessantly.

How did Ghana become the destination for African Americans and peoples of African descent at the same moment that multitudes of African Americans demanded an end to segregation in the U.S. South? As Ghanaians and
others celebrated their newly won independence, many African Americans'
discontent at the persistence of institutionalized racism in the North as well
as the South found expression in the writings of such commentators as
sociologist E. Franklin Frazier.

Frazier, who had studied the effects of urbanization on African Americans
in Chicago and elsewhere, viewed racial integration as a poor substitute for
the wartime progressive mobilizations for racial and social justice, a movement for equal rights that was vanquished by Cold War repression. Although
Frazier did not emigrate to Ghana, his support for African nationalism was
inseparable from his indictment of U.S. society during the 1950s. Frazier
would have agreed with several recent accounts of the long civil rights movement by Martha Biondi, Robert Korstad, and Matthew Countryman. These

studies emphasize the failure of postwar liberalism as they chronicle the rise
and fall of wartime national agitation for civil rights that demanded an end
to racial discrimination in the workplace, housing, and public accommoda-
tions. That wartime movement for integration, focused in northern cities on
struggles for equality in housing and the workplace and defined in the South
by struggles for voting rights and economic justice, was derailed by federal
policies that reinforced residential segregation, Cold War loyalty programs,
and the 1946 repeal of the Federal Employment Practices Committee, which
had been instituted to oppose discrimination in wartime industries. At war's
end, violence against returned black veterans in uniform and the persistence
of segregation mocked wartime appeals for victory against Jim Crow at
home and fascism abroad. The intensification of racial hostilities on the
home front eclipsed wartime efforts to integrate neighborhoods, polling
places, unions, and the workplace. As the Cold War came to dominate the
nation's domestic politics, the progressive wartime agenda of integration
was co-opted by a federal government that promoted racial liberalism as a
gradualist and largely symbolic legal and legislative process of racial change
managed by the courts, Congress, and policy makers.[5]

To Frazier's dismay, many African American civil rights leaders, politicians, and intellectuals assented to this top-down redefinition of integration
bounded by Cold War considerations. This agenda was incapable of addressing the socioeconomic inequalities from which African Americans dispro-
portionately suffered. Equally disturbing to Frazier was that integrationism
under Cold War auspices seemed to require that African American citizenship was predicated on the renunciation of an independent group consciousness. Frazier's black popular front sensibility, including support for African
anticolonial movements, fueled his impatience at the parochialism of the
American scene. For him and other African American radicals, it was not so
much a matter of choosing Ghana and Africa over the promise of integration
and the U.S. civil rights movement. Rather, Ghana's progressive vision of
freedom placed in sharper relief Frazier's critique of a postwar American
liberalism compromised by antilabor and segregationist reaction and the
stifling of dissent. For African Americans, American liberalism failed to practice the freedom it preached.

As historian Nikhil Singh has argued, during the early Cold War years,
Frazier and other black American progressives risked official censure by
articulating a vision of global democracy as a critical alternative to an American liberalism unwilling to interrogate the racism that belied its universalist
claims and aspirations.[6] Frazier remained unrepentant for his associations

with Du Bois and other black progressives and was investigated by the Federal Bureau of Investigation throughout the 1950s.[7] Frazier's outlook casts doubt on a narrative of the civil rights movement that posits an early consensus between civil rights organizations and liberal administrations disrupted by black power militants in the late 1960s. Such a narrative not only is predicated on the exclusion of progressive antecedents from the history of the movement but also requires the erasure of the significance of African decolonization for the struggle over the meaning and content of the formal American citizenship claimed by African American activists and intellectuals. Well before the phrase "black power" exploded into the nation's consciousness, during the late 1950s and early 1960s black militants in the North, including novelist Julian Mayfield, openly defied Cold War protocols and the mainstream civil rights movement's adherence to nonviolence. Mayfield and other rebels fled political repression in the United States, ending up in Ghana with scores of activists, professionals, and technicians seeking refuge from constrained opportunities. They were welcomed by Nkrumah, who, perhaps more than any other African head of state of his time, encouraged blacks from the Western world to emigrate and lend their skills to building the new nation.

If African Americans remained in a crucial sense strangers in their own land, excluded from the nation's vaunted freedom and prosperity, black activists and dissenters were doubly estranged for holding political opinions that exceeded the limits of the Cold War American nation. These expatriates' decision to situate their hopes for meaningful change in Ghana was not an act of political escapism; if anything, they left behind the restrictions on political discourse that outlasted the witch hunts of the McCarthy period. Thus, to assert that they rejected the United States for Ghana erroneously implies that they had a choice between these options. Prominent within the group of expatriates was the category of political refugees, not unlike those South African freedom fighters driven into exile by the apartheid regime in the early 1960s. Some, like W. E. B. and Shirley Graham Du Bois, who had been deprived of their passports for most of the 1950s, had bid an angry farewell to a United States defined for them by the violation of their citizenship rights and the persecution of the black Left. Black American anticolonial activist and literary scholar W. Alphaeus Hunton had served six months in a segregated federal prison for his leftist commitments during the 1950s. After his release, no university would employ him. Leftists such as the Du Boises and Hunton were not the only ones so targeted. Mayfield and Preston King were also political exiles but of a different sort. King, a political scientist, was convicted of defying his Georgia draft board after it refused his request to cease the demeaning racist practice of referring to him by his first name only. Facing incarceration on his return to the United States, King remained in exile until he received a presidential pardon in 2000. Like King, Mayfield, a writer, actor and former communist, did not choose exile in Ghana. That nation was merely the terminus of his flight from a federal manhunt in connection with his involvement with black activists engaged in armed self-defense in North Carolina. However varied their trajectories, the common plight of these dissenters suggested that the U.S. government was more committed to containing black activism than to implementing desegregation and protecting civil liberties.

African American emigration to Ghana (or a general support for African independence) was not an either/or proposition rooted in a rejection of the American nation or the African American freedom movement. Frazier's critique of American liberalism was shared by such leftist exiles as Du Bois, Hunton, and Mayfield as well as by noncommunist pacifists Bayard Rustin, Bill Sutherland, and St. Clair Drake, whose support for African independence movements went hand in hand with their advocacy of racial and economic justice in the United States. The perception that African Americans faced an irreconcilable choice between America and Africa—between the U.S.-based civil rights movement and African national independence movements—belied the transnational outlook of such figures as Rustin, Sutherland, and Drake. Indeed, that presumption of a zero-sum "choice" between Africa and America suggests the persistence of the dominant view that the American Negro was strictly American, an assertion whose political intent was the delegitimization of Afro-diasporic solidarities. In espousing a global democratic and anti-imperialist vision that informed their struggles for justice in the United States and abroad, African American expatriates in Ghana and such renowned figures as Paul Robeson, Lorraine Hansberry, and Malcolm X disputed declarations of the Negro's essential Americanism. These black radicals refused to accept the Cold War assumption that solidarity with African peoples and their struggles for independence was tantamount to disloyalty.

The lingering cloud of official suspicion that plagued African American intellectuals and the depth of resistance to desegregation by southern white political and civic leaders informed attempts by African American civil rights leaders to appropriate the rhetoric of anticommunism and national security for their own purposes. After returning from Ghana's independence festivities, Martin Luther King Jr. navigated the treacherous straits of acceptable African American political expression, downplaying his interest in the transnational pan-African movement and seeking to legitimize his appeal for civil rights as essential to the national interest. King's subsequent decision to rhetorically situate the cause of civil rights within the American dream, muting the implications of his understanding of the socialist political economy of African nationalism, represented not so much a choice as the likelihood that that he had absorbed the lessons of the disciplining of black radicals during the 1950s. When toward the end of his life King broke with the prescribed ground rules of domestic race relations leadership to which he and others had been confined, linking racism, imperialism, and materialism in his indictment of American foreign policy, he became a pariah from the standpoint of the civil rights establishment and American officialdom.

Whether or not they were literally pushed by the repressive policies of the U.S. state and the apartheid regime of South Africa, many of those who emigrated to Ghana were attracted by the boldness of Kwame Nkrumah's vision of pan-African emancipation. Nkrumah spoke of asserting the "African personality," which meant that Africans would exert military, political, and diplomatic leadership in world affairs and take the initiative in resolving conflicts on the African continent. Ghana served as the political base for Nkrumah's agendas of African union government and West Indian federation. State power in Ghana provided the vehicle for Nkrumah's pursuit of the inter-African political, economic, and military cooperation central to his strategy for the liberation and development of Africa. Ghana was unrivaled among African nations in its willingness to provide sanctuary to black (and nonblack) radicals from the United States, the Caribbean, Africa, and Europe unable to function politically in their countries of origin. For many of these expatriates, this willingness made Ghana a destination of radical hope. Nkrumah reinforced that image by his willingness to provide political asylum for exiled freedom fighters from southern Africa and to extend material and political support to nationalist movements and parties still fighting to oust white minority regimes. While Ghana's appeal to black American radicals was inseparable from their view of an American liberalism distorted by white supremacy, that small nation of some 4.5 million inspired black intellectuals and leaders across the political spectrum and throughout the black world. From the early 1950s until Nkrumah's overthrow by a military coup in 1966, a number of prominent African Americans and West Indian advisers and

heads of state visited or resided in the West African nation, including those
mentioned previously as well as Richard Wright; Martinique-born intellectual and activist Frantz Fanon; West Indian economist W. Arthur Lewis;
Jamaican novelist Neville Dawes; Trinidad's prime minister, Eric Williams;
African American civil rights leader James Farmer; newly crowned heavyweight boxing champion Muhammad Ali; and numerous others.

The story of the African American expatriate community in Nkrumah's
Ghana illuminates the challenges and contradictions posed by Cold War
liberalism and American hegemony during the 1960s. The American nation's declared support for desegregation, formal equality, and decolonization masked the repression of black radicals. As several scholars have established, the period was defined by comprehensive official attempts at the
manipulation of black politics, public culture, and group consciousness, from
clandestine Federal Bureau of Investigation surveillance and counterintelligence against black intellectuals and civil rights organizations and leadership[8] to covert government funding of the American Society for African
Culture, an organization that fostered dialogue between African American
and African intellectuals, to domestic and international propaganda that
sought to mitigate the pan-African solidarities pursued in Nkrumah's Ghana.
The African American intelligentsia's forays into African and foreign affairs
risked official censure throughout the 1950s and 1960s. Even as such critics
as Du Bois and Frazier claimed that the Negro American leadership remained blithely indifferent to the struggles of African peoples, Ghana's independence, along with the nonaligned movement, fueled a black nationalist
awakening among northern urban African American writers, artists, musicians, and activists. Their outspoken condemnations of white supremacy at
home and in U.S. policy toward Africa animated the transformed outlook of
Malcolm X after his departure from the Nation of Islam. But in response to
Malcolm's emergence as a radical voice on African affairs and more cautious
attempts by mainstream civil rights leaders to formalize their support for
African liberation struggles, U.S. officials discouraged an independent African American perspective on the nation's foreign policy toward Africa. Silencing African American leadership on African and foreign affairs was a
major priority, particularly amid the nation's escalating war in Vietnam and
continued U.S. political and military support for neocolonial and white minority regimes in central and southern Africa, where the stakes included substantial American financial investments and control of strategic resources.
Although black radicals in Ghana represented a small segment of African

American opinion, the potential that their assaults on the legitimacy of U.S. liberalism would spread, whether domestically or internationally to other African nations, led to concerted strategies of containment.

An account of African American expatriates' engagement with African national liberation struggles and a global nonaligned movement resituates the history of the U.S. civil rights movement within one of the most important, if neglected, developments in twentieth-century international politics—that is, the challenge to the bipolar vision of postwar global order posed by the emergence of new African and Asian states. Cold War rivalry with the Soviet Union heightened the significance of racial discrimination against African Americans. The all-too-frequent incidents of antiblack brutality throughout the postwar era imperiled U.S. attempts to secure the allegiance of this global majority of nonwhite nations. Thus, for African Americans to criticize U.S. racism from abroad was certain to provoke an irate response from U.S. officialdom. U.S. policy makers hoped to counter such criticism by sending African American spokespersons and civic officials abroad to defend the nation by asserting that atavistic outbursts of racism were giving way to the essential rectitude and perfectibility of American institutions.[9] When African American radicals and dissenters such as Du Bois, Robeson, and others diverged from the official script, they were accused of disloyalty and their passports were seized, cutting them off from overseas audiences.

Although Du Bois and Robeson were scapegoated, their accusers conflating the two men's advocacy for African anticolonial movements with their pro-Soviet leanings in a manner that demonized the cause of decolonization (just as segregationists used the Red Scare to discredit demands for civil rights), Cold War anticommunism in and of itself does not explain the disciplining of black American radicals and militants. Despite the fact that such advocates of African freedom as Richard Wright and George Padmore were staunch anticommunists, U.S. officials considered these men subversive because of their opposition to American and Western systems of racial and colonial oppression. Frazier's criticisms notwithstanding, not all African American intellectuals caved in to political pressure. The same can be said of African American expatriates in Ghana, whose presence, while numerically small, points to the broadly contested issue of African American political consciousness during an era of escalating challenges to the legitimacy of U.S. power around the world. During the early 1960s, Ghana provided an independent forum for black American radicals largely unavailable in their country of origin, offering them the opportunity to participate in a transnational culture of opposition to a Western culture seeking the preservation of colo- nial and neocolonial dominance over the majority of the world's peoples. Watching the world from the vantage point of Ghana, as did the expatriates and such intellectuals as Frazier and Lamming, these commentators articulated a neutralism resistant to the dictates of both the United States and the Soviet Union. While the paths leading individuals to Ghana varied, these distinct trajectories add up to a larger account of a nascent African diasporic political culture in confrontation with the active engagement of U.S. and Western power in African affairs from the late 1950s to the early 1960s.

During the 1950s, as the U.S. federal government embraced desegregation partly to counter international criticism of American racism and as African Americans in the South quickened the pace of their demands for full citizenship, the birth of Ghana along with other emergent African and Asian states led intellectuals of African descent to reflect anew on the relation of black peoples to Western culture. The image of Africa on the march to freedom and modernity, sloughing off almost a century of European colonial rule, energized African American, Caribbean, and African intellectuals, many of whom had recourse to histories of transnational black solidarity and resistance against racial and colonial oppression.

The pan-African movement and its historical precursors informed a lengthening shelf of scholarly and popular writings by blacks on the historical agency of black peoples, anticolonialism, and the varieties of systemic racial discrimination around the world.[10] These writings comprised a collective assessment of the place of peoples of African descent in Western culture. At such international meetings as the First World Congress of Negro Writers and Artists, held in Paris in 1956, African and African diaspora intellectuals articulated demands for political and cultural emancipation, elucidating the transformation of colonial subjects to self-determining citizens. Energized by the watershed moment linking Ghana's independence and African freedom, the decline of European empires, and the rise of African American demands for equality in the postwar world, these writers built on the work of their predecessors. Ralph Ellison, speaking of Richard Wright, aptly characterized their shared project as the dual endeavor of depicting the meaning of black experience while disclosing to blacks and whites the psychological and emotional problems that arise between the two groups when they strive for mutual understanding. Ellison and Wright anticipated and shared the work of Frazier, Lamming, and such contemporaries as Aimé Césaire, Frantz Fanon, and other writers of African descent: articulating the racialized condition of black and African peoples in Western culture with the ultimate objective of democratizing Western and metropolitan cultures through the exposure and eradication of racist and colonial habits of thinking.[11]

As civil rights leaders, activists, and their supporters in the United States struggled to maintain hope against violent resistance and faced a federal government hesitant to enforce and implement desegregation measures, black radicals in Ghana, in tandem with their allies in the United States, articulated criticisms of American liberalism that could not be articulated within black movement circles in the United States. Black American expatriates in Ghana occupied a front-row seat for the consolidation of U.S. neocolonial influence on the continent, a process that was perhaps facilitated by the American nation's halting progress toward racial integration and formal equality. By contesting an American officialdom intent on manipulating black political expression, the expatriates engaged in a struggle over the meaning and content of the American citizenship being extended to African Americans. For African American radicals in Ghana and their stateside allies, the official project of integration was deeply flawed insofar as it demanded conformity to an America whose undemocratic policies at home and abroad had, in their view, undermined the nation's legitimacy.

Although the expatriates reveled in the utopian and revolutionary potential of Nkrumah's Ghana, their sojourn was clouded by the tension between their radical hopes and the imperatives of a Ghanaian state whose stability and survival came increasingly under siege by internal and external opposition. From 1961 on, Nkrumah relied heavily on his senior ministers and leftist expatriate sympathizers to promote his socialist and anti-imperialist objectives and to counter U.S. efforts to blanket the African continent with propaganda asserting progress in U.S. black-white race relations. The Ghana government and its ruling Convention People's Party (CPP), like any political organization, contained progressive and conservative factions, a conflict that increasingly found expression in the tension between statist and pan-Africanist objectives. Expediency and compromise defined Nkrumah's relationship to the CPP and its conservative elements. He relied on patronage to secure the allegiance of Ghanaian professionals and chiefs and tolerated opportunism and corruption on the part of ministers and party loyalists. Younger leftists within the Ghana government were the closest allies of the African American expatriates. In addition to promoting Nkrumah's political goals, including African unity, nuclear disarmament, an all-African military force, and the government's economic development policy, the expatriates and their Ghanaian allies espoused a militant anti-American agenda that occasionally clashed with Nkrumah's pragmatic objectives. These tensions

surfaced most prominently with Nkrumah's reluctance to lend official sanc-
tion to the visit of Malcolm X, who had come to Ghana at the behest of the
African American expatriates.

For Nkrumah, positive nonalignment in practice meant playing the super-
power rivals against each other, just as he found it necessary to mediate
between rival political factions in his party, taking sides as the political
situation warranted. Such a delicate balancing act was vital, for Nkrumah
both faced the limitations of the CPP and issued his powerful ideological
challenge to the West from a weak strategic position. Ghana had little of
strategic or military value to offer to the West. Moreover, Ghana remained
dependent on foreign investment for its industrial development and the
expansion of its infrastructure. The pilgrimage of radicals and progressives
to Ghana was more than matched by the migration of foreign business exe-
cutives and investors seeking to capitalize on the new nation's promises of
development. The centerpiece of Ghana's plan for industrialization was the
Volta River project, a hydroelectric dam that British colonial officials had initially proposed but that Nkrumah championed on symbolic as well as pragmatic grounds. The dam would provide the power necessary for the nation's
fledgling industries, and Ghana planned to sell electricity to its neighbors,
illuminating the region. Just as important, the Volta River project would
demonstrate Ghana's rapid progress in emulating the West's large-scale industrial might and modernity. Yet Ghana's lack of bargaining power and
Nkrumah's attachment to the symbolism of the project ultimately worked to
the exclusive benefit of the American-based Kaiser Corporation, which had
imposed on Ghana neocolonial terms and conditions that mocked Nkrumah's initial vision of economic development.[12] Ghana's other partner in the
Volta River project, the U.S. government, rationalized its support on the
likelihood that the Soviet Union would gain a crucial foothold by providing
financial and technical assistance if the United States did not. Nkrumah's
strongest hand may have been playing the superpowers against each other,
but this strategy subjected Ghana and its leaders to intense political and
diplomatic pressures.

The contradictions and vulnerabilities of the regime hampered the African American expatriates who had envisioned themselves in partnership
with Nkrumah. Even as they shared Nkrumah's revolutionary aims, some
may have perceived in Ghana a vivid manifestation of the bourgeois nationalism that Frantz Fanon condemned in *The Wretched of the Earth*, much
of which he wrote while in Ghana immediately after the debacle of the
Congo Crisis. As early as 1960, Fanon and C. L. R. James understood that

revolutionary hopes met their match in the human frailty of those Ghanaian officials who used state power as an instrument for self-aggrandizement. The gendered character of state power and expatriate existence in Ghana and to a great extent the masculinist content of that vision of liberation and development contributed to undemocratic tendencies in Ghana in particular and of 1960s African and black freedom movements generally. If racism represented the Achilles heel of the U.S. government's postwar foreign policy, male dominance functioned similarly as a liability for revolutionary and radical social movements and projects. The "big man" created by the post-independence African states became a target for numerous literary critiques of the betrayal of the democratic aspirations of African peoples.[13]

The diversion of the state's resources and the displacement of collective goals of development by self-seeking masculinist perquisites of power, privilege, and hedonistic entitlement that prevailed among Western and non-Western political leaders alike—this was also the era of John F. Kennedy and James Bond movies—contributed to the wide-scale and ultimately damning corruption among Ghanaian elites contemptuous of the democratic aspirations of the Ghanaian people that undermined mass support for Nkrumah's government.[14] Just as expectations of sexual license as an entitlement among Ghanaian "big men" gave the lie to their revolutionary rhetoric, a certain sexual adventurism, evident in several memoirs and other writings by black American expatriates, mitigated for some men of all backgrounds the radicalism of the expatriate experience.[15] In addition, while Nkrumah and other nationalist leaders welcomed the contributions of women to African liberation, opportunities for African American women expatriates to lend their skills to nation building were limited within a hierarchical Ghanaian political culture. When a military coup overthrew Nkrumah's government in 1966, such gender hierarchies, combined with the masculinist exercise of power and privilege in Ghana, figured in some of the expatriates' criticisms of their "failures" in Ghana as well as their critiques of Ghanaian society. As a result of their internationalist politics and their immersion in the gendered politics in Accra, African American expatriates including Sylvia Boone, Julian Mayfield, Maya Angelou, and Shirley Graham Du Bois contributed to the formulation of an independent African American feminist discourse.

This book is divided into three parts that explore the world of expatriates in Nkrumah's Ghana. The first part examines the intellectual and political expressions of pan-Africanism that both contributed and responded to the emergence of Ghana. Chapter 1 considers the interwoven diasporic and anti-colonial routes of passage that influenced the political formation of pan-African nationalist leaders and intellectuals, including Kwame Nkrumah, George Padmore, and St. Clair Drake. The intersecting institutions and movements of international communism, Garveyism, and pacifism; the cosmopolitan spaces of African American colleges; and wartime social and political ferment all helped align the struggle against segregation in the United States with the African political renaissance of nationalism and anticolonialism. These converging tributaries of political formation brought these and other individuals from the United States, the 'West Indies, and the African continent together within Gold Coast nationalism and independent Ghana. Chapter 2 situates Richard Wright's travel narrative on nationalism in the Gold Coast, *Black Power* (1954), within the broader phenomenon of the anticolonial critiques of Western culture of such black intellectuals as George Lamming and E. Franklin Frazier. Chapter 3 examines the moment of Ghana's independence and its impact on Martin Luther King Jr., whose exposure to a wider world of transnational anticolonial radicalism was mediated by the imperatives of the Cold War understanding of civil rights as a national security imperative. The chapter also chronicles Ghana's postindependence projections of what Nkrumah and other contemporaries termed the African personality as exemplified by such initiatives as the All African People's Conference (1958) and Ghana's sponsorship of the protest campaign against French nuclear testing in the Sahara (1959). Such expatriates and visitors as Padmore, Drake, Bill Sutherland, and Bayard Rustin were instrumental in these attempts to assert the African personality. The chapter concludes with the death of Padmore, Nkrumah's adviser and comrade.

The second part of this book examines the deepening confrontation between Ghana and the West led by the United States. Chapter 4 marks a pivotal juncture, focusing on the short-lived expatriate status of African American civil rights attorney Pauli Murray, whose time in Ghana was complicated by the Congo Crisis (1960) and by Nkrumah's political offensive against opposition attempts to destabilize the Ghanaian government. This chapter marks a turning point in the relationship between Ghana and the United States, as 1960 was widely heralded as the Year of Africa, when the prospect of more than thirty nations achieving independence fostered widespread expectations of peaceful political change on the continent. But such hopes of an orderly transition were dashed by secessionist threats to the independent Congo and the assassination of its democratically elected leader, Patrice Lumumba. African American outrage at Lumumba's death was followed by

18   journalistic assertions debunking solidarity between African Americans and Africans as illusory, a discourse Murray played an inadvertent though hardly insignificant role in formulating.

The Congo Crisis abruptly curtailed the idealism fueled by liberatory struggles and hopes for peaceful political change. It also marked Nkrumah's shift from a pro-Western and American stance to open appeals for assistance from the Soviet bloc in addition to the ongoing appeals for U.S. aid. The period also saw Nkrumah's use of increasingly autocratic power to banish his opposition from the processes of parliamentary government. To counter U.S. propaganda and the conservatism of the Ghanaian elite, Nkrumah relied increasingly on leftist sympathizers from America, the West Indies, and other parts of the African continent in tandem with Ghanaian officials to promote his independent ideological blueprint for socialist transformation and development (Nkrumahism). The arrival of W. E. B. and Shirley Graham Du Bois in Ghana helped attract such black leftists as Alphaeus Hunton, Julian Mayfield, Victoria Garvin, and others. Chapter 5 surveys this development, focusing on the arrival in Ghana of Mayfield, whose political activism hastened his flight from the United States.

With the ouster of Malcolm X from the Nation of Islam in 1964, the militant Muslim leader was free to pursue the activism and radical internationalism that he had somewhat deemphasized as the Nation of Islam's national spokesman. Chapter 6 concerns Malcolm's visit to Ghana as part of his extensive tour of Africa and the Middle East. Invited by Mayfield to update African American expatriates on the accelerating struggle back in America, Malcolm welcomed the company of like-minded Afro-Americans and sought to transcend the constraints on the U.S. movement by soliciting African governments' political support for the 22 million African Americans, including those brutalized in the South for demanding full citizenship. Malcolm's visit exposed the tensions between his and the expatriates' pan-African radicalism and a Ghanaian state wary of further antagonizing the United States by openly endorsing the controversial Muslim leader. Malcolm's visit energized the expatriates, who anticipated a new tendency in the U.S. black movement that reflected their radical internationalism. Such hopes would be all but dashed by Malcolm's assassination in February 1965.

Chapter 7 explores the tensions leading up to Nkrumah's ouster in 1966. As Nkrumah faced a host of challenges to his government, African American expatriate loyalists found themselves subject to the vicissitudes of Ghanaian politics. With the regime weakened by corruption and declining revenues from a precipitous decline in the price of cocoa, Ghana's main source of

foreign exchange, Mayfield, although disillusioned by these developments   19
and by Malcolm's death, soldiered on as editor of the *African Review*, a
journal of political economy that represented the major intellectual artifact
of the black expatriate presence in Ghana. As Nkrumah pushed for an African union government and threatened to deploy Ghanaian troops in the fight
against colonialism in southern Africa, conspirators in the police and army
plotted his overthrow. Ironically, by driving his opposition underground or
into exile, Nkrumah left political violence as the only means of challenge to
his rule. While warning signs had been evident, Nkrumah's ouster while on a
peace mission to North Vietnam dealt a devastating blow to the revolutionary hopes of Mayfield and other expatriates. The depth and intensity of their
support for Nkrumah and their commitment to an emancipatory African
politics led them to engage in soul-searching and painful criticism of what
had gone wrong.

The concluding chapters consider the aftermath of the coup and the legacies of the black expatriates' experiences in Ghana. Chapter 8 discusses the
post-Ghana careers of Nkrumah, Mayfield, Drake, and others. Both chapter 8
and the epilogue consider the transnational dimension of African American citizenship through the legacy of Nkrumah's pan-African project and
through the lens of the contemporary memory of the slave trade.

This book builds on recent scholarship that has reframed the study of U.S.
race relations and the civil rights movement within an international perspective. It also builds on an important body of scholarship on transnational
black politics and radicalism.[16] But while much of this valuable work has
taken the form of literary, intellectual, or cultural histories that have illuminated transnational routes of migration, communication, intellectual and
cultural production, and movement activism, *American Africans in Ghana*
analyzes how transnational black subjectivities inspired by Ghana and African struggles for national independence sparked political contests in both
the United States and Africa over the image of the American nation and the
formation of modern black and African subjects. What is most at stake in this
study is not so much the image or legacy of Nkrumah himself or the extent to
which the expatriates succeeded or failed to integrate themselves into Ghanaian life and culture. While these are important issues, what is most significant about the story of black expatriates in Ghana is their involvement in a
transnational political struggle waged both within and beyond the boundaries of the United States over the content and parameters of African American citizenship and consciousness, which, at the nexus of U.S. and African
freedom struggles and during the Cold War, had profound consequences for

20   U.S. domestic and foreign policy makers. Citizenship, as Frederick Cooper reminds us, "is a dynamic concept, whose meanings are not intrinsic to the construct but are shaped in political, social, and cultural debate and confrontation." This understanding of citizenship informs my account of how the political struggle over the meaning of African American citizenship was informed not strictly within the national terrain of the civil rights movement but by global issues of nonalignment, the Cold War, anticolonialism, and African decolonization.[17]

If Nkrumah is remembered at all, it is primarily as an icon of anti-imperialist resistance by those of the global South and their allies engaged in contemporary struggles against Western hegemony and militarism. He, his times, and the struggle over African American consciousness that he in part inspired have been largely airbrushed from public memory. Who remembers Nkrumah and the "African personality" or recalls the images of African diplomats holding forth at the United Nations when African Americans were still violently barred from voting throughout the South? Perhaps such memories still stir within a few Americans of a certain age. It is as if the appearance of new African nations on the world stage never happened.

Of course, fragments persist, remnants of this largely forgotten history. But such artifacts often fail to convey the intensity of the moment and the passions that generated them. Some sense of that period can be retrieved from microfilms of major newspapers or gleaned serendipitously from the dusty shelves of used bookstores or library stacks. As with the handful of surviving veterans of a war concluded generations ago, only a dwindling few can testify to the depths of joy, admiration, and hatred generated by Nkrumah and Ghana or even Martin Luther King Jr.

Two examples of inscribed texts from the period will suffice in recalling the passions of that era. My personal copy of Nkrumah's autobiography is inscribed by the author to John Wesley Dobbs, an African American civic leader from Atlanta. Dobbs attended the Ghanaian independence ceremonies, and his heavily underlined copy bespeaks an avid interest in Ghana and Africa (which coexisted with an equal commitment to the cause of desegregation). The book contains several inlaid sheets of paper with jottings reflecting that interest, perhaps written after a personal interview with Nkrumah, including the statement, "they prefer bad gov[ernmen]t of their own [to] good gov[ernmen]t by outsiders—to walk, must crawl." Contrast this with a copy of a sympathetic political biography of Nkrumah by British journalist Douglas Rogers located in the Harvey Firestone Library at Princeton University. On the title page, near the author's name, is written an

A 1959 political rally in Ghana is interrupted by an enthusiastic supporter of Kwame Nkrumah. (Time Life Pictures/Getty Images)

anonymous inscription, "Nigger Loving Red." Examples of this conflation of white racism and anticommunism abound in the historical record among apologists for white supremacy from South Carolina to South Africa. As for the perspective of Dobbs, similar examples can be found in the African American and West Indian press, the archives of historically black colleges, and other such repositories for the aspirations and activities of generations of African Americans, West Indians, and Africans.

Another artifact of African American cultural memory evokes the largely forgotten world of black transnational affiliations that are at the heart of this book. Ntozake Shange's 1987 poem "Mood Indigo" recovers the vibrant political culture of black internationalism in the Harlem of the poet's childhood against a contemporary condition of neglect if not crisis:

> it hasn't always been this way
> ellington was not a street
> robeson no mere memory.

Shange fondly recalls visits to her family home by these African American icons, including W. E. B. Du Bois, who "walked up my father's stairs," humming a tune over her as she slept "in the company of men / who changed the world." Shange nostalgically recalls the presence of black political and musical luminaries (Ray Barretto and Dizzy Gillespie), a protective, progressive, and loving community of men she likened to "our daddy's arms . . . children growing in the company of men," an implicit commentary on the contemporary absence of such a community. The poem's concluding lines mobilize a defiant collective memory against the erasure and amnesia that Frazier feared would overtake African Americans in post–civil rights America:

> we belonged to a whole world
> nkrumah was no foreigner . . .
> it hasn't always been this way
> ellington was not a street.

For Shange, although the legendary composer may be enshrined in public memory by the street that bears his name, this civic recognition scarcely does justice to the poet's depiction of an internationalist black public sphere, suffused with heroic black male leaders and artists and synonymous with the intimate spaces and structures of feeling understood literally and figuratively as home.[18]

In many respects, this book examines the forces, both contemporaneous and retrospective, that have largely extinguished the memory of Ghana, the vision of black modernity and the prominence of Africa in global affairs it symbolized, and the hope and enthusiasm it inspired. Today, it is a commonplace in the West that Nkrumah undermined his own cause and helped obliterate that memory with his own mistakes and authoritarian rule. While Nkrumah is hardly blameless, I believe that such a focus on his flaws merely rehashes the vilification of his leadership while he was in power. At a deeper level, such condemnations of Nkrumah, while pro-American dictators— euphemistically referred to as "strongmen"—such as Mobutu Sese Seko of Zaire were absolved of their criminal theft and brutality as long as political expediency was served, suggest an underlying contempt for African liberation. This preoccupation with flawed "charismatic" African leadership obscures the independent challenge waged by new Asian and African states to the bipolar Cold War vision of global order. The erasure of the Afro-Asian nonaligned project and the vanquishing of its revolutionary aspirations by the dominant Cold War paradigm is not just a matter of historiographic neglect. Both U.S. policy makers and subsequent Americanist historians of the postwar era have been ill served by their willingness to subordinate the interests of a majority of the world's peoples to bipolar Cold War strategic rivalries and frameworks. These failures of political vision and historical imagination have had dire potential consequences for national and global security.

The story of the destruction of Ghana's radical vision is more than an account of the destruction of the radical hopes of Ghana's sympathizers. It is also ultimately the story of the hollow triumph of American hegemony during and after the Cold War. Such an engagement with the unfulfilled aspirations of the formerly colonized world helps us understand what is obscured by predictable denunciations of Nkrumah: the sense of optimism and resolve with which many black radicals, Ghanaians, and former colonials elsewhere surveyed the world and sought meaningful change. Their belief that the world's oppressed peoples could fulfill their human potential helped define an era that is dismissed or forgotten at our peril. The neglect of this history virtually abandons us to the cynicism of a U.S. foreign policy locked in the unsustainable pursuit of a neoimperial military crusade against fundamentalist extremists whom the United States once supported as part of its misbegotten and cynical Cold War containment policies and proxy wars and who now ominously occupy the political vacuum created by U.S. policies' removal of secular nationalist governments.[19] Within the space of two generations, we have seen the chilling transmogrification of the former colonized world's dreams of freedom and modernity, their memory now eclipsed by

24   the suicidal desperation of fundamentalist terror and widespread ethnic and
religious violence.

While the overwhelming majority of African Americans kept faith with
the United States and its struggle to dismantle systemic racial discrimination, an important segment of the African American population remained
skeptical of the nation's commitment to racial liberalism. In pursuing a politics based on an American citizenship defined by solidarity with African
liberation struggles, African American activists caused establishment voices
to reiterate assertions of the fundamental Americanism of the Negro in the
United States. But for black activists coming of age during the postwar years,
Americanism was defined by the long-standing catalog of the horrors of Jim
Crow segregation, including restrictions on civil liberties; vicious attacks
against African American men and women, soldiers in uniform and civilians
alike; judicial and extralegal lynchings for alleged sex crimes against white
womanhood; barriers to full employment; and restricted educational and
professional opportunities. For a significant number of African Americans,
such systematic inequality in the United States made Africa a more appropriate locus for civic and political identification. While the number of African
American critics of integration and expatriates was small, an American officialdom already contending for the allegiance of "uncommitted" nonwhite
nations in the Cold War viewed this potential mobilization in solidarity with
Africa and anticolonialism as an affront to U.S. foreign policy designs and
management of desegregation on its own terms.

In matters pertaining to race at home and abroad, U.S. officials were inconsistent in their application of liberal principles. The formal commitment
to justice for African Americans at home was not matched by an egalitarian
concern for African peoples. Although compelled by Cold War rivalry with
the Soviet Union to endorse desegregation and enact antidiscrimination
laws that reaffirmed African Americans' right to full citizenship, American
policy makers provided political cover and occasionally military assistance to
repressive white minority governments in Africa and for U.S. and Western
investments in those regimes. U.S. officials were keenly sensitive to African
American criticism of this inconsistency. The prevailing view among officials
was that making the constitution color-blind obliged African American citizens to unlearn the lessons of racialized experience and history and to aspire
to an unhyphenated American nationality.

This mentality is evident in the memoirs of George Ball, undersecretary of
state for economic and trade policy during the Kennedy administration. Ball
strongly criticized the administration's support for new African leaders and

had contempt for the new self-consciousness of American blacks, which he felt was driving misguided pro-African policies. "Though few of them had ever been to Africa or even thought much about it, sociologists and social workers were busily urging black Americans to seek 'identity' by attention to their African roots." This was a mistake, not only "politically distracting but [also] a cruel joke" on black Americans, who were "after all, Americans, and their problem was to cope effectively in American society."[20]

Ball's remarks provide a revealing snapshot of the liberal ideology that held sway among U.S. officials. One might begin with his assertion that blacks could "cope effectively in American society" only as Americans, implying that ethnic consciousness posed a disadvantage toward that end. One is tempted to argue to the contrary, that ethnic consciousness has been and remains a crucial resource of mobility for many groups in American society, including African Americans. Then there is Ball's paternalistic claim that black Americans' identification with Africa was instigated by experts from the academy and the helping professions. That assertion evokes the widespread speculation in public discourse on the sources of black activism during the early 1960s, speculation that often revealed an inability to imagine an indigenous political tradition and historical understanding of group interests among black Americans independent of external organization.

Paradoxically, then, despite its adherence to color-blind ideals in its antidiscrimination agenda, U.S. officialdom and its media auxiliaries arrogated to themselves the role of prescribing normative Negro American civic identities, seeking to delegitimize and discourage transnational solidarities for black Americans. The official opposition to an African American citizenship and activism guided by solidarities with black and African peoples epitomized the racially circumscribed nature of the citizenship extended to African Americans during the 1960s.

The story of the expatriates' presence in Ghana thus sheds revealing light on an articulation of American liberal ideology that, far from being a race-neutral abstraction, was formulated in direct response to an oppositional black politics skeptical of integration and animated by anticolonialism. Nkrumah's global leadership from Ghana of a radical anticolonial movement inspired many African Americans to assert a global citizenship in solidarity with African liberation struggles. Nkrumah provided a haven and a platform for African American radicals silenced by the combined repressive forces of the Cold War and Jim Crow segregation. While their numbers were by no means large, their experience suggests that restrictions on black political expression were far more pervasive than is suggested by the fate of such proscribed individuals as Robeson and Du Bois. Even as it focused its concern on a minority of African Americans, the U.S. government's interest in curbing this particular form of black political and activist expression provides a revealing glimpse at the extent to which dominant American citizenship and liberal ideology were, in fact, racially inflected, marked by the suppression of independent black solidarities. This history belies the claims of some scholars who assert that the United States had an exemplary civic national culture into which African Americans ought to have sought integration.[21] That assumption drastically underestimates the extent of massive resistance in the South and institutionalized racism in the North, factors that led a significant number of African Americans to resist the rhetoric of integration. Some of them found greater possibilities and hope for a truly desegregated existence in Nkrumah's Ghana.

As a beacon for the black world's liberatory aspirations and a political sanctuary for exiles from American and colonial racial oppression, Ghana was the product of generations of struggle waged from the margins of segregated black institutions and global radical and anticolonial movements. The political awakening that united peoples of African descent within anticolonial and antiracist movements throughout the twentieth century is the subject of the next chapter.

I

MAPPING THE ROUTES
TO GHANA

Black Modernity, Subjecthood, and
Demands for Full Citizenship

Six years before Ghana's independence, a biographical account of George Padmore published by a radical West Indian newspaper illustrated the convergence of multiple histories of slavery and colonization in the life and career of the journalist and leading publicist of African anticolonial movements. Born in Trinidad, educated in African American universities, based in London, and now, as the article reported, bound for the Gold Coast colony to assist the nationalist movement there, Padmore symbolized a renascent black world overcoming the fragmentation of enslavement. On this occasion, the narrative of Padmore's life story consciously evoked the shared historical origins of peoples of African descent residing in the United States, Brazil, Latin America, and the West Indies whose genesis could be traced to what had been known as the Slave Coast of West Africa. According to this account by L. H. A. Scotland, Padmore's great-grandfather had been an Ashanti warrior who was taken prisoner and sold into slavery on Barbados, where his grandfather had labored on a sugar plantation. The genealogy of Padmore's slave origins reminded readers of the metropolitan foundations of slavery and colonization. Duly noting the slave-owning origins of members of British royalty and nobility, Scotland laid waste to the mystique of primordial Englishness and royalism. The sugar plantation on which Padmore's grandfather toiled was "owned by the ancestors of the present Earl of Harewood, the son of the Princess Royal, sister of King George VI." Padmore's grandfather had migrated to Trinidad after the abolition of slavery in 1834, working as a stonemason and living to the age of 105. The article selectively sketched Padmore's background, claiming that Garveyite race consciousness had sparked Padmore's efforts on behalf of African emancipation and omitting mention of his tenure as the Communist International's foremost expert on colonial peoples. Appearing as the movement for self-government in the Gold Coast gathered momentum in 1951, the article portrayed Padmore's impending visit to West Africa as the closing of a circle, the resolution of a historical cycle of enslavement and impending freedom, exile and return.[1]

Padmore's peripatetic career provided a fitting symbol for the historical routes of mass migration, cultural and political formation, and movement building furthered by a global black press that converged in the independence of Ghana in 1957. The Trinidadian activist intellectual was hardly unique in this regard; this chapter is concerned with mapping the distinct but overlapping routes of political engagement traversed not only by Padmore but also by Ghana's first president, Kwame Nkrumah, and African American sociologist and anthropologist St. Clair Drake. Though originating from disparate locations, all three men were linked by histories of racial subordination and anticolonial struggle. Moreover, these three figures were longtime political allies and worked together to promote pan-Africanism in Ghana after independence. In tracing the paths to Ghana of these and other individuals, I seek to endow the abstract notion of diaspora with the specificity of political projects, lived experience, and emancipatory hopes.[2] I do not just emphasize the layering of international historical and cultural influences that shaped the perspectives of these individuals and of African, West Indian, and African American peoples in the postwar period generally. I seek primarily to account for the social and cultural movements that led peoples of African descent to imagine themselves anew as political subjects and that informed their demands for freedom and full citizenship. The short African century of decolonization movements was advanced by the social transformations wrought by mass labor migrations, military service in world wars, intellectual attacks against Western white supremacy and the spread of antiracist consciousness, and literary and expressive cultures that articulated black peoples' aspirations for cultural and political freedom.

Afro-Modernity and the Short African Century

The activism of Padmore, Nkrumah, and Drake exemplified what political scientist Michael Hanchard has described as an oppositional culture of "Afro-modernity," the result of black people's liberatory engagement with the institutions, ideologies, and technologies of the Western world.[3] Over the short African century of anticolonial struggle and pan-African nationalism, multiple histories of migration, a variety of institutional settings, mass communications technologies, and social and cultural movements provided the basis for a global culture of black modernity linking colonies with metropolitan centers, forging a new sense of a unified black world out of once-disparate diasporas. The vibrant cosmopolitanism of Harlem and its traditions of black nationalist and left-wing agitation, along with those of other black urban enclaves, including Paris; London; Chicago; Washington, D.C.; and Philadelphia, were important sites for the development of transnational black activism. At such African American universities as Fisk, Howard, and Pennsylvania's Lincoln, the legacy of New Negro radicalism shaped interactions between African Americans and foreign-born students from Africa and the Caribbean. Elsewhere, countless African Americans and colonial subjects from the Caribbean and Africa were politicized by the international communist movement and its global agitation on behalf of the Scottsboro defendants as well as the involvement of the organized Left in black popular front movement activism during the 1930s and 1940s.[4]

A major catalyst for the creation of a global culture of black modernity during the early twentieth century was the unprecedented mass migration of peoples of African descent spurred by the demand for labor within industrial mass-production regimes. As Thomas Holt has written, "[M]illions of colored peoples on four continents were quite literally pulled or pushed out of 'their place' " at the bottom of racially oppressive systems of coerced labor.[5] Moving from colony to metropole, from rural villages to cities, they encountered a succession of similar yet distinct systems of racial subordination that exposed them to the promise and discontents of modernity. Describing the formative experiences of Caribbean-born black labor organizer Ewart Guinier, who worked in wartime New York City, historian Martha Biondi has also delineated a collective experience of emigrants, former colonials from the Caribbean, politicized by their encounters with American racism whether in the urban North or in the U.S.-controlled Panama Canal Zone.[6] Kwame Nkrumah and George Padmore underwent a similar passage through the crucible of Western racism. Traveling to the United States in search of education and professional training, Nkrumah and Padmore worked as laborers to subsidize their studies. The belated incorporation of peoples of African descent into mass-production industries spurred demands for political and economic rights within trade union movements. Whether in search of education or employment, migrants to European and American metropolitan urban centers from the rural U.S. South, from the West Indies, and from the country to cities throughout West Africa exemplified not only black and African peoples' quest for greater economic opportunity but increasingly their demands for political change as modern historical subjects.[7]

Mass migration to metropolitan centers fueled anti-imperialist political organizing in London. Since the 1930s, African nationalist student activists and West Indian intellectuals, including Padmore and the exiled Marcus Garvey, agitated in London around pan-African concerns. Such efforts took on greater urgency after Italy's 1935 invasion of Ethiopia, which heightened nationalist sentiment among outraged black and African peoples throughout the world.[8] World War II accelerated demands for freedom and rights consciousness as the dissonant experience of African American and colonized black and African soldiers fighting for democracy on the side of imperial and segregationist powers honed resistance to systemic racial oppression. In London, migrants and students from Africa, the South Asian subcontinent, and the West Indies envisioned themselves as a commonwealth of colonial freedom movements. In the United States, African Americans agitated for civil and voting rights within the March on Washington movement, which campaigned against discrimination in defense industries, housing, and the military and thereby initiated what scholars have recently termed the "long civil rights movement."[9] Just as African Americans looked to the federal government and the courts to declare unconstitutional racial segregation in the South, so did many young blacks of the postwar era draw inspiration from anticolonial movements. The victorious example of Gandhian nonviolence powerfully influenced the U.S. peace movement, facilitating the participation of such black American radicals as St. Clair Drake, Bayard Rustin, and Bill Sutherland in the politics of Gold Coast nationalism.

Black Expressive Cultures of Modernity: Highlife and Negritude

The main cultural artifacts of this urbanization of the black world, which led racialized and colonial subjects to imagine themselves anew as self-determining citizens, were West African highlife, Afro-Cuban music, Trinidadian calypso, and African American modern jazz, or bebop. During the 1950s, the calypsos recorded by Trinidadian singers in London offered wry commentary on the postwar migration of West Indians to England.[10] In Nigeria and Ghana and throughout West Africa, highlife demonstrated a seemingly limitless capacity to absorb other Afro-diasporic musical influences such as calypso and mambo. Highlife, like calypso and African American modern jazz, epitomized the transnational routes and processes of migration and exchange that merged the cultures and struggles of peoples of African descent during the postwar era. As a form of expressive culture synonymous with the anticolonial movement, highlife, as its name suggests, connoted popular African aspirations for freedom and modernity. The music also promoted nationalism by synthesizing a cultural unity out of tribal and ethnic differences. Indeed, the variety of songs and their origins reflected the hybridity of a pan–West African culture defined by migration, ethnic intermarriage, and cosmopolitanism. According to Wolfgang Bender, "Singers would perform in different languages, and the music's changing rhythms reflected many musical cultures. The language used could be Yoruba, Fante, Ewe, Ga, Urhobo, Efik, Igbo, English, pidgin English, and others." During the early 1960s, highlife and West African percussion styles would feature prominently in the compositions of modern jazz drummer Max Roach, and his collaborations with lyricist Oscar Brown Jr., vocalist Abbey Lincoln, and Nigerian percussionist Michael Olatunji articulated African Americans' solidarity with African liberation struggles. Such collaborations between African American and African musicians contributed to a broader articulation of a global, democratic vision of African American consciousness and citizenship.[11]

In literature, the transformative spirit of black modernity found expression in Negritude, which emerged during the 1930s as a literary and cultural movement of Francophone African and black Caribbean intellectuals. Negritude crystallized a growing awareness among black intellectuals throughout Africa and its diaspora of a black voice, an African and diasporic vernacular rearticulation of modern culture through literature, music, and the arts. Before Negritude became known as such, the artistic evocation of a distinctly black vernacular animated the efforts of many artists, including the work of such poets as Afro-Cuban Nicholas Guillen, Jamaican-born Claude McKay and Louise Bennett, and Afro-Americans Paul Laurence Dunbar and Langston Hughes. Specifically, Negritude as cultural movement and manifesto represented black Francophone intellectuals' response to the alienation produced by French colonial policies of assimilation that inevitably denigrated the ancestral African cultural heritage while patronizing the intellectuals as elite *evolués* for their mastery of Francophone language and·culture. Against

European contempt for Africa, advocates of Negritude affirmed African origins and recovered the submerged history of the continent's ancient civilizations. Just as African scholarship and contributions in the arts and sciences represented crucial elements of Western civilization, so in modern times would black and African cultural innovation make singular contributions to universal world culture. As formulated by Senegalese poet Léopold Senghor, Martinican writers Paulette Nardal and Aimé Césaire, and a host of others, Negritude appropriated and synthesized such disparate Western and Afro-diasporic historical and cultural influences and touchstones as Bergsonian philosophy, surrealism, Marxism, Afro-Cuban literary *negrismo*, the Haitian revolution, the New Negro Renaissance, and European anthropology. These intellectuals' declarations of black and African cultural autonomy, their assertion of the cultural unity of peoples of African descent, and their rejection of European cultural imperialism provided deracinated and exiled black and African peoples with a means of spiritual return to their African origins. Negritude also galvanized anticolonial resistance, as such figures as Césaire and Senghor translated its values into the political realm of decolonization. At its genesis, Negritude represented nothing less than a global assertion of black emancipatory modernity.

Cosmopolitan Afro-Modernity: The Diaspora Comes to Africa

As suggested by the multiple histories that converged in highlife and Negritude, throughout the black world, local subjectivities and demands for freedom were invariably enacted within what was widely understood as a global setting. With the postwar collapse of Europe's empires and African Americans' escalating demands for full citizenship, peoples of African descent increasingly regarded themselves as part of a global community of struggle. West Africans of the postwar era, for example, came of age within a diasporic culture that had long been cosmopolitan and a part of the West. As Paul Gilroy and Manthia Diawara have shown, mass communications technologies and expressive culture are crucial vehicles for the ongoing formation of transnational modern black and African subjectivities.[12] Indeed, as the culture of highlife suggests, "local" African cultures were inherently cosmopolitan and outward looking. For a youth in Lagos during the 1940s and 1950s, confirmations of the worldwide African presence were an everyday matter, from the local community of Portuguese-speaking repatriates from Brazil to American cinematic images of blacks. There was also Afro-Cuban dance

music and such Afro-American heroes as boxing champions Joe Louis and
Sugar Ray Robinson. In this sense, the Anglophone West Africa of Kwame
Nkrumah's youth was truly a part of the black diaspora, with its dense layer-
ing of intellectual exchanges and historical and sociocultural movements.[13]

For example, such Afro-diasporic influences as Garveyism, a cornerstone
of the U.S.-based New Negro movement, contributed to a burgeoning African renaissance during the 1920s through which an Anglophone West African intelligentsia proclaimed Africa's membership in the modern world and
articulated popular aspirations for national self-determination. Such was the
milieu that Nkrumah carried with him to the United States and Harlem,
where he pursued an informal political education in addition to formal study
at historically black Lincoln University. And the New Negro renaissance in
America helped launch George Padmore on the path to radicalism and anticolonial agitation at such black American colleges as Fisk and Howard. Such
African American institutions—including churches, colleges, fraternities,
and newspapers—were major sites of anticolonial ferment, venues for what
historian Penny Von Eschen has called a "politics of the African Diaspora."
Relocated to London, Padmore's pan-African organizing brought him into
contact with Francophone West African labor organizer Tiemoko Garan
Kouyaté, a collaboration that, as Brent Edwards has written, demonstrated
not only the crossing of boundaries between different colonial regimes and
languages but more importantly the inherently international character of
black radicalism in the interwar period.[14] Along these routes of communication and within these hybrid diasporic settings that in a sense could not be
considered strictly African, West Indian, or African American, anticolonial
black activists and intellectuals articulated the emergence of a modern political community defined by self-determination and freedom.

As colonial subjects from Africa and the Caribbean kept abreast of African American politics and institutions, a segment of the African American
intelligentsia linked its struggles for full citizenship in the United States
with the global anticolonial movement. Taking for granted the congruence
of their distinct struggles, members of this worldwide network of activists
and intellectuals pooled educational, political, and intellectual resources
in the service of pan-African emancipation. The organizing and planning
for self-government by Nkrumah and Padmore in London paved the way for
the nation-building efforts of Drake and others as the Gold Coast colony
became the new nation of Ghana. Indeed, the extent to which African
nationalism framed the activities of such African American intellectuals and

activists as Drake, Bill Sutherland, and Bayard Rustin has been greatly underappreciated.

From Trinidad to America, West Africa, and England: George Padmore's Transatlantic Odyssey

George Padmore was the leading theoretician, strategist, and publicist of anticolonialism and African liberation, linking metropolitan agitation to the nationalist movements on the African continent. As with so many other West Indian intellectuals, exile was an essential condition for his life's work. Padmore left Trinidad for the United States in 1927, seeking professional training. Instead, he joined the Communist Party the next year. Padmore quickly ascended to leadership as the Comintern's expert on colonial peoples but was expelled from the party in 1934 when he objected to its pursuit of an alliance with Britain and France in return for its withdrawal of support for anticolonial challenges to those imperial nations. Beginning in 1935, Padmore based his political work in London until he relocated to Ghana in 1957 and became a special adviser to Nkrumah.

Born Malcolm Ivan Meredith Nurse in Tarcarigua, Trinidad, on June 28, 1903, Padmore was the second child in a family of five. His father, H. A. Nurse, had achieved distinction as an agriculturist and botanist. Among blacks of Padmore's father's generation in Trinidad's middle class, racial pride and solidarity were necessary responses to metropolitan racism. An insulting tract by an English writer, J. A. Froude, *The English in the West Indies* (1888), received a swift rebuttal from Jacob Thomas, Trinidad's leading black intellectual. In his aptly titled *Froudacity: West Indian Fables Explained* (1889), Thomas rebutted Froude's "childish insults of the blacks" and called for the unification of the scattered peoples of the African diaspora on behalf of African emancipation. Thomas's appeal was answered by another prominent contemporary of Padmore's father. Harry Sylvester Williams, a Trinidadian barrister, organized the first Pan-African Congress in London in 1900.[15] Malcolm Nurse received his secondary education in Port of Spain and worked as a journalist. Hoping to study law or medicine, Nurse sailed for the United States when his name came up on the U.S. immigration quota. In the mid-1920s, he attended Fisk University, where he joined the student newspaper and made a name for himself as a much-sought speaker on colonial issues. Nurse subsequently entered Howard University in Washington, D.C., where he came into contact with prominent black American scholars including Alain Locke, Ralph Bunche, and Charles Houston. Throughout the

1920s, Howard was a cosmopolitan center of black aspiration, with approximately two hundred foreign students from colonial territories, mostly the
British empire.[16]

Many years later, a roommate from Padmore's days at Fisk and Howard
provided a memorable account of Padmore's political coming-of-age. At
Fisk, Padmore, still known as Malcolm Nurse, studied English literature and
spoke around Nashville and occasionally at Vanderbilt University. He kept
abreast of the doings of the New Negro, following the efforts of Fisk alumnus
Du Bois and Garvey. Padmore read H. L. Mencken and the radical journalism
of the *American Mercury*. Nashville, though moderate, was nevertheless part
of a region where recorded lynchings still averaged between thirty and fifty
annually. Padmore's outspokenness under these conditions enhanced his
appeal as a speaker at nearby colleges. At Fisk, he attended seminars and
achieved renown (or notoriety, according to some) by challenging the racism
of visiting speakers, sometimes heckling them outright. Yet he withdrew
short of obtaining his degree. His wife had arrived in New York, leaving their
baby daughter, Blyden, with grandparents in Trinidad. Padmore moved to
New York, ostensibly bent on obtaining a law degree.

The couple spent the summer of 1927 in New York, where Padmore enrolled at New York University, although he dropped out the following December without ever having attended a class. Padmore did maintenance
work in the *New York Times* building and came into contact with Communist
Party members around Union Square. His biographer, James Hooker, claims
that Padmore was subject to party discipline from mid-1927 onward. Party
officials sent the young man to a youth camp in upstate New York, where he
lectured and immersed himself in party activities and objectives. According
to a Howard classmate, Legrand Coleman, Padmore had come to regard the
Communist Party as the only organization willing to do anything about the
plight of black people.[17]

Padmore transferred to Howard in 1928, again intending to study law.
Howard's foreign students included many West Indians seeking that institution's opportunities for professional training. By now, Malcolm Nurse had
adopted the name George Padmore as a cover for his political activities. But
Malcolm Nurse was no less active a participant in campus politics than the
man answering to Padmore, making it difficult to believe that many observers were taken in by the ruse. Bunche, one of Padmore's instructors,
disclaimed any knowledge of Padmore's party membership and recalled that
the young firebrand gave a speech "one noon in the center of campus in

36 which he denounced just about everybody and everything in fluent, ringing rhetoric."[18] Another incident at Howard suggests Padmore's readiness to confront authority. The school's president, Mordecai Johnson, had invited Sir Esme Howard, the British ambassador to the United States, to speak at the dedication of the university's International House. Padmore and another West Indian student, Cyril C. Ollivierre, president of the campus Garvey Club, organized a protest attacking the ambassador as an apologist for empire and for his likely involvement in Garvey's deportation. Padmore and Ollivierre distributed leaflets identifying Padmore as secretary of an anti-imperialist youth organization, and Padmore's shouted objections to the ambassador's defense of British imperialism in Africa echoed through the hall. So vehement was the young man's heckling that a scandalized board of trustees sought to have Padmore expelled. Johnson, who had admired Padmore and shared platforms with him while he attended Fisk, put a stop to the effort, claiming with tongue in cheek that no George Padmore was enrolled at Howard.[19]

Padmore took full advantage of Howard's tolerant climate, organizing during the day, reading economics at night, and conversing into the wee hours with his roommate, a medical student, on such matters as economic waste and materialism in the United States. His legal studies languished as his party activities consumed most of his time. He commuted frequently between Washington and New York, where he coedited the *Negro Champion* with Richard B. Moore in Harlem.[20]

Padmore's arrival in the United States coincided with the New Negro militancy that had exploded in student strikes deploring the conservatism and white philanthropic control of several black colleges, including Fisk, where a strike occurred in 1927.[21] African American discontent also found expression in the Garvey movement's anticolonial stirrings and the National Association for the Advancement of Colored People's campaign for federal antilynching legislation. Black assertiveness often represented a direct response to attempts in northern cities to keep blacks in their place. African Americans remembered the Red Summer of 1919—so named for the frequency of lethal white mob assaults on black urban communities that season—primarily for black efforts at armed self-defense and retaliation. After the war, the resurgent Ku Klux Klan further spread the viruses of racial polarization, mob violence, and xenophobia. Migrants from the rural South as well as the immigration of Afro-Caribbeans and growing numbers of African students swelled the size of black urban communities. These transformations had a radicalizing effect on African American public culture. The spread of radical ideas was far from a one-way process, however. Already an avid reader of J. J. Thomas, Du Bois, and Garvey before departing from Trinidad, Padmore's political formation did not begin with his membership in the Communist Party. His activities suggested the reverberation of New Negro militancy throughout the Americas and the internationalism of many black U.S. college campuses as sites of African and West Indian nationalist challenges to the British and French empires. Indeed, Robin Kelley's argument that African American communists in Alabama brought cultural traditions and the lived experience of Jim Crow segregation to their membership in the party is instructive for understanding Padmore's attraction to organized Marxism.[22] Those who recruited Padmore capitalized on his background of colonial oppression and black consciousness and resistance, which first began in Trinidad and continued through his exposure to Jim Crow and New Negro agitation in the United States.

Padmore's association with the party coincided with one of its noteworthy periods of receptivity to African and black struggles. His talents were speedily rewarded when he was named secretary to the International Trade Union Committee of Negro Workers and assumed editorship of the *Negro Worker*. In 1930, Padmore toured West Africa, recruiting delegates for the First International Congress of Negro Workers, which was held that same year in Hamburg. Padmore became the Communist International's expert on anticolonial movements. The product of these years was Padmore's *The Life and Struggles of Negro Toilers* (1931), which impressed T. Ras Makonnen, a British Guiana–born pan-African activist who would work alongside Padmore in the Ghanaian government. Like Padmore a product of black American universities, Makonnen, who had taken the name of Haile Selassie's father in solidarity with Ethiopia's struggle against Italy, viewed Padmore's book and its bracing anticolonial rhetoric as a "magic weapon." Padmore resigned from the party in 1934 when the Comintern liquidated the anti-imperialist International Trade Union Committee of Negro Workers as part of an attempt to improve relations with the Western colonial powers. Padmore later wrote that he considered the party's abandonment of the young national liberation movements of Africa and Asia "a betrayal of the fundamental interests of my people, with which I could not identify myself."[23] Beginning in the early 1930s, Padmore was based in London, where he wrote prolifically as a journalist in the anti-imperialist and African American press and continued his agitation on behalf of the colonized world.

The Afro-patriotism that animated Padmore's break with the party was

MAPPING THE ROUTES TO GHANA

38   magnified among peoples of African descent when Italy invaded Ethiopia in
1935. According to Makonnen, the war transcended ideological and cultural
differences among blacks, making it clear to Garveyites, communists and
noncommunists alike, and African Americans only recently arrived from the
rural South that imperialism was the chief scourge of African and black
peoples. Few could remain indifferent to the reports of Ethiopia under siege
or to the Pope's blessing of the war effort against one of the two independent
African nations. St. Clair Drake, Lawrence D. Reddick, and another young
African American instructor at Dillard University in New Orleans risked
physical violence when they disrupted a "Victory Parade" of two thousand
Italian Americans by driving several times through the marchers in a car
bearing the sign "We protest against this celebration of aggressive war and
fascism." The professors' bold maneuver was backed by an African American
community mobilized against the war and its supporters.[24]

The specter of prostrate Ethiopia helped unify disparate and scattered
black peoples. The international black press fanned outrage at the Ethiopian
invasion. Hearing of the Pope's blessing, African nationalist leader Nnamdi
Azikiwe, a future president of Nigeria, and Sierra Leonean trade unionist
and founder of the radical West African Youth League Isaac T. A. Wallace-
Johnson published a bitter editorial in the West African press, "Has the
African a God?" British authorities promptly had the two men arrested on
sedition charges. Both had published articles throughout West Africa attacking British rule and were critical exponents of nationalist movements on the
continent. The war remained front-page news in African American newspapers. In letters to the *Chicago Defender*, black citizens declared their readiness to take up arms to liberate Ethiopia. In 1937, Wallace-Johnson, Makonnen, and a boyhood friend of Padmore from Trinidad, Trotskyist intellectual
and anticolonial activist C. L. R. James, cofounded the International African
Service Bureau. Based in London, the bureau built on the organizational
precedents established by members of the colonial intelligentsia. Its publication, *International African Opinion*, promoted the connectedness of the freedom struggles of Africans and peoples of African descent in the United
States, the West Indies, and Africa. Its frequent demand, "Africa for the
Africans," echoed the pan-African tradition of the U.S.-based Garveyite
newspaper, the *Negro World*, and its pre–World War I precursor, London's
African Times and Orient Review, and *International African Opinion* took up
the cause of black peoples worldwide. For example, it published a poem by
Langston Hughes condemning the scheduled execution of one of the Scotts-
boro defendants alongside a brief history of the case.[25] Padmore's defiant

voice dominated the globetrotting features "Politics and the Negro" and "The
African World," evident in the journal's condemnations of Fascist and democratic imperialists, its opposition to the impending global war on anticolonial
grounds, and its extensive coverage of the labor unrest coursing through the
West Indies. While quick to celebrate such symbolic events as Joe Louis's
defeat of Max Schmeling, hailed as "a victory for Africans and people of
African descent the world over," the *International African Observer* also
excoriated such colonial outrages as French troops' shooting of striking railway workers in Dakar in which six were killed and forty wounded. The
journal's fiercely united anticolonial front had room for some internal disagreement. In an otherwise favorable review of James's *A History of Negro
Revolts*, a contributor took exception with James's negative assessment of
Garveyism.[26]

James recommended Kwame Nkrumah to Padmore. Padmore recruited
Nkrumah, who was pursuing graduate studies in the United States, as the co-
organizer, along with himself, of the fifth Pan-African Congress, held in
Manchester, England, in 1945. At this pivotal meeting, the leadership of pan-
African movement shifted from New World blacks to Africans who sought a
grassroots following through trade union organizations and mass political
parties. Padmore met Nkrumah at Euston Station when he moved to England in 1947 to continue his political involvement in West African nationalist politics.

From the Gold Coast to America and England: Kwame Nkrumah and the African Renaissance

While Padmore was acquiring his political education in Trinidad and African
American universities, including his brief passage through the international
communist movement, colonial strictures and economic depression were
radicalizing young Africans in Britain's Gold Coast colony, including those
who laid the groundwork for Kwame Nkrumah's future efforts. Nkrumah,
born in Nkroful, in the southwestern corner of present-day Ghana, was the
product of the crisscrossing paths of nationalism forged by Padmore and
others like him throughout West Africa, African American communities, and
anticolonial circles in London. Indeed, Nkrumah's route to the leadership of
postindependence Ghana was as steeped in the circuitous routes of diasporic
black modernity as the path forged by any of his expatriate allies.

The global depression of the 1930s brought unemployment, falling wages
and prices, and labor unrest to the Gold Coast colony. Cocoa farmers pro-

40 tested falling prices by withdrawing their crop and boycotting imported goods. A likely target of colonial officials' attempt to suppress seditious literature was the *Negro Worker*, which Padmore edited. During his tour of West Africa, Padmore had recruited distributors for the paper and cultivated ties to nationalist leaders and newspaper editors. Yet another expression of this African renaissance in the Gold Coast was the founding in 1930 of the African Academy at Sekondi by Bankole Awoonor-Renner, who had studied in Moscow during the 1920s. The academy promoted African initiatives in the arts and sciences and encouraged the publication of the works of African writers, poets, composers, and inventors. At its inaugural meeting, members of the academy claimed African authorship of the best of Western thought and culture. According to E. Tackie-Otoo, "[I]t is no longer possible to regard Western Civilization as a just and permanent testimonial to the superiority of a Colour, a Race, a Nation." Tackie-Otoo reminded his listeners that the most eminent philosophers and scholars of the early Christian church—Tertullian, Augustine of Hippo, Clemens, Alexandrius, and Cyril—were Africans and that "Solon, Plato, Pythagorus and others of the Master spirits of ancient Greece performed pilgrimages to Africa in search of knowledge."[27]

In the early 1930s, Isaac Wallace-Johnson and Nnamdi Azikiwe arrived in the Gold Coast, and Nkrumah is almost certain to have read their incendiary editorials. In 1934, Wallace-Johnson cofounded the West African Youth League with Awoonor-Renner. They, along with Ben Tamakloe, the Cambridge-educated son of a Nigerian chief, had agitated against the sedition bill and later Italy's invasion of Ethiopia. Tamakloe had previously spoken at an Accra meeting publicizing the plight of Alabama's Scottsboro defendants. Azikiwe arrived in the Gold Coast in 1934 after completing his education at Lincoln University in the United States. He took up the editorship of the *African Morning Post*, using the paper to demand the repeal of the sedition ordinance and to support the radical nationalist Maambi Party.

During these years of nationalist agitation in the Gold Coast, Nkrumah was planning his sojourn abroad for his collegiate education. Having shown promise under the tutelage of Catholic missionaries, Nkrumah began the course for teacher training at Achimota College in 1927. In this Nkrumah was a rare exception within a colonial education system unable to provide post-primary schooling to massive numbers of elementary school graduates. The Gold Coast's education pyramid thus had an exceptionally broad bottom that led during the early postwar period to the creation of a social group with limited prospects that became a major constituency for Nkrumah's nationalist Convention People's Party.[28] At Achimota, Nkrumah encountered the

influential U.S.-educated Kwegyr Aggrey, assistant vice principal of the college, which provided the equivalent of a secondary school education. Aggrey
did much to awaken nationalist ideals among youth of Nkrumah's generation, though Achimota, in its refusal to employ Africans as teachers, remained consistent with a colonial system that restricted Africans to the low-
est levels of the civil service, paying them half the salary received by British
civil servants. Aggrey returned to the United States in 1927 to complete his
doctorate but died suddenly shortly after his arrival at Columbia University.
Nkrumah paid tribute to his mentor as a founding member of the Aggrey
Students' debate society at Achimota. Later, he would write in his autobiography that his admiration for Aggrey had given him the idea of continuing his studies in the United States, although his goal to attend college in
England, shared by many Africans under British rule, was thwarted when he
failed the London matriculation examination. After graduating from Achimota in 1930, Nkrumah held a series of teaching positions and became even
more deeply immersed in the African renaissance.[29]

What is known of Nkrumah's plans for study abroad while in the Gold Coast
is sketchy, but other mentors seem to have filled the void left by Aggrey's
death, encouraging Nkrumah's aspirations to study in the United States.
While teaching grammar school in Axim, Nkrumah was befriended by nationalist leader S. R. Wood, secretary of the National Congress of British
West Africa. Nkrumah may have been directly acquainted with and certainly knew of nationalist intellectual Kobina Sekyi and kept up with literature published by the National Congress. In his autobiography, Nkrumah
acknowledged the influence of Azikiwe, omitting mention of the radical
Wallace-Johnson's likely influence. When Nkrumah visited Azikiwe's newspaper office in 1935, the older man advised Nkrumah to apply to Lincoln
University, from which Azikiwe had graduated and at which he had subsequently taught. Azikiwe introduced Nkrumah to a friend and fellow Lincoln
graduate, Thomas Dosumu-Johnson, then studying at Columbia University's
Teacher's College. Nkrumah named Dosumu-Johnson as a friend in his application to Lincoln (his personal statement quoted Cecil Rhodes, "So much
to do, so little done") and had received a letter from Dosumu-Johnson as
early as 1933 pledging his assistance and mentioning their mutual friend
Wood, a fact that suggests that Nkrumah had set his sights on Lincoln University before he met Azikiwe.[30]

Nkrumah established a strong academic record at Lincoln, and many
fellow students recalled him as serious, affable but quiet, and selective in his

42 dealings with them. During Nkrumah's tenure, Lincoln's student body numbered about three hundred, of which more than a dozen were African. The yearbook of his graduating class records Nkrumah's selection by his fellow students as "most interesting," with an accompanying verse:

> Africa is the beloved of his dreams
> Philosopher, thinker, with forceful schemes
> In aesthetics, politics, he's all "In the field,"
> Nkrumah, "tres intérresantes," radiates appeal.

Nkrumah's autobiography, published in 1957, is reticent on his social life and political activities in both Philadelphia and Harlem, where he spent summer vacations. Nkrumah is also largely silent on personal encounters with white racism, although he does mention one incident. Nkrumah and a friend were stranded in Philadelphia without lodging and elected to sleep on a bench at the bus station. A policeman told the two men, "[M]ove on chums, you can't sleep here." Regardless of whether Nkrumah softened his account of the policeman's conduct, it is clear that the politician studiously avoided alienating his audience of American policy makers and potential well-wishers. Nkrumah does allude to his constant difficulties in supporting himself, mentioning such odd jobs as peddling fish from a pushcart in Harlem, an equally brief stint working in a soap factory, and working at sea during summers as a member of the National Maritime Union. Nkrumah was chronically behind in paying his tuition fees to Lincoln and benefited from the institution's commitment to African students, particularly those like Nkrumah who had solid academic records.

Nkrumah's account of Harlem was more picturesque than political. He recalled revivalist church services there as a source of "entertainment," implying that his youthful religious ardor had waned considerably. By all accounts, he participated in Harlem's rich cultural life, frequenting Louis Micheaux's bookstore specializing in Africana and reading at the Schomburg Library, where he must have encountered its curator, Lawrence Reddick. Reddick had published an article in the *African Interpreter*, the voice of the African Student Association in Canada and the United States, urging African Americans to educate themselves on the contemporary mass movements in Africa. The same issue of the *Interpreter* carried a photo of Nkrumah as president of the association.[31] John Henrik Clarke remembered seeing Nkrumah at meetings of the Blyden Society, which was devoted to the study of African history. Nkrumah probably became aware of the anticolonial Council of African Affairs as early as 1937, though his autobiography puts this involvement at a later date. Harlem may well have exerted a much greater impact on Nkrumah than his autobiography discloses. Nkrumah received a raucous welcome when he returned to Harlem as Ghana's prime minister in 1958. Two years later, he shared a platform with Malcolm X, Adam Clayton Powell, and other Harlem luminaries at an outdoor rally.[32]

After graduating, Nkrumah avoided deportation by enrolling in post-graduate seminary studies at Lincoln. Marika Sherwood surmises that this was an expedient decision on Nkrumah's part to ease the pressures of living expenses and mounting academic fees. Having obtained the Presbyterian seminary's preliminary preacher's license, Nkrumah appeared regularly in the pulpits of Washington, Philadelphia, and New York. Collections and minister's fees provided him with a source of income, and Nkrumah further benefited from the discount in travel expenses routinely given to ministers. Nkrumah's oratorical talents were well established. One member of a congregation he visited recalled his unique approach: "[H]e would twist around to Africa very quickly from wherever he began."[33] Whatever motives lay behind Nkrumah's ministerial endeavors, they facilitated travel and provided opportunities to articulate African aspirations to African American audiences. In 1941, while enrolled at the Lincoln seminary, Nkrumah earned a master's degree in education from the University of Pennsylvania. That same year, Lincoln hired Nkrumah as a part-time philosophy instructor. Nkrumah joined the Fellowship of Reconciliation, a radical pacifist organization whose leadership included Bayard Rustin and Bill Sutherland. Classmates at Penn recalled his voracious reading in philosophy and above all his enthusiasm for the cause of African freedom.[34]

Nkrumah never received his doctorate from the University of Pennsylvania. He had insisted on writing his dissertation on colonialism, which the philosophy department deemed unacceptable. While at Penn, he assisted the new section on African studies by teaching a course in the Fanti language and compiling a guide to Fanti grammar, and he worked part time in a Philadelphia shipyard, which landed him in the hospital with acute bronchitis. He continued to teach philosophy and "Negro civilization and history" at Lincoln, where one student remembered his magnetic personality, his grounding in Marxist thought, and his conviction that socialism should be the basis of independent African societies.[35]

While in Philadelphia, Nkrumah participated in the public activities of the Africa-conscious segment of the African American intelligentsia. The wartime interest in African affairs bolstered Nkrumah's efforts at forging intellectual and political links with African Americans and African students in the

United States. Nkrumah also frequented the campus of Howard University, where he renewed his friendship with Ralph Bunche, who had relied in part on Nkrumah for a 1944 report to the Office of Strategic Services on nationalism in British West Africa.

In 1947, Nkrumah moved to London and set himself to organizing an active community of West African nationalists in the metropole. There, he continued to forge enduring alliances among members of the African American intelligentsia. Furthermore, most likely through Padmore, Nkrumah made the acquaintance of an African American graduate student and activist, St. Clair Drake, who would serve the future prime minister for years as a pan-African colleague and friend.

In 1951, Nkrumah was named leader of government business after being released from detention in the wake of the Convention People's Party's electoral victory. Fresh from this triumph, Nkrumah returned to Lincoln to receive an honorary degree. In his commencement address, Nkrumah appealed for financial and technical assistance for "our own Tennessee Valley Authority," the Volta River hydroelectric power project. He hoped that African Americans would join others in providing assistance as nurses, agricultural specialists, electrical and civil engineers, teachers, doctors, and architects. His presence in the United States, along with that of other African students, and his extensive contacts with the black intelligentsia proved foundational for the presence of black expatriates in postindependence Ghana. Ghana's status as a beacon for African-descended peoples and indeed in many minds as a synecdoche for modern Africa can be explained by Nkrumah's active recruitment of African Americans and West Indians for the tasks of nation building.[36]

From America to England and the Gold Coast: St. Clair Drake and Independent Black Radicalism

Padmore accumulated innumerable contacts in his political work, and one of the most important African Americans who passed through his Cranleigh House residence in London was social science scholar St. Clair Drake. Drake had met Padmore while pursuing doctoral research on the community of immigrant West Africans, West Indians, Arabs, and Somalis in Cardiff, Wales. Drake received Padmore's instruction in the pan-African political philosophy he had developed in large part through association with the organized Left. Years later, Drake recalled how Padmore "rapped" energetically with a deliberately affected lower-class accent, pounding home his message. Padmore

instructed Drake to read and study Marx, Lenin, Engels, Trotsky, and Stalin
and to interpret and apply their writings in accordance with the needs of
black peoples. "Ideas don't know no color line, man. Black man would be
stupid not to learn from them because they white." Padmore advocated
studying the organizational methods of communist parties but not joining
them. "Build the Black Man's international. But don't red bait the others
either." The Russian Revolution and its rapid achievement of industrial development was a model for Africa, "[b]ut don't let no Russians, or Chinese or
anybody else tell you how to run your business. And don't sign no military
alliances with them." Nonmilitary alliances were fine, but Padmore insisted
that blacks' most natural allies were other black people.

The tenor of Drake's reflections on Padmore's advice appeared to have
been occasioned in part by the contentious separatism Drake had encountered as a founding member of the black studies program at Stanford University during the 1970s. According to Drake, Padmore ranked those with whom
it was possible to have alliances: pan-Africanism came first, followed by
other colored peoples everywhere who had experienced white racism and
finally by the white working class, some of whom had interests or ideological
commitment in common with blacks. Don't be a racist by rejecting potential
allies, Padmore counseled, but don't trust them to liberate you. "If Africans
free themselves they'll force the European working-class to the left." Newly
independent African and West Indian states should be organized as socialist
states. Capitalism was useless, outmoded, and unjust, and black exploiters
must not be allowed to replace white ones. Federate the West Indies and
unite the new African nations. If such unity were not achieved, a "lot of little
Black banana republics will be the result." Finally, "Afro-Americans can't
organize no nations because the man ain't gonna let them. But they got
people and knowhow to give to Africa, and a strong Africa's gonna help them
too. Study Israel and the Jews scattered all over the world." For African
Americans, a transnational identification with African and West Indian nationalism provided an antidote to subordinate status in the United States.
Drake believed that Nkrumah followed Padmore's teachings to the letter,
though federation and regional unity were also objectives of West African
nationalism during the 1930s.[37]

Drake would later adopt Padmore's advice as well as his collaborative
method of building a worldwide public relations network for pan-African
liberation and nonalignment. Though not as prolific (or as combative in
print) as Padmore, Drake published numerous anticolonial articles during
the 1950s that sought to educate American and African American audiences

on nationalism in Africa. In England, Drake spent much time in the company of Padmore and Makonnen.

Drake's interest in Africa was rooted deeply in his background. Born in Virginia in 1911 to a Barbadian Baptist minister father and an African American mother, Drake attended Hampton Institute, where he befriended Mbiyu Koinange, the first Kikuyu to study in the United States and a future Kenyan nationalist leader. At Hampton, Drake learned that Afro-Americans held the duty of "uplifting" Africans, serving as secular missionaries of a sort. These experiences, combined with his father's membership in the Garvey movement and Drake's later work with the pan-African federation, led him to select African studies as means of combining his academic career with his pan-African connections and commitments.

After graduating from Hampton in 1931, Drake became involved in Quaker organizations working for peace and interracial harmony, an affiliation that shaped his subsequent political outlook. Drake moved on to Dillard University in New Orleans, where he worked as a research assistant to social anthropologist Allison Davis. During the late 1930s and the early 1940s, Drake divided his time among graduate study at the University of Chicago, political activism in the National Negro Congress and the peace movement, and a Works Progress Administration–sponsored research project on Chicago's black community, which led to the publication (with coauthor Horace Cayton) of a classic sociological study, *Black Metropolis* (1945).

Drake married in 1942 and served during the war in the nonsegregated Merchant Marine. After the conflict ended, he resumed his graduate studies at the University of Chicago at his own expense since members of the Merchant Marine were ineligible for the GI Bill's benefits. In 1946, Drake joined the faculty of Roosevelt University in Chicago, where he taught until 1968. In 1947, with funding provided by the Julius Rosenwald Foundation, Drake traveled to England to study race relations in the British Isles, conducting his field research in Cardiff. During this stay he met Padmore, Nkrumah, Richard Wright, C. L. R. James, and other pan-Africanist activists and intellectuals.

Drake and his black expatriate associates shared not only a deep interest in African freedom but also an anticommunist outlook. To Wright, Drake reported that he and Padmore had organized a demonstration in Trafalgar Square in the wake of the uprisings in the Gold Coast sparked by the shooting by British troops of Ghanaian ex-servicemen marching in peaceful protest against high-priced imported goods. The Gold Coast's accelerating nationalist movement, which served as the catalyst for Nkrumah's return to the colony, sparked a similar flurry of activity from Padmore, Makonnen, and other members of the Pan-African Federation in London.[38]

Drake's anticommunism ultimately was more pragmatic than ideological, as he believed that red-baiting could become a diversion from fighting those responsible for racist practices.[39] Another factor explaining Drake's anticommunism was the government persecution of a black anticolonial organization, the Council on African Affairs, and its leading proponents, Paul Robeson and W. E. B. Du Bois. Sharing Wright and Padmore's view of the Communist Party's opportunism with respect to African American and African anticolonial struggles, Drake insisted that the pan-African movement maintain its independence from the organized Left as a pragmatic necessity. As an alternative to the left-wing Council on African Affairs, Drake cofounded with fellow Chicagoan trade unionist George McCray and attorney Edith Sampson the Afro-World Fellowship, which sought to generate popular interest in African affairs.

Drake also worked closely with African American journalists in Chicago. He was a close associate of Claude Barnett, founder of the Associated Negro Press, a national news service that placed articles in black newspapers. Another journalist with whom Drake enjoyed a cordial relationship was John Johnson, the African American publisher of Chicago-based *Ebony* magazine. A flood of writing on political change in Africa and the international implications of U.S. racism issued from Drake's pen during the 1950s. Drake's versatility was evidenced by his ability to produce the sort of detailed political reportage associated with Padmore while contributing pieces tailored to African American audiences' identification with the continent and its peoples. Drake contributed to *Ebony* during the early 1950s. One article concerned racism against black West Indian migrants in Britain. An unsigned article on Nkrumah and Gold Coast nationalism may also have been authored by Drake and portrayed Nkrumah, recently appointed the first African prime minister in modern history, as a solemn man of action, a "socialist with a small 's.' The only capital letter ideology he announces is Nationalism." Nkrumah's movement was described as the vanguard of aspirations for self-rule for the African continent. The writer added that "many Africans look to him for continental leadership." Alluding to the high-stakes litmus test of modernity imposed on African peoples and indulging readers' hunger for black achievement (a subheadline read "Nkrumah Is Highest Ranking Negro in All British Empire"), the article mocked the "Colonel Blimps," doomsayers who claimed that public health would revert to witch doctors.

"So far nothing dreadful has happened. Trade flourishes, and the crop disease which was ruining cocoa farmers is . . . being brought under control."[40]

As further illustration of Padmore's influence, when Drake returned to Roosevelt, he sought to merge his political activism and research agenda by becoming a specialist on Africa. Drake and his friends and fellow academics Reddick and Horace Mann Bond enjoyed a long-standing association with Padmore, Nkrumah, and other African nationalist leaders. Indeed, they were among Nkrumah's guests at Ghana's independence ceremonies. Bond, who as president of Lincoln University had presided over Nkrumah's triumphant return to receive an honorary degree as the Gold Coast's leader of government business, was a founding member of the American Society of African Culture and recruited Drake to that organization patterned after the Paris-based Society of African Culture. All three had been inspired by the New Negro radicalism of the 1920s and 1930s, which combined antiracist militancy with leftist perspectives and politics. As insiders within the fraternity (an apt description of what, despite the contributions of Maida Springer, Una Marsen, and Amy Jacques Garvey, was a community of men) of African anticolonial politics, Drake and Bond hoped to institutionalize these linkages in African studies programs based in historically black colleges such as Lincoln. As applicants for the foundation support earmarked for the establishment of university African studies programs, Drake and Bond became known to these philanthropic auxiliaries of the U.S. foreign policy establishment. But they failed to obtain a share of the resources being poured into these new programs. The victorious programs in this competition included Northwestern University under Melville Herskovits and Boston University under William O. Brown. Drake's Roosevelt University, Bond's Lincoln, and Howard University were all left out in the cold, in large part because the scholars associated with these historically black institutions were regarded as politicized and lacking the requisite objectivity for knowledge production in the national interest. Throughout the early 1950s, the repeated failures of Drake's pursuit of individual foundation grants left him wondering if his past affiliations with such radical and by then proscribed organizations as the National Negro Congress had disqualified him.[41]

Drake's experience demonstrates that mobility remained a struggle for politically engaged black scholars and intellectuals during the early 1950s. Unable to rely on their underfunded institutions to support field research in Africa, Drake was at the mercy of the foundations. This dependency undoubtedly led many people to welcome the resources provided by the American Society of African Culture, even as some observers raised questions—

Kwame Nkrumah and Horace Mann Bond, Lincoln University, Pennsylvania, June 1951. (Special Collections, Lincoln University)

presciently, as it turned out—about the organization's possible covert funding by the U.S. government.

With the electoral success of the Convention People's Party having propelled Nkrumah from prison to leadership in the Gold Coast, Drake set his sights on West Africa. A part-time position with Boston University's African studies program facilitated an exchange that landed Drake at the University of Liberia, whose president was Max Bond, Horace Mann Bond's brother. Demoralized by an onerous teaching schedule and the stranglehold over the country exerted by foreign companies and the Americo-Liberian elite, Drake sought deliverance in the form of a position in the sociology department at the University of the Gold Coast. In 1954, his luck transformed by the timely receipt of a Ford Foundation grant of ten thousand dollars to study the mass media in West Africa, Drake moved his wife, Elizabeth, and two small children to the Gold Coast.[42]

Elizabeth Drake, a sociologist also trained at the University of Chicago, and her husband conducted a study of the role of mass communications and

MAPPING THE ROUTES TO GHANA

literacy among urban youth in political change in the Gold Coast. The Drakes focused on that crucial group of young people with some schooling, which the Drakes termed a "transitional elite." Members of this group were crucial disseminators to the nonliterate masses of ideas gleaned from books, magazines, and newspapers. The Drakes also conducted research on the audience reception of selected movies, including *Something of Value*, a Hollywood rendition of the conflict between white settlers and African nationalists.

Drake divided his time between Ghana and Roosevelt University in Chicago, where he was a member of the sociology department. At Roosevelt, Drake was part of a community of Africanists with strong ties to the international labor movement. Moreover, as a Quaker, Drake joined those members of the interracial peace movement who were involved in African freedom movements, including Bill Sutherland, Bayard Rustin, and George Houser, the founder and director of the lobbying group American Committee on Africa. In casting their lot with the future of Africa, Drake and his pacifist colleagues hoped to internationalize the peace movement. They were inspired by the examples of nonviolent social change provided by Gold Coast nationalism and the Defiance Campaign in South Africa. Indeed, Nkrumah's invocation of nonviolence sought to emulate the success of Gandhian *satyagraha* in achieving Indian independence. For his part, Drake also led the campaign to block the deportation of Mugo Gatheru, a Lincoln University student whom the Justice Department had investigated for possible involvement in the Kenyan Mau Mau movement. During the 1950s, Drake remained in close contact with Padmore and other Ghanaian nationalists who relied on the African American scholar's wide contacts, authoritative grasp of the African scene, and gregarious personality to recruit talented African Americans and West Indians to help build the emergent nation.[43]

Drake was one of several African Americans whom Padmore steered toward Africa and the Gold Coast. Padmore did the same for African American novelist Richard Wright, whom Padmore had befriended in the late 1940s after Wright moved to Paris to escape the political repression and conservatism of Cold War America. Padmore had suggested that Wright, at the height of his international renown, visit the Gold Coast and write an account of the nationalist movement. Padmore had advised Wright throughout the latter's involvement in France's Présence Africaine grouping of anticolonial Francophone African and Caribbean intellectuals. Padmore undoubtedly served as a sounding board for Wright's reflections on modernity and anticolonialism. During the early 1950s, Wright learned of the growing number of West

Indian writers who had emigrated to London to refine their craft, men such as George Lamming, whose reflections on the condition of black peoples within Western culture paralleled those of Wright. For Wright and Lamming, the paths to African freedom blazed by Padmore and Nkrumah proved irresistible, as they would for many more intellectuals and activists in the years to come.

2

RICHARD WRIGHT
IN GHANA

Black Intellectuals and the Anticolonial
Critique of Western Culture

At the time of his sojourn to the Gold Coast colony in 1953 to report on the nationalist movement led by Kwame Nkrumah's Convention People's Party, Richard Wright, like his friend George Padmore, was a staunch anticommunist who nevertheless avowed a Marxian framework for interpreting human and social relations.[1] In a development as crucial as his embrace of Marxism, Wright's previous exile to France had prompted him to situate the plight of the American Negro within the modern world. In his journal, Wright recorded a conversation with Gertrude Stein about his autobiographical novel *Black Boy* (1945) as a quintessentially modernist text. That exchange prompted an earnest statement of purpose: "When the feeling and fact of being a Negro is accepted fully into the consciousness of a Negro, there's something universal about it, something saving and informing, something that lifts it above being a Negro in America. Oh will I ever have the strength and courage to tell what I feel and think; and do I know it well enough to tell it?"[2]

Wright's self-exile from the United States and his subsequent travels were vital for his ability to tell such a story. Taking issue with the critical consensus that Wright's departure from the United States contributed to his literary decline, Paul Gilroy has affirmed the importance of exile for Wright's analysis of Western modernity from the perspective of black peoples.[3] Against the restrictions of U.S. Cold War nationalism, Wright pursued a "saving and informing" linkage of African Americans to an anticolonial, nonaligned world.

Wright added his voice to other anticolonial intellectuals inspired by a wider world of democratic struggle, extending his influence to U.S. debates on the relation of blacks to a nation reluctantly pursuing racial integration. Global exigencies had decisively redefined U.S. discussions of national and social affiliations. Accordingly, throughout the 1950s, Wright's advocacy of African independence, building on his earlier fiction exploring the repercussions of the poverty and exclusion that eroded urban African Americans' faith in American integrationist ideals, reflected the growing influence of decolonization. Instead of the inarticulate rage and nihilism of a Bigger Thomas, Wright and many other urban African Americans were increasingly drawn to a transnational culture of black modernity and a sense of a shared destiny with the rising nonwhite anticolonial world. The protagonist of Wright's 1953 novel, *The Outsider*, Cross Damon, a self-destructive African American intellectual, overhears uproarious speculation in a Chicago bar that authorities are concealing the fact that the inhabitants of flying saucers are colored men from Mars: "They didn't want the world to know the rest of the universe is colored!" Wright made clear that this absurd scenario was rooted in an awareness that "most of the folks on this earth is colored" and in the knowledge of their subjugation under regimes of white supremacy. The "rebel laughter" of these "rejected men" inspires Cross's utopian reverie: "Were there not somewhere in this world rebels with whom he could feel at home, men who were outsiders not because they had been born black and poor, but because they had thought their way through the many veils of illusion?"[4]

Cross is a lonely rebel doomed by hubris and his stubborn aloofness from such a community. Wright was not. His mobility along the routes of black modernity to Chicago from Mississippi, then across the ocean to exile in Paris and eventually to the Gold Coast, brought him in contact with a community of exiled black intellectuals. Along with fellow exiles George Padmore and C. L. R. James, Wright was engaged in theorizing the transformative significance of black and African peoples' struggles with Western oppression. Indeed, Wright's embrace of the condition of exile and particularly his travel writing on Africa provided a model for such West Indian writers as George Lamming and Edward Braithwaite. Lamming and Wright were key contributors at the First World Congress of Negro Writers and Artists, organized by Présence Africaine in Paris in 1956. There, both writers joined others who articulated African-descended peoples' struggles for political and cultural emancipation from Western dominance. The travel writings of Lamming and Braithwaite emulated yet revised Wright's impressions of Africa, and his discussion of Africa, anticolonialism, and black modernity is best understood

54   as part of this group endeavor shared by such diverse contemporaries as
Lamming, Braithwaite, and E. Franklin Frazier.[5] Thus, Wright demands our
attention for his contribution to a larger anticolonial critique of the West. But
before turning to Wright's place in this anticolonial world, one must consider
the vexing issues that have haunted the reception of *Black Power*.

Black Power *Reconsidered*

Wright's ambivalent account of Gold Coast nationalism and "African culture"
frustrates the expectations raised by its prophetic title. *Black Power* (1954)
appears to undermine Wright's avowed anti-imperialism with its problematic assertions about African culture. Wright's suspicion of the folk cultures
of peoples of African descent places him at odds with major currents of black
radical thought that regard African peoples' cultural resistance as an imag-
inative response to their subordination.[6] Wright's view of the backwardness
of African peoples and cultures and his inability to question the era's prevailing teleology of modernization have clouded his legacy and hindered recognition of *Black Power*'s importance for theorizing black radicalism and the
transnational dynamics of black consciousness in relation to both Western
culture and American nationhood.

In *Black Power*, Wright advanced a historical account of the making of
black modernity and radical consciousness as the collective condition of
mobility, both forced and elective, shaped Africans and people of African
descent. Little in *Black Power* suggests the popular understanding of diaspora describing a state of alienation resulting from a physical exile or displacement from an ancestral homeland.[7] Modernity rather than diaspora
formed the key concept in *Black Power* and Wright's other writings from that
period. As the outcome of the sedimented legacies of slavery, exploitation,
and labor migrations in which choice and compulsion were often indistinguishable, black modernity was a forward-looking concept within which
Africa, romantically figured as an ancestral homeland, was utterly irrelevant.
Wright engaged with the past of the slave trade and its centrality for Western
modernity in the service of the coalescing anti-imperialist revolt of black
peoples against the West, articulating broad aspirations to global political
community, solidarity, and liberation.

Yet despite Wright's historical approach, many readers of *Black Power*
have approached the book with assumptions of a romanticized diaspora/
homeland binary. Viewed as a diaspora narrative of return to one's presumed ancestral homeland, *Black Power* raises expectations for romantic

solidarity that the narrative thoroughly disappoints. This is not a matter of Wright's failure to critique conservative colonialist clichés. Wright's excoriation of British racism in the Gold Coast served as a coup de grâce for an image of empire left reeling at the end of his merciless assault throughout the text. However, many readers found such a critique undermined by Wright's refusal to provide vindicating truths about African culture. Nevertheless, the difficulties Wright's text poses for us are actually illuminating insofar as we read them as expressions of Wright's struggle to glean critical perspective and political solidarity across national and cultural boundaries.

Wright's *Black Power* departs from the diasporic discourse of "return" to the ancestral homeland because it links—indeed, equates—the profound alienation, both material and spiritual, of the diaspora condition with colonialism's psychological devastation of Gold Coast Africans. It would have been strange if Wright had found himself "at home" in Africa. Wright's unsentimental account of the poverty and limited education of Gold Coast Africans provided little corroboration of the popular view that Africa offered a haven for diaspora blacks. Rather than a therapeutic "return," Wright's narrative suggested the necessity of a collective coming to terms with the extraordinary historical circumstances of forced migration and modernity that might overcome the racism and parochialism that denied self-knowledge and freedom to both Africans and people of African descent in the West.[8]

Migration to urban metropoles was far more salient to Wright than the pilgrimage to a mythic conception of an ancestral homeland. That "urban passage" paralleled the colony-to-metropole migrations of African nationalist leaders and African Caribbean writers in pursuit of literary, artistic, and political development. Like countless other African Americans, Wright escaped the brutality of southern Jim Crow by migrating to the city and later by fleeing the repressive U.S. racial climate for Paris. However, his commercial and artistic success—unprecedented for an African American writer— did not insulate him and his family (his wife, Ellen, was of East European Jewish background) from the hostile racial climate in the postwar United States. Upon Wright's departure from the Communist Party in protest of its wartime appeasement of Jim Crow practices, vindictive party members retaliated in part by joining racists who sought to block the Wrights' purchase of a Greenwich Village apartment. Wright seized the chance to leave behind these petty harassments, government surveillance, and the fear rooted in the constant threat of racist public encounters, accepting an invitation from the French Ministry of Culture. After some difficulty in obtaining a visa, Wright spent a year in France with his family as the honored guest of the government, reveling in what then impressed him as the more humane social environment of Paris. After returning to the hostile stares and occasional violent harassment of interracial couples and groups in the Village, Wright permanently moved his family to France.[9]

In London, Wright met Padmore, Kwame Nkrumah's friend and political adviser. Wright had for years harbored the desire to see Africa, though in *Black Power* he portrayed the trip as a more spontaneous idea.[10] Padmore (along with his British common-law wife, Dorothy), Nkrumah, and Wright hoped that Wright's visit to the Gold Coast would publicize the independence struggle to Western audiences and help recruit members of the black diaspora for the tasks of nation building. The similarity of Padmore's and Wright's experiences as former communists certainly contributed to their friendship. Padmore defended *Black Power* to a disapproving W. E. B. Du Bois, pointing out that whatever its flaws, Wright had captured "the challenge of the barefoot masses against the black aristocracy and middle class." In 1956, Wright contributed an introduction to Padmore's *Pan-Africanism or Communism?*[11]

It is well worth delving into the ambiguities and contradictions in *Black Power*'s account of the drive toward self-government in the Gold Coast. Understandably, Wright's text has widely been judged as problematic or even a failure. Chester Himes believed that the book constituted "a mistake."[12] Not without justification, other critics have identified several problematic areas, including Wright's misguided application of modernization theory to Africa, what they perceive as his Western ethnographic gaze, and his dubious generalizations about African "distrust" and the distortions of African personality bred by colonialism. These and Wright's rather numerous expressions of culture shock have fueled speculation by some readers about his identity confusion if not his racial self-hatred. Finally, critics have seized on Wright's notorious injunction that Nkrumah overcome the inertia of traditional religion, colonization, and ethnic loyalties by "militarizing" Ghanaian society in the service of building a modern state. With the continent plagued by coups d'état and kleptocratic military regimes, hindsight would permit some observers to accuse Wright of crypto-fascism and outright hostility to the cause of African freedom.[13]

At their harshest, these critical appraisals read history backward from the narrow standpoint of a postcolonial Africa subverted by military dictatorships and their Western sponsors. And in defense of Wright's ill-advised forays into cultural interpretation, he qualified many of his statements with a speculative tone, often accompanied by ellipses that marked the provisional nature of his claims, his outright admission of his limited understanding, or occasions on which Wright was satirizing his own earnestness.[14] In a more serious vein, Wright was responding with understandable emotion not only to Ghanaian culture but also to the poverty, misery, and exploitation he witnessed. The notion that Wright was hostile to African freedom is not sustained by even the most cursory reading of *Black Power*. To be sure, Wright's objections to what he perceived as the irrationality, dependency, and inscrutability of many of the Ghanaians he encountered, which he naively generalized as "African" characteristics, tend to undercut the book's insights. And Wright is badly served by his numerous expressions of shock at female nudity, public urination, and what he perceived as homosexual behavior. Still, Wright's puritanism and foibles, however distracting, require contextualization rather than ad hominem condemnation and dismissal.

More sympathetic appraisals of *Black Power* and its author have resisted this tendency to diminish the author's legacy. For Diawara, *Black Power* establishes Wright as an exemplary and prophetic advocate of modernity at the dawn of Africa's independence. Noting the decline and lingering poverty of African states, Diawara regards Wright's prescription of modernity rather than traditional religion as the path to authentic freedom for Africa as relevant today as it was during the 1950s. While acknowledging the book's flaws, Diawara insists that "*Black Power* may unsettle many readers, but one thing is certain: Wright was for Africa."[15]

For some critics, the extent to which Wright was, in fact, "for Africa" is compromised by his reliance on what emerged as the West's modernization theory (let alone his advocacy of militarization) as a framework for his discussions of the relations among culture, decolonization, and development. It would be misguided, however, to claim that his use of the language of modernization and development suggested a complicity with Western power. Wright is better understood as a Marxist advocate before a skeptical if not racist Western public on behalf of anticolonialism, neutralism, and a notion of development predicated on redistributive justice.[16] I believe that this agenda also informs Wright's preoccupation with transcending claims of a racial mystique, rejecting "Negritude" as the basis for a community of opposition. This rejection of racialism is evident in both *Black Power* and his earlier novel, *The Outsider*, an agenda that by no means constituted a denial of the persistence of racism in American and Western institutions and ideologies. Yet to fully comprehend Wright's understanding of modernization, it

58 is helpful to regard both that term and militarization historically, from the perspective of anticolonial movements, marking as well the circumstances through which peoples of African descent encountered the Western world.

Perhaps Wright's view of the necessity of black peoples' confrontation with putatively Western tenets of reason, secularism, and individual freedom lay behind his rejection of a racial sentimentality that refused to acknowledge the benefits of modernity. Wright saw himself as the beneficiary of a black experience of Western modernity whose secular, rational character would give rise to universalist antiracist struggles. In light of this pivotal moment of African-descended peoples' confrontation with the Western world through forced and voluntary labor migrations and anticolonial struggles, Wright's invocation of "militarization" is less ominous. Well before it was possible to speak of "militarization" as a project of centralized nation building, military service was a major catalyst for black modernity in that it acquainted black peoples with the wider world and facilitated contact with other African-descended peoples. Modernizing experiences of war and mobility, although decidedly not of black peoples' making, provided them with a historical framework for understanding the meaning of their lives. During World War II, the military service of African colonials and New World blacks under conditions of segregation and colonialism fostered a pan-African critique of the West that politicized African-descended peoples the world over. With the accelerating collapse of European empires and the heightened rights consciousness of African, West Indian, and African American soldiers who believed that military participation entitled them to full citizenship, militarism could also have positive connotations, enabling struggles for freedom.[17]

In this connection, Diawara's discussion of Wright's recommendation for the "militarization" of African society takes on different connotations. Diawara invokes the experience of a Senegalese scholar who fought for the French resistance against the Nazis. For his generation of Africans, to militarize had positive, anticolonial connotations, signifying equalization and empowerment. Ironically, that empowerment occurred within the rubric of service to colonial and segregationist regimes. Nevertheless, militarization was synonymous with the idea of "the modern" as a term of aspiration, desire, and positive value. In addition to the interactions between African-descended peoples from different parts of the world, military service provided technical skills that could be put to later use on behalf of Africa. Among the more important members of the African diaspora expatriate community in Nkrumah's Ghana were technicians trained in the U.S. military who lent their skills to building the new nation's infrastructure. In addition, Ghanaian ex-servicemen (many of whom served with British forces in Burma) played a significant role in the struggle for national independence. In 1948, three ex-servicemen were gunned down by British troops at a peaceful demonstration protesting the high prices of import goods. Mass anger and rioting in protest of the killings provided the catalyst for the mobilization of Nkrumah's nationalist movement.

Despite Wright's criticism of the moral and religious hypocrisy exhibited in the West's conquest of Africans and native peoples, he identified himself as a man of the West. Yet even as he championed what were widely considered to be the virtues of Western modernity—secularism, scientific method, reason, individual rights, and artistic freedom—Wright was at pains to dissociate himself from the West's tendentious anticommunism. While the Cold War continued to exert a shadowy influence over his activities, toward the end of his life it became less salient in his analysis of the challenges facing Ghana and other emergent African states. By then Wright believed that communism posed less of a threat to African independence than did the combined forces of the exploitation of tribal identities by the colonial powers, corruption, and the antagonism of Western powers to authentic political and economic emancipation.[18]

Wright's trip to the Gold Coast would allow him to witness firsthand a democratic movement that would sharpen his conception of the revolutionary potential of peoples of African descent. The optimism of *Black Power* is muted by Wright's uneasiness at those aspects of Ghanaian culture and society that he perceived as obstacles to the Ghanaian independence movement and African freedom. In other words, while Wright hoped to feel at home politically in the Gold Coast, as a self-described man of the West he harbored a deep suspicion of traditional culture as a barrier to the modern consciousness required for the struggle for independence. Wright identified the anthropological project of interpreting Akan culture so thoroughly with British imperialism that any consideration of an autonomous realm of culture unmediated by colonialism was anathema to him.[19] Wright's criticism was directed not so much toward African culture per se as toward the hybrid of Akan tradition and the missionaries' Christian imperialism. This hybrid culture represented to Wright Gold Coast Africans' psychological adaptation to oppression.

Against the dead hand of traditional culture, Wright foregrounded the memory of the slave trade and simultaneous historical formation of the black diaspora and the Western world. Wright also expressed reservations about the nationalist movement's ambiguous embrace of modernity. Although he expressed dismay regarding Africans' participation in the slave trade, Wright was unequivocal about the West's hypocrisy in orchestrating the slave trade, a critique that was intended to undermine the West's contemporary claims of moral authority as the leader of the "Free World."

Wright began his book with a historical overview of the slave trade and the European settlement of the Americas. Seeking to disperse the fog of Western racialism, Wright stressed the economic origins of enslavement. "Slavery was not put into practice because of racial theories; racial theories sprang up in the wake of slavery, to justify it. It was impossible to milk the limited population of Europe of enough convicts and indentured white servants to cultivate, on a large and paying scale, colonial sugar, cotton, and tobacco plantations. Either they had to find a labor force or abandon the colonies, and Europe's eyes turned to Africa, where the supply of human beings seemed inexhaustible." Wright concluded from his brief visit to Liverpool and his reading of history that "the foundations of the city were built of human flesh and blood."[20]

Wright noted the presence of many Africans in Western dress at London's Euston Station, where he caught a train to Liverpool to sail to Ghana. He sensed that he and those other Africans were retracing in reverse well-worn historical paths of forced migration: Liverpool "was the city that had been the center and focal point of the slave trade. . . . Suffice it to say that the British did not originate this trading in human flesh whose enormous profits laid the foundations upon which had been reared modern industrial England." While that infamous distinction had fallen to the Portuguese, England had developed the slave trade into a system "whose functionings in some manner would touch more than half of the human race with its bloody but profitable agitations—the consequences of which would endure for more than four hundred years."[21]

Wright's descriptions of his arrival in Africa at the port of Takoradi and his trip by bus to the Ghanaian capital, Accra, invoked historical memory as the antidote to the shock he expressed at the poverty and difference of African life. Indeed, this theme of enslavement was framed by a Ghanaian's innocent query about Wright's untraceable African ancestors and Wright's resentment at his inability to answer the question. Wright's narrative suggests an utter lack of preparation for the alienation he experienced. "The kaleidoscope of sea, jungle, nudity, mud huts, and crowded market places induced in me a conflict deeper than I was aware of; a protest against what I saw seized me." Wright's protest was not against Africa or its people but against "the unsettled feeling engendered by the strangeness of a completely different order of life." Stunned by the "absolute otherness and inaccessibility" of this new world, Wright could not be altogether free of racial preconceptions in his perception of such difference. His reaction was, however, a visceral rebuttal to the idea of Negritude and other romantic visions of Africa. At such moments, Wright's narrative shifted to the familiar terrain of historical knowledge, which offered a more valid basis for human identification. As the bus passed Elmina, Cape Coast, and Anomabu on its seaside route, these "historic Gold Coast place names . . . stirred me to a memory of dark and bloody events of long ago." These were the beaches across which "hundreds of thousands of black men, women and children had been marched, shackled and chained, down to the waiting ships to be carted across the ocean to be slaves in the New World."[22]

Having begun with an account of the slave trade's European origins, Wright concluded his narrative with his visit to the slave castles, the sites of the genesis of the African diaspora and of Western industrialism and modernity. There, the American-born Wright confronted the physical monuments of the slave trade, the stark fortresses lining the western coast of Africa, where Portugal, Sweden, Denmark, France, and England battled for control of the lucrative trade. Wright wrote movingly of the castles where captive Africans had been imprisoned before being forced onto the ships that carried them to the Americas as human commodities. "I was told that the same iron bolts which secured the doors to keep the slaves imprisoned were the ones that my fingers now touched." He invited his readers to contemplate along with him the tangible memory of the horror and suffering of the captives, a memory that dwelled in the dungeons of the castles. With powerful and poetic imagery, Wright burnished the memory of enslavement, subjecting the legend among Ghanaians of the existence of gold treasure within the walls of the castles to an inversion that recalled the human suffering that preceded and produced the West's vast wealth and industrial revolution:

If there is any treasure hidden in these vast walls, I'm sure that it has a sheen that outshines gold—a tiny, pear-shaped tear that formed on the cheek of some black woman torn away from her children, a tear that gleams here still, caught in the feeble rays of the dungeon's light—a shy tear that vanishes at the sound of approaching footsteps, but reappears when all is quiet, hanging there on that black cheek, unredeemed, unappeased—a tear that was hastily brushed off when her arm was grabbed and she was led toward those narrow, dank steps that guided her to the tunnel that directed her feet to the waiting ship that would bear her across the heaving, mist-shrouded Atlantic.[23]

Writing from Ghana in a state of bewilderment and enervation, Wright related to the Padmores the difficulties he encountered in obtaining the political knowledge he had sought. He had hoped that the Convention People's Party nationalists would serve as guides and translators and would take him into their confidence as a political ally, but he found the nationalist leaders uncommunicative and reserved. Instead of writing a report on the political situation, Wright was thus compelled to concentrate on the life of the people despite his lack of knowledge of their Akan languages. He described a trip with Nkrumah through Accra as "inspiring." In *Black Power*, Wright praised the nationalists' "streamlined, modern political organization" and marveled at the enthusiastic response of crowds of Ghanaians as Nkrumah's motorcade passed. "[T]hey shouted a greeting to the Prime Minister in a tone of voice compounded of passion, exhortation, and contained joy: 'Free-dooom! Free-doooom!'" Wright believed that these Africans demonstrated a deeper comprehension of the meaning of freedom than did the West. "At a time when the Western world grew embarrassed at the sound of the word 'freedom,' these people knew that it meant the right to shape their own destiny as they wished."[24]

Later, at a women's political rally, Wright was astonished by the synthesis of Christian and Akan prayers and rituals that preceded pro–Convention People's Party speeches in both English and tribal languages. Wright was deeply impressed with Nkrumah and his party's fusion of religion with modern politics. Nkrumah had understood the need for a religious basis for the mass political mobilization that Wright believed would fill the void in the people's lives created by the missionaries' assaults on indigenous culture. On further reflection, he claimed that only a native African such as Nkrumah could have accomplished this blend of Christianity, religion, nationalism, and socialism. Wright regarded Nkrumah's nationalism as the unintentional outcome of British colonial education. This dubious claim, possibly intended to foster Western audiences' identification with Gold Coast nationalism, glossed over the complexity of Nkrumah's formation, which owed as much to such paragons of black modernity as Aggrey, Garvey, Padmore, and Du Bois.[25]

Wright was truer to the cosmopolitan spirit of black modernity when he added that Nkrumah and the Gold Coast nationalists were the product of another synthesis that the British had hardly anticipated—of Marxism and a "racial and class solidarity derived from the American Negro's proud and defensive nationalism." Wright admired Nkrumah's organizational acumen, which Wright claimed far outstripped the Soviet Union's attempts to gain influence in Africa with ideas that were "backward" compared to those of the Convention People's Party. But if Marxism had been a factor, its relevance to the Gold Coast situation was limited, as the Convention People's Party had sought to address the alienating effects of colonialism and modernity:

> [B]ack of it all was something much deeper and more potent than the mere influence of Marxist thought. . . . [T]he twentieth century was throwing up these mass patterns of behavior out of the compulsive naked-ness of men's disinherited lives. These men were not being so much guided as they were being provoked by elements deep in their own per-sonalities, elements which they could not have ignored even if they had tried. The greed of British businessmen and the fumbling efforts of mis-sionaries had made an unwitting contribution by shattering the tradi-tional tribal culture that had once given meaning to these people's lives, and now there burned in these black hearts a hunger to regain control over their lives. . . . White [colonizers] could never realize how taunting were their efforts to save Africans when their racial codes forbade their sharing the lives of those Africans.[26]

Wright was impressed but remained torn about whether this synthesis of politics and religion ("politics *plus*," as he referred to it) could effectively produce industrial and technical mastery.

Wright's uneasiness at the tensions between tradition and modernity in Gold Coast nationalism suffused his account of his reaction to Nkrumah's use of a quasi-religious oath through which women at the rally swore their allegiance to the Convention People's Party and its leader. An astonished Wright regarded this deployment of charismatic authority as radically out of step with the modern politics of the twentieth century, let alone an emanci-patory project. Just as troubling was Nkrumah's refusal to share with Wright the text of the oath. There was a sinister undercurrent to Wright's retelling of the incident, as Nkrumah, in response to a request for a copy of the oath, si-lently looked off into the distance and "slowly, seemingly absent-mindedly," pocketed the slip of paper containing the oath. Wright struggled to reconcile the contradictory presence of religious authoritarianism within a modernist political movement. His uneasiness at Nkrumah's tendency toward self-glorification was prescient in light of the subsequent cult of personality pro-mulgated by the Ghanaian leader.[27]

Richard Wright with unidentified Ghanaians, 1953. (Yale Collection of
American Literature, Beinecke Rare Book Library, Yale University,
New Haven, Connecticut)

Wright's reservations about Nkrumah's appropriations of indigenous culture in the struggle against the petit bourgeois Ghanaian opposition were
rooted in his view that the psychological consequences of colonialism on the
people of the Gold Coast were far more serious than their material exploitation. What he described as the psychological distance between Africans and
Westerners posed the most profound threat to the achievement of true independence. The "travesty" of colonial education and the missionaries' assault
on the Ashantis' capacity for military resistance had wrought psychological
damage to the African personality. Even Westernized elite men of the opposition reflected a sort of bad faith, cynically clinging to the trappings of an
Ashanti culture in which they did not believe. Wright observed mutual self-
deception between Western colonizers and Africans, as the British, pursuing
their economic and religious aims, "cannot escape lending a degree of recognition" to African belief systems, thus reinforcing the African's distance from

modernity. Wright remained skeptical at admonitions from Britishers that juju, the magic of fetish priests, was not some mere superstition to be dismissed out of hand. But Wright wondered why the Africans had not used such supernatural power to defend themselves against the colonizers and why it had taken a Westernized African to lead the fight for freedom.[28]

Wright was keenly and presciently attuned to the problems Nkrumah faced. "[F]rom where would come the men to handle the work of administration when self-government came? Would Nkrumah have to impose a dictatorship until he could educate a new generation of young men who could work with him?" Such trepidation suffused Wright's account of Nkrumah's "Motion of Destiny" speech before the Legislative Assembly petitioning for self-government, the landmark event Wright had come to witness. Ironically, because the country's best-trained men were members of the opposition to the Convention People's Party, Nkrumah was compelled to rely on British administrators and civil servants: "In coming to power Nkrumah had to import more Britishers to serve in technical capacities than had ever been in the Gold Coast." Wright believed that without the expatriates, not only the business of government but Nkrumah's promises of social reforms in health, education, and housing for the masses would have been deferred. Still, Wright was justified in his concern that the British were dictating the pace and terms of the transition to self-government. And he prefigured the incipient analysis of neocolonialism in observing that "the mining, timber, and mercantile interests, all foreign," were unfazed by the petition and "had their own ideas about what was happening."[29]

Wright believed that colonialism had warped human relationships and communication between Africans and Europeans caught in its web. The deracinated Gold Coast petit bourgeoisie that resisted the popular movement for freedom was a product of colonialism. But colonialism also produced conditions from which some hope might be salvaged. Colonial economies and forced labor cheated Africans but also brought them in contact with labor organization and what generally constituted "the most progressive and dynamic aspects of the Western world." The future, Wright hoped, resided with these young nationalists who had been impressed by the techniques of Western industrial production.[30]

Wright would reassert this notion of colonialism as a modernizing process in a paper, "Tradition and Industrialization," given at the 1956 Congress of Negro and African Writers in Paris. This thesis, along with Wright's equally controversial claim that traditional culture was complicit in colonial sub-

66   jugation and potentially posed an obstacle to freedom, had been reinforced during Wright's Gold Coast sojourn.[31] Wright subsequently remained a consistent advocate of African liberation, a position that obliged him to pursue an unsentimental reckoning of the movement's internal contradictions and weaknesses.

The class, cultural, and political contradictions within Ghanaian society were no doubt what Nkrumah had in mind when he remarked to Wright that the "ideological development here is not very high."[32] Nkrumah's reliance on expatriates thus held tremendous significance. In this context, Wright's reflections on the psychological distance between Africans and Westerners were trenchant. He had discerned the most crucial challenge that Nkrumah's emancipatory project faced. Had the ratio between expatriates and Africans within Nkrumah's movement and government been more equitable, the notion of black diaspora and European "strangers" might have been less salient as a potential source of conflict. As it was, despite their impassioned support for African independence, the foreign status of Wright, Padmore, and others—including notably Nkrumah's attorney general, Labour Member of Parliament Geoffrey Bing—represented an internal cleavage within Ghanaian politics.

Black Power was far too candid in its criticisms of virtually every segment of Ghanaian society to be well received in that country. Still, Wright was disappointed at not receiving an invitation to Ghana's 1957 independence celebrations. At the request of the Ghanaian government, Padmore worked to establish Nkrumah's Bureau of African Affairs, which oversaw Ghana's attempts to forge political unity on the continent and to provide assistance for ongoing anticolonial struggles. Wright followed developments in Ghana through correspondence with the Padmores. According to Dorothy Padmore, her husband, who died suddenly in October 1959, had encountered petty obstructions from resentful Ghanaian officials but at the time of his death was beginning to gain recognition in Ghana and throughout Africa for his contributions to Africa, particularly in the critical area of international affairs.[33]

The year 1960, widely touted as the Year of Africa, with more than thirty nations slated to gain independence, ended with the political stalemate of the Congo Crisis. Wright was financially strained, chronically ill, and demoralized by publishers' rejections and incessant political pressure and surveillance. He had absorbed a series of setbacks over the past few years. He contemplated another book on Africa but was unable to secure funding from

American Society of African Culture (AMSAC) and other sources for a trip through French West Africa. After a prolonged application process, England had denied him a residency visa that he had fully expected to receive. Hearing that Padmore was in London being treated for liver disease, Wright, himself weakened by amoebic dysentery, briefly visited Britain in September 1959 but was detained by British immigration authorities. Wright attributed his difficulties with the British home office to racism and suspected the instigation of U.S. authorities. Paris had ceased to be a haven, as U.S. government intelligence agencies had thoroughly infiltrated the black expatriate community with informants. The mobility so essential to Wright was wholly compromised by the state control he had sought to escape through exile. From early 1959, when George Padmore was still alive, to October 1960, when unrest in the Congo dominated headlines, Wright angled for an invitation to Ghana. From there, he planned to tour Africa and report on the political situation in hopes of countering anti-African propaganda in the West. Dorothy Padmore, who had remained in Ghana to take a government position and work on her late husband's biography, discouraged Wright on several grounds. She feared that Western powers would interfere, keeping him out of Africa. Moreover, she confided, Ghanaian officials lacked an "appreciation of your efforts and your motives."[34]

Wright's efforts to return to Africa did not succeed. Dorothy Padmore's letters to Wright from Ghana report a litany of disappointment at what were already the emerging signs of corruption, mismanagement, espionage, and a tendency to appease potential opponents through bribery. She realized that a major threat to true independence resided with the African petit bourgeoisie as instruments of economic imperialism and wanted her new preface to the French translation of her husband's *Pan-Africanism or Communism?* to make it known that Africans must close ranks. Of course, this was the thesis of Fanon's *The Wretched of the Earth*, an exposé of neocolonialism in part occasioned by the debacle of Patrice Lumumba's assassination in the Congo. Dorothy Padmore's explanation for anti-African coverage in the Western press, the threat posed to U.S. and Western interests by the "potential influence of [the] African viewpoint on international affairs," might have served equally well in placing Wright's political travails in perspective.[35]

In his November 1960 Paris speech, "The Negro Intellectual and the Artist in the U.S. Today," Wright noted the vested interests of the U.S. government and its philanthropic and cultural apparatuses in controlling black intellectual discourse and stifling dissent. Wright's analysis echoed that of Dorothy

Padmore, Fanon, and such African American contrarians as E. Franklin Frazier inasmuch as U.S. authorities relied on African American celebrities and intellectuals to discipline independent black thinkers within their ranks. Much of what Wright had to say on this reflected his personal experience, including the attribution of wholly fabricated anti-American statements to him in *Time* magazine in 1958. He claimed that Ralph Ellison, who the same article reported had been living in Rome, had hastened to write to *Time*, insisting that his sojourn in Italy was not politically motivated. Wright contended that Ellison's letter was actuated by fear. This climate of fear plaguing African American and West Indian intellectuals made pan-Africanism and African nationhood a compelling alternative to a level of self-censorship required of black intellectuals in the United States that Wright believed even exceeded that of communist countries. According to Wright, pan-African ideology, refracted through the New World condition of unfreedom and propagated by the ex-communist Padmore, "finally produced Ghana, the first pan-African state," and "lives . . . in the Congo . . . in the person of Lumumba."[36]

After his sudden death in Paris in November 1960 at age fifty-two, the depth of Wright's commitment to Africa was obscured by the accelerating U.S. freedom movement, which opinion leaders and government officials would increasingly come to view as the preferred alternative to a disorderly radical black nationalism.[37] Enduring links remained between Wright and a later cohort of radical expatriates in Ghana. Indeed, Accra under Nkrumah became a beacon of radical hope for exiled African freedom fighters, black intellectuals, writers and artists, and European leftists.[38] In Paris, Wright had been acquainted with African American novelist William Gardner Smith, though political intrigue clouded their relationship. In Ghana, Smith contributed articles to the Ghanaian press and served as director of the country's state journalism institute. Wright's daughter, Julia, was for a time a member of the black expatriate community in Ghana and an ardent supporter of Nkrumah's pan-Africanism. The expatriates generally were inspired by Nkrumah's invitation to members of the African diaspora (and sympathetic others) to contribute their talents and skills to Ghana and the African revolution. In this regard, Ghana had supplanted Paris as the preferred destination for some black radicals, in keeping with the conviction of Wright and others that the struggles of Africans, in tandem with those of black peoples in the West, would determine whether Western culture would realize its vaunted ideals of freedom and democracy.

A preoccupation with the idiosyncratic nature of *Black Power* obscures the broader project of black intellectuals who believed that Afro-modernity offered the best hope of transforming Western culture. Although the writings of George Lamming and E. Franklin Frazier diverged from Wright's view that traditional culture posed obstacles to authentic liberation, all three men shared a fundamental solidarity with African liberation movements. Like Wright, both Lamming and Frazier reflected on African Americans' and West Indian blacks' relationship to emergent African nations. Lamming, who visited Ghana in the year after independence, found it an exhilarating place. In an implicit rebuttal to Wright's belief in Western culture as a modernizing influence, Lamming's enthusiasm for Ghana highlighted his view that black peoples in the United States and the Caribbean remained too afflicted with a colonized consciousness to claim the spirit of modernity he witnessed in the new Africa. Lamming reveled in the self-confidence of Ghanaians who had emerged from colonialism. Their rapid expansion of a national infrastructure of roads, schools, harbors, and hospitals made Lamming all too aware of the absence of such a self-determining spirit in the West Indies.

Frazier no doubt felt a similar enthusiasm at the example of Ghana—he donated his library to the University of Ghana at Legon. But, as with Lamming, the alacrity with which Ghana and Africa were redefining the terms of human freedom prompted Frazier to make an invidious comparison with the status of American blacks. During 1957, the year that saw Ghana's independence and the resistance of white mobs to federally mandated school desegregation in Little Rock, Arkansas, Frazier published *Black Bourgeoisie*, an indictment of an apolitical, materialistic black middle class that he saw as eager to sacrifice its historical and cultural identity in exchange for its newly gained freedoms. A year later, Frazier again played the contrarian, this time as part of AMSAC's attempt to foster dialogue between African and African American intellectuals. While generally supportive of AMSAC's vision of cultural exchange, Frazier provocatively claimed that African Americans were ideologically and materially unfit to make any meaningful contribution toward the development of African societies.[39]

Extending his assault on the black elite to a heretical challenge to civil rights orthodoxy, Frazier remained convinced that the southern civil rights movement could not remedy the dispossession of a substantial segment of the northern urban African American population. At the suggestion of an African intellectual in the aftermath of the turmoil in the Congo, Frazier penned his essay "The Failure of the Negro Intellectual" in the year before his death in 1962. Here, Frazier distinguished the necessary economic and social integration of blacks into American life from the question of assimilation or cultural identity. While welcoming integration in the socioeconomic sense, Frazier rejected assimilation, which he believed amounted to a complete identification with the majority society and culture. Recalling the congresses of Negro writers held in Paris in 1956 and Rome in 1959, Frazier held that African American intellectuals lagged behind African intellectuals in their willingness to engage "the impact of Western civilization on the traditional culture of the Negro peoples." This was symptomatic of the larger problem Frazier addressed in *Black Bourgeoisie*, an anti-intellectual black middle class "that would slough off everything that is reminiscent of its Negro origin and its Negro folk background." If African intellectuals did not shrink from the question of the impact of the colonial experience on African personality, such was distressingly not the case with African American intellectuals. Instead of reflecting on the impact of slavery and segregation on African American consciousness, they preferred to discuss "superficial" matters such as the group's material standard of living or the degree to which it enjoyed civil rights. Frazier could have been referring to the speech of James Ivy, a member of the Afro-American delegation to the 1956 Paris congress.[40]

For Frazier, echoing Wright's conclusions in his final address in Paris, the myopia of African American intellectuals was explained—though not justified—by the political constraints of the Cold War and the limits of postwar American democracy. To reinforce his view that the gradual integration of blacks was "bought at the price of abject conformity of thinking," Frazier referenced the recent volume of poetry by Langston Hughes, *Ask Your Mama*, the poet's insouciant declaration of militant black internationalism. In Frazier's eyes, Hughes claimed that the African visitor to America found that in the American social supermarket, blacks for sale ranged from intellectuals to entertainers.[41] African American intellectuals, according to Frazier, had cut themselves off from the crucial questions facing the group, foremost among them the impact of urbanization on blacks. Frazier sounded the alarm at the emerging cleavage between a growing black middle class and an increasingly demoralized black proletariat. Contrary to some observers' fearful predictions, Frazier believed that these disillusioned, uneducated masses would shun the Communist Party, instead joining nationalistic or racial religious sects or cults. Frazier could muster only two cheers for the sit-in movement.

Thank goodness that African American youth had risen against segregation and a complacent older generation of African American leadership. But with their goals limited to integration, the students ironically echoed the myopia of Negro intellectuals. They were merely deferring an inevitable confrontation with economic inequality in U.S. society.

With the exception of Hughes and a handful of others, black writers and intellectuals had flown from their heritage, neglecting heroic rebels against slavery and disowning such dissidents as Du Bois and Robeson. In language reminiscent of Aimé Césaire's "Return to My Native Land," Frazier emphasized the African American intellectual's "failure to dig down into the experience of the Negro and bring about a transvaluation of that experience so that the Negro could have a new self-image or conception of himself." Frazier reiterated his view that the American Negro had little to contribute to Africa, but the African, in achieving freedom, might save the American Negro's soul "in providing him with a new identification . . . and a new sense of personal dignity."[42]

Frazier's scathing dismissals of black American intellectuals may obscure the main target of his critique—that is, an American political culture that forced black leaders to banish issues of economic democracy, pacifism, and African anticolonialism from their political vocabularies on pain of prosecution (Du Bois) or internal exile (Robeson). Nevertheless, Frazier's maverick criticism of black American mandarins—particularly those selected to represent the United States abroad at the congresses in Paris and Rome—were both influential for and influenced by such writers as Lamming.

While the organized Left historically had provided support to anticolonial struggles, the project of Frazier, Wright, Lamming, and other anticolonial black intellectuals and activists (including, among others, Césaire, Padmore, Fanon, and the Trinidad-born Claudia Jones) was in many respects analogous to the nonaligned movement. Nonalignment as a global political formation was launched by the 1955 conference of Afro-Asian nations held in Bandung, Indonesia, at which newly self-governing and emergent nations declared their independence from both the United States and the Soviet Union, insisting on a neutral path to the development of their societies. The political resolve behind nonalignment was reinforced in part by the solidarity of nonwhite nations with shared histories of colonial racism. Accordingly, U.S. foreign policy makers sought to win over the nonaligned or "uncommitted" nations by supporting desegregation to counter international criticism of American racism.[43]

While Lamming and other anticolonial spokespersons were unwilling to take sides in the Cold War, they could not remain above the fray. Even as they sought neutralist alternatives to dominant Cold War narratives, they invariably confronted the American leviathan. For these African and African diasporan intellectuals, the image of Africa casting off almost a century of European colonial rule signaled new prospects for human freedom. An interrogation of dominant American precepts was central to this project, rooted in the conviction that struggles against systems of colonialism and U.S. racial segregation were synonymous with the democratization of metropolitan centers of power.

Lamming's collection of essays, *The Pleasures of Exile* (1960), elaborated his conception of the simultaneous gift and burden of writers of African descent, the task James Baldwin called "the necessity to remake the world in their own image, to impose this image on the world, and no longer be controlled by the vision of the world, and of themselves, held by other people." The book, based in part on visits to West Africa and the United States during the 1950s, was as much a manifesto rooted in anticolonial liberation struggles as was Richard Wright's work. Lamming's meditations on travel, migration, and exile chronicled the transformations wrought by West Indian expatriate writers in London and by the migration during the 1950s of thousands of black West Indian colonials to the "mother country." Whether or not *The Pleasures of Exile* had a place in Frazier's library, the sociologist probably would have endorsed Lamming's examination of the impact of Western culture on the self-conception of colonized blacks. At the same time, the black presence in Britain was redefining metropolitan culture. Lamming's first visit to Anglophone West Africa and in particular Ghana induced an attempt to recall his earliest ideas, the "fragments of rumour and fantasy" about the continent retrieved from the memory of his colonial education. Lamming was energized by Ghana's jumble of modern nation building and "ancient communal living," and he remarked on the ubiquitous construction and monuments of state (including the statue of Nkrumah outside Parliament House, with its inscription, "Seek ye first the political Kingdom") alongside the splendor of multicolored African dress, tenacious vegetation, and the "declining magic of chieftaincy." "It is this amalgamation of the various styles of living, this feeling of ambiguity toward the future, that gives the country its special quality of excitement." A democratic sense of confidence marked Ghana as a place where two elderly Ashanti women in traditional dress could stop into a popular hotel in Kumasi for drinks, fully expecting to be welcomed alongside their younger, more urbanized fellow citizens.[44]

While on the surface more upbeat than Wright's account of the Gold

Coast before independence, Lamming's exhilaration on his introduction to 73
Ghana's equipoise of ancient and modern cultures yielded to more sobering
reflections on the clash of the old and new. The uncertain future of Ghana's
experiment was poignantly evoked in Lamming's account of two young men,
part of Accra's substantial population of unemployed persons with only an
elementary school education, who fatefully reenacted at a taxi stand the
confrontation between the hero and villain of the previous night's Hollywood Western. Carried away by the images and action, the youth imper-
sonating the film's protagonist broke his rival's nose, bloodied his own shirt,
and landed both men in police custody. Lamming imagined the youths before a magistrate, unable to explain themselves as they faced the penalty of a
legal system blind to the truth of the moment—of spirit possession by cinematic fantasy—that brought them to court. Their tragedy would be private,
mourned by relatives: "society will not notice their absence from this corner." Lamming struck a cautionary note about the fate of such young men
similar to that voiced by Frazier in his prediction of a persistent class inequality among African Americans: "Vagrant, free and defenceless as the birds,
they are learning to travel from moment to moment, from accident to accident. Their desires may grow as lawless as the celluloid gangsters they dra-
matise; for their energy is great, but their hands are idle."[45]

Recounting his trip to Nigeria, Lamming employed his subversive anticolonial reading of Shakespeare's The Tempest to describe British officials'
desperate efforts to justify their increasingly unwelcome presence in West
Africa. In Pleasures, Lamming frequently invoked The Tempest to figure the
altered balance of power between the colonizer and the colonized, symbolized by Prospero and his oppressive magic and Caliban, his rebellious
former slave, who has appropriated the "gift" of Prospero's language—that
is, Westernization—as a weapon against foreign rule.[46] Traversing Nigeria as
the guest of Africans and West Indian expatriates, Lamming mused about
the assistance bestowed on him by strangers. Why did one Nigerian take the
trouble to host Lamming, a stranger, and to talk at length with Lamming
about his country and its politics? Because this Nigerian was married to a
West Indian woman? Lamming concluded that the man "was simply concerned about the future of the African continent, and in particular Nigeria.
He had a . . . moral stake in the future of colonial territories. The West Indies
was his concern, and Nigeria was mine. Hence the spontaneity," the sort of
hospitality, Lamming ironically observed, that had gotten poor Caliban in
such trouble. The solidarity Lamming experienced was born of an impassioned anticolonialism, a bond reinforced in some cases by marriage be-

tween African men and West Indian women, who, often as not, served the emerging nation as professionals, as in the case of a female Trinidadian lawyer Lamming met.[47]

Lamming recounted his visit with a Nigerian friend, Alex, an Oxford-educated research scientist serving as a medical research fellow at University College, Ibadan. Here, Lamming presciently explored the tension between a more democratic notion of national development and the opportunism of a parvenu petit bourgeoisie. Lamming returned with Alex to his hometown of Sapele, where the Nigerian "doesn't doctor for money": his research centered on conquering a blood disease that claimed the lives of Nigerian infants. As if to demonstrate the unremarked coexistence of traditional living and modern aspirations, Alex introduced Lamming to his polygamous extended family. Alex's father, a chief, and Lamming discussed at length the son's future. The elder man believed he had been wise to support his son's education and medical training, but "now he is worried." He sees "all sorts of little people spring up in politics and private practice; and he wonders why his son should earn so much less than these men. . . . It seems a strange providence which allows such things to happen." In Lamming's view, the old man had chosen wisely but had been overtaken by unforeseen new arrangements. Still, Lamming believed that both father and son were united by the same enterprise of modernity as service to the nation and its people. Presciently, Lamming argued that this enterprise would endure "if Nigeria can learn one basic fact . . . that there is absolutely no connection between value and price. Alex can sell his services at any price; but no man can buy the meaning of the old Chief's decision."[48]

The moral imperative Lamming derived from his conversation with Alex's father became a reproach later in the essay in Lamming's depiction of anti-intellectual and status-obsessed African Americans that he encountered on his sojourn in the United States. This was nothing, however, like the scrutiny Lamming endured while entering the country on the sails of a Guggenheim fellowship. He had thought himself above any suspicion of subversive affiliations, never having been a member of any political party. Yet after a lengthy Customs interrogation, his credentials and publishers' letters disregarded by his inquisitor, Lamming was submitted to a loyalty oath, his release coming after only he swore that he would never overthrow the U.S. government. "Citizenship had assumed new and terrifying responsibilities," he remarked, finally free to "to breathe the air which had often haunted [his] childhood." Lamming had received a taste of the abridged citizenship and political harassment visited on African American intellectuals and such resident aliens as C. L. R. James, detained at Ellis Island during the anticommunist witch hunts of the early 1950s.[49]

Lamming recalled the exhilaration of his first days in New York City, of endless nighttime walks "through the acrobatic illumination of Broadway. . . . American nights of pure magic: the repetition of small bars, the sound of jazz . . . a rhythm of impermanence which seemed to impose a surface of energy on everything." After a few weeks, Lamming moved from his downtown hotel to Harlem. He soon met "that group of American Negroes who come within the category of the black élite," imparting, as did Frazier, a decidedly caustic edge to his impressions of them. Invited by a woman journalist from one of the world's largest Negro magazines, Lamming accompanied a group to a party on Long Island given by a social celebrity "on the occasion of her departure from a fabulous white mansion." Accompanying the group on the drive to Long Island, Lamming found the conversation of the three women in the car revealing for some of the sources of income among affluent blacks. "'When did Judas sell his place?' someone would ask." Lamming learned that "place" had a variety of meanings ranging from liquor store to funeral parlor to life insurance brokerage or could mean an operation with no specific physical location. The tellingly named Judas symbolized the type of American Negro whom Lamming met, spending large sums of money (perhaps whites were the same, he mused) and measuring his success by the price of things. Lamming was intrigued to discover that those in the rarified American Negro world into which he had landed had not read his books or those of James Baldwin. Indeed, his lowly status as a writer was elevated by the fact of his presence in the United States at the invitation of white money. They didn't know Baldwin, "but Guggenheim was synonymous with millionaire. . . . I learnt now that I was in the midst of Negro society at its very highest level of colonial achievement." Viewed in the context of his denunciation of the imitative self-denigration of West Indian colonial culture as well as his distinction between value and price, on which the future prospects of independence rested, Lamming's observations on the philistinism and ostentation of the black petit bourgeoisie were as scathing as anything Frazier might have written on the subject. "I felt no ill will towards the people, but Negro or not, my blood rebelled against the colossal myth which, in rewarding their ambitions, had fatally impoverished their spirit."[50]

If Lamming drew on Frazier along with Shakespeare and others for a project (shared with many other West Indian writers) of specifying a modern West Indian sensibility forged by the dynamics of migration, exile, anticolonialism, and the recovery of such landmarks in Caribbean history as the

Haitian revolution, it is equally plausible that Frazier found in Lamming a resource for critiques of the deracination of the African American intelligentsia. As Anthony Platt has noted, Frazier reformulated his long-standing critique of the black elite during the 1950s within the context of cultural debates around anticolonialism.[51] Frazier and Lamming's expansive outlook presented an alternative to the rejection by African American delegates to these congresses of analogies between the condition of African and West Indian colonial subjects and African Americans forged by histories of slavery and segregation. Referring to their own societies, both writers rebutted claims of African American or West Indian exceptionalism that sought to deny the deleterious effects on black consciousness of a Western culture defined by colonialism and institutionalized American racism.

In their various ways, Wright, Frazier, Lamming, and others such as Lorraine Hansberry and James Baldwin saw black and African peoples poised uncertainly between a fading past of colonial and racial oppression and the precipice of an emergent modern world whose ultimate shape they might determine through their demands for freedom. Within the United States, increasingly riven by racial discord, this issue had a potentially combustible political resonance. Wright's intellectual trajectory might thus be seen as a metaphor for the postwar challenges facing African Americans and the American nation. In his earlier fiction, Wright had exposed to the nation the racial terror of the Jim Crow South and the bitter alienation and nihilism of African American men in urban ghettoes. For uprooted urban African Americans, bereft of the certainties of traditional faith and denied a sense of national belonging, an identification with African anticolonial demands promised a lifeline to a wider community of struggle that might transcend the barren soil of American racism.

Who—what—were African Americans becoming in relation to modern political change in America and Africa? Would they simply become unhyphenated Americans, or, in gaining formal equality, would they enact a transnational American citizenship in solidarity with African peoples and in so doing participate in the democratization of America? The independence of Ghana and its attempts to project a new Africa inspired the efforts of Wright and other black intellectuals to forge an equally new path for African American consciousness. Thus, only through his exile could Wright finally return, so to speak, to engage these issues within what he always understood as an inherently fraught and troubled American nation. He did so through his influence on subsequent discussions of race, nation, and African American citizenship.

3

PROJECTING THE
AFRICAN PERSONALITY

*Nkrumah, the Expatriates, and
Postindependence Ghana, 1957–1960*

Writing from Accra soon after the independence celebrations, George Padmore commiserated with W. E. B. Du Bois, sharing the distress felt throughout Ghanaian and African governmental circles at his absence. African reporters, Padmore informed Du Bois, had challenged U.S. Vice President Richard Nixon on the decision to deny Du Bois a visa. The reporters had made it clear that he "would be a more welcome visitor to the country than the Vice President." If U.S. officials had hoped to isolate Du Bois, the octogenarian was still very much in the loop among Ghanaian leaders. Padmore apprised Du Bois of plans to convene two conferences in Ghana as soon as possible. The first would consist of prime ministers and foreign ministers of independent African states—Egypt, Tunisia, Morocco, Sudan, Ethiopia, Liberia and Ghana—"to discuss the creation of an African community within the Asian-African Bandung grouping." The other would convene representatives of all political organizations in non-self-governing territories struggling to gain independence along the lines of what he generously termed "our Pan-African idea."[1]

With these pan-African conferences held in Accra—the First Conference of Independent African States held in April 1958 and the All African People's Conference held the following December—Padmore and Kwame Nkrumah laid down the framework for African leadership within the nonaligned movement of new Asian and African states that sought to pose an alternative, a "Third Force," to the bipolar Cold War vision of global order.[2] These conferences sought to implement their vision of continental unity—a United States of Africa—without which independent African nations would remain politically weak and economically dependent on foreign financial and corporate institutions. After independence, Nkrumah and Padmore strove to give content to what they called the African personality—an ideology of African liberation reminiscent of Negritude but emphasizing the quest for political unity rather than Negritude's assertion, as formulated by Léopold Senghor, of the unity of African cultures. Though vague, the concept of the African personality evoked a radically new structure of feeling inflected by a modernity both particularly African in origin and sensibility—affirming that African peoples could manage their own affairs—and universal in its implications. Central to the concept was a redefinition of the idea of the African, which Padmore had provided shortly before independence. Padmore identified an African as anyone born on the continent, regardless of race, color, or religion, who believed in "one man, one vote" and in political, economic, and social equality.[3] In the context of the First Conference of Independent African States, this inclusive conception of the African acknowledged the limitations of racial pan-Africanism or Negritude as a guide for African unity. Such a view of racial solidarity clashed with the prevalence of Arab and North African nations at the conference. Hence, Nkrumah declared at the conference that "the Sahara no longer divides us; it unites us."[4]

Ghana asserted its demand for the total liberation and unity of Africa and its inclusive vision of African political solidarity through government initiatives such as the 1958 Ghana-Guinea union and the international protest team opposing French nuclear testing in the Sahara Desert in 1959. Both initiatives registered defiant opposition to France's attempt to maintain its African empire. These conferences and initiatives represented the political fruition, with the assistance of such black expatriates as Bill Sutherland and St. Clair Drake, of Padmore and Nkrumah's long association. For Nkrumah, Padmore, Drake, and Sutherland, black people from outside Africa had a vital role in building Ghana and in helping to project the African personality. Indeed, from Nkrumah's affinities and alliances with activist intellectuals and politicians across the black world to the problems he faced as he sought U.S. support for development projects, the paths and perils of nation building were continually woven back and forth across the Atlantic.

In inviting Martin Luther King Jr. to Ghana's independence festivities, Sutherland hoped to bring the young leader in contact with Nkrumah and other African nationalist leaders. The invitation also conveyed Nkrumah's expansive vision of solidarity with the struggles of people of African descent

all over the world. Perhaps better than anyone, Sutherland perceived the
similarity between King and Nkrumah, both prominent leaders of successful
mass movements dedicated to nonviolent direct action. But the two were
more alike than Sutherland or perhaps even they could have known. Each
walked a tightrope of political expediency, downplaying his radical and socialist leanings to maintain the indispensable support of his dominant society. Both relied heavily on leftist advisers—King on Bayard Rustin, Nkrumah on Padmore—whose presence was controversial if not resented within
their movements. Both leaders would come to question their optimistic belief in the prospects for substantive change. Forced to abandon that optimism, openly dissenting from American and Western empire and militarism,
each would experience a dispiriting fall from grace. Nkrumah learned of
King's assassination while in exile in the West African nation of Guinea,
vainly planning his return to Ghana. Nkrumah had long since abandoned
what had been a strategic commitment to nonviolence and mourned King's
passing, incensed at the "arrogance and hypocrisy" of eulogies in the American and British press. Nkrumah, who as Ghana's head of state had weath-
ered two attempts on his life, wrote, "The final solution of all this will come
when Africa is politically united. Yesterday it was Malcolm X. Today Luther
King. Tomorrow, fire all over the United States."[5]

The murder of King and Nkrumah's downfall make it extraordinarily difficult in hindsight to recapture the sense of possibility at the moment of Ghanaian independence. Yet only in light of the devastation of King's dream of
color-blind citizenship and a free society and the eclipse of Nkrumah and
Padmore's vision of African unity and liberation can we begin to grasp the
exhilaration that the moment carried for many Africans and black Americans as well. That widely shared sense of possibility and the imminent fulfillment of liberatory hopes cannot be grasped without a careful consideration
of the ideas and projects of those first years of independence. Black American expatriates such as Sutherland and Drake would dedicate themselves to
these tasks, both assisting Padmore in organizing the December 1958 All
African People's Conference. In addition, Sutherland recruited Rustin for the
international protest against French nuclear testing in the Sahara.

While King was too preoccupied with persuading the Eisenhower administration to take action on civil rights to lend more than rhetorical support
to Ghana, the euphoric experience of Ghana's independence probably bolstered his optimistic faith in America's capacity for meaningful change. As
much as his own efforts, Ghana's independence and the potential damage to
the nation's image abroad as a result of racial crises in the South led the

administration into a more proactive stance on the issues of civil rights in the United States and independence movements in Africa.

Martin Luther King Jr. in Africa, England, and America

Fatigued by the Montgomery campaign and frustrated by the Eisenhower administration's silence in the face of retaliatory bombings and sniping incidents during and after the campaign that desegregated that city's bus system, King and his wife, Coretta, welcomed Nkrumah's invitation to attend the independence celebrations in what would soon be Ghana.[6] Kept abreast of the nationalist ferment in Africa by King and the other ministers leading the movement, King's congregation at Dexter Avenue Baptist Church readily allocated twenty-five hundred dollars for a trip that was much more than a vacation. In New York, the Kings boarded a plane with other dignitaries, including Congressman Adam Clayton Powell; labor leader A. Philip Randolph; Ralph Bunche, who had taught Padmore at Howard University; Lucille Armstrong, the wife of legendary jazz trumpeter Louis Armstrong, who had performed in Accra the year before; and Norman Manley, a future prime minister of Jamaica. More than the others, a crowd of reporters gathered around King at the airport.[7]

By inviting King, Ghana's leaders declared their solidarity with African American leaders and their cause. King's invitation was a fitting gesture, as contemporaries in the peace movement drew parallels between the nonviolent direct action so successfully deployed in Montgomery and that used not only in the positive action phase of Ghana's nationalist movement but also in South Africa's Defiance Campaign against segregated bus facilities and pass laws.[8] Also present were African Americans with a long-standing commitment to African independence, including Congressman Charles C. Diggs Jr. of Detroit; Lester Granger, director of the Urban League; and Horace Mann Bond, former president of Nkrumah's alma mater, Lincoln University.

Arriving in Ghana after stopovers in Dakar and Monrovia, the Kings lodged with a British family at Achimota College. Like many first-time visitors to Africa, they were depressed by the poverty they witnessed. They were also pained to observe the submissiveness of the servants who worked for their hosts. Remarking at their surprise at finding the school as well as the capital city, Accra, so modern, they realized their susceptibility to Western stereotypes of African backwardness. Representatives of seventy-two nations, including the United States and unofficially the Soviet Union, were on hand for

Ghana's birth. Vice President Nixon headed the U.S. delegation, visiting Ghana as part of a fact-finding tour through several African countries that would establish guidelines for future U.S. policy toward the continent. As vice president and years later as president, Nixon showed little inclination to question racial stereotypes of Africans, referring to them in Oval Office conversations with aides as uncivilized, barely "out of the trees."[9] In any case, there was Nixon, bringing the glad tidings of his fellow Americans and, more important, studying Africa's strategic Cold War importance.

From the standpoint of King and the movement, Ghana's novel terrain yielded something that had been impossible to achieve in the United States—high-level contact with the Eisenhower administration. Having ignored King's open invitation to President Eisenhower to come to the South and condemn the violent resistance to desegregation, the administration found that it could not easily avoid King on African soil. King and Nixon met for the first time at a reception in Accra on March 5. "I'm very glad to meet you here," King remarked, no doubt pleased by the irony of the encounter, "but I want you to come to visit us down in Alabama where we are seeking the same kind of freedom the Gold Coast is celebrating." Nixon promptly invited King to Washington for a meeting. At the stroke of midnight, King was among the crowd of fifty thousand at the Old Polo Grounds in Accra as a jubilant, weeping Nkrumah and his colleagues, attired in Northern Territories smocks and prison graduate caps, presided over the raising of Ghana's flag. After a moment of silent prayer, the crowd erupted with shouts of "Freedom" and other exclamations of joyous celebration. Caught up in the moment, King wept, as did many others. The next morning, King gave a radio interview to Etta Moten Barnett, a jazz singer and the wife of Chicago journalist Claude Barnett, founder of the Associated Negro Press service. The Barnetts were longtime supporters of Nkrumah and prominent and staunch Republicans who were members of Vice President Nixon's official delegation. Ghana's independence, King told Etta Barnett and her radio audience back in Chicago, would have repercussions for oppressed people throughout Africa, Asia, and the American South. The occasion renewed King's hope that "somehow the universe itself is on the side of freedom and justice." King was confident of the ability of Nkrumah and the Ghanaian leadership to meet the difficult challenges ahead. To those who claimed that Africans were unprepared for self-government, King approvingly quoted Nkrumah: "I prefer self-government with danger to servitude with tranquility."[10]

The next day, King contracted a fever that kept him bedridden for days. Coretta King was stricken as well, though not as severely. After recovering, the Kings attended a private lunch with Nkrumah, an honor usually reserved for those with official or diplomatic credentials. King was moved as Nkrumah related how the spirit of the people of Montgomery had given him hope in his struggle. Ghana, in Nkrumah's view, "would never be able to accept the American ideology of freedom and democracy fully until America settles its own internal racial strife."[11] The prime minister explained the need to industrialize and diversify the economy from its weak foundation of cocoa production. The meeting profoundly impressed King, who, as Lawrence Reddick wrote, gained inspiration from the fact that Gandhi, Nehru, and Nkrumah had also been jailed. In addition, Sutherland and Dr. Robert Lee, a recent African American emigrant to Ghana, had arranged a dinner for King with Julius Nyerere, a Tanganyikan nationalist and fellow advocate of nonviolent struggle.[12]

Over the next several days of festivities, Lucille Armstrong presented Nkrumah with a copy of *Satchmo the Great*, the new U.S. Information Service film of her husband's triumphant visit the previous year to the Gold Coast. The film, which included Armstrong dedicating to the prime minister the New Negro protest anthem from the 1920s, "What Did I Do to Be So Black and Blue," premiered as part of the independence celebrations. At the State Ball, the Duchess of Kent, representing the Queen of England, danced a foxtrot with Nkrumah (thanks to a last-minute primer on ballroom dancing administered to the Ghanaian leader by Lucille Armstrong). In the wake of reports anticipating violence and disorder, several news accounts marveled at the peaceful nature of the transition.

After the Kings departed Ghana on March 12, they traveled to Nigeria and then on to Rome, Geneva, Paris, and London. They crammed the requisite sightseeing into their four days there, visiting Buckingham Palace, Parliament, and Westminster Abbey. In London, where for a time blacks from the Caribbean euphorically referred to themselves as Ghanaians, the Kings spent the afternoon of March 24 in a discussion with George Lamming; C. L. R. James, Padmore's boyhood friend from Trinidad; and activist David Pitt. King briefed them on the Montgomery movement, its organization, and nonviolence. James told of his plans to write a book on Nkrumah and the revolution in Ghana. King sufficiently impressed James that he wrote to colleagues in Detroit to urge them not to underestimate the Montgomery movement's revolutionary potential.[13]

After returning to the States, King, Randolph, and Roy Wilkins issued a call to convene a mass march on Washington that the organizers called a "Prayer Pilgrimage for Freedom," its overt religiosity in part an attempt by

organizers to deflect accusations of communist influence on the movement.
At that demonstration, civil rights groups would call on the federal government to enforce existing desegregation laws, support black voting rights, and intervene against antiblack violence in the South.[14] King's speeches delivered immediately after his return translated Nkrumah's vision of African nationalism and pan-African solidarity for African American audiences. At the same time, to white liberals and American officials he invoked the awakened aspirations of Africans during the Cold War as leverage to elicit support for desegregation.

In his early speeches and sermons, King's engagement with Gandhian nonviolence had led him to associate colonialism with antiblack oppression in the United States. Being present at Ghana's birth and conversing with Nkrumah, Nyerere, James, and Lamming enhanced King's sense of the global dimension of freedom struggles. The impact of King's travels and discussions is evident in the first sermon after his return to his congregation at Dexter Avenue. King's April 7 address, "The Birth of a New Nation," prepared with Nkrumah's autobiography as a reference, explored the implications for the African American freedom movement of Ghana's birth and the impending demise of the British empire.

King began by giving his congregation a primer on the history and geography of Africa and the Gold Coast, relating how the legitimate commerce between its chiefs and the Portuguese during the fifteenth century deteriorated into the slave trade. King stressed that colonialism was a system of economic exploitation. In revolting against it, Ghanaians expressed their fundamental humanity. King related the story of Nkrumah and the rise of the Gold Coast nationalism. Despite his humble origins, Nkrumah made his way to America for an education, working hard to support himself. Later, as a student in England, Nkrumah applied himself to the question of "how to free his people from colonialism." And so he returned to Africa, determined to lead "continual agitation, continual resistance," until the British realized they could no longer rule the Gold Coast.

King relived his elation at the "great day" marking Ghana's independence. "[I]t was a beautiful experience to see some of the leading persons on the scene of civil rights in America on hand to say 'Greetings to you,' as this new nation was born." After the Union Jack was replaced by the new flag of Ghana, children and the elderly alike yelled "Freedom!" King's identification with the exultant Ghanaians was strong, as he eased into a now familiar peroration: "And I could hear that old Negro spiritual once more crying out: 'Free at last, free at last, Great God almighty, I'm free at last.' . . . And everywhere we turned, we could hear it ringing out from the housetops. . . . 'Freedom! Freedom!'"

King reminded his audience that difficult days lay ahead. "This nation was now out of Egypt and had crossed the Red Sea. Now it will confront its wilderness." That wilderness was the underdevelopment of a colonial one-crop economy, making it crucial to diversify and industrialize. Cocoa provided too flimsy a foundation for Ghana's economy. "Nkrumah said that one of the first things he will do is work toward industrialization." Universal free education was needed to battle illiteracy. King hoped that Americans by the "hundreds and thousands" would emigrate to Ghana to lend their technical assistance. Noting the rich opportunities, King told his congregation that "American Negroes can lend their technical assistance to a growing new nation. . . . And Nkrumah made it very clear to me that he would welcome any persons coming there as immigrants and to live there."[15]

King related the situation in Ghana to the continuing struggles of blacks in Montgomery and throughout the segregated South. As with Ghana's independence, the desegregation of mass transportation in Montgomery marked the beginning rather than the end of struggle. More important, Ghana taught that "the oppressor never voluntarily gives freedom to the oppressed." Persistent agitation and revolt marked the only road to freedom: "We've got to keep on keeping on in order to gain freedom." Ghana also demonstrated that oppression could be overcome without violence. Resistance would lie ahead as the oppressor reacted with bitterness and violence against those seeking their freedom. Despite the violence against the black community in Montgomery after the court order desegregating the bus system, "Ghana tells us that the forces of the universe are on the side of justice." The raising of the new flag of Ghana was no ephemeral, evanescent event but instead signaled "that an old order is passing away. . . . An old order of colonialism, of segregation, of discrimination is passing away now. And a new order of justice, freedom and good will is being born."

King concluded by recalling his visit to London. Despite their fascination, Buckingham Palace and Westminster Abbey appeared to King to be monuments of empire, symbols of a dying system. King emphasized the finitude of British imperial power and welcomed the rise of the Afro-Asian bloc of new nations emerging from colonial rule, the anticolonial bloc "that now thinks and moves and determines the course of history in the world." He marveled that the Church of England never took a forthright stand against this immoral system of exploitation. Taking a somewhat mystical turn, King argued that where organized religion failed to oppose oppression, "the God of the universe eventually takes a stand." Those who struggled for justice did not struggle alone. "God grants that we will . . . start marching with God because we got orders now to break down the bondage and the walls of colonialism, exploitation and imperialism." Reporting to his congregation on his trip, King articulated Nkrumah's political vision, his standing offer to people of African descent to devote themselves to nation building in Ghana, and the anti-imperial sensibility of such supporters as James and Lamming.[16]

As King brought the message of pan-African solidarity to his congregation, Vice President Nixon drew different conclusions from his tour of Africa, which took him to Morocco, Liberia, Uganda, Ethiopia, Sudan, Libya, and Tunisia in addition to Ghana. Nixon recommended increased government aid and foreign investment for African nations to counter the threat posed by international communism. Nixon also requested greater support for U.S. Information Agency programs and a strengthening of the caliber of U.S. diplomatic representation. Sounding like a liberal—albeit one with priorities dictated by the Cold War—in the context of the Eisenhower administration, Nixon warned that continued racial discrimination of African Americans undermined U.S. influence in Africa, making desegregation a matter of urgent national interest as well as a moral concern.[17]

King's next major speech, which occurred at an interracial St. Louis fundraiser for the Montgomery Improvement Association, suggested that the reverend had taken Nixon's report to heart. But as other African American leaders had done since the late 1940s, King used the Cold War as leverage to demand justice for African Americans and the nonaligned world.[18] King urged his audience to keep up the fight against segregation, which was "nothing but slavery covered up with certain niceties of complexity." "We are not fighting for ourselves alone," King argued, "but we are fighting for this nation." The United States must coexist with the two-thirds of the world's population that was colored and that had recently thrown off the yoke of colonialism. "They had assembled in Bandung several months ago, and [this] was the word that echoed from Bandung: 'Racism and colonialism must go.'" That was the refrain he heard from African and Asian leaders throughout his trip to Africa and Europe. Subjecting Nixon's report to the critical perspective of Nkrumah and Ghana's minister of finance, Komla Gbedemah, King observed that while Ghana's leaders were disposed toward the United States, "we are making it clear in the U.N. and . . . around the world that beautiful words and extensive handouts cannot be substitutes for the basic simple responsibility of giving freedom and justice to our colored brothers in the United States."

King insisted that the upcoming Pilgrimage for Prayer in Washington would not be an occasion for confrontation or "threats." But in arguing for the importance of desegregation, King waxed apocalyptic, subsuming the rhetoric of anticolonialism to Cold War anxieties to jolt an unresponsive administration into action. "Oh, the hour is getting late. . . . For if America doesn't wake up, she will one day arise and discover that the uncommitted peoples of the world will have given their allegiance to a false communistic ideology." King served notice to segregationists in Congress that "the civil rights issue is not some ephemeral, evanescent domestic issue" to be exploited by reactionary and hypocritical politicians; rather, "it is an eternal moral issue which may well determine the destiny of our nation in its ideological struggle with communism." King hammered away at this point, reiterating it in his address during the Prayer Pilgrimage, a gathering of fifty thousand at the Lincoln Memorial that foreshadowed the 1963 March on Washington. As Mary Dudziak and Thomas Borstelmann have shown, American administrations would resist this understanding of the issue of civil rights until chaos reigned in Birmingham during the spring of 1963.[19]

Responding in part to Nixon's report highlighting Africa's strategic importance for the Cold War, King argued along similar lines that the maintenance of segregation weakened the nation in its global struggle against communism. However tepid the president's response, Eisenhower apparently was initially more responsive to King's appeal than to Nixon's. The civil rights issue was far more pressing, as time and again angry mobs' resistance to desegregation resulted in internationally publicized incidents of violence that brought shame on the nation. A diluted version of the civil rights bill proposed by the Justice Department was passed in late August despite a record-breaking filibuster by segregationist senator Strom Thurmond. Despite the first passage of civil rights legislation since Reconstruction, Eisenhower's prosouthern leanings and apathy toward desegregation led to the 1957 Little Rock school desegregation crisis. Worldwide press headlines and photographs of black schoolchildren besieged by enraged white mobs, egged on by segregationist Arkansas Governor Orval Faubus, exposed the racial antagonisms that U.S. officials insisted were disappearing. In late September, Eisenhower ended his standoff with Faubus by sending federal troops into the state to maintain order as nine black children attended previously all-white Central High School.

His energies taxed by Little Rock, Eisenhower faced another racial incident, this time involving a visiting African politician, that again sent the administration into damage-control mode. When Gbedemah, visiting the

United States on a trade mission, was refused service at a Howard Johnson's
restaurant in Delaware, Eisenhower invited Gbedemah to breakfast at the
White House. The incident occurred while Gbedemah was accompanied by
Bill Sutherland and two black American professors who had invited the
minister to speak at their Delaware college. Incredulous when the professors
noted that local custom prevented them from being served in Delaware,
Gbedemah insisted on stopping. While Sutherland knew what would happen, "it wasn't my job to take care of the U.S.'s dirty linen," he recalled. After
the snub, Gbedemah delivered his lecture; when he returned to New York, he
broached the incident with reporters. Soon, E. Frederic Morrow, the lone
African American on the White House staff, was on the phone, extending
Eisenhower's invitation. Gbedemah appeared at the White House resplen-
dent in full-length kente robes, while Sutherland was shown to Morrow's
office. According to Sutherland, an African affairs specialist in the State
Department suggested to Eisenhower that the impromptu breakfast with
Gbedemah would be an opportune moment to discuss the Volta River project. In a bizarre conclusion to the affair, Gbedemah was handed what a State
Department official termed "a scurrilous crank letter addressed to him in
care of the White House." Once again, officials scrambled to appease Gbedemah and Sutherland while they investigated the source of the letter.[20]

State Department officials need not have worried about any damage to
relations with Ghana. While Gbedemah had been a trusted ally during Nkrumah's imprisonment, he was now the prime minister's most powerful political rival. Nkrumah shared with the U.S. ambassador his annoyance at
Gbedemah for making a fuss over the incident and suspected Sutherland of
manipulating his boss. Whether or not Nkrumah's disapproval of Gbedemah's handling of the incident was merely a performance for the ambassador's benefit, Nkrumah was sufficiently miffed by Gbedemah's breakfast
with Eisenhower to order a halt to further Ghanaian radio and press coverage of the incident. More incensed at what he perceived as Gbedemah's
grandstanding than the actual slight, Nkrumah assured an apologetic State
Department that he would have handled the incident differently.[21] Nkrumah's conciliatory response reflected Ghana's pro-Western stance at that
time and its need for U.S. investment in the Volta River project. Even as
Nkrumah subordinated his pan-African opposition to American racism to
what he perceived as his own and Ghana's political self-interest, Gbedemah's
encounter with Jim Crow ironically initiated high-level discussions between
the two nations on vital U.S. economic assistance.

In the months following his return from Ghana, King often argued that desegregation was the crucial standard by which newly independent non-white African and Asian nations would judge the United States in its rivalry with the Soviet Union. Rarely—and only to African American audiences such as his congregation or the National Association for the Advancement of Colored People when accepting that organization's Spingarn Medal for his contribution to the cause of civil rights—did King speak proudly of Ghana and its significance for African Americans' struggles for equality. Segregationists had accused King and the Montgomery movement of having been influenced by communists, and he was careful to appropriate the rhetoric of anticommunism to deflect criticism on this issue. With the nation's leadership more focused on the Soviet threat and the Hungarian invasion than the struggle against Jim Crow, King insisted on the importance of the anticolonial movement for the containment of international communism.

Although the worst of the Red Scare of the 1950s was long past, King remained highly sensitive to the dictates of Cold War America in crafting his message and the nature of his claims for African American citizenship. The serviceability of anticommunism for segregationists' intransigence compelled King and other civil rights leaders to limit their claims to citizenship to civil rights, advocating the incremental integrationist agenda that E. Franklin Frazier and others found inadequate for the socioeconomic plight of working-class blacks. King played the hand dealt him with eloquence and aplomb as well as with a low tolerance of political risk. When King adviser Bayard Rustin, an African American pacifist and socialist who had convinced an initially skeptical King of the importance of nonviolence as a principle, urged King to highlight the cause of organized labor in his address at the Pilgrimage for Prayer, King remained silent on the issue. Tacitly permitting the movement's terms and tactics to be dictated by the enemies of change, King also saw Rustin's private life as a threat to the movement's image. Although an indispensable counselor, King and the rest of his circle of advisers viewed Rustin as a potential liability as an ex-communist and homosexual with a previous arrest on a morals charge. In 1960, Rustin was devastated when King severed ties after rival African American leaders threatened to disclose that the two were involved in a sexual relationship, an allegation lacking even the slightest basis in fact.[22] In a Cold War environment defined by official suspicion of communist influences, and given the difficulties of building a consensus for civil rights in the face of antilabor, red-baiting strictures in the United States, King would downplay the vision of pan-African solidarity and social citizenship he had encountered in Ghana and London.

King and Nkrumah shared a pragmatic view of pan-Africanism. Both drew

parallels between distinct and far-flung black movements in support of their
respective local struggles for freedom. At the same time, each prioritized the
needs of his movement in light of the immediate political challenges it faced.
Just as Nkrumah, incensed at Gbedemah's political windfall, downplayed his
opposition to U.S. racial discrimination, King selectively deployed anticolonial and pan-African rhetoric, primarily before black audiences. With a wilderness of difficulties looming ahead for both leaders and their constituen-
cies, Nkrumah and King had little time to bask in their public acclaim. Each
may well have recognized in the other the fundamental tension between
their people's democratic aspirations and the impossible task of negotiating
concessions from the architects of their domination. In years to come, Nkrumah's willingness to view the U.S. government as a potential ally would be
sorely tested by the long-standing and occasionally violent opposition to his
government and the Congo Crisis of 1960. For his part, King's occasional
declarations of support for African nationalism were subordinated to the
need to defend the movement from charges of communist influence.

Projecting a New African American Personality: Nkrumah's Visit to the United States

In July 1958, Nkrumah visited the United States, providing many African
Americans in the North an intimation of their anticipated future as self-
determining citizens, a glimpse of who they aspired to be as a people. After a
state visit in the nation's capital, the prime minister received tumultuous
greetings from African Americans in Harlem and Chicago, where Claude
Barnett headed the Civic Reception Committee. The contrast between Nkrumah's reception in Washington and that of African American civil rights
leaders was striking. That group, including King, was begrudgingly granted
an uneventful Oval Office meeting with Eisenhower. But during his visit,
Nkrumah met with Eisenhower, Nixon, and Secretary of State John Foster
Dulles; addressed sessions of Congress and the National Press Club; and
appeared on NBC's *Meet the Press*. Nkrumah remarked that he had been "all
but overwhelmed by hospitality."[23]

Public officials in New York and Chicago scrambled to duplicate Nkrumah's red-carpet treatment in Washington. Nkrumah received a far more
demonstrative welcome from African Americans in Harlem and Chicago. If
King was the internationally acclaimed leader of the southern black freedom
movement, for Harlemites as well as many residents of such black urban
enclaves as Detroit, Chicago, Philadelphia, and Cleveland, Nkrumah occupied the first rank of enlightened African leadership. In Harlem, crowds lined

the parade route, and ten thousand people thronged to a speech and reception held at the 369th AAA Group Armory building (named for the regiment of decorated African American World War I veterans whose parade through New York City created a similar excitement among crowds of Harlem residents in 1919). Such eminences as Jackie Robinson, Roy Wilkins, Lester Granger, and A. Philip Randolph headed the official welcome committee. St. Clair Drake, soon to take the helm of the sociology department at the University of Ghana, described the reception to Barnett, who was finalizing the program for Nkrumah's visit to Chicago. Nkrumah spoke at the armory hall before a vociferous, enthusiastic crowd that mingled Harlem's upper crust with the nationalist masses, including Garveyites, Muslims, and others. Their unreserved adoration for the Ghanaian prime minister affirmed that this tangible symbol of African power and leadership carried a greater immediacy for them than the prospect of integration in the South.

The New York tribute to Nkrumah had been organized by the Harlem Citizens Committee of One Hundred, and more than five hundred of those in attendance fought their way in to see the prime minister up close during a VIP reception. As the crowd waited for Nkrumah and his delegation in the sweltering heat, George Schuyler, an acerbic journalist, whispered to Drake to make sure the Chicago affair would take place in an air-conditioned facility. Nkrumah and his aides finally arrived. Their posing for press photographers was interrupted by a man and woman who broke through to embrace the prime minister, a familiar occurrence for a leader who obviously reveled in the demonstrative affection of his supporters. At the ceremony in the main hall, the Ghanaian national anthem and the *Star Spangled Banner* were played, to much applause. Ralph Bunche, who heard his share of boos from the crowd, introduced Nkrumah, describing his achievement as the embodiment of black aspirations for freedom and dignity.

Thrilled by the reception and the boisterous crowd, Nkrumah declared himself a son of Harlem, where he had learned politics. He promised not to rest until all Africa was free. When he asked teachers, doctors, and dentists to come to Ghana to assist their African brethren, the crowd roared its approval. Nkrumah was presented with a large sterling silver bowl "to hold the tears wept by African mothers for 300 years over their children torn away and sold into slavery." Thinking ahead to the Chicago festivities, Drake insisted that the reception for Nkrumah at Roosevelt University stress interracialism. The tribute at Roosevelt was repeated in Ghana the following fall when Drake, on loan from Roosevelt to begin a senior appointment in the university's sociology department, presented Nkrumah with a small bust of

Franklin D. Roosevelt, for whom the university was named. A photo of the presentation, with a smiling Drake and a somber Nkrumah gazing at the sculpture, appeared on the front page of the *Accra Daily Graphic*.[24]

The All African People's Conference (1958)

Drake had negotiated an exchange between Roosevelt and the University of Ghana that would have based him in the sociology department for three years. But when Drake arrived in the fall of 1958, the department chair, Kofi A. Busia, a prominent opposition politician, informed Drake that he would be the new department chair, enabling Busia to devote himself entirely to politics. Drake reluctantly shouldered the responsibility and in time restored the department's morale and had affairs running smoothly.

Drake also found time to provide various political services to the Ghanaian government. He had previously helped to formulate the list of African American invitees to the independence festivities. More significantly, he had authored a sheaf of well-informed articles on Ghana's independence and Padmore's role in it for various African American and liberal publications. Now, with the approach of the long-planned All African People's Conference, an overextended Padmore asked his friend to write a paper on "racialism" for the conference. Padmore allowed Drake to assist in planning meetings and even to record the proceedings, although what became of what were presumably audio recordings is unknown.

The All African People's Conference that met in Accra in December 1958 sought to implement Nkrumah's commitment to the total liberation of the African continent. Nkrumah and Padmore, the gathering's principal organizer, hosted well over two hundred delegates representing sixty-two nationalist organizations and parties from twenty-eight African countries. The conference forcefully demanded African freedom and independence and pan-African unity as speaker after speaker excoriated the evils of colonialism under the slogan "Hands Off Africa! Africa Must Be Free!," emblazoned across the front of the dais. Independent African states were called on to render maximum assistance to those still struggling for self-government. The militancy of the conference was a tonic for many of the nationalist leaders, who upon returning home labored to keep pace with the surge of popular nationalist sentiment. Bringing together such rising African nationalist figures as Kenyan labor leader Tom Mboya, the conference cochair; Patrice Lumumba of the Congo; and Frantz Fanon, a Martinican psychiatrist who represented the Algerian struggle against French rule, the conference established Accra, according to historian Adu Boahen, "as the Mecca of freedom fighters and nationalist leaders and [turned] Nkrumah into the greatest and most popular of the heads of state of independent African countries."[25]

Exiled South African writer Ezekiel Mphahlele, then based at the University of Ibadan in Nigeria, praised the confident leadership of Nkrumah and Mboya while noting the tensions indicated by those participants who failed to share Nkrumah's enthusiasm for pan-African unity. Delegates from the not-yet-independent Nigerian federation resented Ghana's leadership, wondering aloud why their vast and populous nation and others should cast their lot with the tiny (population 7 million) Ghana-Guinea Union, forged with Sekou Touré in November 1958 after Guinea's emphatic rejection of membership in the French community in that imperial nation's referendum for its colonial peoples. Ghana had come to Guinea's rescue with an emergency loan of $28 million after France's vindictive withdrawal of resources and the gutting of its colonial infrastructure, making good on the diplomatic union between the two West African nations.

A more important tension emerged in the debate over whether liberation struggles should maintain a commitment to nonviolence. A resolution binding the conference to Gandhian nonviolence in the struggle against colonialism was rejected after criticism from a delegate from the United Arab Republic. Fanon electrified the gathering with his testimony regarding French atrocities against Algerians that left the nationalists no recourse but to fight back. His impassioned speech, widely reported in the Western press, received the longest ovation of all those presented. Fanon's remarks seemed to sway the gathering, though the Liberian delegation "drag[ged] the tone down," in Mphahlele's view, when its leader claimed that advocacy of violence threatened his government's sovereignty.[26]

The conference represented a watershed in the history of pan-Africanism, and both supporters and skeptics closely monitored the events. The doubters inherently distrusted the neutralist global political forums created by decolonization after World War II, which posed forthright challenges to U.S. power and prestige. America's status as the leader of what was often prematurely referred to in the American press as the Free World was contested by new Afro-Asian delegations at the United Nations and most prominently at the 1955 Bandung Conference. At such gatherings, which might now be characterized as meetings of the global South or the Third World but which constituted at that time a nonaligned political project that sought an independent Third Force in global affairs that refused to take sides in the conflict between Cold War antagonists, the United States and its institutionalized

George and Dorothy Padmore greet Sekou Touré, president of Guinea, Accra, November 1958. (Ghanaian Times)

racism faced criticism from nonwhite nations with colonial histories. U.S. officials, sensitive to worldwide criticism in these settings, relied on articulate American defenders to counter the damage done by the nation's detractors. In a sort of Newton's law of geopolitical discussion, every anti-American utterance demanded an equal and opposite rebuttal. Representative Adam Clayton Powell rendered this service at the Bandung conference—unsolicited, as it turned out. In so doing, Powell amassed a measure of political capital from the U.S. foreign policy establishment. By the All African People's Conference, U.S. authorities appeared to have relented in their determination to prevent the attendance of such African American dissidents as W. E. B. Du Bois, who had been kept from Ghana's independence celebrations. Although granted a visa to attend the conference, Du Bois could not attend for health reasons, although his wife, Shirley Graham Du Bois, attended and read his message to the gathering.

At global congresses hosted by neutral nations that struggled to introduce a political and diplomatic Third Force within the bipolar global order, U.S. authorities hoped that Americans would quickly tamp down any brush fires ignited by embarrassing criticisms of their country. To deflect challenges from leftist organizations as well as from the neutralist nations, Western intellectuals of the noncommunist Left signed up for cultural organizations such as the Congress for Cultural Freedom. These groups opposed Soviet totalitarianism and defended the West at conferences and in publications. Along with such American and Western European intellectual heavyweights as Richard Wright, Stephen Spender, and Arthur Koestler, the Congress for Cultural Freedom enlisted the services of rising black and African intellectuals, including American novelist Ralph Ellison and Mphahlele. Generally, *hommes d'culture* of African descent were members of the French Society of African Culture and its U.S. counterpart, the American Society for African Culture. While the members of these organizations ranged across the political spectrum, a major function of their publications was to interpret decolonization and global affairs from a pro-American, noncommunist perspective that above all valued political stability in the image of Western political institutions and ideals.[27]

In accounts of the Accra conference published in an anthology of African writing edited by Langston Hughes, African sympathizers such as Mphahlele and Frederick Arkhurst, a senior official in the Ghanaian government, conveyed pan-African objectives to the American public. Arkhurst noted that the conference's endorsement of a boycott of South African goods by Ghanaian and Kenyan trade unions was joined by Jamaican trade unions. Such transnational solidarity epitomized Ghana's vision of freedom and modernity binding together Africans and peoples of African descent.[28] The sizable U.S. delegation contained many pan-African allies, who, like Padmore, stressed the noncommunist nature of African liberation movements. Yet for others, Ghana's ideological and political independence and the legitimacy of the neutralist Third Force remained an open question. But those who wished to score propaganda points for America at the Accra conference were undermined by U.S. diplomatic indifference. The Eisenhower administration refrained from sending an official high-level greeting to the conference, fearful of jeopardizing its North Atlantic Treaty Organization alliance with such colonial powers as France, England, and Belgium. The deafening silence from Washington angered Nkrumah and many of the Africans in attendance.

Frustration with U.S. apathy was apparent from several of the reports of the conference, penned for official and quasi-official consumption by American observers. Mercer Cook, a black American scholar of Francophone literature and future U.S. ambassador to Senegal, covered the proceedings for the Congress for Cultural Freedom, whose covert funding from the Central Intelligence Agency (probably unbeknownst to Cook and many of the group's members) was exposed in 1967. Cook praised Mboya, the victim of political murder in Kenya in 1969, as the African leader of the future, whose "sustained performance" was "electrifying." In Cook's estimation, Mboya repeatedly "steered the conference away from the shoals of extremism." Cook regarded Mboya as the responsible alternative to Fanon, restoring calm after Fanon had brought the audience to its feet with his declaration that Algeria was not a part of France. Mboya had effectively countered Fanon by reiterating his stand for a policy of nonviolence, albeit one allowing for retaliation. In their shared preference for Gandhian methods, Cook compared the "impressive" Mboya to Martin Luther King Jr.

Cook complained that the conference was badly organized and protested the apparent demotion to observer status of fraternal delegates such as himself and Alioune Diop, secretary-general of the Paris-based Society of African Culture. As observers, they were denied access to the closed sessions where delegates drafted the conference resolutions. (Soviet observers were similarly restricted.) Cook also reported that French-speaking delegates protested the inadequacy of translation and disapproved of the gathering's Anglophone emphasis (a perception evidently not shared by the French-speaking Algerian delegation). Léopold Senghor, present on behalf of his party, the Union Progressiste Senegalaise, aired his dissatisfaction in *Le Monde*, which his friend Cook quoted at length:

"We have never refrained from criticizing the French government when we felt that criticism would serve the interest of Africa and of France. But we cannot allow Pan African conferences to condemn France while white-washing Anglo-Saxon colonialism. Nor can we accept English as the official language of Pan African conferences. We respect the English, but we prefer French culture, which we consider more progressive and more humanistic. . . . Opportunists of a revolutionary verbalism attack us in Africa because we try to keep a cool head, because we prefer the reality of an independence prepared and organized collectively, to the risk of an immediate pseudo-independence. . . . [W]e shall persevere along this middle road."

Cook's respect for Nkrumah seemed miserly after his lavish praise of Mboya. Perceptively, Cook quoted a statement from Nkrumah's keynote address that sparked much discussion. "Do not let us also forget that colonialism and imperialism may come to us yet in a different guise and not necessarily from Europe." Delegates debated whether Nkrumah meant the United States, the Soviet Union, or the United Arab Republic. Indeed, after the Afro-Asian solidarity conference held in Cairo in 1957, the United Arab Republic had generated alarmist coverage in the Western press that claimed that the republic had procommunist leanings. While the large delegation from the United Arab Republic spared no expense in courting African delegates, raising suspicion of its motives in some quarters, Mphahlele, for one, believed such suspicion to be unfounded. According to Cook, Cairo had overplayed its hand, though, not surprisingly, he remained silent on the question of American intentions. Putting the best face on his skepticism, Cook claimed that despite his claims of neutralism, Nkrumah was "more attracted to the Free World because of his background and friendship with numerous U.S. Negroes." Nkrumah's opening speech had started the conference on a note of moderation, stressing that his vision of pan-Africanism was founded on non-racialism. Moreover, Nkrumah decided against reading messages to the conference because Khrushchev had sent a lengthy missive while nothing had come from Washington. Vice President Nixon sent a message in time for the final session after Representative Charles Diggs warned the administration that its silence was damning. African delegates concluded from Nixon's belated greeting that the U.S. government cared far more about containing communism than supporting African freedom. Uncomfortable at Nkrumah's apparent political inscrutability, Cook described the Ghanaian leader as seeming to be a different person each time Cook saw him. The best Cook

could muster was wary praise for "a master politician, a force to be reckoned
with in world affairs." In spite of the considerable disorganization and conflict manifested at the gathering, Cook believed that by bringing together
such a variety of African perspectives on independence and unity, the conference represented an important achievement.[29]

Quite different in tone and intent from Cook's pro-American depiction of
the conference were the reports written by African American labor activist
George McCray and the white liberal executive director of the American
Committee on Africa, George Houser. Both McCray and Houser were part of
Drake's extended network of supporters of African freedom. Along with
Drake and Claude Barnett, who also attended the conference (wiring home a
human interest dispatch on a dinner with Nkrumah and his Egyptian bride,
the former Fathia Rizk), McCray was a member of the Chicago-based Afro-
World Fellowship. Moreover, as a State Department labor specialist and
member of the noncommunist International Confederation of Free Trade
Unions (ICFTU), McCray had worked since independence to provide training
and assistance to the Ghanaian labor movement. Houser, whose pacifism
within the Fellowship of Reconciliation had embraced the cause of African
freedom, attended the conference as a representative of the American Committee on Africa, which lobbied in support of African nationalism and assisted African nationalists visiting the United States.

McCray supported the autonomy of African aspirations to a greater degree than did Cook. That said, the influence McCray sought with his conference report was a complicated matter. As an ICFTU delegate affiliated
with the international labor division of the American Federation of Labor, his
reports circulated among that organization's leaders, including its president,
George Meany, and the director of international labor, hard-line anticommunist Jay Lovestone. Like Lovestone, McCray believed that American foreign
policy should support African and Asian anticolonial aspirations. The two
men agreed that America's unwillingness to do so capitulated to the Soviet
Union's pursuit of the allegiance of these "uncommitted" peoples. But while
Lovestone's anticolonialism placed him to the left of the Eisenhower administration, his view of Soviet communism as the ultimate evil also fully
accorded with that of the White House and the intelligence community.
Indeed, Lovestone was working as a paid Central Intelligence Agency informant, serving as the covert link between the American Federation of Labor
and U.S. intelligence. The reports he received on African labor (as well as on
labor movements throughout the Third World) circulated among high-level
U.S. officials, including Meany, and Central Intelligence Agency officials,

including director Allen Dulles. By sending reports to Lovestone, Meany, and other labor officials, McCray hoped that his analyses might positively influence U.S. labor's position on Africa and ultimately official policy. It is doubtful that he suspected that his efforts fed the insatiable maw of U.S. global intelligence. If he did, he may have reconciled this fact with his anticommunism and with Lovestone's support for the new Africa. McCray may also have willingly accepted as a trade-off the mobility afforded by the state and its auxiliaries to work and travel throughout Africa.

McCray read the conference through the lens of a pan-African anticommunism that was closer to George Padmore's worldview than Lovestone's. For McCray, both the U.S. government and the free trade union movement were not doing enough to support African aspirations. McCray was a forceful advocate for Nkrumah and his quest for a unified and liberated Africa, emphasizing Africans' determination to rid the continent of foreign control. McCray believed that the colonial powers backed Nkrumah's vision of pan-Africanism over the radical alternatives of the United Arab Republic's nationalism and communism. For all the talk of socialism, Nkrumah remained friendly to foreign investment and capitalism. He and his colleagues, labor activists Irving Brown and Maida Springer (both longtime associates of Lovestone), constantly debated Africans who charged that the United States was showing its hand as the main support of colonialism and imperialism in Africa through its political alliances and private investments. They went to great lengths to make amends for the silence of American politicians while greetings from the communist bloc were applauded. McCray said that U.S. Ambassador to Ghana Wilson Flake refused to solicit such greetings from Washington despite the urging of U.S. embassy officials ("shades of the ugly American"). McCray welcomed the permanent organization of the conference as a mechanism for reconciling the tensions Cook emphasized. McCray and his American associates opposed a plan by the labor delegates to convene an all-African labor conference largely because it was sponsored by left-leaning and neutralist parties seeking to minimize the influence of the non-communist ICFTU, whose British, French, and Belgian member unions were tainted by their support for colonialism. While a neutralist All African Labor Federation expressed the justifiable demand for an African labor movement predicated on nationalism and economic democracy, McCray and the American Federation of Labor delegates feared that such a movement would be prone to communist subversion. "Accordingly, we persuaded Tom Mboya and the Ghanaian trade union leader John Tettegah to defend the ICFTU," pointing out that not all of its unions were apologists for colonialism. Both

Mboya and Tettegah mentioned support from the American Federation of Labor–Congress of Industrial Organizations in the United States as an exception. McCray warned that the ICFTU was losing the battle by failing to mobilize the staff and resources in Africa that would persuade Africans that the West sympathized with their desires for freedom and unity. It was fortunate, in McCray's view, that he and his colleagues had been present and able to call on their close, friendly relations with Nkrumah, Mboya, and Tettegah. Otherwise, the prestige of American labor and the ICFTU would have been irreparably diminished.

McCray saw no contradiction between his pan-African and black nationalist sentiments and his anticommunism. Padmore and Drake shared this perspective. Nkrumah, Padmore, and Drake likely pragmatically regarded the work of trade unionists McCray, Springer, and Brown (who was legendary for his work in undermining communist-dominated trade union movements throughout postwar Europe) as a source of technical, material, and political support and on the whole compatible with pan-Africanism. Indeed, the alliance between the Ghanaian government and the U.S. labor movement was mobilized as part of Ghana's diplomatic protest of the death sentence given to Jimmy Wilson, an African American in Alabama. Tettegah lobbied Meany and the U.S. trade union movement to intervene on Wilson's behalf.[30]

Compared with Cook's and even McCray's, Houser's account of the conference was more closely attuned to African concerns. Insofar as Houser invoked the Cold War, he did so to pressure the U.S. government to alter its policy of neglect. Houser urged the Eisenhower administration unequivocally to endorse African nationalist aspirations. The failure to do so would forfeit the continent to Soviet influence. Houser considered the conference the most representative gathering of African leaders ever assembled. It was also significant that the leaders from the continent's English- and French-speaking areas were in contact for the first time. Less troubled than Cook by the difficulties of translation, Houser emphasized the importance of contact across language and colonial barriers. The depth and high level of African nationalist participation compelled the colonial powers to take seriously the conference's demands. Noting the controversy over armed struggle, Houser reported the conference's resolution to endorse nonviolent methods but not to rule out other methods if the choice were imposed on independence fighters.

In noting the conference's promotion of a pan-African agenda through regional federations' pursuit of the ultimate goal of a United States of Africa, Houser singled out St. Clair Drake's paper on racialism, which added a new dimension to the pan-African concept. No doubt drawing on his experience as part of a progressive interracial culture of pro-African labor and peace activists, Drake described a shift from pan-Africanism as a racial concept ("Africa for the Africans") to a more inclusive political framework. As Houser described Drake's formulation, "Anyone living in Africa, white or black, could be a part of the Africa of the future so long as the basic principle of democracy ('One man one vote') is accepted." In expounding on Padmore's and Nkrumah's rejection of racial chauvinism in his opening address, Drake, like Richard Wright, envisioned a new Africa defined in universalist political terms rather than by race and color. While the movement's essential African leadership was taken for granted, progressive whites from Africa as well as from the West could also contribute.

As King had done, Houser invoked the Cold War primarily to jolt American policy makers out of their complacency. He believed that the conference's articulation of a foreign policy defined by nonalignment and positive neutrality represented a concrete expression of the projection of the "African personality" in world affairs. Houser believed that Soviet presence and influence on the continent were minimal but were certain to increase if the conflicts in the multiracial areas of the continent and in Algeria were not quickly resolved. It was fortunate that, in addition to the delayed message from Nixon, the bland, unsigned statement from an anonymous official U.S. spokesperson went unmentioned; otherwise, American prestige would have suffered even further. The Soviets were anxious to dispense material support to African political parties. Houser argued that the American Committee on Africa could provide nongovernmental assistance in the service of the U.S. government by raising special funds to support concrete projects in support of equality and freedom in Africa.[31]

In the provisional court of world opinion convened at the 1958 Accra conference, the attempt to project the African personality elicited a range of responses that illustrated both the promise and the precariousness of these independent global forums during the Cold War. The war of position waged within these forums and beyond at base concerned the meaning of black and African aspirations and solidarities. Houser's view that the U.S. government needed to change its policy in accord with Africans' essentially legitimate objectives of freedom and pan-Africanism reversed the official presumption that obliged Africans to adapt their politics to the imperatives of U.S. national security. Because Drake and Houser were members of independent and nongovernmental organizations concerned with gaining African aspirations a fair hearing in the West, their noncommunist rhetoric sought to engage the dominant assumptions of Cold War officialdom. Focused on forg- ing alliances with anticolonial allies within a seemingly divided American foreign policy establishment, Drake, Houser, and McCray, like King, believed that the Cold War provided moral and political leverage to lobby the U.S. government actively to support African peoples' aspirations. Yet while these advocates and others believed that they were playing their strongest hand, Nkrumah only briefly enjoyed latitude after independence, as the Cold War almost instantaneously eclipsed the promise and optimism sparked by Ghana's independence and its continuing fight for African freedom. Even as Lord Kitchener sang of the unforgettable achievements of Ghana and Nkru- mah and as black peoples in the West celebrated the first years of Ghana's independence, what Africans and their allies understood to be the winds of change were in fact the persistent gusts of Cold War machinations distorting African aspirations and stifling Ghana's dynamism as the vanguard of black and African hopes.

Although King and Padmore may have overestimated their autonomy in phrasing their demands for freedom and citizenship within the terms of Cold War anticommunism, at the All African People's Conference and subsequent pan-African gatherings hosted by the Ghanaian government, Nkrumah could at least dictate his independent agenda. By comparison, few members of the American Society for African Culture suspected the extent to which govern- ment officials monitored the group's deliberations on African American iden- tity within the context of African freedom. In June 1959, the society held its second annual conference in New York City. The organization had assem- bled an impressive program of African American and African intellectuals, perhaps capitalizing on the momentum of the Accra conference. Keynote speakers included Kenyan politician J. Gikanyo Kiano; Senator John F. Ken- nedy, chair of the newly established African Affairs Subcommittee of the Senate Foreign Relations Committee; and Detroit's Representative Charles C. Diggs Jr., who called for increased African American investment and par- ticipation in the affairs of the New Africa: "The American Negro should have as much interest in the development of Africa as the American Jew has in the development of Israel." Kennedy endorsed African independence, position- ing himself for the upcoming presidential election by voicing support for the aspirations of the African people while holding the volatile domestic civil rights issue at arm's length. In a rebuke to the Eisenhower administration, Kiano insisted on the primacy of Africans' desire for freedom over the West's concern with keeping communism out of Africa. Graced by the presence of distinguished Africans including Mboya and Arkhurst, the gathering was also a virtual who's who of that segment of the black American intelligentsia interested in African affairs, from left-wing internationalists (John Henrik Clarke, Harold Cruse) to literary eminences (Langston Hughes, Sterling Brown, Lorraine Hansberry) to Africanist scholars (Elliott Skinner, Martin Kilson) to members of the status- and office-seeking black bourgeoisie. Entertainment was provided by Babatunde Olatunji and his ensemble of drummers and dancers as well as by singers Camilla Williams and Todd Duncan.

An intelligence report prepared for the State Department's African Affairs Desk summarized the conference papers, discussion periods, and informal conversations. Sounding relieved that the mostly black audience "included a healthy number of whites," the report's anonymous author seemed predisposed to characterize interactions between African Americans and Africans as fraught with misunderstanding. The writer's ears pricked up whenever discussion turned to Africans' attitudes toward the United States and "the reactions of African students to racial discrimination and their relations with American Negroes." The author approvingly quoted one of the presenters to the effect that African students generally felt that their relations with the white Americans were more pleasant than relations with African Americans because whites showed greater understanding of the students' status and aspirations as Africans. Possibly hoping to curtail the production of more Nkrumahs and Padmores, the author suggested that it might be preferable to place African exchange students in integrated rather than historically black colleges.

The report also monitored African Americans' attitudes on "racial questions and the African continent" and characterized as the prevailing sentiment at the conference the view that affirmed the American Negro's roots in Africa and stressed African ancestry and cultural heritage. By so doing, the report went on, African Americans would find a new dignity and self-respect through identification with African aspirations. The report recorded other, more integrationist, African American perspectives. There were those who decried any stress on race, considering themselves Americans only and insisting that the Negro was an integral part of American society. The report also identified a position that claimed that the American Negro's ties to Africa were irretrievably broken. Consequently, the quest for identity, dignity, and self-respect was best served by "affirming the distinctive values of American Negro society rather than those of Africa." While the typology of positions on Africa's relevance or lack thereof for African American consciousness was descriptive, the report valued "moderation" above all, as Kiano's "hard-hitting" address came in for criticism. (Interestingly, the report refrained from discussing Diggs's speech, perhaps taking the more prudent course of challenging black solidarities in the abstract.) Whatever the accuracy of the report's characterizations, the official attempt to monitor, interpret, and guide the projection of a new African American personality along politically acceptable lines was unmistakable. At the same time, the interracial nature of the meeting might have raised warning signs to some of the African Americans present, prompting watchfulness and wary questions about whose interests the gathering ultimately served.[32]

Bill Sutherland and the Sahara Protest Team

After France announced its intention to explode an atomic bomb in the Sahara Desert, British antinuclear activists contacted Bill Sutherland, who successfully lobbied the Convention People's Party to back an international team that would attempt to stop the nuclear test with an audacious plan to drive across the Sahara to the test site in Algeria. Sutherland became a liaison between the Ghanaian government, the British antinuclear movement, and the U.S. civil rights and peace movements. He enlisted Bayard Rustin to join the campaign, which included British pacifist and antiapartheid cleric Michael Scott. The team consisted of eleven Ghanaians, two Africans from outside of Ghana, and six persons from Britain, France, and America, including Rustin and Sutherland. The Sahara team caravanned through northern Ghana, stopping for mass meetings at towns along the route. Mobilized by the Convention People's Party, crowds would meet the group in each major center, where Rustin and others would address open-air rallies. In addition to government support, the team raised twenty-five thousand dollars from Ghanaians.[33]

Sutherland had arrived in the Gold Coast in 1954, making him one of the earliest African American emigrants. His path had been traced by Christian pacifism, African American civil rights activism, and imprisonment for his defiant conscientious objector status during World War II. As with so many others, he was recruited to pan-Africanism by George Padmore. As a teenager during the 1930s, Sutherland joined the National Association for the Advancement of Colored People. The Congregational Church in his predominantly white hometown of Glen Ridge, New Jersey, introduced him to pacifist and socialist causes, and through the church he joined the movement to save the Scottsboro defendants as well as Christian peace campaigns. After graduating from Bates College, Sutherland joined the Youth Committee against War. He lived with other pacifists in a Newark commune based on

Gandhian and radical Christian precepts and agitated against U.S. entry into World War II. When Pearl Harbor subsumed his efforts, Sutherland remained true to his antiwar principles and was sentenced to four years in prison by a judge visiting from the South—twice the penalty that any white conscientious objector had received to date. Incarcerated in the segregated federal prison system, Sutherland fasted in protest of Jim Crow, censorship, and brutality. Much later, he recalled that his confinement within an imprisoned "black segregated community" connected him with the "real world" and "black people's techniques of survival and gave me . . . an experience of both the warmth and generosity of an oppressed community (as well as its tensions and destructive violence)" greater than he had ever known in his protected, semi-integrated academic environment.[34]

After leaving prison, Sutherland joined the Workers' Defense League and the Fair Employment Practices Committee, the first federal entity since Reconstruction established to remedy antiblack discrimination. His circle of militant activists spurned legislative and judicial strategies for the direct action of Gandhian civil disobedience. He and his colleagues in the Fellowship of Reconciliation helped found the original Committee for Racial Equality (later the Congress of Racial Equality), which engaged in direct-action protests against segregation in northern cities. Joining the migration of artists and radicals to Greenwich Village during the 1940s, Sutherland counted Richard Wright and C. L. R. James as neighbors. Sutherland was active in the radical wing of the peace movement and demonstrated against the Korean War. In a bold initiative that garnered headlines, Sutherland and three fellow activists cycled from Paris to Moscow to protest nuclear proliferation. During his travels through Europe, Sutherland met Africans involved in national liberation struggles and learned of plans for Gandhian demonstrations in South Africa. Sutherland persuaded two of his associates in the peace movement, Rustin and Houser, to support the Defiance Campaign, a series of nonviolent protests organized by the African National Congress against pass laws in apartheid South Africa. To channel material support to the campaign, led by Nelson Mandela, Walter Sisulu, and Oliver Tambo, Sutherland, Houser, and Rustin formed Americans for South African Resistance, from which evolved Houser's organization, the American Committee on Africa. Sutherland and his pacifist colleagues believed that their commitments to peace, racial justice, and nonviolence could be merged with their support for African independence yet could escape accusations of communist influence. Convinced that Africa offered the greatest hope for progressive change, Sutherland moved to the Gold Coast.[35]

Having secured Nkrumah's blessing to establish chapters of the pacifist War Resisters' League and Fellowship of Reconciliation on the African continent, Sutherland struggled to find paid employment. With the support of the American Committee on Africa, Sutherland moved to rural Ghana and began a family with his new Ghanaian wife, Efua Theodora Morgue, a poet and playwright who later contributed to an anthology of African writing edited by Langston Hughes and who would become a leading figure in the arts and culture in postindependence Ghana. The couple put into practice their belief in rural development and a vision of modernity grounded in traditional culture by participating in the construction of a secondary school in Tsito in the trans-Volta state of Awudome. This was a collaborative effort with Ghanaian educators and the local community, encouraged by a progressive chief who had attended Achimota College. Sutherland penned an account of the school's establishment, praising the determination, financial sacrifice, and strenuous voluntary labor of Tsito's impoverished villagers, many of them women and children, in raising the buildings. In addition to training its citizens for life in a modern rural community, the school's curriculum was grounded in an "appreciation for the best in the local traditions and culture." Employing skilled workers and artisans among the village's residents, the school's planners broadened the scope of the project, introducing a cooperative farm inspired in part by a report on industrialization and the Gold Coast penned by the West Indian economist W. Arthur Lewis, another associate of Padmore and Nkrumah in the black Anglophone pan-African commonwealth. Lewis had recommended that the first priority be the development of subsistence agriculture, an essential precondition for industrial development. The planners believed that sufficient skills existed to launch several village industries, including the manufacture of sugar and soap, food canning, and the production of some vegetable oils. Sutherland's account of the school was intended to solicit material support for the project from his pacifist colleagues back in the States.[36]

Sutherland moved his family to Accra in 1956 when he was appointed personal secretary to Gbedemah, the minister of finance. A friend of Sutherland's from the United States, Marguerite Cartwright, a political columnist for the *Pittsburgh Courier* who had known Nkrumah since his student days in the United States, helped to arrange the position for Sutherland. Sutherland worked alongside Drake in planning the independence celebrations. Dedicated to the cause of nonviolent protest, Sutherland further expanded the pan-African network of leaders and activists by making sure that Martin Luther King Jr. was invited as one of Nkrumah's honorary guests.

　　The Sahara protest, backed by a global antinuclear movement, underscored Ghana's willingness to challenge French colonial ambitions. As Sutherland recalled, "[T]he plan was to get as close to the test site as possible . . . preventing the testing through our physical presence." The team had chosen a route through Upper Volta into French-controlled West Africa, hoping to elude French patrols and somehow reach the test site. The wide publicity the test had received throughout Africa, the United States, Britain, and the United Nations granted a measure of protection when the protesters were detained by French forces in Bittou, Upper Volta. During a standoff of several days, the protesters distributed leaflets, and Rustin and Sutherland, who passed the time rallying the protesters and villagers by singing Negro spirituals, briefly contemplated moving ahead clandestinely on foot. The team finally relented and was escorted back to the Ghana border. Sutherland and Scott again attempted to reach the test site but were quickly apprehended and jailed by French troops and then transported back to Ghana.[37]

　　The protesters again tried and failed to reach the site, and the French exploded atomic bombs in February and April 1960. Yet the international team had focused opposition to French nuclear policy in a manner that strengthened the international initiatives to end aboveground nuclear testing. For months, the team's efforts received highly favorable front-page headlines in the Ghanaian press, supporting Nkrumah's view that Ghana should actively support the antinuclear movement.[38]

"A Great Beacon Is Dimmed"

For many years George Padmore had been a fountain of political advice and material support for the many African nationalists who found their way to his Cranleigh Street flat in London. During the independence celebrations, Nkrumah had loaned his private bungalow across from the statehouse to Padmore and his British wife, Dorothy. Padmore subsequently stayed on, assisting with the departure of British expatriate officials and helping defuse a border dispute instigated by French Togoland and the Ghanaian opposition National Liberation Movement. Although an appreciation of his abilities was far from universal within the government, Padmore received many offers to remain in the newly independent country.[39]

　　Amid the celebrations, Nkrumah initially had invited Padmore to stay and promote the advancement of their idea of African unity. An advisory role for Padmore, so strongly identified with anticommunism, might have been expected to send a reassuring signal to a watchful Western world. But the prime minister hesitated as senior members of the cabinet opposed working alongside Padmore, who, Dorothy Padmore believed, posed a formidable obstacle to their expectations of self-aggrandizement. Pressured by younger radicals in the Convention People's Party who resented the cabinet's neo-colonial elements, Nkrumah relented, appointing Padmore as an adviser on African affairs.

Prior to independence, Padmore had urged Nkrumah to retain personal control over the portfolio of African affairs and foreign relations generally. Both men well knew that his ministers could not be trusted with this linchpin of pan-Africanism and continental unity. Mediating between the left and right wings of the government, Nkrumah was reluctant to endow Padmore's office with the importance and resources it required. Against the interference of ministers and members of the civil service, Padmore secured offices and a staff, though he refused a personal secretary, preferring to entrust his confidential work to Dorothy. While engaged in the planning of the All African People's Conference, Padmore told Nkrumah that under present circumstances, he could not continue as an adviser. Nkrumah persuaded Padmore to remain, granting him an increase in salary, though Padmore was not compensated as lavishly as British expatriates.

Padmore seems to have borne these slights with equanimity. A tireless agitator for pan-Africanism, he had always insisted that Africans should lead in the struggle, with black "strangers" from the New World providing support. The treatment accorded her husband—a paltry reward for many years of sacrifice in London—embittered Dorothy Padmore, however. No one among the ministers was prepared to emulate her husband's selfless example. "All want to take. And so they jostle and scheme and are not for Africa but for themselves." To her friend, Richard Wright, Dorothy contrasted the shabby treatment of her husband with the handsome sinecures bestowed on British hangers-on. In her view, Ghanaians customarily "reward[ed their] enemies in the hope of buying them off! Your friends you condemn."[40]

Dorothy Padmore believed that her husband's difficulties were symptomatic of the failure to transform the Convention People's Party from an electioneering mechanism into a vanguard party committed to an ideological program of pan-African socialism. By the time of Padmore's sudden October 1959 death in London as a result of liver disease, he had vindicated himself with his work placing Ghana in the forefront of African affairs. Despite opportunistic whispering against the "stranger" and claims that it was inappropriate for a West Indian to exercise leadership in African foreign relations, his contribution and incorruptibility were acknowledged by his ene-

PROJECTING THE AFRICAN PERSONALITY

mies and certainly by Nkrumah, who paid Padmore a lavish tribute with a state funeral and a heartfelt eulogy: "[O]ur friendship developed into that indescribable relationship that exists between two brothers." Nkrumah considered it fitting that Padmore's ashes be interred at Christianborg Castle, the seat of the Ghanaian government, where, perhaps "hundreds of years ago, his ancestors stood, as silent sentinels, awaiting their wretched lot. . . . Fate returned George Padmore home to us. . . . While we mourn his loss, the battle for Africa's total emancipation must continue unabated."[41] Dorothy Padmore remained in Ghana, where she embarked on a never-completed biography of her late husband. She was employed by the government as a writer and researcher, remaining in Ghana until her death in 1964.

Through George Padmore's state funeral and the extensive press coverage over several days devoted to his passing, the Ghanaian government reaffirmed its leadership in African affairs. Nkrumah continued to campaign for African unity with undiminished fervor. Unmistakable in the many tributes to Padmore was Nkrumah's transnational vision of nation building. At the time of his death, Padmore had been involved in drafting Ghana's republican constitution, whose adoption in July 1960 would end the Ghanaian government's dependent relationship with the British government and monarchy. As Ghana celebrated its new status as a republic, Nkrumah's diplomatic efforts to resolve the Congo Crisis, precipitated by the Belgian-backed secession of Katanga Province shortly after the Congo's independence in July 1960, would have repercussions throughout Africa and beyond. This crisis would dramatically sour the Ghanaian government's relationship with the United States and the West. Nkrumah told Drake that the U.S. ambassador to Ghana had told the prime minister in a fit of anger, "If you think you can throw your weight around in the Congo the U.S. will cut you down to size."[42]

The Congo Crisis would bring an abrupt end to the period of optimism that characterized the first months of Ghanaian independence, which were marked by attempts not only to define but also to enact the African personality and codify pan-Africanism with projects designed to link African nations so that they could achieve autonomy from their former colonizers. Events in the Congo would sorely test the assertion of the African personality and indeed hopes for peaceful, nonviolent change in Africa. The Congo Crisis, which included the first coup d'état against an independent African government, roiled Ghanaian politics and sparked global outrage and an angry protest by African Americans at the United Nations. Unrest in the Congo also inflamed tensions between black radicals and nationalists (in both Ghana and the United States) and such African American liberals as attorney Pauli Murray, who sided with the U.S. government during her brief residence in Ghana. In emphasizing her view that African Americans were Americans first and foremost, Murray would inadvertently echo the terms of a liberal counteroffensive against African American criticism of U.S. foreign policy toward Africa. That counteroffensive sought to debunk the ideals of pan-African solidarity espoused by Nkrumah and Padmore. Support for Nkrumah's political vision among African Americans would lead to an intense preoccupation in the U.S. media with the relationship between Africans and African Americans, a debate that testified to the high stakes attached to the matter of the political identities of African Americans.

4

PAULI MURRAY
IN GHANA

*The Congo Crisis and an
African American Woman's Dilemma*

In a United States riven during the late 1950s by organized white southern resistance to desegregation, Pauli Murray, an African American attorney and writer, was an impassioned fighter for the cause of civil rights. While her brief stay in Ghana did not alter her fundamental support for civil rights, it worked a profound if fleeting metamorphosis on her politics. Her presence in Africa at a perilous juncture in that continent's struggle against colonialism landed her at the heart of debates over the vexed matter of African American consciousness and citizenship. Murray hoped that living in Ghana would help her resolve what she termed the question of identity for the American Negro. Her singular reflections on African American identity came during her three-year appointment to teach constitutional law at the University of Ghana beginning in February 1960. She relished the task of training the young nation's lawyers and helping construct its judicial system. But overtaken by political turmoil during what was widely hailed in the Western press as the Year of Africa, Murray left Ghana after only eighteen months. She defended her country against the Ghanaian government's criticisms of segregation and U.S. foreign policy during the Congo Crisis. Finding herself caught up in the bitter struggle between Kwame Nkrumah and his opposition, Murray incurred the Ghanaian government's suspicion by advocating the universality of what she understood as American values of democracy and individual rights, values whose application back in the States was at best inconsistent. Unlike Ghanaian officials, Murray was reluctant to consider the

contingent nature of American ideals and was even less willing to regard the
United States as implicated in destabilizing policies that opposed the democratic and nationalist aspirations of African peoples.

Murray's faith in American constitutionalism and color-blind citizenship
placed her at odds with the Ghanaian government and its left-wing expatriate sympathizers of all backgrounds. Murray's adherence to color-blind
ideals, while typical of civil rights attorneys of her era, was also informed by
her personal and professional dilemmas stemming from her outsider status
as a black woman. That said, Murray's political choices in Ghana are best
understood in the context of the struggle over the legitimacy of an expansive, transnational African American citizenship. Murray's politics in Ghana
took a profoundly different turn than would have been the case if she had
remained in the United States. In Ghana, Murray insisted on the Negro's
fundamental Americanism and denied the validity of transnational black
solidarities. Above all, Murray saw herself as defending the American image
in Ghana. The perspective Murray voiced in Ghana raises challenging questions about the specific content of the patriotism she espoused and the policies of the American nation she defended. In retrospect, the pro-American
ideology Murray articulated from Ghana coincided with a recasting of liberal
understandings of race, citizenship, and nationhood at an unsettling moment back in the United States. Although Murray asserted her patriotism in
response to events in Ghana and Africa and racial turmoil back in the United
States, the form that patriotism took also suggests the pervasive influence of
an American liberal ideology that was not race neutral in the disembodied,
platonic sense she had envisioned. Rather, dominant understandings of
American identity and national belonging were being reformulated directly
in response to the activism of black people in the United States and in Africa.

Murray's many talents and varied career have made her a fascinating
subject for historians of the civil rights and women's movements.[1] Yet her
sojourn in Ghana, part of a postwar phenomenon of black women's civic
participation as U.S. representatives abroad, has gone largely unexplored.

Born Anna Pauline Murray in Baltimore but reared in segregated Durham, North Carolina, Murray was among the cadre of lawyers trained at
Howard University Law School under Charles Houston during the 1930s.
Murray's pursuit of education was in itself a struggle, as she was barred from
the graduate school of University of North Carolina and Harvard Law School
on grounds of race and sex, respectively. Murray had been active in New York
City's left-wing culture during the 1930s. She graduated from Hunter College
and participated in the city's vibrant radical politics. During this time, she

and National Association for the Advancement of Colored People (NAACP) organizer Ella Baker became lifelong friends.[2] Joining such prominent African American leaders as Mary McLeod Bethune and A. Philip Randolph, Murray worked on the unsuccessful campaign to save the life of Odell Waller, a Virginia sharecropper condemned to death for killing his employer. Another friend, trade unionist Maida Springer, first met Murray in connection with the Waller defense campaign. Springer recalled her initial glimpse of Murray, a small woman with close-cropped hair speaking atop a table, on fire with indignation at racial injustice.[3] During the 1940s, Murray was arrested in Virginia for her direct-action protest against segregated bus facilities. Murray was also a literary celebrity, author of the widely anthologized poem "Dark Testament" and the book *Proud Shoes* (1956). Through her wartime civil rights activism, Murray met Eleanor Roosevelt and caught her attention with the publication of an angry poem denouncing President Franklin Roosevelt's inaction on civil rights. Later, Murray was active in New York City Democratic politics, working in both of Adlai Stevenson's unsuccessful presidential campaigns. Her civil rights activism and her prior associations with radicals led to a federal investigation in 1953. As a result of this investigation, Murray's application for a visa to serve as a legal consultant in Liberia was denied. Murray fought back, writing the family memoir *Proud Shoes* as a tribute to her grandparents, whose struggles and perseverance during the late nineteenth century represented what Murray saw as a more authentic Americanism than that espoused by the House Un-American Activities Committee (HUAC) and the loyalty boards.[4]

Having earned law degrees from Howard and the University of California, Murray pioneered in the study of race in U.S. law.[5] Her prospects were limited by racism as well as the systemic barriers imposed on women in the legal profession. Murray watched from the sidelines as her African American male peers entered government service as part of New Deal and Fair Employment Practices Commission reforms or joined the NAACP's legal struggle against segregation. During the mid-1950s, Lloyd K. Garrison, a senior partner with Stevenson's New York corporate law firm and a descendant of abolitionist William Lloyd Garrison, hired Murray. True to his heritage, Garrison was a staunch supporter of civil rights; he also served as Langston Hughes's counsel when the poet testified before HUAC. At Garrison's firm, professional fulfillment remained elusive for Murray, as she encountered clients and coworkers uncomfortable with a black woman attorney. Murray remained active within civil rights circles, serving on the defense team of radical NAACP leader Robert Williams. In 1959, the association suspended

Williams, a brash advocate of armed self-defense from Monroe, North Carolina, after he urged blacks to employ retaliatory violence in the wake of the
acquittal of a white man charged with assaulting a black woman. Before the
NAACP board, Murray argued that Williams had spoken out of understandable frustration at the level of antiblack violence tolerated not only by southern courts but also by President Dwight Eisenhower.[6]

Murray's young adulthood was defined by rebellion against dominant
sexual mores as well as struggle against racial and gender barriers. Readers
of Nancy Cunard's leftist *Negro Anthology: 1931–1934* would have been surprised to find a short story by a youthful Murray, not listed in the table of
contents, based on her experience of riding the rails with a female companion as both women masqueraded as men. On this occasion, Murray adopted
the more androgynous name "Pauli." After a brief marriage was annulled by
mutual agreement, Murray engaged in same-sex relationships, though not
without considerable ambivalence. Murray's rebelliousness was tempered by
her wish to maintain leadership status within a black public culture that
required a decorous silence on homosexuality. Noting the evident pride Murray exhibited in transgressing gender boundaries in her body language and
clothes while posing for photographs during her young adulthood, Doreen
Drury has written of Murray's struggle to reconcile "her desire for certain
kinds of freedom—to travel, to write, to play, to love women, to pursue a
masculine persona—with her responsibility for fulfilling her family's and
community's dreams of her respectable achievements as a Black woman."
After years of painful struggles over her sexuality, Murray settled into a
public persona of spinsterhood and the stability of a long-term partnership.[7]
In the face of personal and professional adversity, she achieved an aston-
ishingly active and productive career. She cherished friendships with professional women like herself who battled sexism. Murray was determined,
within the bounds of propriety, to seek her own path against societal or
group norms. She entertained a platonic notion of a sexless self in the public sphere, a demeanor appropriate to her status as a woman in a male-
dominated profession.

In Ghana, Murray emphasized a raceless ideal in defiance of local expectations of racial and political solidarity. Against those expectations, Murray espoused a dominant color-blind American individualism that mirrored
the ideology promoted overseas by U.S. officialdom. As a civil rights lawyer, Murray was powerfully drawn to color-blind principles. It is likely, too,
that her previous encounter with leftist political circles that prioritized class
struggle fostered a skepticism toward racial affiliations.

PAULI MURRAY IN GHANA

The question of identity weighed heavily on Murray on the eve of her voyage. How would she respond to Africa? How would Africans respond to her? She sensed that the answers to those questions would be deeply revelatory at a personal level. Work also held mysteries, though she imagined that the position with the Ghanaian government promised an international horizon of public service. Springer had given Murray a sense of what to expect, having introduced Murray to visiting African nationalists in New York City. George Padmore had recruited Springer to the cause of pan-Africanism in London during the 1940s. An official in the International Ladies Garment Workers Union, Springer provided educational and material assistance to African trade unionists. She frequently hosted and gained the confidence of African nationalist leaders and had pulled strings with Nkrumah on Murray's behalf. Soon, with Garrison's blessing, Geoffrey Bing, Ghana's British expatriate attorney general, recruited Murray to help train the new nation's lawyers. Bing hired a staff that included exiles from South Africa and elsewhere who, like Murray, faced social constraints in their countries of origin.[8]

Murray's reflections on her identity as an American of African descent were shaped by the turbulent politics of Ghana and Africa, which led her to view herself as fundamentally American. Her initial task of building a legal infrastructure in Ghana evolved into a mission to defend U.S. constitutional values and America's image. Springer may well have been a model for Murray's political engagement. At the time, Springer was a frequent observer at pan-African conclaves, representing the international division of the American Federation of Labor–Congress of Industrial Organizations, which sought to promote a noncommunist African trade union movement.[9]

Murray's arrival in Ghana coincided with the ratification of Ghana's new republican constitution and the government's advocacy of socialism as the path to economic development, events that politicized her task of teaching U.S. constitutional law. The transition to republic status completed Ghana's independence from British authority, but the new constitution was also the mechanism by which Nkrumah, as president of Ghana, sought to neutralize his vocal and sometimes violent opposition. Murray's reservations regarding the new constitution's emphasis on executive power at the expense of Parliament and the courts and the curbs on civil liberties she witnessed put her on a collision course with Nkrumah's desire to strengthen his hand against his opponents.

In the classroom, Murray argued for the universality of U.S. constitutional ideals, separation of powers, civil liberties, and the rule of law. The difficulty

for Murray went beyond the emergency powers the Ghanaian government
claimed were necessary for its security. Her case was weakened by the racial turmoil in the U.S. South and the upheaval in the Congo, crises that
led to sharp criticism of U.S. domestic and foreign policy in Ghana's state-
controlled press.[10] Murray defended the United States in the face of such
criticism, but she was hard-pressed to convince Nkrumah, who had studied
in the United States during the 1930s and 1940s, that her idealized vision of
U.S. democracy bore any resemblance to an American society ripped apart
by racial conflict.

Along with Nkrumah's political opponents, Murray clashed with the Ghanaian government over the 1958 Preventive Detention Act, which jailed without trial for up to five years those deemed threats to national security. Defenders of the act claimed that in cases of subversion, the courts were often
hampered when witnesses in criminal trials refused to testify, fearing retribution. Defenders thus viewed preventive detention as a necessary expedient
against threats to state security, including assassination plots against Nkrumah. To members of the opposition and Ghana's critics in the Western press,
preventive detention confirmed reports of Nkrumah's autocratic leadership.
To be sure, critics of the policy also included such longtime allies as African
American pacifist Bill Sutherland, an expatriate employee of the Ghanaian
government who strongly objected to the policy and told Nkrumah so.[11]

Recruited as a presumed sympathizer of the Ghanaian government, Murray broke with her employers in criticizing the concentration of presidential
power in the new constitution and the government's repression of its opposition. Murray had ample occasion to discuss with Bing and others the rationale for strong executive power in Ghana's constitution. She grasped the
need for emergency powers and preventive detention to counter threats to
stability, including political violence. Murray well understood the risks of
speaking against Ghanaian governmental policies and struggled to remain
impartial in her teaching. But her law classes were attended by opposition
members of Parliament and monitored by government intelligence agents.
Undaunted, Murray brought her criticisms to the attention of the Ghanaian government. Dismayed by the surveillance, Murray eventually provided
clandestine assistance to opposition legal challenges to preventive detention.
That affiliation joined her principled commitment to the rule of law with the
opposition's legal defense of its civil liberties. Indeed, Murray shared the
values of her profession with such lawyers as J. B. Danquah and Joseph
Appiah, both of whom were prominent members of the opposition. Alien-

ated by the government's anti-Americanism and with her attempts at dialogue rejected by Nkrumah, Murray joined forces with an opposition that at the time still enjoyed a measure of legitimacy within Ghanaian politics.

The political crisis in the Congo heightened tensions on all sides. In late September, Nkrumah addressed the United Nations General Assembly, condemning Belgium's neocolonial attack on the sovereignty of the independent Congo, urging the United Nations to uphold that sovereignty, and denouncing the Union of South Africa, France, and Portugal for their colonial policies.[12] This, along with the advocacy of socialism by Ghana's ruling Convention People's Party, was the background for a testy exchange of letters between Murray and Labor Minister John Tettegah. Murray defended the American press and capitalism against Tettegah's criticisms, which were prompted by negative coverage of Nkrumah in *Time* magazine.[13] In mid-October Nkrumah angrily refuted "pernicious" reports that Ghana planned to nationalize foreign enterprises; Murray may have come under suspicion for spreading these rumors.[14] In November Murray broached her concerns to Nkrumah, who curtly dismissed her charges of dictatorship. Through his private secretary, Nkrumah refused Murray's request to meet with him. That official rebuff solidified Murray's opposition to the Ghanaian government.[15]

Stung by criticism of the United States in Ghana's press, Murray's self-appointed role as defender of the image of American democracy against criticism by Cold War adversaries framed her discussions of race, identity, and U.S. citizenship. The Americanism Murray espoused was a raceless, unhyphenated ideal with little place for ethnic identification. The appeal of color-blindness for Murray went beyond U.S. Supreme Court Justice John Marshall Harlan's formulation of the principle in his dissent from the majority opinion in *Plessy v. Ferguson* (1896). Insofar as color became shorthand for an array of discriminatory practices under Jim Crow, Murray and other blacks of the wartime generation saw race and color as a badge of servitude and the basis for the Jim Crow South's legal and extralegal deprivation of the full citizenship rights of African Americans. Murray and others saw color-blind constitutional rights as the remedy for all-too-common judicial atrocities such as the Odell Waller execution. In Murray's eyes, color-blind jurisprudence meant due process, equal protection, and fairness in criminal trial procedures such as jury selection. No wonder, then, that on U.S. terrain this color-blind construction of American citizenship epitomized freedom and equality for Murray and many others at a hopeful if uncertain moment of change. Largely unexamined within this mind-set was the assumption that a "color-blind" state ideology obliged African Americans to renounce a black or African identification, an assumption that restricted claims for citizenship to national criteria inflected by the Cold War and white supremacy; it also illustrated the assimilationism among black leadership that E. Franklin Frazier and Lorraine Hansberry, to name two prominent examples, found so troubling. Unlike Frazier, Hansberry, and others, however, Murray seemed unable to distinguish the negative ascription of racism from a positive affirmation of blackness. In retrospect, Murray's ideal of color-blind citizenship overlooked the racialized character of a U.S. citizenship that, as David Roediger has put it, has historically been colored white. Indeed, much of the broad-based appeal of the color-blind ideal resulted from the fact that it left unquestioned structural, economic manifestations of white privilege and power.[16]

Murray's ideological sparring with the Ghanaian government was informed by a dominant, ostensibly color-blind American liberalism that in effect banished an independent black political identity to a Siberia-like realm of otherness, its racialized logic accusing African American dissenters of "thinking like blacks" instead of "like Americans." (Afro-American writer and Ghanaian expatriate Julian Mayfield debunked this dominant logic as late as 1984, when it was invoked during Jesse Jackson's presidential campaign by those hostile to the candidate's progressive politics and criticism of U.S. foreign policy.)[17] While quite valid reasons existed for Murray's belief in color-blind Americanism, the coercive Cold War climate and the traumatic experience of her federal investigation may also have shaped her views, affecting her embrace of the same injunctions of national loyalty wielded by HUAC to bring dissenters and liberals like herself to heel. As we have seen, transnational black solidarities were widely viewed as subversive during the 1950s. Moreover, criticism of U.S. foreign policy was decidedly off-limits for prominent African Americans. Well into the next decade, both black leaders and white officials censured Martin Luther King Jr. when he opposed the war in Vietnam. That unspoken but widely understood restriction of black leadership to the purview of domestic civil rights epitomized the subordinated citizenship of African Americans under the regime of Cold War liberalism. In other words, U.S. officialdom routinely subordinated the rights of blacks to regional, national, international, and corporate interests. In large part, for their attacks on this logic and their advocacy of African liberation, the State Department seized the passports of Paul Robeson and W. E. B. Du Bois during the 1950s. And they were not the only ones disciplined by the Jim Crow state. Liberals with prior radical associations, including Ralph Bunche and Murray, were investigated.[18] Herself a target of such harassment, Murray would not have actively supported this ideological regime of Cold War suspicion of black internationalism and solidarity. At the same time, that regime's potential wrath led many black spokespersons to seek legitimation by disassociating themselves from dissident internationalists. In this fashion, Murray took sides in internal ideological struggles between black liberals and leftists.

Murray's views on the responsibilities of being an American Negro in Africa were in part influenced by the State Department's selection throughout the 1950s of prominent African Americans, including women, as international spokespersons. To counter Soviet and neutralist criticisms of American racism, U.S. officials sent African American intellectuals and public figures abroad, hoping that they could persuade emerging nonwhite nations in Africa, Asia, and the Middle East that the nation was committed to racial equality. Another friend of Murray's, Chicago attorney Edith Sampson, probably influenced Murray's approach to representing the United States abroad. Sampson became a lightning rod for African Americans who objected to her defenses of American democracy to overseas audiences amid the antiblack violence and upheavals of the 1950s. In 1952, as Murray awaited the conclusion of her loyalty investigation, she defended Sampson after radical African American journalist William Worthy disputed the rosy assessment of improving U.S. race relations offered by Sampson in a speech she delivered in Copenhagen. Murray shared Sampson's concern for presenting the United States to overseas audiences in the best possible light. Murray later emulated Sampson's willingness to defend American democracy from attacks by the leftist Ghanaian government.[19]

Before her trip, Murray's friend, Harold Isaacs, urged her to write up her impressions of the encounter between American Negroes and Africans on the continent. Isaacs, a journalist and scholar of international affairs, was researching the impact of emergent African nationhood on black Americans' identity. Through Isaacs, Murray inadvertently helped craft a new journalistic image of alienation between African Americans and Africans that debunked notions of pan-African solidarity as illusory and inauthentic.

In Ghana, Murray viewed herself as fundamentally American. Her experiences led her to view this identification as normative for American Negroes in Africa. As she saw it, American Negroes and Africans could not have been more different in outlook. This premise functioned for Murray as a political litmus test where Ghana was concerned. She was disconcerted by African Americans (or anyone, really) who supported Nkrumah or criticized the

Pauli Murray with Mrs. George D. Carroll, Accra, 1960. (Schlesinger Library, Radcliffe Institute, Harvard University, Cambridge, Massachusetts)

United States and its domestic and foreign policy. Springer recalled that she and Murray had quarreled bitterly over Springer's support of Nkrumah.[20]

In letters home, Murray adopted an upbeat tone as she described coping with unwieldy mosquito nets and the myriad challenges of life in Ghana and related her halting initiation into the ways of indigenous cultures in West Africa. In a spirit of self-examination, however, she confided to her journal a profound loneliness, self-doubt, and sense of isolation from Ghanaians and other African American expatriates and her intense disapproval of the political situation in Ghana. She was further taxed by the chronic malaria she stoically kept from correspondents until her impending departure. Murray felt estranged from Ghana's sympathizers, black and white. In one anguished diary entry in which she reflected on the source of her personal and political estrangement, Murray attributed her unhappiness to "self," a formulation that was both circumspect and telling.[21]

The Congo Crisis and the Struggle over America's Image

Murray's difficulties in Ghana were exacerbated by the worldwide repercussions of the outbreak of civil strife in the Congo on July 5, 1960, almost one week after the ceremony marking its independence from Belgian rule. Congolese troops revolted against continued Belgian control over the military. In response, Prime Minister Patrice Lumumba dismissed Belgian officers, but he was unable to halt the looting, rioting, and violent harassment of Belgians. Lumumba approved the intervention of Belgian paratroopers to restore order, but they worsened the situation with violent attacks against Congolese. On July 11, Belgian officials engineered the secession of the mineral-rich province of Katanga. Demanding an end to the secession and the withdrawal of Belgian troops, Lumumba appealed for international assistance. On July 14, a United Nations military force with a substantial Ghanaian contingent arrived to act as peacekeepers. Thus began what became known as the Congo Crisis, a defining event in Africa's struggle for independence. The Congo became a proxy Cold War battleground for the United States and the Soviet Union and a test for Nkrumah's positive neutralism, which held that African diplomatic and military initiative in concert with the UN should play a leading role in resolving the conflict.

Despite assumptions in the Western press that he had fallen under communist influence, the democratically elected Lumumba was a moderate radicalized by the nationalism of the Congolese people and his attendance at the country's wealthiest region, was a bold attempt by Belgium to maintain neocolonial control over the nation's economy. For several years, the secession, led by pro-Western Congolese politician Moise Tshombe, was subsidized by the Union Minière du Haut Katanga, a Belgian mining company that had historically dominated politics in that region. Backed by Belgian advisers and Union Minière personnel, Tshombe became the poster child for neocolonialism from the perspective of sympathizers of the global anticolonial movement. Under Tshombe's titular leadership, Katanga's military included Belgian troops as well as mercenaries from white-dominated South Africa and Rhodesia and even some former Nazi SS soldiers and Italian Fascists. Belgium fomented other secessions, succeeding in the South Kasai region. As Belgium came under fierce criticism from Afro-Asian nations and the Soviet Union, the Eisenhower administration quietly supported the Katanga secession and the Central Intelligence Agency (CIA) funneled French military planes to Katanga.[22]

In late July, Lumumba traveled to New York and Washington, vainly seeking support from the Eisenhower administration and the United Nations. American officials were convinced that Lumumba was irrational, unstable, and a communist. Lumumba found few allies at the UN, which was effectively financed and controlled by the United States.[23] To Lumumba's consternation, UN troops made no effort to end Katanga's secession. In late August, Lumumba accepted a Soviet military airlift, playing into American fears of a Moscow takeover of the Congo. At the urging of U.S. officials, Congolese president Joseph Kasavubu dismissed Lumumba as prime minister. Lumumba easily outmaneuvered Kasavubu's coup. Appealing directly to the Parliament, Lumumba persuaded the body to honor his mandate.[24]

Lumumba's resourcefulness and popular support led to concerted efforts by the Belgian and U.S. governments to eliminate him by any means. According to Madeline Kalb, the CIA, along with Western embassies in Leopoldville, had financed the Congolese army with infusions of cash to Joseph Désiré Mobutu, an ambitious young officer and former journalist.[25] Finally, after intense international criticism, the UN assisted Lumumba and condemned Belgium's presence in Katanga. UN troops formed a cordon around Lumumba's residence, protecting him from arrest by Congolese officials in league with Belgium. On November 27, while Lumumba was attempting an escape to Stanleyville to rally his supporters, Congolese troops captured him near Thysville. Belgian officers, working in tandem with their Congolese factotums, assassinated Lumumba and two of his aides on January 17, 1961. With Lumumba's death, Belgium and the United States had achieved their objectives in the Congo.[26] The West's role in the assassination of Lumumba was roundly condemned worldwide when Belgium released the news of Lumumba's fate a month after his execution. From Ghana, Nkrumah observed that Lumumba's murder was "the first time in history that the legal ruler of a country has been done to death with the open connivance of a world organization on whom that ruler put his trust."[27]

Well before Lumumba's disappearance and death, the turmoil in the Congo overshadowed all events, including the First Conference of African Women and Women of African Descent held in Accra in July 1960. Murray attended that conference, which, like similar international gatherings, became an ideological battleground over the worldwide image of American democracy. Another conference participant and an acquaintance of Murray's dating back to the Waller campaign was civil rights activist Anna Arnold Hedgeman, who had held a federal appointment in the Health, Education, and Welfare Department during the Truman administration. She was later appointed to the cabinet of New York City Mayor Robert Wagner. As with Murray, Hedgeman's involvement in international affairs provided a refuge from racism and sexism in American public life. After a well-publicized swearing-in at City Hall, Wagner showed no intention of employing her in any capacity. Hedgeman mobilized allies in the black press to prevent Wagner from reneging on her appointment. Shunted to a basement office, Hedgeman, who had previously traveled to India on a goodwill mission for the State Department, hosted visiting African diplomats and their wives, a courtesy repaid by the invitation to deliver a keynote address at the conference.

Hedgeman recalled her visit to Ghana in a 1964 memoir containing a bitter indictment of a northern liberalism defined by a white ethnic chauvinism resistant to sharing power in New York City with African Americans and Puerto Ricans. Hedgeman, who also encountered sexism within the civil rights establishment as the only woman on the executive committee of the March on Washington, described a nation at a crossroads and symbolized by an organized Christian church torn asunder by racism.[28]

Hedgeman recalled that "the shadow of the Congo hung over the convention" and sympathetically portrayed Nkrumah. In her address, Hedgeman balanced candor about the realities of racism at home with a reminder that many whites supported desegregation, stressing "the continuous struggle for

freedom in which Americans of African descent have always engaged." She
believed it important to remind her audience that African Americans "have
had cooperation from like-minded people of many races and creeds." To
ringing applause, Hedgeman encouraged women of new African states to
join the new United Nations Commission on the Status of Women.[29]

While the conference sessions were devoted to the social concerns of
African women (legal status, problems of vocational and professional training, the expansion of educational opportunities, maternal and child health,
and nutrition and disease control), the Committee on Resolutions focused on
the political controversies affecting the continent. Two resolutions sparked
heated debate. First, the conferees called for the UN Security Council to
uphold the Congo's sovereignty against secessionist challenges. The second,
proposed by an African delegate, was "a resolution on discrimination linking
the United States with [French colonial repression in] Algeria, the Congo and
the Union of South Africa." Hedgeman protested the linkage of the United
States with South Africa, but other U.S. delegates (including Shirley Graham
Du Bois) supported the resolution. In the ensuing discussion, delegates from
the United States clarified distinctions between apartheid in South Africa and
racial discrimination in America. In her memoir, Hedgeman praised Murray
for explaining the history of the Constitution and its amendments and the
Supreme Court "as basic to our struggle for freedom." Although twenty of the
delegates, mindful of the frequent reprisals against blacks in the South,
equated white supremacy in the South with the apartheid regime, the minority position advocated by Hedgeman, Murray, and others prevailed.[30]

In her diary, Murray wrote glowingly of Hedgeman's role in this U.S.
diplomatic victory. Murray praised the teamwork of members of the American community, which included personnel from U.S. embassies in Ghana
and Nigeria.[31] Perhaps with this experience in mind, Murray castigated Attorney General Robert Kennedy in a letter for his demand that activists from
the Congress of Racial Equality call a halt to the Freedom Rides. Murray told
Kennedy that his reluctance to enforce federal desegregation law undermined American credibility on race relations, confirming many Africans'
perceptions of the United States and South Africa as partners in white supremacy. What effect this missive had on Kennedy, if any, is difficult to
determine.[32] While Murray, Hedgeman, and other African Americans effectively countered anti-American rhetoric in Ghana, they appeared unable to
dislodge the Kennedy administration's Cold War mind-set, which could not
seem to view racial justice as an end in itself.

Murray set herself the task of writing an essay on the American Negro in Africa for publication back in the States. Her motivation to do so was kindled by a visit from her friend Isaacs, who stayed at her house while attending the Accra women's conference as an observer. Adelaide Cromwell, an Africanist sociologist and member of the U.S. delegation, recalled that some members of the committee on resolutions, which met at Murray's house, were miffed to find Isaacs intent on hearing the deliberations, totally unfazed at being the lone white male in a gathering of black women.[33] Murray later sent Isaacs a draft of her essay, "A Question of Identity," crediting her friend as a major influence on its contents. Based on her encounters with other American blacks and her experiences in Ghana, Murray's essay reflected a dominant liberal construct of a normative black identity. Adopting the prescriptive and gendered tone then common in writing about race and identity, Murray argued that the "American Negro" visiting Africa discovers there that "his peculiar history and unending search for unqualified acceptance . . . have made him uniquely American." From Africa, she continued, African Americans are able to see "the American dream of freedom and equality" as they are unable to see it in America, "in shining perspective." At the same time, Murray acknowledged that Africans had serious concerns about African Americans' loyalties. Educated Africans, she observed, vacillated between viewing American blacks as "our brothers" and as "agents of imperialism." Murray regarded such suspicions not as political differences but instead as emblematic of Africans' psychological and cultural differences from African Americans. Educated Africans seemed unable to view America through any lens other than segregation and neocolonialism. Convinced of this mistrust, Murray disagreed with members of the American Society for African Culture and others who argued for a strategic interest in increasing African American representation in foreign service posts in Africa. Interestingly, given her argument to Kennedy that the Cold War should not outweigh black demands for equality, Murray invoked the Cold War in support of her view that African Americans should not be placed in such sensitive diplomatic positions. Murray argued for a normative black identity aligned with the American nation and its national security imperatives.[34]

Murray hoped that Isaacs, now back in the States, would assist her in placing her essay with a major magazine. Why this never happened is an interesting question. *Harper's* claimed to like the piece but refused it, citing a backlog of material on race and Africa. By late November, Murray had gotten several rejections and had apparently laid the essay aside.[35]

Murray's unpublished essay anticipated a shift in the liberal preoccupation with containing black political expression and limiting the ideological boundaries of citizenship. To the usual Cold War suspicion of black and African movements as instigated by communists was added a new argument, less driven by the terms of Cold War anticommunism and instead involving the question of racial authenticity—or, rather, inauthenticity. Against considerable evidence of African American identification with African peoples and their struggles, this new argument posited a fundamental alienation between African Americans and Africans, debunking linkages between the two groups' freedom struggles.

To appreciate the significance of this new argument, it is instructive to consider the relationship between the Cold War and the black freedom movement. As Penny Von Eschen has shown, the political repression of black leftist supporters of African anticolonialism during the early 1950s led African American civil rights leaders to craft a Cold War rationale for desegregation. Seeking political leverage and distancing themselves from proscribed anticolonial alliances, civil rights leaders shifted the framework of claims for citizenship and civil rights away from Africa and toward the American nation. They insisted that racial justice was essential to U.S. national security and containment of the Soviet threat.[36] That attempt to turn the Cold War into a justification for desegregation was double-edged. Although the Supreme Court embraced this logic as part of the rationale for the 1954 *Brown v. Board of Education* decision, segregationists and ultraconservatives just as often demonized the cause of racial justice by accusing black activists, leaders, and organizations of communist affiliations. Moreover, as Mary L. Dudziak has argued, it was commonplace for liberals, including President John F. Kennedy and his brother, Robert, the attorney general, to prioritize the national security imperatives of the Cold War over African American demands for equality. By this logic, civil rights protesters played into the hands of Soviet adversaries. Some viewed civil rights demonstrators as disloyal to America's national security.[37] The gatekeepers of American liberalism subjected even African American assertions of cultural equality—specifically, the claim that ancient African kingdoms had contributed to Western civilization —to red-baiting and ridicule. For example, *Newsweek* published without attribution reproductions of Afrocentric paintings by African American expatriate Earl Sweeting it had obtained in Accra. The works challenged the racist erasure of Africa from Western modernity by portraying Africans sharing their knowledge with the Greeks. "If you have no history, invent one," *Newsweek* sneered, adding that "Ghana, apparently, has taken that bit of Russian advice." Sweeting unsuccessfully sued the magazine for the unauthorized use of his work.[38]

As *Newsweek*'s contempt for the idea of an African contribution to Western civilization suggested, this version of red-baiting spoke explicitly to those subscribing to Western white supremacy. This was also an example of a generic, Manichaean anticommunism that led many Americans to view the Soviets as incapable of an accurate or truthful assessment of global affairs. These Americans (including, of course, many of African descent) remained highly susceptible to their government's ideological biases and propaganda. For many, the truth—if not God's favor—resided with the "Free World," a belief reinforced by pervasive anxieties at the threat of nuclear annihilation. Thus, within government circles, which included powerful segregationist senators, insurgent African Americans were synonymous with subversion. This synthesis of Cold War anticommunism and white supremacy influenced U.S. opinion on the Congo Crisis. At the height of the turmoil there, many U.S. politicians and opinion leaders believed that the Soviet Union had orchestrated the international criticism of U.S., Belgian, and UN policies. Despite worldwide protests in the wake of Lumumba's death and the validity (as hindsight has shown) of criticisms of Belgian neocolonialism by Afro-Asian nonaligned nations, Soviet officials, and African American radicals and nationalists, many liberal officials and commentators, apparently including Pauli Murray, dismissed those criticisms out of hand as mere communist propaganda.[39]

September 1960 found Murray on the defensive about the Congo situation as well as heightened Cold War tensions as a result of U.S. Secretary of State Christian Herter's assertion of Nkrumah's communist sympathies, which provoked more anti-American rhetoric from the Ghanaian press. Murray balked at Dorothy Padmore's assertion that UN Secretary-General Dag Hammarskjöld was the instrument of Belgian interests in the Congo. *Voice of America* became Murray's balm against criticisms of U.S. policy as well as homesickness. On one occasion she hosted a luncheon for four African American couples, the men employed by the U.S. government or engaged in businesses in Ghana. Murray savored the lengthy discussion of their favorite topics, the American Negro in Africa and the Congo. One of her male guests predicted war between the United States and the Soviet Union within six months.[40]

The actual war, with thousands of military and civilian casualties, would occur over the next several years as Congolese forces loyal to Lumumba's legacy and Antoine Gizenga's Stanleyville government would continue their fight for control over the country. Their revolt was suppressed in late 1964 as Belgian forces, with U.S. air support, invaded Stanleyville and engaged in the mass slaughter of an estimated three thousand Congolese civilians. War in the Congo, if not the suffering of the Congolese, ended only after Mobutu instituted a corrupt and brutal dictatorship that lasted until his overthrow and exile in 1997.[41]

For its part, the American and Western press, preoccupied with the spread of communism and the specter of Congolese violence against Belgians, scarcely felt the need to justify Lumumba's removal to its audience.[42] Indeed, Lumumba's whereabouts remained unknown for several weeks after his execution by firing squad and the grisly destruction of his dismembered remains in sulfuric acid by Belgian troops. Before his death was announced, Belgian authorities reported that Lumumba and his aides had escaped from Mobutu's troops, a patently false account that provoked immediate suspicion among Belgium's critics. This fabrication was the prelude to the official Belgian cover-up of Lumumba's murder: the Congolese prime minister was reported to have been killed by vengeful members of a rival tribe. While laying the cornerstone for a new institute for the training of socialist cadres, Nkrumah denounced the official story of the death of Lumumba and his aides as "the most absurd fabrication, that could emanate only from the diseased brains of Belgian colonialists and their puppet agents."[43]

As tacit U.S. support for Belgium and apartheid South Africa came under attack by Ghana and other African nations, Afro-Americans already angered by racial oppression at home had further cause to doubt their government's goodwill. Such opposition erupted in February 1961 when several African Americans, outraged by Lumumba's death, interrupted a speech by U.S. Ambassador to the United Nations Adlai Stevenson with a demonstration in the gallery of the Security Council. Screams and shouts of "Murderers!" rang through the hall, and the demonstrators, men and women alike, physically resisted UN guards. After calm had been restored, Stevenson apologized for what he called an obviously "organized" disturbance. Predictably, contemporary press accounts (including editorials, opinion pieces, and newsreels) proclaimed that the demonstrators, like the slain Lumumba, were the willing dupes of communists.[44]

Closer to the truth was that the demonstrators reflected the appeal of African nationalism rather than communism among blacks in New York City. In a rebuttal to the widespread charges of communist influence, James Bald-

PAULI MURRAY IN GHANA

win warned that this view exposed white liberals' "dangerous" penchant for self-delusion. When blacks mobilized against southern segregation, their opponents claimed that they were activated by "outside agitators." When northern blacks protested, Baldwin observed, the Kremlin was to blame. For Baldwin, who claimed that he had intended to join the protesters, the belief that the demonstration was orchestrated by communists insulted the intelligence of the many blacks who needed no prodding to sensitize them to the discriminatory conditions of northern ghettoes, including poverty, unemployment, police harassment, and slum conditions.[45]

Of course, Baldwin's analysis did not put an end to such crude red-baiting. Soon thereafter, U.S. periodicals published two widely discussed articles that appeared to steal Murray's thunder in contending that African Americans and Africans were strangers to each other, their relationship defined by vast, insurmountable differences. This argument echoed not only Murray's unpublished essay but also, ironically, Baldwin's prior claim, in his report on the First World Congress of Negro Writers in Paris, that an unbridgeable gulf separated African Americans and Africans.[46] Baldwin and Murray were not the only commentators to voice such sentiments. Like Richard Wright, African American journalist Era Bell Thompson had written candidly of her feelings of estrangement from African peoples and their cultures. Unlike Wright, she affirmed her American identity and loyalties in response to her pilgrimage to Africa.[47] Thompson's pro-American stance, mediated in part by the gender tensions she experienced in Africa, may well have served as a precedent for Murray's reflections.

As these earlier statements suggest, the position taken in these two new articles penned by Murray's friend Harold Isaacs and by Russell Howe, a British-born journalist, was hardly unprecedented. However, the timing of their appearance and perhaps the circumstances of their authorship struck African American supporters of African national independence movements as a none-too-subtle attempt to discourage African American activism on African affairs. Isaacs had written of misunderstanding, hostility, and "mutual prejudice between Africans and American Negroes." According to historian Carol Polsgrove, Isaacs had scooped Murray. Accused of plagiarism by another friend of Murray's, Isaacs insisted that his article, while based in part on conversations with Murray, reflected his findings. Polsgrove also notes that Isaacs told Murray in a letter that his *New Yorker* article was prompted by the UN demonstration. Although the provenance of Howe's article is less clear, like Isaacs, Howe argued in the liberal periodical *Reporter* that the relationship between African Americans and Africans was one of mutual alien-

Audience members listen to Nkrumah's speech in Harlem during his visit to the United Nations, October 1960. (Time Life Pictures/Getty Images)

ation rather than solidarity. Howe claimed that African Americans would do more damage than good in diplomatic and other nation-building tasks. For some African American critics, it was hardly coincidental that the journalistic debunking of pan-African solidarity came so soon after the explosive African American and global outrage over UN and Western complicity in Lumumba's death.[48]

Members of the American Society for African Culture and that segment of the African American intelligentsia with direct ties to Ghana and a commitment to the cause of African freedom strongly objected to Howe and Isaacs's claims and hastened to refute them. But African American critics had a difficult time gaining a hearing in mainstream periodicals. Horace Mann Bond, former president of Lincoln University, which had for many years educated future African nationalist leaders, eventually published his rebuttal in the *Negro History Bulletin*.[49] In his keynote address at the American Society for African Culture conference in June, St. Clair Drake faulted Isaacs for failing to differentiate by political status and national distinctions within the category "African." Noting the preponderance of members of the "non-Communist, socialist left" in Ghana, Drake may have been referring to Murray when he observed that Ghanaians rejected American Negroes propagandizing for capitalism.[50] Even Murray's erstwhile ally, Anna Hedgeman, who

PAULI MURRAY IN GHANA

had by then returned to New York black leadership circles eager to join forces with African nationalists active at the UN, later wrote that "[s]ome so-called experts on Africa and the American Negro present distortions which further confuse the picture for the white American public and even for some Negroes and some Africans." She quoted a prominent African diplomat at the UN who objected to an article that presumed to tell how Africans and African Americans should feel about one another: the author was "merely trying to [drive] a wedge between you and us." For Hedgeman, who added that a major New York newspaper refused to publish her favorable account of Nkrumah, the African diplomat's words rang with truth. She had talked with Isaacs in Ghana, perhaps at Murray's bungalow. Hedgeman and others present shared with him views contrary to the thesis of his article, only to have them disregarded.[51]

Hedgeman quoted Bond's rebuttal at length. Bond saw an insidious pattern behind two prominent articles appearing at roughly the same time, "with remarkably parallel themes. . . . American Negroes were misfits in Africa, and Africans did not identify themselves with American Negroes." Against this view, Bond recounted the detailed history since the nineteenth century of New World blacks' concern for the welfare of African peoples. He emphasized the prescriptive intent of this new line on black identity: "It is not difficult to see that there must be a powerful public feeling, that it *is* dangerous to send Negroes to Africa; and that, whether true or not, American Negroes *ought* to dislike Africans, and vice versa. This is one of the oldest of racial stereotypes." Both Hedgeman and Bond believed that the crux of the matter lay in the hypocrisy of those who presumed to speak for black Americans. Summing up her experiences in Africa, Hedgeman recast the problem of racism in world affairs in terms of Christian morality: "If America, which presents herself as a great Christian nation with a belief in the equality of mankind, does not respect her own citizens of color, what can Africa expect of her?" Although Hedgeman and Murray had banded together to defend America against critics of its racial inequality, the two clearly differed on the question of African American identification with Africans. The different positions they took may well be explained by the different political realms they inhabited. Perhaps Hedgeman's immersion in New York City politics, with its long traditions of bruising ethnic conflict and black nationalism, impressed on her the necessity of group consciousness and solidarity with African peoples. Unlike Hedgeman, Murray's belief in color-blind individualism resonated with her interventions in national and international politics, where articulations of black particularity were suspect.[52]

As the turmoil in the Congo heightened the level of political intrigue in Ghana, Murray risked expulsion by criticizing the Ghanaian government's lack of adherence to Western liberal conceptions of multiparty parliamentary democracy, civil liberties, free market capitalism, and the rule of law. Fearing that Ghana was in danger of "going communist," Murray corresponded with Ghanaian officials and communicated her experiences to politically connected friends in the United States. Keenly attuned to racial integration's importance to overseas audiences, Murray lobbied the incoming Kennedy administration to appoint her law school mentor, William Hastie, as the first African American member of the Supreme Court.

Murray's political activities were driven in large part by her search for community. In March 1960, Murray joined the American Women's Association of Accra, an unofficial group that sought to foster understanding between its members and Ghanaians. The group amassed news clippings and similar documentation to counter hostile propaganda and refute anti-American statements disseminated by the state-controlled press. A year later, Murray recommended that the group seek a more formal relationship with the embassy and other U.S. foreign service missions abroad.[53] Murray found a sympathetic ear for her criticisms of Nkrumah in her friend, Lloyd K. Garrison Jr., a *New York Times* correspondent covering West Africa and the son of her mentor in the legal profession. Like the younger Garrison, Murray viewed Ghanaian criticisms of biased Western press accounts as evidence of a creeping authoritarianism.

The new Kennedy administration sparked a flurry of correspondence on behalf of Murray by the elder Garrison. Missives to members of the foreign policy establishment, including G. Mennen Williams, assistant secretary of state for African affairs, and recent Kennedy appointees George Ball and Chester Bowles, apprised them that Murray had valuable insights into the political situation in Ghana gained from her struggles against the left-wing attorney general over curbs on civil liberties and an independent judiciary. Murray had felt keenly the rigors of a police state. Garrison further confided that an African American on the embassy staff in Accra whom he believed to be a CIA informant was in constant touch with Murray. Garrison quoted from Murray's letters describing her precarious situation in Ghana. He seemed to be angling for a suitable exit strategy for her.

Not much came of Garrison's efforts. Williams, who met Murray during a visit to Ghana, probably found little new in the information Murray had to offer. In any case, official criticism of Ghana potentially undermined congressional support for the Volta River project, a joint venture of the U.S.

government and the U.S.-based Kaiser Corporation. Murray's political views and associations with members of Nkrumah's opposition made it increasingly difficult for her to function in Ghana. She and her colleagues at the law school encountered a climate hostile to academic freedom. The precise nature of Murray's cooperation with a CIA agent (a member of Murray's social circle of African American U.S. government personnel) is difficult to determine.[54] If she confided to Garrison that she was in contact with an African American CIA agent (as Garrison reported to State Department officials), she could have been something more than an unwitting asset. At the very least, Murray championed American influence in Ghana with a steadfastness that made her serviceable to those engaged in gathering intelligence.[55]

Murray's efforts in Ghana and her departure just ahead of what would certainly have been her expulsion are best understood within a broader context of political intrigue. Among Accra's conspicuous community of American expatriates and visitors were personnel from the U.S. embassy seeking intelligence on Ghanaian politics and leadership. The U.S. government and its covert representatives actively sought such cooperation, not only from well-placed African Americans but also from members of the Ghanaian government. Murray's opposition to Nkrumah and her tendency to privilege an identification with America over solidarity with Ghana and African nationalism made her the subject of attention from U.S. government personnel. Springer reintroduced Murray to an old acquaintance from the 1930s, Jay Lovestone, an ex-communist cold warrior, director of the American Federation of Labor–Congress of Industrial Organizations' international free trade union initiative, and CIA operative.[56]

The vicissitudes and intrigues of the Ghanaian postcolonial situation seemed to turn Murray's politics and principles upside down. In Ghana, her commitment to due process and civil liberties, which were transformative in the United States, informed her alliance with opposition lawyers, including John B. Danquah, in their legal challenge to the government's Preventive Detention Act. From the Ghanaian government's standpoint, this stance placed her squarely in the camp of a reactionary colonial iteration of jurisprudence that shielded subversive activities. Her criticism of threats to civil liberties in Ghana expressed a principled faith in American judicial values. Indeed, Murray rendered a crucial service to Ghanaian political culture at a moment when the country's government was turning away from the rule of law. Her efforts did not go unappreciated in government circles. One official was sufficiently impressed to recommend to the State Department that Murray receive an American specialist grant to another English-speaking African country, cautioning, however, that she would not consent to being sent as a Negro, as "[s]he considers herself just an American."[57] There would be no such return engagements to Africa. By the end of 1961, Murray returned to the United States to begin doctoral study at the Yale Law School in the hope that law schools would eventually begin hiring women faculty in greater numbers.

While her response to the volatile political situation in Ghana during the Congo Crisis was singular, Pauli Murray's dilemma was far from unique. Her plight resembled that of Anna Hedgeman, Maida Springer, and other African American women for whom social constraints in the United States made the international arena a vital outlet for activism. At the Conference on Women of Africa and of African Descent, Murray and Hedgeman found common cause, defending the United States against critics of its racial strife and in the process laying claim to the leadership denied to them in the male-controlled domains of American politics and the civil rights movement.

Yet if their plights were similar, Murray and Hedgeman responded quite differently as domestic and international racial crises prompted liberal officials and opinion makers to circumscribe African American citizenship within the narrow dictates of the Cold War, prioritizing so-called national security over the cause of African American and African freedom. The optimism of the Year of Africa had within months unraveled with the Sharpeville Massacre, the prolonged civil strife in the Congo, and the UN disturbance over Lumumba's death. As the Kennedy administration faulted civil rights demonstrators for playing into the hands of America's Soviet adversaries, the transnational vision of African American citizenship in solidarity with the struggles of African peoples envisioned by such African Americans as Hedgeman, Bond, and Drake as well as the nationalists and radicals who revolted at the United Nations became the target of quasi-official liberal propaganda. So it seemed to Hedgeman and other African American advocates of African freedom. For her part, Murray was too preoccupied with events in Ghana to note anything amiss in a construction of American Negro identity that corresponded with her views.[58]

Murray's thoughts on the question of identity that resulted from her brief, unhappy sojourn in Ghana marked a critical moment in the ongoing confrontation over the terms and conditions by which American citizenship would be extended to Americans of African descent. Assertions of estrangement between the African and the American Negro unquestionably differed qualitatively from the outright seizure of the passports of such black internationalists as Robeson and Du Bois or the widespread declarations, uttered by those both in and out of government, that civil rights demonstrators and radical African nationalist leaders were communists. Yet the denial of legitimacy to American blacks' ties to African peoples and their liberation struggles did more than presume to tell African Americans, in effect, who they were or ought to be. It also dictated for blacks a conditional American citizenship with the implicit injunction that they eschew pan-African solidarities and an independent critique of U.S. foreign policy.

Murray's sojourn in Ghana coincided with that nation's embrace of socialism and, after the Congo Crisis, a gradual recasting of its nonaligned stance through increased trade and assistance from the Eastern bloc and China, positions that convinced her as well as hawkish U.S. officials of Ghana's drift toward communism. From that time on, Ghana's African American expatriate community would take on a strongly leftist orientation, far more supportive than Murray of Ghana's anti-imperialist agenda and far more critical of U.S. policies at home and abroad. Working within the Ghanaian government and activated by the political culture of the U.S.-based black Left, these newcomers deplored claims of alienation between African Americans and Africans as an utter falsehood refuted by the African Americans' presence in Ghana. Proponents of this view regarded such propaganda as part and parcel of the U.S. government's repression of black dissenters since the mid-1950s, a phenomenon that some observers, including Julian Mayfield, Shirley Graham Du Bois, Victoria Garvin, and Preston King, knew firsthand.

Murray returned to the United States, graduated from Yale Law School, and later received a tenured position in American studies at Brandies University. She remained active in civil rights and women's rights causes. Years later, Murray wrote in her autobiography of her time in Ghana. Her account consists largely of direct quotations from her letters home, describing her opposition to the policies of preventive detention, the surveillance of her classroom by Convention People's Party officials, and the mundane details and impressions of her daily existence. While she acknowledged the tumultuous impact of the Congo Crisis on Ghanaian politics (though Lumumba's death and the worldwide condemnation of it remained unmentioned) and discussed her clandestine work for opposition members who brought legal challenges to preventive detention laws, Murray disclosed little about her staunch pro-American interventions. As she wrote not long after her arrival in Ghana, "The human spirit is nationless, raceless, sexless. It is, and it will continue to be—whether we have cold wars, hot wars, positive neutrality, Nkrumahism, McCarthyism."[59] This wish to transcend race and sex did not transcend but in fact defined an idealized American nationhood whose virtues were confirmed by her direct experience with Ghana's curbs on civil liberties.

Murray's desire for public influence and recognition through her efforts in Ghana responded to her need to overcome the liabilities she associated with her status as a black woman. Writing years later with considerable evidence that U.S. policies had not lived up to the lofty moral standard she championed in Ghana, Murray was less than candid about her pro-American activities. Murray was hardly unique in engaging in the self-protective filtering of memory, a silencing universally practiced by authors of life writing regardless of political persuasion. Her silences resemble those of Carl Rowan, an African American journalist and director of the U.S. Information Service during the Belgian-U.S. military campaign against Congolese rebels in 1964, which black leaders across the ideological spectrum roundly condemned. Rowan's memoir of a distinguished career in journalism and public service omits any mention of that indefensible policy.[60] Murray may have determined that her staunch defense of Americanism, in retrospect inseparable from the repressive forces of empire and neocolonialism, was untenably anachronistic, incompatible with the progressive image she wished to create for posterity. Such a disclosure would only be a disturbing reminder of her voicelessness and marginalization and the measures she took to overcome them.

5

ESCAPE TO GHANA

*Julian Mayfield and
the Radical "Afros"*

The angry demonstration by African American protesters at the United Nations during the Congo Crisis in February 1961 was a disturbing spectacle for liberal officialdom and mainstream civil rights leaders alike. Domestic racial turmoil further inflamed the debates sparked by the demonstration over black identity, activism, and loyalty to the American nation. In the ensuing debate over the motivations of African American activists, black intellectuals in and around the American Society for African Culture (AMSAC) challenged assertions that the Negro was fundamentally American, with no interest in African peoples. Yet within AMSAC, the controversy exposed an underlying tension between the organization's liberal leadership and those from the black Left who participated in its programs. Some AMSAC members feared that such talk of alienation between American Negroes and African peoples would perpetuate the exclusion of blacks from the U.S. foreign service and weaken their claims to ambassadorial posts in new African states. For their part, black radicals discerned a campaign to head off the rising militancy of northern urban blacks, what one writer approvingly termed the new Afro-American nationalism.[1]

It was fitting that the United Nations was the site of the demonstration, for the Afro-American nationalism on display there was deeply international in outlook. But the label "Afro-American nationalism" was equally telling, articulating a vision of American citizenship shaped by the singular history of American racism. The disillusionment of northern urban blacks a generation or two removed from the tyranny of southern Jim Crow with institutionalized racism above the Mason-Dixon Line—what many people called "Up South"—fueled an identification with the anticolonialism of the world's darker peoples. African Americans in Harlem, Chicago, and other cities took inspiration as the complexion of global politics at the UN was transformed by the expanding membership of nonaligned African and Asian nations, among whom Ghana played a prominent diplomatic role. Also subsumed within Afro-American nationalism was a cultural common sense whose identification with global manifestations of antiracism, including the Cuban Revolution, was born of a deep suspicion of the federal government's complicity with segregation and a growing frustration at unredressed antiblack violence in the South and the civil rights movement's nonviolent emphasis. Indeed, Afro-American nationalists decried antiblack violence wielded by southern whites at home and white minority regimes in Africa. Many joined a patchwork of black organizations, their members running the gamut between redemptionist and rejectionist stances toward the American nation. The most prominent among them was the militant though separatist and culturally conservative Nation of Islam, whose newspaper, *Muhammed Speaks*, publicized the linkage of African American and anticolonial struggles throughout black urban communities. In addition to Nation of Islam minister Malcolm X, the most articulate exponents of this formation were black writers and artists, many of whom had been affiliated with the organized Left.

One such writer, novelist Julian Mayfield, was a prolific advocate of this radical alternative to the civil rights movement, a tendency operating at the lower frequencies of American politics. Mayfield's activism eventually forced him into exile in Ghana, an unforeseen development that perhaps reduced his influence in the United States. Before his exile, Mayfield, who had planned to take part in the UN demonstration, had been an important articulator of this black radical Third Force that diverged from integration and separatism. In this capacity, Mayfield illuminated the debate over the ideological parameters of African American citizenship. In 1959, at an AMSAC-sponsored conference on the future of African American literature, Mayfield rejected predictions that the demise of Jim Crow would facilitate the maturation and mainstreaming of Negro writing as outmoded novels of social protest would give way to fictions shaped by more "universal" themes. While declaring his support for integration, understood as the attainment of full and equal citizenship rights, Mayfield contended that for many blacks, integration into the so-called American mainstream really meant "completely identifying the Negro with the American image—that great power face that the world knows and the Negro knows better." The American dream had remained elusive for the Negro despite its determined pursuit by generations of blacks willing to fight in every war "and regardless of the nature of the war." Given this history, black leadership and intellectuals were obliged to question the society's dominant values. The Negro writer's detachment was a virtue, offering unique insight into contemporary American life. For the black writer, "This alienation should serve also to make him more sensitive to philosophical and artistic influences that originate beyond our national cultural boundaries." In 1959, Mayfield was pessimistic about the prospects for meaningful change in the United States. He foresaw "a tragic future . . . for the American Negro people." For the foreseeable future, blacks' minority status consigned them to political dependency and exclusion.[2]

At that uncertain juncture, Mayfield was not the only black public figure who pondered the impact of racial change on African American politics and culture. Like Mayfield, W. E. B. Du Bois, Lorraine Hansberry, and E. Franklin Frazier viewed integration into an atomized, materialistic, and repressive Cold War American culture as a threat to an African American cultural heritage ennobled by struggles for justice. In effect, they wondered whether the integration of blacks would transform and democratize the nation or whether blacks would be remade in the image of a stultifying, inequitable, and morally bankrupt American society.

Frazier's criticisms of integration as largely irrelevant to the alienation and poverty of African American urban masses who remained strangers in their own land were influential for those who strove to articulate an independent black progressivism. Younger black writers and spokespersons habitually invoked Frazier's *Black Bourgeoisie* to dissociate themselves from the integrationist orthodoxy of the civil rights establishment. Partly under the aegis of AMSAC, ironically, such rhetoric was advanced by such Nigerian intellectuals as scholar E. U. Essien Udom, author of an early and definitive study of the Nation of Islam and an associate of *Freedomways*, and playwright John Pepper Clark, who heard Malcolm X at open-air rallies in Harlem while touring the United States under State Department auspices in 1962.[3] For them and others, the black bourgeoisie reflected national failings. At the AMSAC conference, Hansberry dissected American culture and its myths of normative whiteness, its sexism and hypermasculine militarism, its perverse combination of Puritanism and prurience, and its slavish acceptance of the status quo. The greatest illusion of all was the belief in an indefinite period of time during which the nation "may leisurely resurrect the promise of our Constitution" and achieve equality on American soil. Hansberry contended that such time was running out for a misguided

Julian Mayfield, March 1959. (Carl Van Vechten Photo Collection,
Yale Collection of American Literature, Beinecke Rare Book Library,
Yale University, New Haven, Connecticut)

worldwide minority as "the universal solidarity of the colored peoples of the world" had arrived. Hansberry would not be dissuaded from the central fact of the moment: "that the ultimate destiny and aspirations of the African people and twenty million American Negroes are inextricably . . . bound up together forever." Echoing Frazier on the historical amnesia of the black bourgeoisie, Hansberry defined the work of the black artist as "the vast task of cultural and historical reclamation—to reclaim the past if we would claim the future."[4]

Hansberry's progressive outlook was all the more telling in light of her mainstream success as author of the Broadway drama *Raisin in the Sun*, a work that joined a spate of literary dissections of the American dream by numerous writers, including Mayfield, Gwendolyn Brooks, Alice Childress, Langston Hughes, Arthur Miller, and others. But whether through AMSAC or government intervention, Hansberry's essay, with its invocation of African Americans' solidarity with a global majority of colored peoples, was excluded from the published proceedings of the conference. Whatever the reasoning behind the exclusion of Hansberry's essay, this censorship of black radical opposition confirmed Frazier's irritation at a Negro American intelligentsia anxious to police itself or to submit to such policing by others.

Exile as the Price of African American Dissent

By 1961, as Hansberry defended the UN protesters after they were maligned in the press, the ideological stakes of black dissidence seemingly could not have been higher. It was hardly a coincidence that first Mayfield and soon thereafter Du Bois left the United States for Ghana as this new racialized liberal discourse was mobilized to contain an emergent transnational black political consciousness. The significance of exile can be properly understood only in this context of official uneasiness at black activist challenges to the legitimacy of U.S. domestic and foreign policy. For Mayfield and other expatriates, exile was the price for their civic engagement with the American nation through their outspoken challenges to Jim Crow. Unfortunately for them, they were not in a position to "reject" America or "choose" exile. These formulations ignore that federal and state authorities exacted a prohibitive cost for African American dissent against injustice. Moreover, however unique the circumstances of their exile, their departure must not be seen as anomalous, occurring as it did precisely at the moment when northern African American activists were condemning U.S. foreign policy. For Du Bois, Mayfield, and the other proscribed African Americans who would

seek to reclaim their political voice in Ghana, the United States of free speech
and constitutional rights did not exist. Du Bois's departure was a final gesture of defiance capping a century-spanning lifetime of prolific and largely unrequited struggle. As a radical writer, Mayfield was strongly influenced by Du Bois, but fighting deeds as much as words forced Mayfield's departure from the United States.

Mayfield and other members of this new cohort of radical black expatriates found in Ghana a sanctuary from U.S. political repression. Mayfield and Du Bois were powerfully drawn to the utopian sites of radical hope exemplified by Ghana and the Cuban Revolution. Ghana provided Du Bois; his wife, Shirley Graham Du Bois; Mayfield; and others with a forum for their criticisms of American racism and empire and with a home for their quest for a radical alternative to the U.S. civil rights movement and its officially managed goal of integration. More broadly, Ghana proved irresistible to many African American, West Indian, African, and European radicals who saw it as a bastion of revolutionary and socialist hopes. Ghana afforded them what was impossible in America: the freedom not just to speak but to advocate democratic socialism and economic justice; not just a sanctuary from exile but an external vantage point that enabled critical insight into U.S. overseas propaganda and the nation's relationship to the world. These exiles hoped to give tangible meaning to pan-Africanism from Ghana. Their skepticism toward reformist racial change in the United States was informed by their location in Ghana, at the front lines of not only the African revolution but also the formation of a new American empire as the United States sought to expand its hegemony to Africa and to replace European hegemony there. The hope that Mayfield and Du Bois attached to Ghana and Nkrumah was in direct proportion to their disillusionment with the prospects for racial equality and economic democracy in the United States.

But while Ghana facilitated for African American radicals a transnational solidarity and global citizenship marginalized in the United States, their pan-African convictions were tested by the constant internal and external challenges to the stability and survival of Kwame Nkrumah's government. As Ronald Walters has insightfully written, for all that the black American expatriate community gained in Ghana, political exile imposed certain constraints.[5] Although radical African American expatriates may have criticized certain Ghanaian government policies, the exiles on the whole staunchly defended Nkrumah's government and its aims. In other words, the sort of criticisms by Mayfield and Du Bois of the gulf between American rhetoric and reality that led to their exile in Ghana could not be made about that country, a young nation besieged by internal and external enemies. Indeed, their presence in the country coincided with an intensification of challenges to Nkrumah's leadership and the stability of his government. These threats, including a 1962 assassination attempt on Nkrumah's life, occasioned a ratcheting up of authoritarian executive power. Under these circumstances, the ideology of pan-Africanism and revolution demanded the unequivocal support of the Ghanaian state by its expatriate allies, militating against the sort of criticism voiced by Pauli Murray and conservative critics in Congress and the print media. For Ghana's supporters, the objectives of African liberation and unity outweighed the rights of opposition forces, particularly as the latter had been implicated in political violence against the Convention People's Party (CPP). Ghana's anti-imperialism and support for continental unity thus made it attractive to such sympathizers as Du Bois and Mayfield, mitigating for them the contradictions within what they viewed optimistically as an essentially progressive Ghana.

Sympathetic to the Ghanaian government's efforts to build a socialist society and accelerate the overthrow of colonial regimes throughout Africa, the African American expatriates seized opportunities to articulate pan-African solidarities. Hoping to link their struggle to Ghana's, the black American expatriates staged a demonstration at the U.S. embassy that paralleled the March on Washington. They also paid tribute to Du Bois, who had died on the eve of the demonstration. Yet in fleeing to Ghana from the tense racial climate of the United States, Mayfield exchanged a repressive political situation for a Ghanaian public culture that had its own restrictions on serious internal debate and criticism. Against these limitations, Mayfield and his Ghanaian colleagues projected a transnational black radicalism in support of the Ghanaian government's objectives. Hoping to counter the conservatism of British-trained Ghanaian elites and working in collaboration with like-minded Ghanaian journalists, Mayfield and others sought to convince Ghanaians of the persistence of white supremacy in the United States while reporting events in Ghana to the African American press. Above all, Mayfield hoped to convince Ghanaians that African Americans had a legitimate role in the tasks of nation building and revolutionary struggle.

Only rarely did African American expatriates engage in public, political activity. They were eager publicly to declare their support, but they also fully appreciated the constraints necessitated by protocol. Many of the exiles regarded their presence in the country as a political statement. After all, U.S. officials viewed their residency in Ghana as a repudiation of America if not an expression of pro-Soviet views. The Ghanaian government employed

several "Afros," as many of the expatriates called themselves, downplaying
their Americanness, in ideological and infrastructure-building occupations.
Mayfield worked as a journalist in the Publicity Secretariat, and his wife,
physician Ana Livia Cordero, was an innovative public health provider. Du
Bois was brought to Ghana as the executive director of the *Encyclopedia
Africana* project, and novelist William Gardner Smith would later serve as
director of Ghanaian journalism. Scholar and leftist analyst of African affairs W. Alphaeus Hunton was recruited to assist Du Bois on the encyclopedia project and assumed its directorship after Du Bois's death. After her
husband's death, Shirley Graham Du Bois became the founding director of
Ghana Television. In addition to those intellectuals and professionals, many
African American expatriate technicians, engineers, electricians, and plumb-
ers were literally engaged in nation building. These expatriates saw themselves and their contributions as political although they did not necessarily
engage in public demonstrations or take an active part in Ghanaian politics.

Despite their support for the African revolution, their status as diasporic "strangers" limited their influence on and comprehension of events in
Ghana. Their location in Ghana was fraught with ambiguities. They were of
African descent yet socially and culturally alien to a Ghanaian culture within
which race consciousness lacked the visceral meaning it held for them as
African Americans. Indeed, Ghanaians saw the Americans as potential spies,
and even within the expatriate community or in interactions with other
black American visitors, trust might give way to suspicion and paranoia. The
exiles were remote from the racial controversies of the U.S. scene, yet their
proximity to the global anticolonial movement afforded a unique perspective
on the impact of U.S. power in Africa. They sympathized with the politics of
African liberation yet remained remote from the corridors of power, junior
partners in pan-Africanism within Nkrumah's Ghana.

As challenges to Ghana's stability mounted, the African American expatriates' status became more uncertain, even tenuous. When Nkrumah barely
escaped assassination in 1962, indignant press accounts detected the hand of
American espionage behind such events if not everywhere. Black Americans
found that they were not immune to such suspicion, which surfaced in the
Ghana press during 1963, since several African Americans loyal to the U.S.
government were living in the country or were working at the U.S. embassy.
Such accusations against potentially disloyal African Americans unquestionably had a reckless component. Although understandable and perhaps not
entirely unfounded, such suspicions could also be exploited by those Ghanaians who coveted expatriates' jobs. Mayfield and other radical African Amer-

ican expatriates faced another obstacle in that many Ghanaians did not share the Americans' outrage at the U.S. racism that in large part had fueled their utopian vision of Ghana. More than other expatriates, Mayfield, with his Ghanaian colleagues in the press, worked to build a global print culture that unmasked the realities of brutality and exclusion behind the official American rhetoric of progress in U.S. race relations.

Julian Mayfield, Robert Williams, and the Black Left Challenge to the Civil Rights Mainstream

As a novelist, actor, and journalist, Mayfield had been at the center of Harlem cultural life throughout the 1950s. He was active in left-wing politics, which, as playwright William Branch wrote, "opened up to him a vast new world and promised hope for change of the American racial and social ills he knew all too well, as well as linking him to global struggles against racism and imperialism with which he found instant rapport."[6] At twenty-one years of age, he held his first and only major Broadway role as Absalom in the production of *Lost in the Stars*, a Kurt Weill–Maxwell Anderson musical drama adapted from Alan Paton's *Cry the Beloved Country*. Mayfield was a member of the Harlem Writer's Guild along with Maya Angelou, John Henrik Clarke, John Oliver Killens, and Sarah Wright, all of whom shared a politics of leftist internationalism and southern origins in Jim Crow terror. As a member of the Committee for the Negro in the Arts, which fought racial discrimination in the theater, Mayfield was an associate of such Harlem-based actors and playwrights as Ossie Davis, Ruby Dee, Lonne Elder III, William Branch, Sidney Poitier, Alice Childress, Lorraine Hansberry, and Harry Belafonte. When the writer's group of that organization was disbanded because of anticommunist repression in 1954, Mayfield relocated to Puerto Rico with his new wife, Ana Livia Cordero, a physician and *independentista* from that island. In Puerto Rico, Mayfield worked as a journalist (as a youth in Washington, D.C., he had been barred from employment by the *Washington Post*) and wrote his first two novels, *The Hit* (1957) and *The Long Night* (1958), well-received sketches of Harlem life. *The Hit*, in which the dream world of the illegal numbers lottery game represents the ghetto version of the American dream, concerns the undoing of a desperate middle-aged Harlemite when he finally hits the number yet is unable to collect his winnings. Mayfield's Harlem novels were works of realism that examined the internal lives of northern slum dwellers hemmed in by an American affluence and power that remained beyond their reach. During his years in Harlem, Mayfield's participation in left-wing campaigns and theater productions had attracted federal surveillance. Agents tracked him to Puerto Rico, where in light of Mayfield and Cordero's association with Puerto Rican communists, intelligence that "[s]ubject stays home most of day and appears to do a lot of typing" took on a sinister cast.[7]

Drafting novels at the typewriter paled in comparison to Mayfield's activities after his return to Harlem. During the late 1950s, Mayfield was drawn to the armed self-defense movement and became a staunch supporter of the Cuban Revolution. Dissatisfied with the civil rights movement's gradualism, its emphasis on nonviolence, and its ultimate reliance on white goodwill for legislative reform, Mayfield was inspired by ex-marine and National Association for the Advancement of Colored People (NAACP) official Robert Williams, whose use of armed self-defense against Klan harassment had revitalized the association's branch in Monroe, North Carolina. After the NAACP suspended Williams in 1959 for saying that southern blacks should engage in retaliatory violence when justice in the courts was unavailing, Mayfield and others took up Williams's cause. Mayfield joined other Harlem activists, including John Henrik Clarke and Ora Mobley, and Williams in forming the Coordinating Committee for Southern Relief. That organization, uniting northern and southern black militants, raised funds to send relief caravans of food, clothing (and more discreetly, firearms) to impoverished Monroe residents.[8] Williams, Mayfield, Clarke, LeRoi Jones, Harold Cruse, Sarah Wright, and others traveled to Cuba in July 1960 as part of a delegation of African American writers headed by Williams and arranged by the Fair Play for Cuba Committee. The victory of the Cuban guerrilla forces strengthened Mayfield and others' belief in the tactical value of armed self-defense in the United States. In late-night conversations in Havana, Williams impressed Mayfield with his fearlessness and his selfless leadership in Monroe.[9]

Revolution was in the air, and Mayfield viewed Williams and Monroe's black people through the lens of Castro's Cuba. During the summer of the harrowing events in Monroe that sent him into exile, Mayfield published several essays, including a review of James Baldwin's *Nobody Knows My Name*, and a discussion of the Cuban Revolution's significance for U.S. society.[10] The revolution's antiracism convinced Mayfield that social change need not wait on the "patient education and persuasion of the bigot and reactionary." If the U.S. government marshaled its full legal and moral resources to end discrimination, dramatic change would occur practically overnight. The lack of such a commitment led Mayfield to conclude that government leaders and the "non-colored" U.S. majority condoned racism. Mayfield noted the statement he signed along with other black public figures condemning the Bay of Pigs invasion of Cuba, which appeared in the *New York Post* and the *Baltimore Afro-American*. That declaration had been a defiant rejoinder to the Cold War silencing of black intellectuals. If Jackie Robinson could assert outside the Hotel Theresa that black Americans were just like all other Americans, Mayfield stood amid cheering crowds welcoming Castro and insisted that some black Americans were prepared to link arms with antiracist allies overseas, even those who lacked State Department approval. In the Baldwin review, Mayfield highlighted Baldwin's debunking of the accusation in the press that the UN demonstrators had been inspired by communists. Mayfield also noted that he and Baldwin had intended to be among the demonstrators. Mayfield's Harlem novels had portrayed the desperation of northern urban blacks mired in poverty amid plenty. Had Mayfield been able to remain in the United States, black working-class militancy and an anticapitalist critique of the limits of integration may well have found a more consistent and effective articulation.[11]

Mayfield emulated Williams's approach, forging international allies whose condemnations of racial abuses would embarrass the federal government and thereby compel it to intervene on the side of aggrieved blacks. But events in Monroe had careened out of control, exposing the complicity between federal and local authorities that forced Mayfield and Williams into exile. Mayfield and Williams were not communists (though Mayfield had been close to the party if not a member during the early 1950s), but the federal government nevertheless construed their internationalism and their advocacy of armed self-defense as subversive, forcing them into exile.

In 1961, Mayfield commuted between a Harlem energized by the presence of Castro at the Hotel Theresa during the general assembly of the United Nations (Nkrumah was also at the Theresa, though overshadowed by Castro) and Monroe, where he and Clarke delivered food, clothes, and guns to sympathizers in the black community. In June, Mayfield met with Williams and others, including former communist Mae Mallory, to formulate a response to escalating armed attacks against blacks in Monroe. That summer, Mayfield helped supply Monroe with rifles, pistols, and submachine guns (obtained from New Jersey gangsters with the assistance of writer LeRoi Jones). On his last run to Monroe in August, Mayfield took Mallory, neither suspecting that the visit would land her in prison for months and result in his and his wife's flight to Ghana.[12]

Mayfield and Mallory, who had scuffled with guards at the 1961 UN protest, reached Monroe as a white mob menaced an interracial group of nonviolent demonstrators outside the town courthouse. The nonviolent demonstrators had descended on Monroe hoping to convince Williams of the rightness of their approach. The unarmed demonstrators, who included James Forman of the Student Nonviolent Coordinating Committee, were attacked and viciously beaten by the mob, some of whom had come from afar to menace the protesters. Mayfield, Williams, and his followers decided that they had to rescue the besieged marchers. Years later, Mayfield described joining an automobile caravan led by Williams for a show of force intended to disperse the mob. When a car filled with white youths attempted to ram Mayfield's car off a bridge high above railroad tracks, Mayfield grabbed his .38-caliber pistol. His passenger, a young upstate New Yorker committed to nonviolence, cried, "No, no Julian, that's not the way!" Mayfield ignored his passenger and aimed straight at the youths, who retreated when they realized that their intended prey did not practice nonviolence. While members of the rescue caravan accompanied the demonstrators to Newtown, the black section of Monroe, they exchanged fire with whites shooting from the overpass where Mayfield had been attacked.[13]

A heedless middle-aged white couple ventured into Newtown and was ordered out of the car by an angry crowd. In a fateful act, Williams intervened, leading them to safety inside his house. Fearing a bloody confrontation with white law enforcement authorities and vigilantes, Williams decided to leave Monroe. After nightfall, Mayfield drove Williams; his wife, Mabel; their two children; and Mallory out of Monroe, eluding National Guard roadblocks. Within days Williams was on the Federal Bureau of Investigation's most-wanted list, sought on federal kidnapping charges for having sheltered the white couple. Williams was described as armed, dangerous, and psychotic in what appeared to be a thinly veiled invitation to authorities to shoot him on sight. Mayfield and Cordero mobilized a network of middle-class leftists to harbor Williams and his family and to secure their escape to Canada and then to Cuba. Less well connected, Mallory was betrayed to authorities while hiding out among relatives in Cleveland. Mayfield went into hiding, traveling to Canada and then London, where he joined Ana Livia Cordero and their five-year-old son. The family departed for Ghana months before Cordero's contract with the government as a public health physician was scheduled to begin.

W. E. B. Du Bois: Blacklisted, Unbowed, and Bound for Ghana

Although U.S. authorities prevented Du Bois from attending Ghana's independence and illness kept him from the All African People's Conference, his relocation to Ghana in 1961 aided Nkrumah's efforts in recruiting a cadre of black expatriate supporters. For members of the black Left, a younger generation of politically aware African Americans, and the handful of African American intellectuals, including John Hope Franklin, who stood by Du Bois as others abandoned him, Du Bois was a hero for having defiantly withstood the full force of official censure.[14] When the Supreme Court restored Du Bois's passport in 1958, he and his wife traveled to Russia, China, Sweden, and England. To their delight, Du Bois was feted in Russia and China, receiving state tributes and audiences with Nikita Khrushchev and Mao Zedong. At Du Bois's suggestion, the Soviet Union established an African studies program. Exhausted by his travels, W. E. B. Du Bois rested at a resort near Moscow while Shirley Graham Du Bois read his message to the All African People's Conference in Accra. Du Bois shrugged off criticisms of the Soviet system discreetly aired by friends. In China, the famine caused by the Great Leap Forward remained invisible to the couple as they received VIP treatment and saw staged scenes of happiness and cooperative efficiency.[15]

Du Bois's regard for these problematic powers was underscored by their support for the anticolonial cause and African liberation and strengthened by his complete disillusionment with the United States. In the context of pan-Africanism, however, Du Bois evidenced greater flexibility. Throughout the 1950s, Du Bois and George Padmore had debated the relationship of communism to the cause of pan-African freedom. In those friendly exchanges, both men were committed to finding common ground. The two agreed to disagree over the merits of Richard Wright's *Black Power*. The staunchly anticommunist Padmore elaborated to Du Bois his vision of a pan-African neutralism that selectively borrowed from Soviet models of economic development while remaining essentially pro-Western, given the necessity for foreign investment.[16] Deeply appreciative of the campaign orchestrated by Padmore in the global black press defending Du Bois during his prosecution by the U.S. Justice Department, Du Bois was won over by Padmore's formulation of an independent pan-African Third Force that resisted the blandishments of East and West alike. Nevertheless, Du Bois warned Padmore of American capitalist designs on African labor and resources. Yet where Du Bois might espouse a hard Left position, as he did in a speech to African students in Chicago in 1958, his endorsement of pan-African socialism read by Shirley Graham Du Bois to the Accra Conference acceded to Padmore and Nkrumah's preference for a stance of positive neutrality.[17]

Nkrumah and Padmore's view of neutrality was evident in their willingness to cooperate equally with those close to the Communist Party, such as

Du Bois and Alphaeus Hunton, and with noncommunists such as St. Clair Drake, who justified his public embrace of Du Bois as a revered icon of pan-Africanism despite Drake's discomfort with Du Bois's leftist views and associations. For their part, Nkrumah and Padmore saw no need to justify their long-standing loyalty to Du Bois: they had previously honored him at the historic Manchester pan-African conference in 1945 and had publicly lobbied U.S. authorities to rescind the ban that kept him from the Ghanaian independence celebrations. During his 1958 visit to the United States, Nkrumah had invited Du Bois to come to Ghana for state-sponsored research. With their right to overseas travel restored, the Du Boises attended the ceremonies ushering in the new republic of Ghana in July 1960. (On that visit, Shirley Graham Du Bois spoke at the Conference of Women of Africa and African Descent and served on the Resolutions Committee.) Again, the Du Boises were honored and deeply moved by the occasion, though it was somewhat marred by Padmore's death less than a year earlier. Nkrumah informed Du Bois of the proposed secretariat for the *Encyclopedia Africana*. In February 1961, Nkrumah cabled with news that the project had been approved and generously funded. The Du Boises planned their departure while collaborating with other black progressives, including Esther Cooper Jackson, Margaret Burroughs, Mayfield, Hunton, and Hansberry, in founding a new black radical journal, *Freedomways*.[18] The recent rise of the student sit-in movement and events in the Congo necessitated an alternative voice that the new journal would provide, its name alluding to its predecessor, Paul Robeson's newspaper, *Freedom*.

Du Bois's view that American political institutions were beyond redemption was confirmed in his eyes by the Supreme Court's decision to uphold the constitutionality of the 1950 McCarran Internal Security Act, which required left-wing organizations to register with the U.S. government under threat of fines and imprisonment. The law also barred foreigners whose writings were deemed to contain communist ideas from entering the United States. Threatened once again with the possible seizure of his passport, Du Bois accelerated plans for his departure to Ghana. As a parting shot against what seemed to be a revival of the Red Scare inquisition that had targeted him a decade earlier, Du Bois joined the Communist Party in October and traveled with his wife to Ghana. He was ninety-three years old.[19]

Unable to work full time on the encyclopedia, Du Bois relied on his assistant, Hunton, a literary scholar and authority on the political economy of neocolonialism in Africa, to manage the project. Frail and weakened by a prostate condition, Du Bois settled into a ceremonial role, receiving African

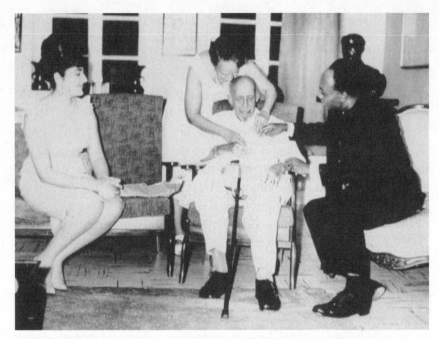

Nkrumah and his wife, Fathia, with W. E. B. Du Bois and Shirley Graham Du Bois on the occasion of Du Bois's ninety-fifth birthday, February 1963. (Schlesinger Library, Radcliffe Institute, Harvard University, Cambridge, Massachusetts)

and Asian diplomats at his residence in the once-colonial quarters of Cantonments Road. There and on automobile tours through Accra's hills, he may have mused on the corruption and the entrenchment of foreign capital in Ghana about which he had warned Padmore. Whatever qualms Du Bois may have had remained private. W. E. B. and Shirley Du Bois published optimistic firsthand accounts of the young nation in progressive publications. In addition to his duties with the encyclopedia, which provided a focal point for Ghana's promotion of Africanist scholarship, Du Bois completed *Worlds of Color*, the final volume of his historical novel, *The Black Flame Trilogy*.[20]

When Du Bois celebrated his ninety-fifth birthday, Conor Cruise O'Brien, the vice chancellor of the University of Ghana, conferred on Du Bois an honorary degree. As guests clustered around the honoree on the veranda of the vice chancellor's residence on a hill above the Accra plain, Du Bois sat impassively in his wheelchair. When conversation turned to James Meredith's attempt to desegregate the University of Mississippi, Du Bois's clipped cadence silenced the gathering. "The only thing . . . I can't understand about that young man . . . is why anyone would want to go . . . to the University of Mississippi." Later, when a young admirer likened Booker T. Washington to Katanga secession leader Moise Tshombe as a stooge of powerful whites, Du Bois objected, apparently viewing the comparison as unfair to the Wizard of Tuskegee: "When I was young, I once spoke like that about him. My aunt told me: 'Never let me hear you talk like that again.' Booker T. Washington was born in slavery and bears the mark of the lash on his back. He lives in the South. You were born free. You live in the North. He does what he can for his people in the South, in his own way. You do what you can here, in your own way, but don't insult him.'" Du Bois concluded, "I have never forgotten that."[21]

Hounded out of the United States, where he had damned America with his praise of the Soviet Union, Du Bois had become a citizen of Ghana. But from O'Brien's hillside veranda and at the end of a long life of ceaseless struggle, Du Bois could wax philosophical on past disputes with such long-departed adversaries as Washington and Marcus Garvey. Those rivalries were mitigated by time and the freedom advancing across the continent under Ghana's Black Star. For Mayfield, such equanimity would have been difficult to muster after his brush with violence in the South and a federal manhunt.

"Taking the Good with the Bad": Making the Best of Exile in Ghana

In Ghana, the circumstances of Mayfield's exile strengthened his resolve to debunk U.S. overseas propaganda asserting black progress. A major theme of Mayfield's writings was exposing for African audiences the distance between official U.S. pronouncements of racial progress and the persistent realities of antiblack violence and repression. While his political writing in Africa served an important purpose, Mayfield's exile disrupted his stateside efforts to promote radical alternatives among the black working class, North and South, to a civil rights liberalism tailored to the Cold War.

Mayfield's December 1961 arrival in Ghana coincided with a period of intense political turmoil. Resistance to Nkrumah's agendas of socialist development and continental unity would have been unmistakable to any newcomer. The government had incurred British criticism by detaining fifty people, including opposition leaders J. B. Danquah and Joe Appiah, on allegations of subversion. In November, two explosions took place in Accra, and one of them damaged the bronze statue of Nkrumah outside Parliament House. The incidents prompted the British press to call for Queen Elizabeth to cancel her planned trip to Ghana later that month. Nevertheless, the queen followed through with her visit, which was a resounding success.[22]

ESCAPE TO GHANA

Spurred by the Congo Crisis, Nkrumah accelerated his efforts to forge an anticolonial bloc of African nations. Heads of state from Ghana, Guinea, Libya, Mali, Morocco, Tunisia, and the United Arab Republic met in Casablanca to declare their support for Algerian and Congolese nationalists. Nkrumah urged the formation of a joint African high command that could deploy troops to assist any African territory that might find its sovereignty threatened. The African American press closely followed these developments. Praising the leadership of Egypt's Gamal Abdel Nasser, *Muhammed Speaks* reported that the anticolonial Casablanca bloc envisioned a military Third Force that would challenge East-West conflict. Nkrumah pointedly criticized South Africa at the Commonwealth conference and sought increased trade with Eastern bloc nations and China. While visiting the United States in 1961, however, Nkrumah took pains to distinguish Ghana's anticolonialism from any propensity toward communism.[23]

The birth of a son, Emiliano Kwasi, soon followed Mayfield and Cordero's arrival in Ghana. The new parents were touched by their Ghanaian neighbors' insistence on welcoming the baby with a traditional Akan outdooring ceremony. There was much to celebrate in the family's relocation to Ghana. Mayfield wrote to his friend John Henrik Clarke of an indescribable feeling of liberation and happily contemplated the years he would now have to focus on his writing (a series of novels he planned to call *Songhay*). Mayfield was reserved in relating his experience of the usually overwhelming first trip to Africa. It was not a matter of liking or disliking Ghana but of taking the good with the bad. For the present, he was wandering around, slowly forming impressions.[24]

His son's birth delayed Mayfield's engagement with Ghanaian politics, but he must have noticed relatively quickly the turbulent state of affairs. As Nkrumah's April "dawn broadcast" condemning corruption suggested, the grasping maneuvers of ministers and CPP members was becoming a liability. As early as 1960, C. L. R. James put his finger on the problem while addressing a party gathering. His lavish praises of Nkrumah's policies of nonalignment and socialism were frequently interrupted by applause until James warned of the threat to the Ghanaian revolution posed by bribery and corruption and the failure to build a mass socialist party that would effectively forbid these counterrevolutionary tendencies. James's warnings dampened the festive mood, and the audience received them with dead silence. Since at least the time of independence, if not before, Nkrumah had contended with political opponents and his more conservative ministers in the right wing of the CPP. As the unity of the nationalist struggle gave way to internal conflicts

Ghanaian outdooring ceremony, 1961. Ana Livia Cordero Mayfield
(holding Emiliano Kwasi) and Julian Mayfield are second and third from right.
(Julian Mayfield Collection, Schomburg Center for Research in Black Culture,
New York Public Library, New York)

over economic development policy, Nkrumah empowered a radical faction of
the CPP to organize a mass party. In tandem with the leftist faction, led by
Tawia Adamafio, Nkrumah purged senior ministers from office. With the
pro-Western Padmore gone, leftists in the party tilted Ghanaian rhetoric and
policy toward the Soviet Union. In September 1961, Nkrumah was touring
the Soviet Union and the Eastern bloc when railway workers went on strike
in Sekondi-Takoradi, protesting provisions in the new budget that taxed
wage and salaried workers to compensate for budgetary shortfalls caused by
a decline in cocoa revenues. The strike occurred in defiance of a government
law prohibiting such actions. When the struggling opposition movement
aligned itself with the railway workers, Nkrumah sent Adamafio back to
Ghana to put an end to the uprising, calling it a "neo-colonial conspiracy."
Nkrumah returned and crushed the revolt, jailing opposition leaders, journalists, labor leaders, and market women. After Finance Minister Komla
Gbedemah spoke in the National Assembly criticizing the Preventive Detention Act and a newly proposed measure criminalizing sedition, treason, and
unlawful assembly, for which there would be no appeal, he went into exile.[25]

As Mayfield continued to write for the Ghanaian press, he took to the
country, writing to a friend that he wished to remain there indefinitely. He

154   and Cordero had rented a roomy bungalow that had housed British colonial civil servants, and the Du Boises' residence was visible across the backyard. Mayfield relished the freedom of expression for his activist journalism. He corresponded regularly with Clarke, one of the editors of *Freedomways*. They exchanged newspapers and materials, trying to cultivate a transatlantic print culture of pan-African radicalism. Mayfield assisted Clarke in getting *Freedomways* distributed in Ghana, though Mayfield admitted that the task was complicated by some Ghanaian officials' indifference to the Afro-American struggle.[26] One of Mayfield's first columns for the *Ghana Evening News* was an account of Mallory's imprisonment on the trumped-up federal kidnapping charges. Throughout his days in Ghana, Mayfield often published exposés of American racism and the plight of such dissidents as black journalist William Worthy, who faced prosecution for an unauthorized trip to Cuba. Such journalism earned Mayfield the ire of U.S. embassy personnel, and Mayfield's activities were duly reported back to the State Department and intelligence agencies.[27]

Mayfield bluntly related his impressions of how the Cold War was playing out in Ghana—the Americans were stupid about Africa, the Soviets even more so. Mayfield held no illusions about the many problems the Ghanaian government faced, including an opposition willing to employ violence. "But if Nkrumah sticks to his guns and *really* wipes out corruption and *indifference* (which I think is the major danger) he may get somewhere." Mayfield inadvertently sparked a major corruption scandal by mentioning to Ghanaian visitors a small item he had seen in the Nigerian press on the purchase of a £3,000 golden bed in London by Mary Edusei, the wife of senior CPP minister Krobo Edusei. Such actions compounded Edusei's vulnerability to charges of corruption, and he was dismissed from his post, although he was later rehabilitated.[28]

Having fled a federal manhunt, Mayfield scoffed at accusations from other Americans in Ghana that he was selling out his country. He was certainly not alone in his criticisms of the United States. Mayfield sought to replicate in Ghana the northern U.S. urban African American culture of opposition. Its members hailed an African American consciousness remade in the image of African freedom and independence, exploding Hollywood stereotypes of African savagery. Northern-based black intellectuals—many, including Mayfield, Clarke, and writer John Oliver Killens, with southern origins and time served in the segregated U.S. military—regarded American white supremacy as a global phenomenon, perpetuated by collusion between South African supporters of apartheid and local authorities and vigilantes in the South.

Their outlook was shared by the Nation of Islam Minister Malcolm X, who was both voicing the antiwhite eschatology of Elijah Muhammed and quietly defying Nation of Islam prohibitions against political agitation by cultivating a network of African diplomats, freedom fighters, and Harlem activists. At a June 1961 rally held by the New York–based Liberation Committee for Africa, Killens defended the new spirit of black nationalism evidenced by the demonstration in the UN gallery protesting Lumumba's murder. Other speakers denounced U.S. interventions in the Congo and Cuba, reminded U.S. officialdom that Jim Crow undermined American foreign policy toward Africa, and proposed civil disobedience campaigns opposing not only racial discrimination but also neocolonial foreign policies. *Freedomways* and the Liberation Committee's magazine, *Liberator*, published essays by Mayfield from Ghana, and both publications opened their pages to African nationalist leaders. *Freedomways* reprinted Nkrumah's speech to an Accra conference of African freedom fighters in June 1962. With the experience of the Congo still fresh, Nkrumah warned of the advancing forces of imperialism and neocolonialism, citing the recent Portuguese massacres of nationalists in Angola, Mozambique, and Bissau. Against the balkanization of small, unviable states created by retreating colonial powers, Nkrumah insisted on the necessity of African unity, economic cooperation, and a coordinated African trade union movement and foreign policy.[29]

The arrival of Mayfield and Cordero, W. E. B. and Shirley Graham Du Bois, and Alphaeus and Dorothy Hunton signaled a transformed black American expatriate community whose allegiance to Nkrumah set it apart from the American community in Ghana. While this group joined the first wave of elective expatriates, which included pacifist Bill Sutherland and dentists Robert and Sarah Lee, a substantial number of this latter group were political refugees from Jim Crow America and the Cold War repression of the black Left. This was true of Hunton, a pioneering scholar of Victorian literature and empire whose incarceration under the Smith Act for his left-wing and anticolonial politics during the 1950s made him unemployable in the United States. The Huntons had been living in Guinea, where Alphaeus taught English, until Nkrumah and Du Bois beckoned with the invitation to work on the encyclopedia. Another such refugee was Victoria Garvin, a left-wing trade unionist, who was victimized by McCarthy-era purges that targeted black radicals.

Preston King was an altogether unique example of a black American in flight from a repressive U.S. society. King, who came from a prominent Albany, Georgia, family, was a graduate student in political philosophy in

London, where he attended anticolonial meetings and, like other African Americans abroad, thrived in the more hospitable racial climate of European intellectual circles. Everything changed when his draft board in Albany, belatedly realizing King's African descent, adopted the demeaning Jim Crow practice of addressing him by his first name in correspondence. In protest, King refused to cooperate with the draft board until it accorded him the respect shown to others. King was summoned back to Albany and convicted of failing to cooperate with the draft in the sort of judicial farce common in the Jim Crow South. King returned to Britain to complete his doctoral studies, only to learn eventually that through federal and local collusion, his passport had been declared invalid and the British had revoked his visa status. In effect, King was being extradited to the United States to face certain imprisonment. The Ghanaian government provided King with a passport, and he remained in exile for more than thirty years, until Bill Clinton granted a presidential pardon in 2000. King's experience resembled that of Mayfield and others who had searing encounters with a Jim Crow American nation determined to crush black dissidents.

Pan-Africanism in Ghana: Interventionist versus Idealized Perceptions of Ghanaians

The African American expatriate presence in Nkrumah's Ghana belied the American propaganda asserting that Africans and American Negroes were strangers to one another. While the expatriates and their allies insisted on the indivisible nature of the freedom struggles of Africans and African Americans, such a claim hardly did justice to the nuances of African Americans' perceptions of Ghanaians and of the Americans' role within Ghana's pan-African project. Members of the group varied considerably in their understanding of their function as expatriates, and frequent debate concerned the level and political significance of involvement. The political activists among the expatriates had taken Nkrumah's ideological mission to heart, assisting what might be described as a campaign of public persuasion. At the same time, differences existed among the expatriates with respect to whether Africa was "home," and beneath the general support lay internal criticism of Nkrumah's policies and performance.

Expatriates differed in their perceptions of their role in Ghana. Heuristically speaking, two distinct levels of political involvement existed, one driven by the agendas of the Ghanaian state, the other expressing the expatriates' subjectivity. The nature and scope of their sense of purpose hinged on their

perception of African peoples and Ghanaians. Expatriate intellectuals in the
Ghanaian government were frankly interventionist, seeking to radicalize
Ghanaians and their political culture by promoting a militant diasporic pan-
Africanism; those not directly involved with Ghanaian politics tended to
idealize Ghanaians as exemplars of human dignity, beauty, and black power.
Nkrumah's expatriate propagandists, working through the state press, radio,
and television, sought to rally the Ghanaian public's political support. This
group, which included journalists, academics, and government employees
and was not limited to people of African descent, argued the case for socialism and continental unity and opposed the residual Anglophilia and conservatism of British-educated Ghanaian elites and university students, some of
whom considered themselves aloof from if not superior to African Americans, the descendants of slaves. Nkrumah's expatriate allies campaigned
against tribalism as a counterrevolutionary force and welcomed statist modernization as a necessary detribalizing process. Working with allies in the
press, Mayfield and others offered Ghanaians a crash course in American
racism past and present. Mayfield and his allies hoped that exposing the
Ghanaian public to the harsh truths of the oppression of Afro-Americans
would generate more active support for the new country's government, helping citizens to resist U.S. efforts to expand American political and economic
influence on the continent.

Attempts to impress on Ghanaians the entrenched racism of their imperialist adversaries were contested not only by the U.S. embassy but internally
as well. Ghanaians often did not share African Americans' sensitivity to white
racism. Indeed, some African Americans questioned the emphasis on racism.
Following Padmore, St. Clair Drake, for example, saw pan-Africanism as
evolving from a racial ideology to a political vision of continental unity and
mass democracy. To be sure, Nkrumah's position was complex, race conscious in appealing for the assistance of diaspora blacks for nation building
yet maintaining a principled commitment to nonracialism in solidarity with
the struggles of Africans, peoples of African descent, and colonial peoples the
world over. At the same time, Nkrumah, who had resided in America and
England, knew that racism was intrinsic to colonialism and the ongoing
imperialist exploitation of Africa. Armed with such knowledge, Ghanaians
would remain vigilant against neocolonial subversion and could more objec-
tively assess official American claims of racial progress in the United States.
While Mayfield and other expatriates labored in this ideological vineyard
with mixed results, the greatest success in promoting an antiracist diasporic
consciousness among young Ghanaians and Africans was arguably achieved

158   by Malcolm X during his 1964 visits to the African continent. Malcolm failed, however, to lobby African heads of state to forge an alliance with Afro-Americans at the Organization of African Unity meeting held later that year in Cairo.

Quite distinct from this interventionist impulse was a diasporic idealization of Ghanaians and Africans that regarded their proud existence in a majority African society as the antithesis of the alienation of black people in white America. For many expatriates and particularly the visual artists among them, Africans had been spared the psychological traumas of slavery and racism and had survived intact the short century of colonial rule. Subjected to demeaning images of African savagery in America, these expatriates, like many African Americans back in the United States, were thrilled at encountering self-determining African peoples, particularly those whose technical skills and leadership placed them at the controls of modern African statehood and global affairs. Moreover, African American expatriates' fascination with African peoples and their cultures made tribal differences less troubling. The exiles were perhaps more likely than their counterparts in the Publicity Secretariat to explore African roots; learn the Ga, Fanti, or Twi languages; wear Ghanaian dress; or travel across the country to see how rural Ghanaians lived. These expatriates emphasized the liberating and healing effects they experienced as a result of residence in Ghana and exposure to its people and cultures. For them, living in Ghana relieved the existential burden of racialization, of being seen as black in a white majority society. The visual artists who resided in Ghana constituted themselves as a group within the black expatriate community, and their affirming depictions of the Ghanaian (or African) man, woman, and child opposed racism, countering Euro-American hierarchies of beauty and aesthetic value. By representing an African-diasporic vision of beauty, strength, dignity, and revolutionary spirit, their work essayed an important statement of survival, resilience, and black power and modernity.

Of course, such an idealized vision of the new African was a political intervention in its own right. Accordingly, Julian Mayfield incorporated such images in the *African Review*. The cover of the June 1965 issue exemplified this vision, with its photograph of three Ghanaian women, perhaps members of the influential grouping of "mammy traders." These formidable, stout women, attired in traditional dress, are shown smiling and applauding as part of a larger crowd at what appears to be a political rally. Their revolutionary consciousness is signaled by Mayfield's earnest caption, "The People Are Ready Now!" The depiction of the revolutionary African masses as market women represented both a progressive acknowledgment of the importance of women in African nationalism and an implicit reproach against the male-dominated pursuit and exercise of political power.

A certain level of immersion in Ghanaian culture, traditional or otherwise, was inevitable for many of the expatriates, though some would have been too busy with their government-appointed tasks to avail themselves of local cultural experiences. Mayfield wrote somewhat guiltily of participating with Cordero in a traditional durbar ceremony as guests of a paramount chief, all the while hoping that none of the photographs of them taken at the event would find their way into the newspaper. On another occasion, Ghanaian friends in and out of the government treated Mayfield and Cordero to an outdooring ceremony in honor of the birth of their son, Emiliano Kwasi.[30] William Gardner Smith described being awakened at night by the distant sound of Ghanaian drumming and driving off in search of the source of the music several times, without success. When finally he was taken to the scene of the drumming and dancing, he was warmly welcomed by the Ghanaians there and plunged into festivities that lasted until dawn.[31]

Some African Americans undoubtedly could not adjust to their surroundings, as Richard Wright seemed unable to do. The black expatriate experience in Africa involved a complicated negotiation of cultural differences. Such is to be expected in any encounter with a foreign culture, but for many black Americans, travel to Africa bore a unique emotional significance. For example, Frank and Dona Irvin spent several years in Ghana without becoming actively engaged in Ghanaian politics. Frank Irvin, a professor of chemistry at the University of California, Berkeley, had met African and Ghanaian students, and he and his wife were eager to see the new Africa for themselves. They seized the opportunity when Irvin was invited to teach chemistry at the University of Ghana in 1962. Though saddened by their initial exposure to the poverty of Accra's slum dwellers, they soon warmed to life in Ghana. Like most expatriates, they hired a steward, an unlettered man from the Northern Territories named Adongo who walked from where he stayed in Accra to do their cleaning. When Frank obtained a carved walking stick, Adongo took it to his home village and had it anointed with medicine for their protection, covering it with leather. "That was a very loving gesture," Dona Irvin remembered. The Irvins honored that gift by taking the walking stick with them on all their travels. "For a long time, we enjoyed the protection of that stick."

Before arriving in Ghana, the Irvins had heard talk about mutual distrust between African Americans and Africans and about Africans, believing themselves superior, who shunned association with black Americans. While the Irvins eventually found this to be untrue, Dona acknowledged a division between the two groups. Both groups brought preconceptions to their encounter. The idea that Africans held themselves aloof from African Americans may have been as much a product of misplaced African American expectations as a result of dominant liberal propaganda. "We expected to be welcomed with open arms. . . . That didn't happen . . . because they had been told we were coming with this superiority complex." For the Irvins and other African Americans, visiting and living in Ghana was a corrective to assumptions born of social conditioning. "We [were] thinking that the Africans think they are better, and the Africans think we think we are better. But we learned that when we showed that we identified with Africans, and respected them, they really went all out for us. But we had to earn that." After returning to the United States, the Irvins were chagrined to encounter the same misconceptions and ignorance about Africa and Africans, even from black Americans.[32]

On the whole, such direct encounters with Ghanaians and their culture challenged the preconceptions of African Americans and Ghanaians alike. At the same time, some African Americans possessed an idealized and even romantic diasporic perception of the African as endowed with a natural purity, and this perception could take more problematically gendered forms—as an Afro-kitsch sentimentality that thoughtlessly ventured into the dubious province of the male tourist's hedonistic quest for sexual gratification. Some Afro-American men's appreciations of African women's beauty could venture into the realm of erotica. Reflecting a standard expression of the exoticizing imperial gaze, this perception of African women might find expression in the production or consumption of commodified, mass-produced sexualized images of female nudity. This mind-set led black American male expatriates, along with other male (particularly unmarried) tourists and expatriates, to avail themselves of the casual drinking and carefree sexual relationships that were commonplace within the Accra nightclub scene. A certain racialized romanticism prevented them from viewing their conduct as exploitative. African American artist Curtis Morrow wrote in eroticized terms of his arrival in Ghana: "It was a perfect landing. When the airplane door was opened, the hot humid air engulfed me and all the butterflies in my stomach disappeared. It felt like a hot juicy kiss. I walked down the gangplank and at the end of it stood the most beautiful black woman I had ever seen. I must have been staring because she smiled and her whole face lit up as she said, 'Ma Akwaaba' (welcome). I didn't know what it meant but I knew it had to be

good and just replied, 'Thank you sister.'" Not much further along in the
narrative, Morrow writes of the consummation of his romantic yearning. In
the autobiography of African American expatriate Leslie Lacy, the pleasures
of consorting with Ghanaian and African women were enhanced by the
casual and noncommittal character of such liaisons. Lacy appeared unwilling to spoil his fantasy by acknowledging that his participation in such sexual
exchanges was driven by impoverished life in an underdeveloped country.
He implied that such relationships with African women offered a welcome
contrast to the burdensome familiarity and tension of historically fraught
relationships with African American women. In Ghana, some African American men experienced their own version of the so-called sexual revolution.
Yet the actions of Lacy and others often mimicked the sexual tourism and
colonial cohabitations of white Western expatriate men.[33]

Those who sought to politicize Ghanaians and those who idealized African peoples and their cultures were indistinguishable in their support of
Nkrumah, however. Moreover, these perspectives overlapped to a considerable extent. In addition to Mayfield and the other political refugees from
racial and Cold War repression, this new cohort of black American expatriates included entertainer and aspiring writer Maya Angelou, who had been
active on behalf of African freedom and the civil rights movement in New
York City. Fellow expatriates remembered Sylvia Boone, whose study of the
aesthetics of female beauty among the Mende people of Sierra Leone was the
magnum opus in her far too brief career as a historian of African art, as an
active contributor to the expatriates' political discussions and as someone
keenly attuned to cultural differences and similarities with Ghanaians.[34]
Tom Feelings, an artist from Brooklyn's Bedford-Stuyvesant neighborhood,
spent the mid-1950s stationed in England with the U.S. Air Force. After
returning to the United States, Feelings contributed to the black press a
comic strip on African American history. In 1965, in search of greater opportunity than that available in the States, Feelings went to Ghana to pursue
a career as an illustrator specializing in black subject matter. Even at the
height of the U.S. civil rights movement, Feelings had found that magazine
art directors still preferred white illustrators for depictions of blacks. Frustrated that the few assignments he received called for images of junkies and
the like, Feelings headed for Ghana: "I knew where the pain came from, I
wanted to find out . . . the source of the joy."[35] Herman Bailey, a Howard
University–educated artist from Chicago, resided in Ghana from 1962 to
1966. Mayfield recalled that instead of catering to tourist demand for images
of African primitivism, Bailey chose the less lucrative option of portraying

the Africans of the future, "people who looked upward and outward, toward power."[36] Another couple, Max Bond and Jean Carey Bond, arrived in Ghana in August 1964. He became Nkrumah's personal architect, while she contributed to *Freedomways* and worked with Mayfield on the *African Review*. Frank Robertson, originally from Los Angeles, was part of a corps of highly skilled black American technicians, many of them trained in the U.S. armed forces, who provided vital assistance in infrastructure building and construction. These and other members of the radical black American group associated with junior officials of the CPP left wing and South African exiles and freedom fighters. Maryse Condé, who taught black Francophone literature at Winneba, referred to her colleagues, including the African American expatriates, as a family, unconcerned with issues of language and nationality. "We were brothers and sisters."[37]

These progressive newcomers to the black expatriate community in Ghana were uniquely situated to reflect on the gender dynamics of life in that rapidly changing society. Gender politics were a major concern of women who were part of the black cultural Left in Harlem and who participated in the groundswell of black nationalism in Harlem inspired by African national independence movements. Left-wing mobilizations during the late 1940s and early 1950s in defense of black women victimized by southern Jim Crow violence led to the formation of a group of black female progressives, the Sojourners for Truth and Justice. A glance at the editorial boards of Paul Robeson's *Freedom* newspaper and its successor, *Freedomways*, and the membership of such organizations as the Committee for the Negro in the Arts demonstrates that women played a prominent role in the literary and cultural activities of what Mary Helen Washington has called the "Black leftist cultural front." Many of these female activists shared with their male comrades an avid interest in African independence movements. Shirley Graham Du Bois, Eslanda Goode Robeson, Esther Cooper Jackson, Lorraine Hansberry (an important feminist thinker before the advent of second-wave feminism), Jean Carey Bond, Alice Childress, Paule Marshall, Sarah Wright, Rosa Guy, Maya Angelou, Abbey Lincoln, and Ora Mobley-Sweeting were associated with *Freedomways*, AMSAC, and other pro-African cultural organizations that articulated the northern urban critique of liberal integrationism and U.S. foreign policy. As members of the Cultural Association for Women of African Heritage, Lincoln, Angelou, and Guy participated alongside male colleagues and members of several black nationalist organizations in the demonstration at the United Nations protesting its complicity in Lumumba's death.[38]

This new group of African American expatriates was more closely attuned to Nkrumah's leftward turn than was an earlier cohort of African Americans with ties to Nkrumah that dated to before independence. Such members of this previous cohort as academics Horace Mann Bond, Adelaide Cromwell, Lawrence D. Reddick, and especially St. Clair Drake remained staunch supporters of Nkrumah, even as his stance evolved to a position to the left of theirs. One of the earliest arrivals, Bill Sutherland, left Ghana in mid-1961, a casualty of the power struggle between Nkrumah and Gbedemah, whom Sutherland had served as private secretary. Sutherland and Nkrumah had discussed plans for a center to train activists in nonviolent positive action, but the Congo Crisis and the Sharpeville Massacre pushed Nkrumah away from a Gandhian stance. At loose ends and with his marriage dissolving, Sutherland took a position with an Israeli center for Afro-Asian cooperation and eventually settled in Dar es Salaam, Tanzania.[39] From the United States, Drake discreetly sought to intervene against what he perceived as the dominance of the "Du Bois–Graham–Mayfield–Hunton" line on American racism in CPP circles. He proposed to his expatriate colleague William Gardner Smith that a tour of the United States be arranged for young Ghanaian journalists as a means of grooming future leaders. In America, they could witness firsthand African Americans' struggle for equality and the importance of hydroelectric technology in the United States. Drake hoped such a trip would make the Ghanaians less prone to gratuitous attacks on the United States.[40]

Through their ties to AMSAC, Drake, Cromwell, Bond, and others expressed their commitment to African American advocacy and activism in the service of African freedom. But although deeply immersed in Ghanaian life and with friendships with Ghanaians from all walks of life, Drake and his family were never expatriates in the same sense as Mayfield, Du Bois, Hunton, or Preston King. Whereas those individuals were exiled from America, Drake maintained a foothold in the United States through Roosevelt University, AMSAC, and the foundations vital to funding academic field research in Africa. By 1962, Drake served as a consultant for the Peace Corps, charged with training volunteers to serve as high school teachers for Nkrumah's ambitious plan for secondary school expansion. At the same time, as the influx of black radicals continued apace, Drake sought through his contacts at the university to arrange teaching posts in Ghana for such old friends as Bond and Reddick. Drake hoped to stem the negative effect of the magazine articles claiming that Africans did not want Afro-Americans to come to Af-

164   rica. While Nkrumah supported Drake's recruiting, such efforts met with frustration because of a lack of resources both at the university and among Drake's colleagues.[41]

Throughout the early 1960s, Drake defended Nkrumah against right-wing criticism of Ghana in American politics and mainstream publications. He tirelessly advocated Nkrumah's outlook and industrializing objectives, particularly the Volta River project. That linchpin of Ghanaian modernization had been imperiled by reports of political strife emanating from Ghana, amplified by accusations by U.S. Senator Thomas Dodd and such Ghanaian exiles as Kofi A. Busia, that Ghana was a communist satellite.[42] Calmer heads in the State Department ignored such attacks, fully aware that the overwhelming majority of Ghana's trade occurred with the West. In the black American press, Drake assumed the task of shaping black Americans' discourses of pan-African solidarity.

Mayfield's hard-hitting columns in the *Ghanaian Times* led to his employment by the Publicity Secretariat to promote the Ghanaian government's ideological agenda. Mayfield edited and published *The World without the Bomb*, the proceedings of a June 1962 conference on nuclear disarmament, the Accra Assembly. An impressive group of scientists and public figures, including Bertrand Russell, Linus Pauling, Conor Cruise O'Brien, and St. Clair Drake, gave papers at the conference.[43] Mayfield sought to jolt Ghanaian youth, particularly university students, out of an uncritical attraction to American wealth. He complained to Clarke that the university was a hotbed of opposition to the Ghanaian government.[44] Mayfield provided the Ghanaian press with unsparing criticisms of American racism, often illustrated by graphic images of blacks being brutalized by white southern police, including a gruesome photo of Emmett Till in his open casket. These exposés formed a counterpart to a sharp increase in anti-American editorials and coverage in the Ghanaian press after the August 1962 attempt to assassinate Nkrumah.

Nkrumah became convinced that the attempt on his life had been instigated by the U.S. Central Intelligence Agency (CIA). Passing through the town of Kulungugu on his return from a diplomatic mission in Upper Volta, Nkrumah paused to greet schoolchildren and was receiving a bouquet from one student when a grenade exploded, killing the child and several others. Nkrumah was wounded by shrapnel and hospitalized in Bakwu, although his advisers claimed that he had been unhurt. Nkrumah convalesced at the hospital in Tamale for a week before returning to Accra. Two weeks later, three of his aides—Tawia Adamafio, Ako Adjei, and August Coffie Crabbe— were arrested in connection with the attack, even though the case against them was circumstantial. The arrests failed to dissipate the climate of intrigue and distrust that had descended on the government. A shaken Nkrumah closed all borders and detained more than five hundred people, many of whom remained jailed until the 1966 coup overthrowing Nkrumah. Adamafio's removal enabled the return of senior ministers Krobo Edusei, Nathaniel Welbeck, and Kojo Botsio and increased the authority of more committed leftists, including Kofi Batsa, John Tettegah, and Eric Heymann.[45]

Maya Angelou recalled that the assassination attempt ended the black expatriates' honeymoon in Ghana. Whispers and accusations spread throughout Accra, some targeting African Americans as covert agents of American imperialism. None of their number had been accused, but from then on, according to Angelou, they felt marked and less secure. The violence continued even after the arrest of Nkrumah's ministers. By late September, terrorist bombings had killed or wounded three hundred people. Later that year, African American anthropologist Hugh Smythe greeted Nkrumah at an Accra conference of Africanist scholars and reported that the president looked older, had lost weight, and was visibly under great tension. Smythe also noted that the extensive security was impossible to ignore.[46]

Nkrumah had good reason to feel besieged. His security agents had unearthed CIA contacts with Gbedemah and Busia in Togo, exacerbating the violent feud between Ghana and Togo. Busia next turned up before Dodd's Senate committee on internal security, where the exiled opposition leader testified that Ghana was the center of communist subversion in Africa. Nkrumah retaliated by threatening to expel all Peace Corps volunteers, a rebuke that jeopardized U.S. support for the Volta River project. Nkrumah did not carry out the expulsion but maintained his suspicions of covert CIA support of subversion based in Togo. Another bomb exploded in Accra in January 1963. Soon thereafter, the government requested that the U.S. embassy withdraw two officials implicated in financing terrorist activity from Togo. On January 13, 1963, President Sylvanus Olympio of Togo was assassinated by disgruntled Togolese troops led by future president Gnassingbe Eyadema. But according to historian Richard Mahoney, the conflict between Nkrumah and Olympio led some African leaders to suspect Nkrumah's involvement in the assassination.[47]

Nkrumah's predicament was not lost on Mayfield. Mayfield learned from Ghanaian press colleagues of an American physician on the U.S. embassy staff who had been caught with a terrorist courier on a Ghana Airways jet.

Mayfield's fellow journalists, part of the CPP's left wing, wanted to report the story. But Nkrumah, intent on preventing a breach with the United States, stayed their hand despite strong evidence of CIA involvement in subversion. He quietly had the American physician expelled.[48]

By March 1963, Mayfield and Cordero were planning to move to East Africa. In the meantime, Mayfield prepared an essay on James Baldwin for *Freedomways*, defending the celebrated writer against black militants who criticized him and his work in heated, ad hominem tones. While sharing younger writers' suspicion of Baldwin's art-for-art's-sake putdowns of protest literature and his upstart assaults on the reputations of Richard Wright and Langston Hughes, Mayfield recalled having organized a meeting while still in the United States to allow Baldwin and his critics to clear the air. The desired rapprochement did not come off, but Mayfield was won over after the departure of the other writers as a visibly relaxed Baldwin held forth with "rampaging insight and brilliant flashes of humor," taking his leave at sunrise. Mayfield served notice to Baldwin's African American critics that even if the writer was not radical enough for them, he was nonetheless a powerful critic of the U.S. establishment and thus was an ally, despite their suspicion.[49]

By June, Mayfield, still underemployed by the Ghanaian government, contemplated relocating his family to East Africa, perhaps Kenya; in the meantime, however, he asked Clarke to send camera-ready photos of whites brutalizing blacks for a new feature in the Ghanaian press called "Is This America the Beautiful?"[50] If Nkrumah was compelled to treat the United States with discretion, militants in the press openly proclaimed their suspicion of U.S. attempts at subversion. Against the propaganda of racial progress and friendship generated by the U.S. Information Service and the new U.S. ambassador, William Mahoney, Ghanaian journalists, with Mayfield's help, sought ever-more-visceral depictions of an America still largely defined by white supremacy at home and abroad. Mahoney and the State Department were outraged by what they viewed as anti-American propaganda. But to Mayfield, the quotidian abuses of Jim Crow had gone unreported in the U.S. press for far too long. He and others were thus determined to redress this whitewashing of black suffering.[51]

The critical outlook of Mayfield and his colleagues in the Ghanaian press was reinforced by the state of emergency in the United States. The spring and summer of 1963 saw a sharp escalation of racial unrest that furnished Mayfield and the Ghanaian press with a steady supply of shocking images of the repression of black American demonstrators. Mayfield probably shared these images with Cameron Duodu, who edited the Ghanaian edition of

and *Ebony*, *Drum* was staunchly pan-African and Nkrumahist in orientation
until after the 1966 coup, when, at the behest of the military junta, it yielded
to the pent-up fury of Nkrumah's opposition. Mayfield authored a *Drum*
article buttressed with stark images of brutality from the Birmingham campaign that sought to impress on Ghanaians the terror experienced by African
Americans in the South and the persistence of white supremacy throughout
American history.[52]

African newspapers extensively reported the shocking events in Birmingham. Images of police use of attack dogs, high-pressure hoses, and beatings
brought home the violence of segregation to audiences across America and
worldwide. The chaos imperiled hopes for racial reconciliation held out by
such figures as James Baldwin and the musical bards of black American consciousness, Curtis Mayfield and Nina Simone. In June, a sniper killed Medgar
Evers, the leader of the Mississippi NAACP and a mentor to young activists in
the Student Nonviolent Coordinating Committee, in his driveway. The cost
was searing, but the civil rights movement gained moral authority in the
United States as President John F. Kennedy, his hand forced by mounting
chaos, called for an end to segregation to avert further damage to the nation's image abroad. Martin Luther King Jr. and other major civil rights
leaders had again planned to march on Washington as a massive show of
support for civil rights legislation. After some hesitation, Kennedy embraced
the march to ensure its overall friendliness to the administration. Keeping up
the pressure against the U.S. embassy, the Ghanaian press dutifully reported
incidents of U.S. antiblack violence or discrimination, which sometimes targeted African students and diplomats. Mayfield may well have had a role
in the publication in the *Ghanaian Times* of a letter signed by a group of activists from the Student Nonviolent Coordinating Committee, including
Stokely Carmichael and Bob Moses, that incensed U.S. officials in Ghana
with its suggestion that members of an African "Peace Corps" be sent to the
United States "to civilize the barbaric racists here." The U.S. activists also requested, as Malcolm X would do during his travels through Africa a year
later, that African leaders bring the plight of American blacks before the
United Nations.[53]

In June, Nkrumah appointed Mayfield editor-in-chief of a new monthly
magazine, the *African Review*, to be published by the president's Publicity Secretariat. Nkrumah was impressed with *Freedomways*, published from
Harlem by John Henrik Clarke and Esther Cooper Jackson, and coeditor
Shirley Graham Du Bois made sure the journal was required reading in

Flagstaff House, the site of Nkrumah's government offices. Mayfield envisioned a magazine independent of political orthodoxies and enlisted Clarke's help in getting it off the ground. This new venture, matching Cordero's work in significance, enabled the couple to cast their lot with Ghana.

Mayfield apprised Clarke of recent discussions in Flagstaff House of how to facilitate the recruitment of qualified African Americans needed in Ghana and throughout Africa. Beneath the strident editorials denouncing Afro-Americans as imperialist stooges, Ghanaian insiders recognized that African Americans offered a valuable pool of talent underutilized in America. Clarke had a standing invitation from Mayfield to visit and possibly relocate to Ghana. Mayfield promised Clarke that Shirley Du Bois and others could muster support from Ghana and Tanganyika, East Africa, to create a pipeline for skilled and progressive Afro-Americans that would provide an alternative to the political screening exercised by the foundations and the U.S. government. Contrary to certain views expressed in the U.S. press, African governments did not oppose Afro-Americans as a whole: as Mayfield put it, "They just do not want the finks." Mayfield had described the problem of untrustworthy African American visitors to Ghana in "Uncle Tom Abroad," an essay published in the States. Mayfield's vision of recruiting African Americans to Ghana was far less visible than Nkrumah's appeals to New World blacks in the wake of independence. But with the Ghanaian government unstable and under siege and its leader upbraided in the Western press as a dictator, Nkrumah became more selective regarding those African Americans willing to relocate to Ghana. As with Drake's attempts to bring Afro-Americans to Ghana, Mayfield's recruitment efforts failed to live up to his and the government's expectations.[54]

Against the unrest in the United States and broadsides in the Ghanaian press alleging Afro-American disloyalty in the aftermath of the Kulungugu attack, Mayfield and his fellow black expatriates felt it necessary to reaffirm the connection between the Afro-American struggle and the African revolution. The expatriates joined their support for the movement in the United States with the cause of Ghana, the African revolution, and global anti-imperialism, with denunciations of U.S. foreign policy thrown in for good measure. The March on Washington on August 28, 1963, provided an occasion for these efforts, as did Malcolm X's May 1964 visit. In addition, the illness and death of W. E. B. Du Bois in Accra on the eve of the march on the U.S. embassy transformed the protest into a somber memorial to the pan-Africanist visionary and intellectual.

For fellow activists back in the States, Alice Windom penned an account of the expatriates' demonstration at the U.S. embassy that described how that event had been organized out of the mundane details of daily existence in Ghana. Four days before the march, expatriates Windom, Frank Robertson, Carlos Allston, and John Makunga, a South African biochemist, discussed staging a demonstration coinciding with the Washington event. They soon abandoned the idea, thinking that not enough time remained to organize it. But that night a sleepless Robertson became convinced of the need to express solidarity with the Afro-American freedom movement. Robertson, Windom, and an unnamed comrade from Basutoland contacted members of their community, including African Americans, Ghanaians, and southern Africans. The lack of telephones among many of them increased the legwork of visiting, which went on until midnight.

After obtaining the CPP's permission for the demonstration, Windom and Robertson visited Mayfield's house, where they found Makunga. They envisioned a demonstration that would go beyond an expression of solidarity with the Washington march. In Windom's account, the demonstration "would make an independent statement against American racialism and imperialism. Also, our consciousness of the connection between the Afro-American and African freedom movements would be stressed." As they brainstormed slogans, they realized that such criticisms of U.S. domestic and foreign policy risked alienating some African Americans in Accra, but there was no turning back. Mayfield publicized the demonstration through his press contacts, and the group notified other African Americans, avoiding those employed by the U.S. embassy, although several secretaries attended the demonstration with official permission to do so.[55]

Before their meeting adjourned, Vusumsi Make, an exiled South African nationalist and Accra representative of the Pan-Africanist Congress, arrived. He requested that Cordero, who served as W. E. B. Du Bois's personal physician, go to the Du Bois residence. Make and his wife, Maya Angelou, were lunching with the Du Boises, the doctor had taken ill, and he needed medical attention. At age ninety-five, Du Bois's activities with the *Encyclopedia Africana* had been greatly reduced. He had received an honorary degree from the University of Ghana on his birthday, and the Du Boises had dined that evening with Nkrumah and his wife. Du Bois, who had become a citizen of Ghana, had saddened them all by asking Nkrumah to forgive him for being unable to see through the task of completing the encyclopedia. Despite his failing health, he remained lucid and very much the spiritual leader of the black expatriate community.[56]

Taking leave of Mayfield and Cordero, Windom, Robertson, and Makunga visited Du Bois's colleague on the encyclopedia project, Dr. W. Alphaeus Hunton, and his wife, Dorothy. The Huntons were enthusiastic about the planned demonstration and agreed to take part. A prominent member (along with Du Bois) of the Council on African Affairs and author of *Decision in Africa* (1957), a detailed account of American and Western economic incursions in Africa, Hunton had published numerous articles along similar lines in the left-wing U.S. press and continued to do so from Ghana.[57] At the Huntons', the group also encountered Lou Gardner, a plumbing contractor in partnership with Allston, and his wife, Lois. The organizers also visited Robert and Sarah Lee, dentists who had been among the first African Americans to move to Ghana. The Lees had arrived before independence and by 1963 were naturalized Ghanaians, having renounced their U.S. citizenship. The initiative rapidly gained momentum, and the demonstrators planned to gather the next night at Mayfield and Cordero's house.

The next morning, Windom visited Hunton at the *Encyclopedia Africana* secretariat and learned that Du Bois was gravely ill. That evening, forty people attended the meeting at Mayfield and Cordero's house. Windom reported that the majority were African Americans: some, such as artist Camille Billups and playwright William Branch, were visiting Ghana, but most were residents of the country. Windom counted about six South Africans, the Ghanaian husband of an African American, and the white American spouses of two African Americans. Among the black Americans, only two were employed by the U.S. government—a married couple who apparently shared the expatriates' politics "and did not ask 'permission' from the embassy." The attendees drafted a petition to be presented to the head of the embassy (Ambassador Mahoney was on leave) and conveyed to President Kennedy.

The next morning, several people gathered at Mayfield and Cordero's residence to work on placards and iron out more details. Windom and Mayfield visited Flagstaff House to secure the support of John Tettegah, leader of Ghana's Trade Union Congress. Tettegah promised the participation of members of his group. Mayfield informed the U.S. embassy that a delegation of Afro-Americans would arrive the following morning to present its petition for transmittal to the president. The planned demonstration was announced over Ghanaian radio that afternoon, and Mayfield's commentary linking the Washington and Accra demonstrations was heard that evening. Among the reporters who visited Mayfield was Julia Wright Hervé, Richard Wright's daughter. She and her husband, a French leftist, worked for a progressive French publication and had been in Accra for two weeks; soon thereafter, the couple moved there. The first demonstration, a torchlight parade at the embassy, was scheduled for midnight on Tuesday. There would be three demonstrations picketing the embassy on Wednesday, one early in the morning and two in the afternoon.

On Tuesday, Mayfield heard of Du Bois's deteriorating condition from Cordero, who had attended him that day. Windom was typing the final copy of the petition when Mayfield and Herman Bailey arrived at 10:45 with the news of Du Bois's death. When Windom arrived near the embassy just before midnight, fifty people were there, carrying placards and torches. The somber news had reached the group, which solemnly marched to the embassy. The demonstration had become a memorial to Du Bois. Windom recalled being at the embassy for about half an hour before the group noticed that half a dozen or so U.S. Marines in uniform were surveying the scene from the roof. The march lasted roughly an hour, with the demonstrators singing "Freedom, freedom, no more slavery over me . . . and before I'll be a slave, I'll be buried in my grave and go home to my Lord and be free." The song erupted spontaneously, against the wishes of some, including Windom, who insisted that there be no singing. But the loss of Du Bois seemed to warrant such a display of feeling.

A larger group assembled for the march scheduled at 8:00 the next morning. Windom and Robertson held up a placard with Du Bois's name. As embassy personnel snapped pictures, the marchers circled in front of the building. Later that morning, a delegation of five—Windom, Mayfield, Hunton, Angelou, and Wendell Jean Pierre, a professor of French literature at the University of Ghana, Legon—presented the petition to the acting head of the embassy. Hunton made a brief speech. The petition blasted Kennedy for the shortfall between his administration's rhetoric on African American civil rights and African freedom and its tacit support for the status quo both at home and on the African continent. That indictment was reiterated in an unsigned article in the *Ghanaian Times*, accompanied by a photograph of a police dog lunging at an African American demonstrator in Birmingham and the subhead, "The Blackman Is Also God's Son."[58]

The protest scheduled for noon took place in a driving rain that soaked the forty or so demonstrators and bled the lettering on their signs. Later that afternoon, they were joined by twenty members of the Ghanaian Trade Union Congress, whose chanted slogans represented a dramatic change from the restraint that marked the earlier demonstrations. When a marine emerged to lower the American flag at the end of the day, the marchers heckled him. The march continued until 6:30, with the embassy staff remaining on the premises until the marchers had left. Windom felt that the

Julian Mayfield, W. Alphaeus Hunton, Alice Windom, Wendell Jean Pierre, and Maya Angelou at a demonstration at the U.S. embassy, Accra, August 28, 1963. (John Henrik Clarke Photograph Collection, Schomburg Center for Research in Black Culture, New York Public Library, New York)

demonstration was a success, but she noted subsequent investigations and intrigues involving efforts by American officials and "Afro-American stooges" to determine who was responsible for the demonstration and for "booing the flag." In fact, of all the demonstrations in sympathy with the March on Washington held at various U.S. embassies throughout the world, including Paris, Munich, Oslo, Cairo, and Tel Aviv, the picketing in Accra attracted the most detailed scrutiny by U.S. authorities. The State Department received from the embassy a thorough summary of the demonstration, with the petition to President Kennedy and signatures attached, revealing the participation of T. Ras Makonnen and Ghanaian journalist Eric Heymann along with the other demonstrators. (Mayfield followed his signature with a defiant "USA.") Appended to the document were clippings from the *Ghanaian Times* about the massive gathering in Washington and the more modest one in Accra, one with a banner headline referring to Kennedy, "Afro-Americans Challenge Jack on Racism—Accra Joins."[59]

The community's attention shifted to the funeral rites for Du Bois. Their demonstration over, most of the marchers proceeded to visit Shirley Graham Du Bois to give their condolences. They listened to that evening's radio commentary, Mayfield's tribute to Du Bois, which began, "A mighty tree has fallen." Shirley Du Bois informed the gathering of arrangements for a state funeral personally supervised by Nkrumah. A pictorial feature in the Ghanaian edition of *Drum* magazine linked Du Bois's funeral in Ghana with the massive demonstration in Washington, D.C., with images of marchers (including demonstrators at the U.S. embassy in London) framed by photographs of the rites for Du Bois. One showed Nkrumah standing next to Shirley Graham Du Bois and somberly gazing into Du Bois's open casket.[60]

Conor Cruise O'Brien and CPP Conflicts with the University

The vice chancellor of the University of Ghana, the affable and urbane Conor Cruise O'Brien, was for a time an important ally for Mayfield and the culture of opposition based in Ghana. O'Brien and Mayfield remained friendly well after O'Brien came under attack by members of the Ghanaian government for resisting CPP interference in university affairs. Nkrumah had appointed O'Brien to head the university after his role as the UN's representative in opposing the Katanga secession in the Congo. Moreover, O'Brien had won praise throughout Africa for his exposé of United Nations' failures and complicity in Lumumba's death. O'Brien had participated in the disarmament conclave in 1962 and was later cultivated by Mayfield as part of his duties as editor of the *African Review*. An intellectual of wide-ranging interests, O'Brien's writings from Ghana attacked the anticommunist West's hostility to African aspirations and generally took effective aim at the hauteur of Western liberalism. He was a natural ally for Mayfield and other black radicals in whose political imaginations the death of Lumumba loomed large. Well before the disclosures of covert CIA funding for the Congress for Cultural Freedom and its flagship journal, *Encounter*, O'Brien had diagnosed that publication's close adherence to U.S. foreign policy. O'Brien caustically noted that *Encounter*'s avowedly nonideological defense of liberty showed a greater concern for Hungary than for the freedom of black Americans or South Africans. No doubt prompted by Mayfield, O'Brien read *Freedomways* and was conversant in black militants' and radicals' literary polemics.

In 1964, O'Brien reviewed in the *New Statesman* James Baldwin's two volumes of essays on race, literature, expatriation, and American nationhood— *Notes of a Native Son* and *Nobody Knows My Name*. O'Brien echoed Mayfield's defense of Baldwin in *Freedomways*. Baldwin's essays had ended the voicelessness and invisibility of blacks, shattering the white majority's indifference. Baldwin had forced white Americans to regard their nation from the viewpoint of blacks, which represented no small feat. O'Brien noted that

Baldwin had stood the so-called Negro problem on its head, conquering the fear and hatred of his youth to examine why white Americans needed to invent and institutionalize the racist fiction of the "nigger." In posing this question to white Americans, Baldwin was not so much inveighing against injustice as "probing for the roots of a sickness."

In the eyes of some black militants, however, Baldwin's success implicated him as an Uncle Tom. While this suspicion was understandable given both the accommodationist tradition in African American leadership and Baldwin's participation in meetings convened by the anticommunist Congress for Cultural Freedom, O'Brien defended on principle the writer's independence from the strictures of the group. O'Brien, like Mayfield, claimed Baldwin as solidly in the fold of progressives, citing Baldwin's defense of those African Americans who protested Lumumba's murder at the United Nations. The writer's apparent detachment, so infuriating to some observers, might also be understood as a measured rhetorical style that compelled whites to face the "unattractive facts" of black rage and alienation. O'Brien defended Baldwin's writing about homosexuality as an expression of the writer's fidelity only to his own artistic compass, not to the dictates of others.[61]

While O'Brien was penning several similar examinations of black radical discourse and politics for the London press, he was battling the Ghanaian government's attempts to take over the university, long a site of internal dissension. In a 1963 speech at the university, Nkrumah had warned that the institution's academic freedom should not be used as a shield for efforts to destabilize Ghana. Nkrumah believed academic freedom was best expressed in the service of socialist nation building and development. Nkrumah's views challenged what was widely perceived as the entrenched legacy of colonialism in the academic culture at Legon. For O'Brien, however, the government's steady erosion of the university's autonomy made for a stormy conclusion to his three-year term. From the start of 1964 onward, the CPP staged several demonstrations against the university and O'Brien's leadership. The vice chancellor blocked the government's attempt to siphon off university faculty positions as sinecures for party loyalists and unsuccessfully resisted the government's 1964 expulsion of four professors on charges of subversion. Not surprisingly, he found it difficult to recruit faculty to fill these sudden vacancies.

In an essay published in the United States in 1962, Mayfield had noted the deep conflict between much of the university's faculty and the Ghanaian government. Mayfield believed that behind their agitated appeals for academic freedom, the lecturers were contemptuous of the government's avowed socialism. They seemed sympathetic to students opposed or indifferent to the government's aims. Mayfield approvingly cited Nkrumah's insistence that true academic freedom was compatible with serving society's needs and praised O'Brien for creating a more stimulating, progressive environment at Legon.[62]

The issue of academic freedom hit home for African American expatriates when one of their number, Wendell Jean Pierre, was expelled for alleged subversive activities. Jean Pierre had been informed that his presence was injurious to the nation and was given twenty-four hours to leave the country. Jean Pierre's expulsion put to the test Mayfield's defense of the government's position on the university's social obligations. Mayfield, Preston King, and Leslie Lacy, a black American university student and friend of Jean Pierre's, defended the scholar of Francophone literature and Negritude against the charges of subversion. Before coming to Ghana, Jean Pierre and his family had lived in France, where the scholar had looked to Richard Wright as a mentor. His defenders saw Jean Pierre as loyal to Nkrumah and Ghana. Mayfield, whose suspicion of African American visitors to Ghana some observers saw as verging on paranoia, had received assurances of Jean Pierre's loyalty and wrote to Nkrumah on Jean Pierre's behalf.[63] In what Lacy described as an "ugly experience," efforts to elicit support for Jean Pierre met with chilling silence among members of an African American community unwilling to invite suspicion upon themselves by closing ranks with Jean Pierre. His few supporters—Mayfield; Preston King and his wife, Hazel; and Lacy—saw Jean Pierre and his family off at the airport. The matter of precisely who orchestrated Jean Pierre's deportation is probably impossible to determine. If Jean Pierre was innocent, as his supporters believed, then he may have been the victim of slanderous intrigue by a Ghanaian official resentful of expatriates. Another possible scenario was that Jean Pierre was brought down by the personal vendetta of an Afro-American expatriate.[64]

None of Jean Pierre's supporters, particularly those based at the university, found themselves similarly targeted by Ghanaian authorities. But for O'Brien, the political heat was stifling. He stood his ground. In March 1964, in a convocation address warmly received by faculty, students, members of the diplomatic corps, politicians, paramount chiefs, and others, the vice chancellor answered the charges against the university that filled the state-controlled newspaper. Acknowledging the government's generous support of the university, O'Brien insisted that the institution was not indifferent to the sacrifices of the Ghanaian workers and farmers in discharging its responsibilities as "a real University." It was "simply not true to suggest that this

University today is a colonialist or neo-colonialist institution, or that, behind a screen of concern for academic freedom it seeks to promote colonialist or neo-colonialist purposes." The values of a real university—respect for and intellectual courage in the pursuit of truth—were not "European" or imperialist impositions but universal values. It was cynical to suggest, as had one critic, that teachers were obliged to teach in accordance with the preference of their paymasters. Such a view would concede the South African government's right to enforce its teachers' adherence to or failure to challenge "its disreputable and unscientific racialist theories." O'Brien buttressed his argument by quoting the core of Nkrumah's speech encouraging "scrupulous respect for academic freedom," without which there could be no university. O'Brien endorsed Nkrumah's "enlightened" view of academic freedom in the service of the community and hoped that Ghanaian authorities would not descend to the attacks on academic freedom that had recently taken place in the United States, the Soviet Union, and Germany.[65]

Nkrumah responded with a conciliatory letter to O'Brien, but relations between the two men deteriorated. State interference continued unabated at Legon. At his final congregation address, O'Brien cited this interference as cause for his resignation. The faculty implored O'Brien to reconsider and fight back, but he refrained from introducing a resolution deploring government meddling in the university's affairs. He believed that although most faculty members sympathized with his calls for academic freedom, they were intimidated from publicly expressing their support. Riding out another onslaught of press attacks, O'Brien completed his term and accepted teaching positions in England and America, where he soon became a prominent critic of Nkrumah.

For David L. Lewis, another African American who taught European history at the University of Ghana, the country's heady promise was clouded by the presence of Ghanaian intelligence agents in the classroom and the tension engendered by the assassination attempt on Nkrumah. One afternoon, he noticed that the usually attentive Ghanaian students sat listlessly through his lecture until a student politely suggested that Lewis might wish to dismiss class because of the president's death. Stunned at hearing that assassins had finally accomplished the destruction of Nkrumah and his revolution, Lewis eventually realized that not Nkrumah but Kennedy had been slain. The U.S. president's death reportedly profoundly affected Nkrumah, who had been sufficiently charmed by Kennedy during a 1961 visit to the White House to mute criticism of U.S. complicity in Lumumba's death. A devastated Ambassador Mahoney confirmed the news to Nkrumah, who seemed to relive

his Catholic upbringing in his prayerful sorrow. When the suspects in the
Kulungugu attack were acquitted in December 1963, Nkrumah dismissed the
chief justice who had issued the verdict and rushed a new law through the
National Assembly empowering the president to overturn any decision in
Ghana's courts in the interest of national security.[66]

On January 1, 1964, Nkrumah survived another attack, somehow escap-
ing injury after a gunman fired at him outside Flagstaff House, although a
policeman was killed. After the dismissal of the chief justice, a dismayed
C. L. R. James implored Nkrumah to reverse his decision and repair the
damage from international condemnation of his action. Receiving no response, James went public with his criticism in a Trinidad newspaper. "All
[of Nkrumah's] closest supporters . . . should have got together to tell him
quite plainly, 'Mr. President, you cannot dismiss your Chief Justice after he
has made a judgment from the Bench. Publicly declare that you made a
mistake. . . . You continue with this dismissal and you dismiss us, all of us.'" If
that suggestion was not enough to anger Nkrumah, he was undoubtedly
infuriated by James's tactless statement that with two attempts on Nkrumah's life, "something was wrong with his regime which demanded serious
attention, otherwise people don't shoot."[67]

Mayfield would experience fallout from the breach between Nkrumah
and James. In the summer of 1964, Mayfield accompanied the Ghanaian
delegation to the Commonwealth leaders' conference in London, hoping to
line up contributors to the *African Review*. Mayfield met with James, who
energetically voiced disapproval of Nkrumah and political developments in
Ghana. Mayfield persuaded James to contribute an article for his magazine.
James proposed an essay on Lenin's deathbed reflections on the failures of
the Bolshevik Revolution. James believed that Lenin's analysis was especially
relevant to Ghana and independent Africa. The essay never appeared in the
African Review. A humiliated and outraged Mayfield returned the manuscript to James, although he was paid for his efforts. Mayfield believed that
James's essay was killed in retaliation for a recent publication in which
James credited George Padmore as one of the leading architects of the new
Ghana. This contention reportedly angered Nkrumah, although Mayfield
could not confirm the president's direct involvement. Mayfield's explanation,
based on hearsay, seems highly unlikely. On the fourth anniversary of his
death, the *Ghanaian Times* remembered Padmore as the architect of African
independence and the Organization of African Unity charter, formulated at
the inaugural June 1963 summit meeting. "How much of this could have
been done without Padmore?" the editorial queried. Though Padmore had

178 not been born in Africa, "Padmore was a part of Africa. He lived for Africa. He died for Africa."[68] If Nkrumah was responsible for keeping James out of the *African Review*, James's public criticism of Nkrumah was a much more likely explanation. Obsessed in later years with this incident and with the larger question of what went wrong in Ghana, Mayfield surmised that the deed had been done by either orthodox communists in Nkrumah's inner circle opposed to the Trotskyite James and the pro-Western Padmore or Ghanaians resentful of the implication that Nkrumah relied on West Indian "strangers." Mayfield recalled that a well-connected Ghanaian friend had informed him that Padmore's sudden death had occasioned rejoicing in Flagstaff House by chauvinistic and ambitious Ghanaian aides. Far more likely than Mayfield's scenarios was that James had become persona non grata by publicly crossing Nkrumah over the dismissal of his chief justice. Mayfield may have witnessed Ghanaian hostility to Padmore, but this probably did not constitute a factor in the suppression of James's article.[69]

Mayfield's frustration at the censorship of James's essay also suggested that James had not been completely forthcoming about the nature of his dispute with Nkrumah. In any case, Mayfield's belief that he could publish James's thinly veiled criticism of Nkrumah captured the struggle of hope against disillusionment that Ghana provoked in Mayfield. His emotional investment in the success of Ghana's revolution was heightened by his exile from America and the civil rights movement. At the same time, more than they realized, Mayfield and other black radicals in Ghana were animated by the dominant American mood of progress that they shared with their liberal antagonists. Many liberals believed that integration was inevitable, as the Cold War and national security concerns had made racial segregation anachronistic. In like fashion, such radicals as Du Bois, Mayfield, and others regarded the Ghanaian state as the engine of revolutionary change, able to impose socialism from above. More than most people, Mayfield perceived the disappointing limits of Ghana's commitment to pan-Africanism and socialist revolution. Yet he refused to abandon hope in Ghana's experiment as he had already abandoned the United States. If Mayfield realized what a flawed vessel Ghana was for his radical hopes, for political refugees like him and the exiled South African freedom fighters, he had nowhere else to go.

6

MALCOLM X IN GHANA

During the chaotic final year of his life, Malcolm X found respite in his deepened Islamic faith, his collaboration with Alex Haley in the production of his autobiography, and his travels throughout the Middle East and Africa and shorter trips to Europe and Canada. In comparing the story of Icarus to his ouster from the Nation of Islam (NOI), Malcolm anticipated the autobiography's conversion of his life story into modern-day myth. Malcolm invoked Icarus to depict his painful separation from Elijah Muhammed, marking the transition from disciple to dissenter. Initially, Malcolm gratefully equated the wings of Icarus with the Islamic faith that helped redeem him from his criminal past. Later, with bitter irony, Malcolm portrayed himself as Icarus and his nemesis, Muhammed, as the father who gave Malcolm his wings. A tangle of rage, gratitude, self-doubt, and self-justification informed Malcolm's Icarus analogy. If Malcolm owed his prominence to Muhammed, Malcolm's identification with Icarus, whose disobedience had been fatal, also suggested Malcolm's guilt over his rebellion. Malcolm's identification with Icarus was both inexact—Muhammed's malevolence contrasted sharply with the protective concern of Daedalus, Icarus's father—and all too apt, as Malcolm fully expected to share Icarus's fate.[1]

However singular Malcolm's plight after his departure from the NOI, as with other African American intellectuals and activists, travel outside the United States provided refuge from the racial constraints of American culture. Although Malcolm's sojourns certainly provided sanctuary from threats of NOI violence, extended travel also had powerful attractions. Malcolm's journeys to the Middle East and throughout Africa, especially Ghana, provided him insight into America's relationship to the rest of the world. His conversations with black American radicals in Ghana, African heads of state, and Third Force revolutionaries immersed him in the global anticolonial movement that had resonated so powerfully in Harlem. His growing popularity with radical student groups and activists in the United States, Africa, and Europe placed Malcolm at odds with American officialdom's attempts to contain the black freedom movement's tactics, objectives, and political language. Before international audiences, Malcolm exposed and excoriated the global dimensions of U.S. racial subjugation. He supplemented his ongoing critique of the federal government's appeasement of white extremists in the South with exposés of U.S. interventions in African affairs, linking U.S. domestic and foreign policy as two sides of the same white supremacist coin.

Just as Martin Luther King Jr. formulated strategy in consultation with a group of advisers, Malcolm came to rely on a group of U.S.-based black radicals whose dissent from Cold War liberalism many black expatriates in Ghana shared. Malcolm's dialogue with such individuals as scholar John Henrik Clarke and novelist John Oliver Killens informed Malcolm's criticisms of U.S. policy and overseas propaganda. Clarke and Killens were involved in the formation of Malcolm's Harlem-based Organization of Afro-American Unity (OAAU). In his association with Detroit-based activists James and Grace Lee Boggs, Malcolm had further recourse to radical and anticolonial traditions well before his pilgrimage to Mecca and his tour through Africa. Through these relationships, Malcolm became the leading heir to the secular black Left tradition of Paul Robeson, W. E. B. Du Bois, and W. Alphaeus Hunton. Malcolm intervened in African politics, soliciting support for his planned United Nations petition to charge the U.S. government with human rights violations against African Americans in the South and indeed nationwide. The solidarity Malcolm enjoyed with black radical expatriates and diplomats in Ghana and with African leaders throughout the continent fortified his commitment to radical truth telling. Those black radicals in Harlem and Ghana who were pessimistic about the liberal state's commitment to civil rights reform saw Malcolm as the potential crystallization of an alternative that encompassed the radical wing of the civil rights movement and the militancy of northern black youth.

Icarus was an apt symbol, then, for Malcolm during his more than six months abroad of the eleven months remaining to him. His travels were an attempt to suspend the passage of time, an attempt to stay aloft, as it were, as long as possible, to sharpen his analysis and enlighten his audiences while evading the political constraints and murderous intrigues that awaited him back in the United States.

The African American expatriates who hosted Malcolm, in collaboration with their allies in the left wing of the Convention People's Party (CPP), saw his visit as an occasion to reaffirm their loyalty to Kwame Nkrumah's revolution. The expatriates' status in Ghana was tenuous as Nkrumah continued to face internal opposition and as U.S. authorities anticipated the Osagyefo's removal. (Nkrumah had bestowed this Akan honorific, meaning "Redeemer," on himself in 1960.) The Ghanaian government's security concerns placed African American expatriates under intense scrutiny, particularly at the University of Ghana at Legon, where intelligence operatives monitored classroom discussions. Remote from the existing struggle in America, the expatriates looked to Malcolm for an update on events there. But through his presence, they also sought deliverance from their marginal situation.

Malcolm had gratefully championed Muhammed and the NOI for salvaging a sense of purpose from Malcolm's debasement and for its mass reclamation of criminals and convicts. By mid-1963, mounting frustration with the NOI's withdrawal from activism, combined with knowledge of Muhammed's sexual misconduct, had made abundantly clear the prohibitive cost of Malcolm's rise within the NOI. The NOI's parochialism entailed for Malcolm a repression of the vibrant subculture of Afro-diasporic modernity, a transnational culture of freedom and an identification with global anticolonial movements propelled by the rhythms of modern jazz, calypso, and highlife. Similar collective dreams of black freedom and modernity inspired those secular militants and radicals who later worked with Malcolm, including Mayfield, John Henrik Clarke, John O. Killens, and actress and writer Maya Angelou. Along with Malcolm, they welcomed the Cuban revolution as a challenge to American racism and were heartened by Fidel Castro's residency in Harlem after his Cuban delegation to the United Nations General Assembly had been denied the use of a downtown hotel. Castro's stay at the Hotel Theresa instantly transformed Harlem from a maligned ghetto to the nerve center of geopolitical affairs. Crowds of local residents cheered visits by such foreign dignitaries as Nkrumah, Egyptian President Gamal Abdel Nasser, and Soviet Premier Nikita Khrushchev. The occasion gave Malcolm and many Harlemites a tantalizing glimpse of the power and modernity emanating beyond the sea from the darker world of nonaligned nations whose mere existence constituted an affront to an American nation slow to relinquish its heritage of white supremacy. Until the spring of 1963, Malcolm's engagement with African, Arab, and Latin American revolutionary nationalism was harnessed to the expansion of the NOI and the glorification of Elijah Muhammed. By departing from the NOI, however, Malcolm would increasingly provide a rallying point for the revolutionary aspirations of young African Americans, Africans, Arabs, and people of African descent in the West.

The confrontation between Malcolm and Muhammed reflected long-simmering tensions but was precipitated by the volatile national and international crisis that gripped the South in the spring and summer of 1963. As radio and television audiences heard Malcolm's condemnations of the Kennedy administration and the civil rights movement, the Federal Bureau of Investigation (FBI) stepped up its counterintelligence, seeking to discredit the NOI and foment discord within it. Since 1962, the Nation had been harassed by police raids of mosques in several cities. The House Un-American Activities Committee investigated the NOI, and J. Edgar Hoover's FBI viewed the movement as susceptible to communist influence. Malcolm refused to back down in the face of this pressure. As Birmingham police deployed violence and mass arrests against black demonstrators, Malcolm faulted Kennedy for taking too long to intervene.

For his part, Kennedy regarded the Muslims as a threat to national security if the turmoil in Birmingham continued. Malcolm declared it strange that Kennedy would single out the Muslims as extremists rather than the Ku Klux Klan and the White Citizens Councils rampaging with impunity in the South. Federal inaction in Birmingham provoked outrage among delegates at a conference of Afro-Asian nations in Addis Ababa. Seeking to halt further damage to America's image internationally, Kennedy made a nationally televised speech endorsing desegregation as a moral issue. At the same time, government harassment of the NOI continued. Muslim inmates filed petitions protesting persecution by prison officials, and the FBI waged psychological warfare against NOI members with fabricated newspaper stories claiming that the movement's founder, Wallace D. Fard, was a white man.[2]

The crisis seemed to be averted by Kennedy's statement and the massive, peaceful assembly at the March on Washington, which Malcolm petulantly criticized from the sidelines. But the image of popular support for racial reform sought by U.S. officials who circulated footage of the march worldwide was shattered by the bombing (with possible FBI foreknowledge) of the Sixteenth Street Baptist Church in Birmingham, killing four girls attending Sunday school. African American Muslims and non-Muslims seethed helplessly at this slaughter of innocents and at the indifference to law and life evident in the FBI's decision not to prosecute suspects in the case arrested by Alabama state troopers. As Kenneth O'Reilly has written, "No single event [did as much to turn] the movement's young people against their most potentially valuable ally, the federal government."[3]

As Malcolm's visibility increased, so did Muhammed's anxiety at his protégé's political outspokenness. The tension between the two men was apparent in the pages of the NOI newspaper, *Muhammed Speaks*. The publication, as one of its secular editors, Leon Forrest, recalled, maintained a dual editorial policy of printing Muhammed's sermons alongside a radical pan-African and anticolonial perspective.[4] Malcolm publicly embodied this tension, dutifully praising "the Honorable Elijah Muhammed" before launching into analyses of the domestic and global dimensions of American white supremacy. Since 1960, Malcolm had spoken to non-Muslim audiences, primarily on college campuses. Muhammed feared that such extracurricular activity, combined with Malcolm's pithy demystifications of domestic and international politics, increased the likelihood of a federal probe of the NOI. Malcolm eventually came to chafe at the restrictions imposed by Muhammed. In 1962, Muhammed forbade Malcolm from pursuing a civil suit against Los Angeles police who had murdered a Muslim and wounded several others in an attack on a mosque in that city. Emboldened by the racial crises of 1963, Malcolm ceased to defer to Muhammed's anodyne religion and apolitical nationalism. Toward the end of that year, Alex Haley detected in Malcolm's private demeanor an abandonment of reverence for Muhammed and discomfort at intimations of a feud.[5] According to Detroit-based activist Grace Lee Boggs, Malcolm was already functioning independently well before he dilated on the significance of Kennedy's death.[6]

On December 1, 1963, Minister Malcolm X spoke to a gathering of seven hundred people in New York City. As national spokesman for the NOI, Malcolm was filling in for the organization's leader, Elijah Muhammed, the self-proclaimed "Messenger of Allah." Muhammed had canceled his speaking engagement after the assassination of President John F. Kennedy on November 22. Fearful that U.S. authorities would target the NOI in the wake of Kennedy's death, Muhammed had ordered Muslim ministers to refrain from any public remarks on the murder. Malcolm delivered a prepared speech on "God's Judgment of White America" that avoided direct references to the assassination. But while fielding questions afterward, Malcolm broke his silence on the president's death, his repressed radical perspective returning with a vengeance. According to Malcolm, Kennedy had fallen victim to the violence his administration had unleashed throughout the world. Explaining that the government had sanctioned violence in the Congo and Vietnam and had tolerated it in Alabama, Malcolm drew a folksy moral from the Dallas

MALCOLM X IN GHANA

tragedy that delighted his audience, overshadowed his analysis, and above all infuriated Muhammed and other leading NOI ministers. For the press, the statement was vintage Malcolm: "Being an old farm boy myself, chickens coming home to roost never did make me sad; they've always made me glad."[7]

As Claude Clegg has argued in his insightful study of Elijah Muhammed, such impolitic—even insensitive—statements had been Malcolm's stock-in-trade. At the Manhattan center, Malcolm probably believed that he could speak out with impunity despite Muhammed's directive. Perhaps he calculated that his knowledge of Muhammed's sexual indiscretions—Malcolm later disclosed that the Muslim leader had fathered several children with young women who worked in the movement—made it unlikely that Muhammed would discipline him. Whatever motivated Malcolm's test of Muhammed's authority, the consequences were swift. Muhammed silenced Malcolm, prohibiting him from public speaking for ninety days. While Muhammed's apparent sympathy for the late president, who in life had been the preeminent "white devil," must have come as a surprise, Malcolm accepted the punishment in a spirit of contrition.

Ironically, Muhammed's immediate reaction to Kennedy's assassination was not unlike that of other NOI members who viewed the president's murder as divine retribution for the Birmingham church bombing and other atrocities, as some ministers had preached. A November 23 FBI wiretap recorded Muhammed's belief that NOI followers would not mourn "that devil's death." Sensing that such gloating might further antagonize the U.S. government, Muhammed made a show of mourning the late president and certainly had Malcolm in mind when he ordered Nation ministers to remain silent about the assassination. Malcolm's defiance confirmed Muhammed's belief that his charismatic spokesman posed a threat to his authority. Jealous senior ministers feared that Malcolm would disclose the moral hypocrisy, financial corruption, sexual misconduct, and violence he witnessed within the NOI. Muhammed was not alone in having a vested interest in purging Malcolm. The FBI eavesdropped on telephone calls between New York, Chicago, and Phoenix, where Muhammed resided for health reasons, and welcomed the dissension. Bureau agents even visited Malcolm to inquire if he might become an informant.[8]

Muhammed stripped Malcolm of his leadership of Mosque no. 7 in Harlem. Malcolm hoped that his protégé, boxer Cassius Clay, would win his upcoming title fight against Sonny Liston and thereby restore Malcolm to Muhammed's good graces. After all, Malcolm had recruited Clay to the NOI

(though his membership was not yet public) and his prefight counsel stead-
ied the jittery contender, a ten-to-one underdog against the fearsome Liston.
Malcolm reasoned that if he left the NOI, Clay would remain loyal to his spiritual adviser. *Muhammad Speaks* gave the fight little advance publicity. Privately, Muhammed dismissed Clay as a loudmouth with no chance against
Liston. But when Clay shocked Liston and the world by winning the heavyweight title in February 1964, the NOI leader embraced the boxer, renaming
him Muhammad Ali. Ali had suddenly displaced Malcolm in Elijah Muhammed's affections. Malcolm was devastated by Ali's betrayal. After the ninety-
day suspension period passed with no statement from Muhammed, Malcolm
realized that the man he regarded as a surrogate father now regarded their
estrangement as permanent. On March 8, Malcolm announced his departure
from the NOI.[9]

Malcolm's ouster from the NOI reflected the larger problem of the exclusion of African Americans within a segregated American public culture. Racial exclusion in the urban North, combined with the repression of such
African American dissidents as Julian Mayfield and W. E. B. Du Bois, fueled a
discontent exacerbated by black voicelessness and invisibility. Other than
more traditional forms of worship, the sole major organizational outlet for
the discontent of northern urban blacks was the internal exile of a distorted
variant of Islam. "The Muslim movement," wrote U.S.-trained Nigerian sociologist E. U. Essien-Udom, "is a grand reaction to the American scene and
especially, the Negro's position in it; yet the scenery . . . shackles and delim-
its the drama—the potential for meaningful political and social action."[10]
Within an ostensibly open northern society defined for black people by racial
discrimination in public schools, housing, organized labor, and machine
politics and by police harassment, the NOI's teaching that African Americans
experienced hell on earth at the hands of white devils resonated among
many impoverished, disaffected working-class blacks. But it is a sobering
irony that first prison and then the autocratic and violent NOI constituted
the vehicles for Malcolm's entry into public life. The NOI's discipline submerged the expansive vision of postwar black diasporic modernity that such
scholars as Manthia Diawara, Robin Kelley, and Ferrucio Gambino have
viewed as crucial for Malcolm's political coming-of-age.[11]

The NOI swiftly retaliated after Malcolm's departure. Malcolm sued unsuccessfully to block the Nation from evicting his family from its home in
Queens. Isolated from Muhammed by the inner circle of Muslim ministers,
Malcolm attempted a conciliatory public appeal to his former mentor, vainly
seeking forgiveness and reinstatement. At the same time, Malcolm fished for

defectors, regaling Muslim ministers with information of NOI malfeasance and Muhammed's adultery. A similar rebellion against the Messenger by his sons, Wallace and Akbar, and the threat posed by an exodus of disillusioned members induced a violent feud between rival Muslim factions. Malcolm went public with reports of Muhammed's dalliances, believing that such disclosures would erode support for the NOI, halt the violence, and expose the dangers closing in on him, affording a measure of protection. To his frustration, major newspapers held back the stories, unwilling to risk libel actions, and Malcolm's desperate exposés only steeled his enemies' deadly resolve. A Muslim confessed that Captain Joseph, the head of the Fruit of Islam, which was the NOI's security force, had ordered a bomb placed in Malcolm's car.[12]

While battling for Muslims' loyalties, Malcolm pursued a more collaborative relationship with the leaders of the black freedom movement. Partly to broaden his appeal, Malcolm softened his criticism of the movement. On March 26, 1964, Malcolm attended the Senate gallery to observe the ongoing filibuster of the pending Civil Rights Act. Martin Luther King Jr. was present, warning reporters that continued stalling would lead to more demonstrations. Ignored by the press and seemingly by King, Malcolm approached King in the corridor. The two shook hands and exchanged pleasantries during their first and only encounter while photographers recorded the unlikely meeting. One of King's advisers, black attorney Clarence Jones, admired Malcolm enough to envision an alliance between the two leaders, but other members of King's camp vehemently opposed the idea.[13] Since the early 1960s, Malcolm had approached such leaders as the executive secretary of the National Association for the Advancement of Colored People, Roy Wilkins. However quixotically, Malcolm sought cooperation and with it a measure of personal vindication from other civil rights leaders. He had debated Bayard Rustin and James Farmer of the Congress of Racial Equality, striking up a friendship with the latter.

In 1964, the movement seemed to be passing Malcolm by. In early July President Lyndon Johnson signed the Civil Rights Act into law. Drawing on the legacy of wartime mobilizations for voting rights, activists from the Student Nonviolent Coordinating Committee (SNCC) had crafted an inventive challenge to federal complacency and the segregationist wing of the Democratic Party with their voter registration campaign during the Mississippi Summer Project.[14] With SNCC organizers, volunteers, and African Americans facing violence in Mississippi (in June, Lemuel Penn, an African American officer in uniform, was gunned down by night riders there), Malcolm perceived the inadequacy of disengaged NOI bombast from above the Mason-Dixon Line. He spoke of building what he called a "united action front." Malcolm's attempted rapprochement with civil rights leaders failed because he could not overcome his media image as an undisciplined fire-brand. Malcolm's name, to many people synonymous with extremism, was invoked by Rev. James Robinson, the director of Crossroads Africa, a non-governmental precursor to the Peace Corps, to establish political respect-ability during testimony before the House Un-American Activities Commit-tee on his ties to left-wing organizations and causes dating from World War II. While anticommunist monitoring of real or imagined subversives within the black freedom movement continued apace,[15] many mainstream civil rights leaders saw in Malcolm the specter of a disorderly and rebellious black nationalism that threatened to displace what was widely viewed as responsible black leadership.[16]

In April, as *Muhammad Speaks* printed violent attacks on Malcolm's apos-tasy, Malcolm borrowed money from his half-sister, Ella Collins, for a one-way flight to Cairo. During his travels, Malcolm continued to recruit dis-illusioned NOI members. Malcolm hoped that his visit to the Middle East and his participation in the hajj (pilgrimage to the Muslim holy city of Mecca) would establish his credibility within orthodox Islamic circles and expose Muhammed's fraudulent Islam. As is well known, the hajj enriched Mal-colm's understanding of Islam as a universalizing world religion. Popular myth enshrines the hajj as the catalyst for Malcolm's renunciation of racism. Malcolm claimed that he had witnessed fellow Muslims who would be con-sidered white in America practicing their faith in a spirit of brotherhood. To be sure, this not entirely new knowledge about blond, blue-eyed Muslims was generally reported as Malcolm's repudiation of the notion of whites as devils. But Malcolm may also have intended his reports of nonracist white Muslims to convince NOI followers that Elijah Muhammed had misled them with the false teaching that Islam was the proprietary religious expression of black people.

If Malcolm had embarked on the hajj for spiritual growth, in Ghana he also continued to seek the counsel of a secular community of revolutionaries. As historian Gerald Horne has suggested, whatever impact the hajj had on Malcolm's racial consciousness, his visit to Ghana and his interaction with so-called white as well as black revolutionaries enabled him to imagine coalitions with nonblacks and therefore to reject the NOI's parochial black nationalism.[17]

Malcolm found Ghana, with its criticism of U.S. racism at home and neo-colonialism abroad, a congenial platform for his views. But while he received a warm welcome from Ghanaians in the press and members of the diplomatic corps, particularly those from Cuba, Algeria, Nigeria, and China, Nkrumah and the Ghanaian government were lukewarm about Malcolm's visit. The months preceding Malcolm's arrival were marked by a crisis in Ghana that paralleled the turmoil in America. At that moment, adding Malcolm's volatile persona to Ghana's already unpredictable situation placed Nkrumah at odds with his African American expatriate supporters.

On January 1, 1964, an assailant fired five shots at Nkrumah, killing one of his bodyguards and rekindling the Ghanaian leader's fears of subversion by the U.S. Central Intelligence Agency. An unscathed Nkrumah detained three alleged suspects, including J. B. Danquah, the doyen of Ghanaian nationalism. The spread of rumors and allegations further strained U.S.-Ghanaian relations. On February 4, the government staged a demonstration at the U.S. embassy. The protesters' denunciations of American imperialism and rumor-mongering by embassy personnel reverberated in the Ghanaian press for several days. Embassy officials voiced alarm at the presence at the demonstrations of Soviet-bloc journalists (along with Julia Wright Hervé, described as the "Left-leaning daughter of Negro author Richard Wright").[18]

An embassy protest a few days later enraged U.S. officials, sparked high-level consultations between the State Department and the Johnson administration, and jeopardized the Afro-Americans' standing in Ghana. When demonstrators pulled the American flag down, an African American political affairs officer on the embassy staff, A. Emerson Player, rushed to secure the flag from the protesters and raised it again. U.S. officials were outraged when the Ghanaian press printed an editorial excoriating his "disgraceful act" and asking rhetorically if he had raised the flag for the children killed by dynamite in the Birmingham church or for slain civil rights leader Medgar Evers. Ambassador William Mahoney and other U.S. officials strongly protested the unsigned editorial (which resembled articles published around that time under the bylines of Julian Mayfield and Maya Angelou), and President Johnson expressed his gratitude to Player in a personal letter.[19]

The furor over Player's patriotic act revealed the U.S. government's sensitivity to Ghanaian attacks. Assistant Secretary of State for African Affairs G. Mennen Williams lodged a strong protest to Ghana's ambassador in Washington, Miguel Ribiero, condemning the invective heaped on Player. Matters were worsened by the Ghanaian government's expulsion of six members of the academic staff at the university, including Wendell Jean Pierre. Since 1961, the emergence of a radical African American expatriate community and its collaboration with leftists in the Ghanaian press raised the stakes for official U.S. efforts to counter Ghana's criticism of the American government or, failing that, to quietly assist ongoing attempts to destabilize Nkrumah's government. But Jean Pierre's expulsion reminded the black expatriates that their support for Nkrumah did not place them above suspicion.

As African American radicals found themselves caught in the middle of the diplomatic feud between the United States and Ghana, unbeknownst to Malcolm, his impending visit assumed the character of a diplomatic mission on behalf of the Afros. Press attacks on alleged Afro-American quislings were nothing new in the Ghanaian press. But in the tense aftermath of the assassination attempt, the Player incident, and the expulsion of Jean Pierre, the political solidarity that had defined the pan-African movement degenerated into distrust. Mindful that opportunists could manipulate such blanket suspicion of Afro-Americans, African American allies of the Nkrumah government perhaps felt more pressure than usual to demonstrate their loyalty. That may well explain African American authorship of a series of editorials attacking U.S. policy and African Americans unfriendly to Nkrumah's Ghana. That some African American supporters of Nkrumah could thus act to fan the flames of suspicion against themselves underscored their vulnerability in Ghana. For the expatriates, Malcolm's timely visit promised to deliver African American supporters of the Ghanaian government from the suspicion of disloyalty.

From Nkrumah's standpoint, however, the timing of Malcolm's arrival was less auspicious. Nkrumah bore the brunt of American officials' ire at the anti-American rhetoric in the Ghanaian press. In Washington, Ambassador Ribiero conveyed Nkrumah's willingness to remedy a situation that had gotten out of hand. A Kaiser Corporation executive told Nkrumah that work on the Volta River project could not proceed if such attacks continued. On February 26, Nkrumah wrote to Johnson, expressing regret over recent events in Accra and reassuring the president of his continued commitment to nonalignment and of Ghana's openness to foreign investment. But Nkrumah insisted that clandestine Central Intelligence Agency operations in Ghana threatened harmonious relations between their governments. After returning from consultations in Washington, Ambassador Mahoney maintained the diplomatic pressure on Nkrumah and worked overtime to divine the Ghanaian leader's true sentiments from such confidants as Hanna Reitsch, the expatriate director of Ghana's flight training school (and previously Hitler's personal pilot). But while Nkrumah extended an olive branch, telling Mahoney (truthfully) that his notion of socialism was gradual rather than revolutionary—how could it have been otherwise among the conservative Ghanaian elite?—his efforts to put his personal stamp on African affairs only confirmed U.S. authorities' fears.

In March, Nkrumah released his philosophical blueprint for the development of colonies and newly independent countries, *Consciencism*. An analyst with the U.S. embassy deplored the volume's anticapitalism and its advocacy of socialism that was "a variant of the system that prevails in the Communist countries." That same month, after high-level discussions between Johnson and the Africa desk at the State Department, LBJ's reply to Nkrumah claimed that there was no basis for Nkrumah's contention that the Central Intelligence Agency was engaged in subversive activities in Ghana. By April, African Affairs Undersecretary Averell Harriman, back from Ghana, advised the president and congressional leaders not to be dismayed by the Ghanaian government's overheated rhetoric. Work on the Volta River project was well under way; moreover, the Kaiser Corporation stood to profit handsomely from its aluminum smelter, run with inexpensive power supplied by Ghana.[20]

Despite Harriman's appeal for calm, Mahoney viewed Malcolm X's prospective visit with considerable alarm. Nkrumah listened, nodding silently as the ambassador explained Malcolm's break with Elijah Muhammed and emphasized the dangers of Malcolm's advocacy of racial violence. Mahoney warned that Malcolm should not be allowed to use Ghana as a propaganda platform. Because Nkrumah's brand of pan-Africanism was decidedly nonracialist, he would have been cool to Malcolm's separatist views, which the latter had espoused immediately prior to his trip to Africa and the Middle East.[21] It was unrealistic to expect that Nkrumah would prevent Malcolm from speaking his mind in Ghana. But in the current climate, Nkrumah probably judged it prudent to keep his distance from Malcolm.[22] With a massive aid package then under consideration by the U.S. government, Nkrumah was loathe to further jeopardize relations with the United States.

Malcolm arrived in Ghana on May 10, taking the African American expatriates, who had been awaiting his arrival for weeks, by surprise. They greeted him at the Ambassador Hotel, where Malcolm stayed courtesy of the Ghanaian press. "How many of us are out here, Julian?" Malcolm wanted to know. "About three hundred," Mayfield replied, exaggerating the number who actively supported Nkrumah. "Beautiful. That's beautiful. . . . What are we doing?" Amused by the question, Mayfield explained that they were trying to help the president with various levels of involvement, to which Malcolm replied, "That's what I call making a real revolution."[23] Mayfield and other members of the Malcolm X welcoming committee organized several speaking engagements for their guest, including a lecture at the Marxist study forum at the university. Over lunch, Malcolm told his hosts of his stay in Saudi Arabia, where he had been a guest of Prince Faisal, and later Nigeria. There, Malcolm had lectured at Ibadan University, and a riot ensued when students mobbed a West Indian lecturer who had criticized Malcolm's statements. The expatriates were eager for news of Malcolm's split with the NOI. According to Alice Windom, Malcolm expressed his desire to work toward the unity of the various civil rights organizations in the United States. Wishing to promote a black united front, Malcolm chose not to publicize the roots of the dissension between himself and Muhammed. While acknowledging the value of the NOI as a redemptive force in the lives of many of its members, Malcolm made clear his fundamental disagreement with Muhammed on the necessity for the Muslim movement's involvement in the struggle for human rights in the United States.

That evening, between thirty and forty Afro-American expatriates joined Malcolm at Mayfield and Ana Livia Cordero's home for lively discussion. Angelou recalled the gathering as a diverse group of "revolutionaries, counter-revolutionaries, petit-bourgeoises, capitalists, communists, hedonists, socialists, humanitarians, and aging beatniks."[24] Leslie Lacy described a festive atmosphere. "We laughed, slapped hands, listened to Bessie Smith, talked some more, ate Ana Livia's curried goat, looked at Malcolm and *felt good*, listened to Miles and *felt good*, and talked about Harlem, West Oakland, Chicago . . . and finally, after all that Soul, we sat down to talk to our leader."[25] Malcolm described his plan to go before the United Nations and charge the United States with human rights violations against its black population. His goal, as described by Windom, was to bypass the civil rights movement's reliance on white goodwill and bring the U.S. government to account before the international community, much as South African blacks had petitioned the UN over the atrocities of the apartheid regime. Malcolm regarded his tour of Africa as a diplomatic mission seeking the political support of heads of state throughout the continent for his UN petition. Windom, anticipating a press blackout in America on Malcolm's trip, recorded the details of Malcolm's visit in a letter circulated to fellow activists in the United States. She was deeply impressed by Malcolm's lack of self-aggrandizement, his patience, and his willingness to consider and value the opinions of all.[26]

Perhaps in part because of his difficulties in joining forces with other African American leaders and activists, Malcolm's message throughout West Africa was one of unity between Africans and African Americans. From Lagos, Malcolm wrote, "[M]y warm reception here in Africa will forever repudiate the American white man's propaganda that the Black man in Africa is not interested in the plight of the Black man in America." In Ghana, Malcolm appealed for increased support between Africans and African Americans. American blacks should forge a global community with African peoples, as American Jews had done with Israel. Malcolm also contended that African governments were obliged to protest the mistreatment of American blacks. He claimed that to fight against apartheid in South Africa or Portuguese colonialism, it was necessary to attack the legitimacy of the U.S. government, whose power upheld those racist regimes. Malcolm's visit to Ghana happened to coincide with that of G. Mennen Williams, the head of the U.S. State Department's African Affairs Bureau. Williams's brand of diplomacy prompted Malcolm to warn Ghanaians and their supporters to be suspicious of friendly Americans in Africa "grinning in your face when they don't grin in mine back home."[27]

Malcolm also gave a public lecture before a predominantly African audience in the university's Great Hall. Lacy had helped organized the lecture as part of a series sponsored by the Marxist Study Group, an organization he had cofounded with a West Indian student and a Ghanaian student as an independent alternative to the CPP's strictures on the university's intellectual life. Lacy had hoped to explain his side of the dispute between the government and the university, knowing that Malcolm was surrounded by party officials and journalists who would skew the issues. As Lacy had feared, Malcolm, who "spoke of Nkrumah like he spoke of Elijah Muhammed," sided with the CPP against the university's defense of academic freedom. But Malcolm quickly recovered his own voice, so thoroughly winning over the students that Lacy believed the Marxist Study Group had scored a victory against CPP interference.[28]

Malcolm's speech targeted the specific acts of white supremacist brutality inflicted on black demonstrators in the South. He condemned the American media's paternalistic notion of "responsible" black leadership and the press's condemnation of Nkrumah and other nonaligned leaders critical of Ameri-

Malcolm X speaks to *Drum* magazine in Accra, May 1964.
(Cameron Duodu/Drum)

can hegemony. In addition, Malcolm spoke of the hypocrisy of American diplomacy in Africa that pursued cordial diplomatic exchanges while seeking tighter economic control over African resources. Malcolm rejected the U.S. government's injunction that black American official visitors to Africa privilege their American identities over expressions of black solidarity.

At Legon, Malcolm laid siege to this prescriptive Americanism and its imposed limits on acceptable political speech: "I'm from America, but I'm not an American. [I'm] one of the victims of Americanism, one of the victims of democracy, one of the victims of a very hypocritical system that is . . .

representing itself as being qualified to tell other people how to run their country when they can't get the dirty things which are going on in their own country straightened out."[29]

It was not a foregone conclusion that Nkrumah would meet with Malcolm. That would have to be facilitated by another of Nkrumah's confidants, Shirley Graham Du Bois. One difficulty was that Du Bois, like so many others, had a negative view of Malcolm. "Just let me have five minutes with her," Malcolm told Mayfield, and Du Bois soon expressed her highest praise by proclaiming Malcolm a son. She paved the way for the meeting with Nkrumah.[30]

Malcolm's private meeting with Nkrumah at the government offices in Christianborg Castle, one of the old slave forts dotting the West African coast, reassured the expatriates of the legitimacy of their presence in Ghana. According to Windom, "Although we could not ask what transpired between [Malcolm and Nkrumah], it was apparent that Malcolm was moved and gratified by the experience." Windom's positive spin on the meeting differs from Mayfield's recollection of the encounter. Writing after Nkrumah's overthrow, Mayfield dismissed an anti-Nkrumah scholar's assertion that the Ghanaian leader had been influenced by Malcolm X. First, it had been difficult to persuade Nkrumah to meet with Malcolm (a fact Windom failed to mention). Moreover, Windom wrote that the two men met for approximately an hour, but according to Mayfield, on the two occasions Malcolm and Nkrumah talked, their meetings were brief—no more than twenty minutes. Mayfield delivered Malcolm to both interviews and picked him up at their conclusion. In his view, "[T]here was no love lost between the two men." Mayfield explained that Nkrumah was pressured by Kaiser Corporation officials during Malcolm's first visit and soon thereafter by representatives of the International Monetary Fund seeking to negotiate ways of easing Ghana's economic troubles. Mayfield believed that Nkrumah felt obliged to keep Malcolm at arm's length. Mayfield also surmised that Nkrumah would have been put off by Malcolm's firebrand image.[31]

Mayfield's account of what transpired between Malcolm and Nkrumah, while tantalizing, is disappointingly cryptic. Although it provides a plausible explanation for Nkrumah's coolness toward Malcolm, it sheds no light on Malcolm's impressions of Nkrumah. Nkrumah, for his part, left little record of his impressions of Malcolm X besides the obligatory eulogy. On one occasion, Nkrumah referred to Malcolm in the context of his mixed assessment of Stokely Carmichael, a militant SNCC leader and black power spokesman. After SNCC collapsed as a result of racial polarization and U.S. government harassment, Carmichael advocated pan-African revolution and

made several visits to Nkrumah in Guinea. Nkrumah thought the younger
man capable but impulsive. (At the time, Carmichael was married to exiled
South African singer Miriam Makeba, who, like Nkrumah, received asylum
from Guinea's Sekou Touré.) In assessing Carmichael, Nkrumah remarked,
"On the whole, Malcolm X was more mature." Combined with Mayfield's
recollections, Nkrumah's tepid praise for Malcolm suggests at best a qualified respect.[32]

Less clear is what Malcolm thought about Nkrumah, though Mayfield's
formulation implies that Malcolm had doubts about the Ghanaian leader. If
that was the case, then Mayfield, known for bluntly articulating the usually
unspoken misgivings of the Afros at troubling developments in Ghana, probably was the source of Malcolm's qualms.

The issue of corruption was broached during Malcolm's brief return to
Ghana in August, during which he had his second meeting with Nkrumah.
Leslie Lacy recalled that Malcolm and Mayfield visited Lacy's residence at the
university. Lacy found Malcolm tired and preoccupied. According to Lacy,
Malcolm asked Mayfield, "Is there much corruption here?" Squirming, Mayfield allowed that there was. "How does Mr. Nkrumah deal with it?" Lacy
believed that Mayfield knew more about the problem than he was willing to
tell. This topic generally was off-limits with Nkrumah's ubiquitous security
men, who were attuned to the slightest criticism of the government. On one
occasion, Mayfield said simply, "We don't need a lot of party loyalists. What
we need are committed men and women who are willing to live on their own
salaries." Mayfield told Malcolm that Nkrumah had taken some steps against
corruption but implied that they were insufficient: "[I]f he were to shoot a
few of his ministers, other crooks might get the point." Mayfield described
the recent fate of Ras Makonnen, a Guyanese restaurateur and an organizer
of the Manchester pan-African Congress who was said to have confronted
Nkrumah on the endemic levels of corruption. Makonnen was summarily
demoted from his position as director of the African affairs center, "to the
status of a caterer, in charge of the state bakery." (Makonnen's new position
was managing director of the Ghana Hotels and Tourist Corporation.) According to Lacy, Malcolm replied, "I guess Mr. Nkrumah knows how to best
deal with his people." Malcolm responded with indifference to Mayfield's
explanation. "I've got twenty million other black people to think about right
now and I guess I should get back to them soon." It is difficult to believe that
Mayfield would not have privately shared with Malcolm his criticism of the
government on the issue of corruption. Perhaps if he had lived, Malcolm
would have expanded his criticisms of accommodationist black leadership in

the United States to the corrupt, self-seeking national bourgeoisie of African nations.[33]

While in Accra, Malcolm's conversations with black Americans contained indications of the danger that awaited him back at home. At mention of the Harlem uprising against police brutality in July, one of the expatriates informed Malcolm, who had been in Cairo at the time, of reports from the United States that some critics felt he should have been in Harlem during the disturbances. Malcolm responded angrily, "Those Negroes don't know what they're talking about—if I'd have been there, I'd be dead."[34]

Although the passage of time made possible an acknowledgment of tensions between Malcolm and Nkrumah,[35] Windom's account of Malcolm's first visit had no room for such internal criticism. Even if Windom and Malcolm were aware of the corruption within the CPP, both had little to gain from a public airing of these problems. Such criticism would have confirmed the swirling suspicions of Afro-American disloyalty to Nkrumah's government. In addition, such information was not conducive to Malcolm's message of unity and mutual support between African Americans and Africans, and Windom would not have acknowledged tensions and contradictions and thereby deviated from her objective of rallying support for the struggles ahead. Windom's purpose, as with Malcolm's report on his first visit to Ghana, which was published in *Liberator* magazine in July, was to break the silence in the U.S. press about his warm reception by African students and heads of state and to publicize his new alliance with African, Asian, and Latin American revolutionary movements.

Far more appropriate news for U.S.-based activists, according to Windom, was an account of Malcolm's speech at the Kwame Nkrumah Ideological Institute in Winneba, a training center for African activists who would advance the revolution. On occasion, such prominent African and Third World revolutionaries as Amilcar Cabral, Ernesto "Che" Guevara, and Agostinho Neto spoke at the institute. All two hundred students attended Malcolm's lecture. "As usual, he was brilliant," recalled Windom, "and he communicated with them at their own high level of political awareness." When a young Afro-American whom the expatriates did not know defended the United States and argued that African Americans had no choice but to employ passive resistance, the other students heckled him, and he was rescued by a teacher and escorted from the hall. While a blanket suspicion of such rare moments of criticism informed Windom's account, one cannot rule out the likelihood that the Afro-American defender of the United States at Winneba may have been, in fact, engaged in U.S.-sponsored covert strategies of psychological warfare against Ghana.

Malcolm seemed to have endless energy for a dizzying pace of engagements followed by nightly conversation into the wee hours with the Afro-Americans. Like other expatriates, African American political theorist Preston King, who had introduced Malcolm at Legon, was pleasantly surprised by his humility and self-critical posture. Malcolm solicited the expatriates' assessments of his speech, wanting to know where he had exaggerated or gotten the history wrong. According to King, Malcolm "wasn't full of himself, there was no pulpit manner. . . . I found him very likeable, not just impressive." Malcolm was endearingly straightforward, "determined to be a better person, to tell a more persuasive story—for however long the storytelling should last, or be allowed to last."[36] Windom emphasized Malcolm's message of unity. Able from bitter experience to distinguish between potential allies and true enemies, Malcolm cautioned the expatriates against sectarianism. According to Windom, Malcolm explained, "Last year I was busy attacking [Martin Luther] King and he was busy attacking the Muslims, and nobody was really attacking the devil." Windom attached particular significance to the fact that Malcolm was the first Afro-American leader of national standing since W. E. B. Du Bois to make an independent trip to Africa. "This may be the beginning of a new phase in our struggle. Let's make sure we don't give it less thought than the State Department is . . . giving it right now."[37]

When not engaged in marathon late-night conversations with African American expatriates, Malcolm was feted at a series of gatherings hosted by the Chinese ambassador, the Nigerian high commissioner (where Muslim members of the Ghanaian diplomatic corps welcomed Malcolm), and the Cuban ambassador. At the conclusion of the round of diplomatic tributes, the Malcolm X committee escorted the guest to the airport. Malcolm encountered Muhammad Ali and his entourage outside the Ambassador Hotel. In his autobiography, Malcolm reported a terse exchange with the uncharacteristically "monosyllabic" boxer who had so abruptly ended their friendship. Years later, Ali expressed regret for turning his back on Malcolm and described him as a "great, great man."[38]

With Malcolm's departure, the battle over the meaning and significance of his visit began in Ghana and the United States, as if to anticipate his highly contested apotheosis in the wake of his martyrdom. *Muhammed Speaks*

198   would consolidate Ali's usurpation of Malcolm's status as Muhammed's protégé, adding insult to injury by appropriating Malcolm's language calling for a united black front. The same issue of the NOI publication featured an account of "How Africa Acclaimed Muhammed [sic] [Ali]" that quoted Ali's statement, lifted from Malcolm's talks in Ghana, "I haven't been home in 400 years." Giving Muslims little doubt of whose authority was supreme, a scowling, bowtie-clad Ali glared out from a tiny photograph on the cover of that issue, adjacent to the much larger portrait of Elijah Muhammed that usually appeared on the tabloid's front page.[39]

In his autobiography, Malcolm dwelled fondly on the recognition accorded him in Ghana and throughout Africa as the unofficial representative of African Americans. The Ghanaian press coverage of Malcolm's visit was subdued, however. The several items on Malcolm and the lack of any mention of his audience with Nkrumah were far more restrained than the ecstatic banner headlines and front-page photographs that celebrated Ali's visit. One, under the caption "Mohammed [sic] Ali Meets His Hero," featured Ali in kente robes shaking hands with the Osagyefo, who beamed straight into the camera, overjoyed at the coup of appearing with the champion. (There was precedent for such symbolic displays of pan-Africanism—Nkrumah had personally invited African American boxer Floyd Patterson to Ghana when he regained the heavyweight title in 1960.)[40]

The coverage of Malcolm's visit in the *Ghanaian Times* was even upstaged by the controversy that ensued immediately after his departure. Exiled South African journalist H. M. Basner angered Mayfield and the African American expatriates with a column criticizing Malcolm X's speech at Legon. According to Basner, Malcolm was preoccupied with racialism rather than a more proper attention to the global struggle against capitalism and imperialism. Basner did not specify what Malcolm had said to warrant this appraisal but claimed that Malcolm was excluding from the struggle progressive whites such as Basner. In criticizing Malcolm, Basner invoked the doctrinaire leftist view of racism as a by-product of capitalist exploitation. Basner's call for interracial solidarity was sensible, but the reductionism of his emphasis on class over racial oppression and the high-handed manner of his attack on Malcolm were too much for many of the African Americans who hosted Malcolm.[41]

Mayfield's response came swiftly, appearing the next day in the *Times*. With all due respect, Basner was out of his depth on the condition of black Americans and Malcolm X. Mayfield professed that he had heard nothing in

what Malcolm said to contradict a basically Marxian analysis of racial oppression in the United States and the need for a socialist restructuring of
society. Here, in much the same manner as the others who assessed Malcolm's speech, Mayfield projected his ideals onto Malcolm, evidently hoping
that the ex-NOI spokesman would soon overcome his reluctance to embrace
a socialist analysis. To Basner's objection that Malcolm's emphasis on black
unity marginalized white workers and progressives, Mayfield referenced the
history of the compromises and betrayals of black peoples by the "so-called
Left." The American Communist Party had joined establishment and moderate African American leaders in condemning what Mayfield (perhaps alluding to Robert Williams and Malcolm) considered to be the most militant
and effective voices among blacks. Malcolm's call for solidarity among New
World blacks and with Africans did not constitute racialism or a rejection of
Marxism but was predicated on simple pragmatism and common sense.[42]

According to Basner, Nkrumah resolved the matter in Basner's favor before a meeting of the CPP Central Committee, declaring that Basner's repudiation of Malcolm was correct. The cloud over Basner immediately lifted.
Despite the self-serving nature of Basner's account, a measure of credence
may go to his description of the dispute's outcome, given his insider status
and credibility with the government as a prolific and authoritative anti-
imperialist critic and defender of Nkrumah in the Ghanaian press.[43]

African American expatriates such as Mayfield, Shirley Du Bois, and Lacy
viewed Basner's criticisms of Malcolm as an affront. Basner's attack on Malcolm constituted more than yet another exhibition of white leftist conde-
scension; it was an attack on Afro-Americans' legitimacy as revolutionary
allies, a legitimacy that was already being eroded in the press. For that
reason alone, Basner's initial criticism of Malcolm demanded an immediate
and forceful rebuttal. Malcolm had become a powerful symbol of Afro-
American radicalism that might counter accusations in the Ghanaian press
of Afro-American disloyalty to Ghana. The space devoted to Basner's criticism in the press suggested that Nkrumah had taken Basner's side against
the Afro-American expatriates. Lacy seemed unaware that Nkrumah had
relied all along on a multiracial ensemble of advisers that included European
as well as African and African-descended expatriates.[44]

In the July 1964 *Liberator*, Malcolm provided a glowing account, as he
would in his autobiography, of his audience with Nkrumah, keeping private
any possible misgivings about the man. Malcolm credited Nkrumah with
being the most advanced pan-Africanist leader on the continent. Consequently, "President Nkrumah is both feared and hated by the White Western

powers who are trying to maintain a neocolonialist foothold on that continent of beauty and wealth." Based on his conversations with African, Asian, and Latin American members of Ghana's diplomatic corps, Malcolm concluded that "the entire Dark World is beginning to see America as the 20th Century's leading neo-colonial power." Malcolm singled out the warmth and revolutionary commitment of the ambassadors from China, Cuba, and Algeria.[45]

Malcolm ended his essay in the *Liberator* with the matter-of-fact observation that "[t]ravel broadens one's scope. My outlook after my five weeks' tour of the Mid-east and Africa is much broader than before I left." Malcolm's enhanced outlook led to the June 1964 founding of the OAAU, a secular organization based in Harlem that promoted an agenda of self-determination, black pride, and community control and sought to bridge religious and ideological differences among blacks in America. Inspired by the Organization of African Unity, launched in Addis Ababa in 1963, the OAAU applied global consciousness to local activism, drawing on generations of Harlem's cosmopolitan black nationalism: "What we do [in Harlem] to regain our Self-Respect, Manhood, Dignity, and Freedom helps all people everywhere who are fighting against oppression."[46] Among the Afro-American expatriate community, Malcolm established an Accra branch of the OAAU, which issued a press release quoting Malcolm's statement to the Organization of African Unity that "thousands of Afro-Americans" were willing to fight alongside Congolese nationalists against South African mercenaries.[47]

In mid-July, Malcolm attended the Organization of African Unity summit in Cairo, Egypt. There, Malcolm appealed to African nations to argue the cause of 22 million black Americans before the United Nations. In Cairo, Malcolm called attention to America's Achilles heel—the worldwide reach of American institutionalized racism and empire. Reminding the African heads of state of the discovery, during the search for three missing civil rights workers in Mississippi, of the bodies of two more victims of violence and of incidents of racial harassment meted out to African diplomats and students in the United States, Malcolm maintained that "[o]ur problem is your problem. It is not a Negro problem, nor an American problem. This is a world problem, a problem for humanity. It is not a problem of civil rights, but a problem of human rights." Malcolm scorned the recent passage of the Civil Rights Act as a concession to world opinion, merely a propagandistic diversion.[48] In Cairo, Malcolm became ill at a dinner; he believed he had been poisoned. From September to November 1964, Malcolm would return to the African continent, meeting with heads of state and addressing the parliaments of several nations. Also traveling through Africa, SNCC activists John Lewis and Don Harris wrote of the "fantastic impressions" Malcolm made in several countries. They ran into Malcolm in Kenya, sharing an exhilarating two days of freewheeling debate.[49] Throughout these travels, Malcolm was shadowed by U.S. intelligence operatives, who noted his facility for connecting with his African audiences.[50]

After Malcolm's departure from Ghana, Julian Mayfield and journalist Cameron Duodu worked to keep Malcolm's defiant image before the readers of the Ghana press. Duodu reprinted extracts from Malcolm's speech in a photo essay in the Ghanaian edition of *Drum*.[51] In a feature intended to disabuse Ghanaians of any illusions about the depth of American racism, Mayfield described the Harlem riots of July as an open rebellion against police violence. Mayfield's hard-hitting captions appeared below photographs selected to familiarize Ghanaian audiences with an African American memory of collective suffering. The article reprinted the famous pairing of the portrait of a smiling Emmett Till with his mother and the photograph of Till's horribly disfigured face after his murder in Mississippi. Mayfield informed his readers, "The two white men who killed him are alive and free. They sold their story to an American magazine for 10,000 dollars." The final image in the feature was one of Malcolm X, holding his daughter, Ilyasah, cropped to show a frowning white policeman looming ominously over his shoulder. Mayfield described Malcolm as "a great admirer of the Osagyefo Dr. Kwame Nkrumah" and approvingly noted Malcolm's appeal for cooperation between Afro-Americans and Africans and unity among Afro-American organizations as a means of more effectively opposing white racialism.[52]

Malcolm's Oxford Debate Union Address

Before his departure from the NOI, Malcolm had isolated himself by condemning a generalized and innate white supremacy. After his travels and discussions with African heads of state and radical members of Ghana's diplomatic corps, Malcolm's analysis of American power focused on institutionalized racism at home and abroad, granted black and African peoples a greater measure of agency in fighting their oppression, and posited a universal moral standard of justice and human rights. By detailing the injustices of the U.S. political system, Malcolm sought to purge the nation of these inequalities. It was impossible to transform American society without exposing its violations of democratic principles both at home and overseas.

Not surprisingly, Malcolm's criticisms of American foreign policy were taken most seriously by foreign audiences. The receptivity of such audiences seemed to restrain Malcolm from the lapses into sensationalism that occurred when he returned to the United States.[53] Of course, Malcolm held no monopoly on extremism in those turbulent times. When Malcolm spoke at the Oxford Debate Union in early December 1964, a event broadcast by the British Broadcasting Corporation, the motion he defended, "extremism in the name of liberty is no vice, moderation in the pursuit of justice is no virtue," seemed tailored to Malcolm's controversial image. But the motion was a direct quotation from Republican presidential candidate Barry Goldwater's defiant acceptance speech at a GOP convention whose Far Right rhetoric and hostility toward African American delegates epitomized the backlash against the black freedom movement and the recently passed civil rights bill.[54] The right-wing provenance of that motion hardly does justice to Malcolm's speech, which responded to two recent events. In late November 1964, Belgian forces, acting with U.S. military assistance, invaded the Stanleyville region of the Congo on the pretext of the humanitarian rescue of European hostages held by Congolese rebels against the central government led by Moise Tshombe. Many African and nonaligned states viewed Tshombe as an accessory to the murder of Patrice Lumumba. The purported humanitarian intervention resulted in the slaughter of some three thousand Congolese civilians. At the United Nations, Afro-Asian critics bitterly noted the hypocrisy of the invasion's stated objective of the protection of white lives in light of the wanton massacre of the Congolese. Kojo Botsio of Ghana had told the Security Council that the United States was no more entitled to intervene in the Congo than Ghana was in the U.S. South, where African Americans were "from time to time tortured and murdered for asserting their legitimate rights." The second event Malcolm referenced was the dismissal of charges against the accused killers of three civil rights workers by authorities in Meridian, Mississippi, who also refused to hear the confession of one of the suspects. Malcolm was not the only person to deplore this travesty of justice. Noting the Western press's lack of condemnation of the Congo massacre, Guinea's UN representative inquired, "Was it because the thousands of Congolese citizens murdered by the South Africans, the Rhodesians, the Belgians and the Cuban refugee adventurers had dark skins just like the colored U.S. citizens murdered in Mississippi?" What is fascinating and generally overlooked about the firestorm of criticism from African diplomats and the nonaligned bloc is that amid the furor, African American civil rights leaders including Martin Luther King Jr., A. Philip Randolph, Roy Wilkins, James Farmer, Whitney Young, and Dorothy Height were pressing the Johnson administration for a complete revision of U.S. policy toward Africa, including a withdrawal of support for Tshombe. Not unlike Malcolm, African American leaders proposed the sort of transnational citizenship and civic engagement that posed a direct challenge to U.S. military-industrial liberalism.[55]

For Malcolm, extremism was the deployment of state-sponsored violence, which he called "cold-blooded murder" in the Congo. The real extremists were the vigilantes in Mississippi and throughout the South who acted with impunity, knowing that local courts would never convict the criminals if they even came to trial. Such extremism, winked at by the federal government, justified methods of self-defense. Malcolm pointed out the double standard by which the State Department and the Western press condoned the slaughter of Congolese under the guise of humanitarianism yet characterized as extremism self-defense by blacks against unredressed violence.[56] The metropolitan press conferred respectability on Tshombe, Belgium's puppet, the same factotum who relied on "hired killers" from South Africa. While much Western press coverage supported the U.S.-Belgian intervention, Malcolm mentioned an unusual item in the British press that noted that the U.S.-Belgian forces and their auxiliaries had killed Congolese who supported Tshombe's central government as readily as they had killed the rebels from the Stanleyville region. Malcolm challenged his audience to reflect on events not as members of different races but as human beings and to reject the racism that resulted in the devaluing of human life and in the denial of the right of the oppressed to defend themselves against oppression.[57]

Malcolm saw U.S. policy in the Congo as the mirror image of the federal government's complicity with black oppression in Mississippi. His voice rising to a higher pitch of fury, Malcolm disputed U.S. claims of racial progress, citing the unpunished murders of the three civil rights workers and the federal government's inaction on the matter despite the recent passage of the Civil Rights Act. Racism was entrenched in the American political system, as many powerful congressional committees were chaired by southern segregationists whose seniority was founded on the denial of voting rights to most of the region's blacks. So integral to American institutions was white supremacy that lasting change within the legal and political system was virtually impossible. If a society refused to enforce the law on behalf of its black citizens, those people are justified "by any means necessary to bring about justice where the government can't give them justice."[58]

This was incendiary rhetoric in those days and sadly prophetic for our own times. As the courts over the past twenty-five years have steadily reversed civil rights reforms in antidiscrimination, voting rights, and affirmative action, who can say that Malcolm's contentions of late 1964 are wrong?[59] Malcolm's emphasis on human rights violations and self-defense were born of his conviction that constitutional reforms and safeguards in America would not protect the rights—and in those days the lives—of black people. Malcolm was unquestionably ill served by his reckless use of the slogan "by any means necessary," on which the American press routinely seized to obscure his fundamental point that black people were entitled to self-defense.

Of course, "by any means necessary" also encompassed Malcolm's diplomatic strategy of forging alliances with African nations to dramatize the plight of African Americans internationally before the UN. Malcolm had informed the heads of state at the Cairo meeting of the Organization of African Unity that if others could threaten to charge the Soviet Union with human rights crimes against its Jewish minority, then African peoples could do the same on behalf of oppressed blacks in America. Some, like Rev. Albert Cleague of Detroit, dismissed this strategy, claiming that Malcolm knew that Africans could not free black Americans. But others, particularly the U.S. government, viewed Malcolm's plans with the utmost seriousness. Nigerian scholar and NOI expert E. U. Essien-Udom quoted an August 1964 *New York Times* article:

> [T]he State Department and the Justice Department have begun to take an interest in Malcolm's campaign to convince African States to raise the question of the persecution of American Negroes at the United Nations. . . .
>
> After studying [Malcolm's memorandum to the heads of state at the Organization of African Unity summit in Cairo], officials said that if Malcolm succeeded in convincing just one African government to bring up the charge at the United Nations, the United States government would be faced with a touchy problem.
>
> The United States, officials here believe, would find itself in the same category as South Africa, Hungary and other countries whose domestic policies have become debating issues at the United Nations. . . . The issue . . . would . . . contribute to the undermining of the position the United States had asserted for itself as the leader of the West in the advocacy of human rights.[60]

This was Malcolm's intention. By countering claims that American blacks were achieving progress in America with criticism of U.S. foreign policy toward Africa, Malcolm articulated a contradiction that historian Thomas Borstelmann noted in his study of race in Cold War foreign policy. With the formal end of Jim Crow as a result of the passage of the Civil Rights and

Voting Rights Acts during 1964 and 1965, respectively, U.S. foreign policy toward Africa aligned itself with the suppression of African freedom, as seen in the U.S. participation in the Congo and heavy financial investments and an indulgent policy toward apartheid South Africa and white-dominated Rhodesia. Such policies, in tandem with U.S. propaganda intended to convince Africans of idyllic conditions for blacks in the United States, provided the context for Malcolm's December 1964 statement that "Afro-Americans" should remain in the United States but "migrate to Africa culturally, philosophically, and spiritually."[61]

At the heart of Malcolm's remarks was an intense, if now largely forgotten, struggle over the terms of African American affiliation. By naming themselves "Afro-American," Malcolm and his followers insisted on the legitimacy and salience of black and African heritage as the basis for their full participation in American life. This oppositional naming amounted to nothing less than a defiant assertion of the expansiveness of blackness as the grounds for national belonging, for international identification, and ultimately for a radical democratic political articulation universal in its applicability. Nothing in Malcolm's understanding of solidarity with the cause of African peoples restricted or confined that vision to black people. Nevertheless, in speaking of the "Afro-American," Malcolm had signaled anew the importance of being black *and* American, with no contradiction between the two.

Malcolm is rightly mythologized today for his insight and fearlessness and for his selfless devotion in giving his life in the struggle for freedom and justice. He is mythologized for the wrong reasons as well, including separatism, hypermasculinity, and brute violence, positions he held before he rethought, clarified, or discarded them. Rightly and wrongly, some who mythologize Malcolm need to honor him almost as an act of penance for not having properly understood his significance while he lived. Speaking at Malcolm's funeral, Ossie Davis may have come as close as anyone in articulating the meaning of Malcolm's life and its application for the lives of African Americans: "I say the word again, as he would want me to: Afro-American— Afro-American Malcolm, who was a master, was most meticulous in his use of words. . . . Malcolm had stopped being a Negro years ago. . . . Malcolm was bigger than that. Malcolm had become an Afro-American, and he wanted— so desperately—that we, that all his people, would become Afro-Americans too."[62] For Malcolm and his followers, "Afro-American" signified the promise of a utopian fulfillment of modern black consciousness. "Afro-American" promised the achievement of a unity through which black and African peoples might know themselves and each other and imagine a world transformed by their action on that knowledge. Today, many people find the designation "Afro-American" innocuous. But as understood by Davis and Malcolm, "Afro-American" (combined with Malcolm's late-in-life immersion in world Islam) offered a glimpse into a promised land of radical liberation movements on a global scale.

Three days after Malcolm was gunned down on February 21, 1965, while speaking at a public meeting in Harlem, Julian Mayfield's eulogy appeared in the Ghanaian press. People of African descent everywhere had suffered a grievous loss, Mayfield wrote. Malcolm was the only prominent black leader who opposed American capitalism and believed that African Americans "would be signing [their] death warrant" by siding with the world's most formidable imperialist power. He was also the only Afro-American leader of national stature who sought to unify Africa with its descendants in the Western hemisphere and who rejected an accommodationist non-violence. In Mayfield's eyes, these uncompromising stands made Malcolm "the most dangerous man in America." Drawing lessons from Malcolm's life that would resonate within a Ghanaian political culture weakened by malfeasance, Mayfield attributed Malcolm's departure from the Black Muslim movement he had built to the moment "when he found that the stench of corruption was setting in." Malcolm was honest, incorruptible, a man with a ready smile. His ascetic lifestyle may have been trying to his friends, but Malcolm remained (unlike Nkrumah, Mayfield seemed to suggest) ever ready to listen to suggestions from all of those around him. Malcolm was the antithesis of Ghanaian big men, Mayfield hinted. The eulogy made a virtue of Malcolm's poverty, his renunciation of big cars and houses, and his immunity to the temptations that had corrupted so many U.S. black leaders. (Leery of offending CPP politicians, Mayfield invited his audience to read between the lines.) Mayfield spoke of Malcolm's intellectual growth over the course of his two trips to Ghana and his calm acceptance of his fate. Malcolm had written to Mayfield, expressing his wish, in the event of his death, that some African state would give refuge to his wife and children.[63]

Nkrumah sent official condolences to Malcolm's funeral and extended an offer to Malcolm's widow, Betty Shabazz, to relocate her family to Ghana. The *Ghanaian Times* regarded Malcolm's murder as a cowardly assault on African Americans' demands for justice. "The green light of the Afro-American's hopes and aspirations is out, leaving behind mountains of fear and hatred, of suspicion and subjugation, to be moved." Malcolm "died as martyr of a living revolution . . . of racial equality and social justice."[64] Such tributes helped enshrine Malcolm in the pantheon of martyred African revolutionary icons. The London-based Council of African Organizations, which represented African residents and students in Britain and Europe, blamed U.S. imperialism for Malcolm's death, noting that the killers of Lumumba and Camerounian nationalist Felix Moumie had claimed another victim in their drive to subjugate the majority of humanity. Malcolm had addressed this group in December 1964, shortly before French authorities barred his entry into that country, preventing him from keeping an engagement to speak to a student organization.[65]

Mayfield and the Afro-American expatriates whom Malcolm had enlisted as the Accra branch of the OAAU, along with their Harlem counterparts, were "in a bad way," as John Henrik Clarke put it. Mayfield thanked Clarke for the clippings he sent on Malcolm, which Mayfield said he used for memorial services and other commemorations. A month after the assassination, however, Mayfield confessed that he could not read the clippings. Mayfield staggered through the round of memorials and his writing and editorial duties with the *African Review*, yearning to mourn in solitude. The Afro-American comrades in Ghana were "depressed, as you may gather." Mayfield described a "sense of personal loss . . . so great—the thing has cut me up in the guts in a way I imagined anything could. . . . Personally and politically that was the way I felt about Malcolm whom I had come to know so well here and in Cairo." As black and white commentators roundly denounced Malcolm in death, only a select group that included the African students who had heard him speak, African Americans in Ghana, Malcolm's allies and followers in Harlem, and members of U.S. intelligence organizations fully appreciated who the slain Muslim leader was and what he might have been.[66]

Given the lineage of black nationalism that tied the NOI to its precursor in the Garvey movement, Malcolm's killing resulted not only from the NOI's corruption but also from its profound lack of historical and political awareness. In this respect Malcolm and the NOI were pawns victimized by the same divisive tactics that the FBI had used to destroy Marcus Garvey and his movement. The sobering fact that mendacity at the top of the NOI permitted the FBI again to undermine a black movement makes a particularly humiliating farce of Malcolm's murder. An uncompromising—indeed, hostile—critic of the civil rights movement and its leadership until nearly the end of his life, Malcolm was never a civil rights leader. Thus, it is a particularly grim irony that the circumstances of Malcolm's death paralleled the vain appeals of civil rights workers for federal protection against white southern extremists. For

Malcolm had pleaded for protection from local police authorities, and his assassination had occurred while he was shadowed by U.S. intelligence and New York Police Department officials who had seemingly abandoned Malcolm to his fate.[67]

That the NOI fell into the same trap of infiltration that brought about the demise of the Garvey movement demonstrates the long arc of U.S. government intervention against independent formations of black internationalism. But by the 1960s, the scope of such interference matched the hegemonic ambitions of U.S. policy makers. In January 1965, the State Department dispatched civil rights leader James Farmer to retrace Malcolm's travels through Africa. U.S. officials hoped that Farmer's influence on African audiences would negate that of Malcolm. However relieved U.S. authorities may have been at the silencing of Malcolm's criticisms of Western and American propaganda on the Congo and African affairs, they failed to halt Malcolm's growing influence on countless African and black youths worldwide. A spate of verse tributes echoed Ossie Davis's eulogy recalling Malcolm's selfless devotion to black liberation. Many people remembered Malcolm as an African American Lumumba. To invoke his memory was an injunction not to forget other African martyrs and the cause for which they had died. In a 1970 concert in Conakry, Makeba praised Malcolm in song. Julia Wright Hervé's tribute appeared in *Présence Africaine* soon after Malcolm's death. When Africans and people of African descent "fight the fundamental fight" for authentic freedom, "[w]e are alone."

> When we challenge the stupor of tradition
> And bare the real earth
> With our weed-stained fists,
> We are assassinated
> In flesh,
> But not in meaning.[68]

With the death of Malcolm X, the transatlantic radical culture that spanned Harlem and Accra became increasingly subject to political repression and sectarian strife. John Henrik Clarke informed Mayfield that the OAAU was in a shambles. Clarke wrote cryptically of intrigues emanating from Washington, probably referring to agent provocateurs who preyed on members of the group. Clarke also complained of the growing schism within the *Freedomways* editorial collective. To Clarke's dismay, a growing emphasis on the southern black freedom movement was steadily eclipsing the pan-African internationalism of the journal's early years.[69]

Malcolm X represented a crystallization of the nascent black urban revolt against the liberal orthodoxies of the U.S. establishment and the civil rights movement. When Malcolm died, he was in the process of forging the African American masses' inchoate aspirations for cultural autonomy into a political analysis of U.S. power at home and abroad and, through the OAAU, into a program for African Americans that situated local activism within a global framework. This project escalated the ideological struggle against U.S. officialdom over African American political consciousness and civic engagement. Despite the hopes black radicals invested in him, in the end Malcolm must have understood that he was alone, cornered by a mounting array of liabilities and intrigues—he was shadowed by U.S. intelligence, denied entry into France, hobbled by a lack of resources and squabbling among members of the OAAU, his warnings about NOI death threats ignored by the mass media as it continued to sensationalize his statements, and finally, stalked by NOI assassins. In the end, Malcolm's effectiveness was severely compromised.[70] What did Malcolm really think about Nkrumah's Ghana and the black expatriate community there, beyond the obligatory statements of praise he left behind? Despite what might be gleaned from his subsequent speeches and the various interpretations of his visit by expatriates, we may never know precisely what Malcolm learned in Ghana about the challenges facing African and black leadership.

7

THE COUP

In her memoir of her years in Ghana as Kwame Nkrumah's private secretary, Erica Powell, who had previously been the secretary to the colonial governor of the Gold Coast, described an incident aimed at her boss that was so horrendous that she kept it from him and was unable to discuss with friends. A narrow parcel arrived from Angola, a foot long and about four inches wide. The outside wrapper was greasy, and a pungent smell seared Powell's nostrils. "To this day I really don't know why I opened it," she wrote. In retrospect, she believed that it was better that she discovered its contents than any of the Ghanaians in the office. Inside was the forearm of an African, cut from wrist to elbow. Attached to the rotting flesh was a message written in Portuguese. She hurriedly wrapped the parcel in newspaper and burned it in an incinerator.[1]

That ghastly instance of colonial brutality belied the West's optimism that the "winds of change," a tellingly passive phrase, would come without violence. By 1965, the intransigence of white minority governments in Rhodesia, South Africa, Angola, and Mozambique made it clear that change would require arms and bloodshed on the part of national liberation movements. Accordingly, Nkrumah committed resources to the training of African freedom fighters and redoubled his pursuit of an African union government. When Nkrumah demanded the rapid construction of a new complex of buildings to house the Organization of African Unity (OAU) summit in Accra, skeptical officials secretly made alternative plans. But the complex, known as Job 600, was completed in time for the conference, aided in part by the contributions of many expatriate African American technicians.[2]

Far from the triumph of the 1958 All African People's Conference, the OAU meeting held in Accra in 1965 had at best mixed success. That it occurred at

all represented an achievement, given the opposition of pro-Western African
nations. The crisis over Rhodesia's recent unilateral declaration of independence from England dramatized the necessity of unity and forged solidarity among those African governments in attendance. In hosting the gathering, Ghana staged an impressive display of pageantry for conference delegates, observers, and members of the international press. Ghana Television, under the direction of Shirley Graham Du Bois, provided live coverage of the proceedings, with the remainder of its programming supplied by all of the independent African nations represented at the conference. Also featured were performances by the exiled South African singer Miriam Makeba and France's legendary African American expatriate chanteuse, Josephine Baker, both of whom entertained at conference galas. Symbolic victories aside, Nkrumah's last conference as head of state failed to sway African heads of state in favor of a continental system of governance.[3]

Michael Dei-Anang, an official in Ghana's African Affairs Secretariat, described Nkrumah's resoluteness in the face of all obstacles. Nkrumah would often stand before a large map of Africa, extolling its vastness and its bounty of agricultural and mineral products: oil, iron ore, diamonds, copper, tin, uranium, gold, cocoa, tobacco, rubber, and many others. "What do we lack? And why should we be so poor in the midst of plenty?" Nkrumah's answer to that question—neocolonialism—led to the final breach between his government and the United States. Matters were not helped by the fact that Nkrumah lent financial support and training to exiled nationalist leaders and freedom fighters from those territories still struggling against colonialism, thereby convincing U.S. officials that his regime threatened national security interests on the continent.[4]

Nkrumah's quest for African liberation justified all, including the autocratic policies and tolerance of corruption that eroded his legitimacy. After several assassination plots and attempts, Nkrumah withdrew behind a phalanx of security, isolating himself from a formerly adoring populace. The conspicuous wealth gained by politicians through graft, nepotism, and patronage bred resentment among a wage-earning and impoverished population burdened with austerity and high taxes for national development. The pluralism and mass participation that had once defined Convention People's Party (CPP) campaigns and government were replaced by the regime's reliance on uncontested elections, executive fiat, and coerced adulation. Nkrumah's opposition had damaged its cause by resorting to violence that killed and wounded many innocent Ghanaians. But by vanquishing his opposition through detentions and by undermining parliamentary government and the courts, Nkrumah had stifled meaningful dialogue, sowing fear, cynicism, and apathy among the populace. Economic troubles compounded his difficulties. As the decline in the price of cocoa proved ruinous for Ghana's balance of trade, inflation and shortages of consumer goods ensued.[5]

Where African unity was concerned, Nkrumah threw caution and cost-accounting to the wind. An ever-expanding list of diplomatic missions around the world and Job 600, whose cost was estimated at £8 million, further depleted dwindling foreign exchange revenues. Critical supporters competed with sycophants and opportunists for Nkrumah's attention. Nkrumah struggled to balance the nation's economic and political difficulties with his foreign policy objectives. His credibility suffered an additional blow with the February 1965 death of J. B. Danquah while in solitary confinement at Nsawam maximum security prison. The death of the man who had given Nkrumah his start in Gold Coast politics and who had named the new nation after the ancient Akan empire of Ghana further tarnished Nkrumah's image both at home and with fellow African heads of state.

Danquah had been the leader of the strident and occasionally violent opposition. A year before his death, he had been detained without trial for a second time after an assailant fired several shots at Nkrumah outside Flagstaff House. As reports of Danquah's failing health emanated from Nsawam, Julian Mayfield and other expatriates, including St. Clair Drake and Ana Livia Cordero, along with Ghanaian scholar K. A. B. Jones-Quartey, petitioned the president for clemency.[6] When Danquah's death was reported, Nigerian president Nnamdi Azikiwe, in his tribute to Danquah, publicly rebuked Nkrumah. Without mentioning his former protégé by name, Azikiwe left no doubt that he held Nkrumah personally responsible for Danquah's death. Indeed, some Ghanaians saw Nkrumah's culpability as taking on patricidal connotations. Fearing a demonstration, Nkrumah banned Danquah's family from holding his funeral in Accra. Despite his alleged involvement in subversion, the death in jail of the doyen of Gold Coast nationalism and the resentment it spawned in Ghana and throughout West Africa gave opposition forces a martyr. Evincing a zeal that outweighed its better judgment, the government's defamatory newspaper assessment promising "The Whole Truth about Danquah" inflicted more damage on Nkrumah than on its deceased target.[7]

As the regime's difficulties mounted, the intellectuals among the black expatriate community made the most of their project, primarily through the *African Review*, of articulating a radical analysis of events in the United States and the world. While Nkrumah's Ghana made their work possible, their political vision was broader than a blind loyalty to Nkrumah. In addition to such contributors as Preston King and Maya Angelou, Julian Mayfield opened the pages of the *African Review* to writers from Africa and the Caribbean, including Bessie Head of South Africa and Neville Dawes of Jamaica. Emulating such African American publications as *Freedomways* and the Nation of Islam's *Muhammed Speaks*, Mayfield and his colleagues extended Malcolm X's critique of the limitations of civil rights and voting rights legislation, insisting that these minimal and belated reforms were a diversion from U.S. political support for and investment in racist white minority governments and from escalating involvement in Vietnam.

Apart from their shared anti-imperialism and skepticism toward U.S. professions of racial progress, the African American expatriates varied considerably in their degree of political involvement and activity. For every Panglossian true believer, several hard-headed skeptics hoped that the Ghanaian government might overcome its flaws. Mayfield, whose journalism in Ghana routinely outraged U.S. embassy officials, fell into the latter category. Mayfield, along with those who maintained lower profiles, such as Sylvia Boone and Preston King, shared an essentially similar outlook. The political support of some expatriates—for example, dentists Robert and Sarah Lee and the businessmen and technicians who helped expand Ghana's infrastructure and raced to complete Job 600—was evident in their self-perception as permanent residents. Those who were more or less transient—particularly academics such as Martin and Marion Kilson, David Levering Lewis, and St. Clair and Elizabeth Drake—hardly shared uniform views regarding the government. The Drakes were astute observers who cherished a deep attachment to Ghana and its moment of global black modernity. Some, like Martin Kilson and Angelou, who had returned to the United States as urban rebellions transformed black activism and the nation's perception of it, felt that the expatriates belonged at home, where their guidance was sorely needed.

Any qualms among Nkrumah's staunchest supporters in Ghana and elsewhere had faded in the face of their conviction that, notwithstanding his errors and the CPP's imaginary "socialism," Nkrumah was the sole African leader willing to lend institutional backing to African liberation struggles. Let detractors throughout the U.S. and Western press belittle his dream of continental unity. Let disingenuous journalists pillory Nkrumah as a dictator while they remained silent on the use of detentions by pro-Western African governments. Behind such anti-Nkrumah propaganda remained the fact that for U.S. and Western governments, at the heart of the matter lay the threat to their objectives and interests posed by Nkrumah's staunch anti-imperialism and his material support for African freedom fighters.

THE COUP

Among many of the expatriates of African descent, then, support for Nkrumah's objectives was animated by a politicized race consciousness. This should not be surprising; indeed, it would truly be surprising if this were not the case. Not only had the expatriate "Afros," as some referred to themselves, come of age in a society defined for them by egregious racial exclusions, but they were also acutely aware that U.S. propaganda agencies were assiduously working to minimize the scope of discrimination in America for African audiences. From the Congo Crisis to U.S. diplomatic backing and investments in South Africa, the expatriates and their allies in the United States held no illusions about the heart of white supremacy beating behind a veneer of racial liberalism.

But it is crucial to understand the complexity of their race consciousness. "Race" was no abstract variable for the African American expatriates; rather, what some would call race was suffused with multiple narratives of systemic and personal humiliation, family stories of resistance, and collective dreams of freedom. For the expatriates and African Americans back in the United States, a racialized subjectivity, buttressed by expansive global democratic solidarities, was foundational for demands for equality, citizenship, and national belonging. Far from parochial, separatist, or even racist, the Afros' analysis of racial oppression and socioeconomic analyses of the plight of Africans and black peoples worldwide exemplified pan-African universalism. Nkrumah's Ghana welcomed the participation of persons of conscience regardless of race, and the Drakes, Richard Wright, and George Padmore shared Nkrumah's nonracialism. In Ghana, tensions might erupt along race/class lines, as when H. M. Basner clashed with Mayfield regarding the significance of Malcolm X, possibly at Nkrumah's behest. Nevertheless, the Ghanaian leader's anti-imperialism elicited pride among Africans and peoples of African descent even as it held a transracial appeal for many non-African expatriate supporters, including Geoffrey Bing, Thomas and Dorothy Hodgkin, Conor Cruise O'Brien, Hanna Reitsch, and many others.

Whatever doubts expatriate and Ghanaian supporters quietly held about conditions in Ghana, Nkrumah's Ghanaian and expatriate staffers in the Publicity Secretariat struggled to match the frenetic pace set by their leader to enact his vision. This was true of Mayfield, charged in the months leading to the OAU summit with making the intellectual case for continental unity in the pages of the *African Review*. Yet while Mayfield, a militant leftist, became disillusioned and informed a friend that he was "bursting to get away," the pragmatic, politically moderate St. Clair Drake ironically remained a staunch supporter of Nkrumah's government.[8]

Drake and others saw corruption and preventive detention as both serious problems and weapons of propaganda wielded by a hostile Western press. Drake was far from alone in his view that continental unity and socialism represented the only solution to Africa's poverty and political weakness. He and his generation of pan-African allies would not abandon the dream of pan-African revolution and Afro-diasporic modernity unless forced to do so.

During Drake's intermittent stays in the country since 1955, he limited his duties to teaching and research, declining Nkrumah's offers of political appointments. Drake believed that he could best serve Ghana and the pan-African cause by defending the young nation's objectives and interests within the American press. With his many contacts in the U.S. Africanist nexus of academia, government, and foundations and within the African American press and with his acquaintance with many African nationalist leaders, Drake provided Nkrumah with a valuable asset. When Nkrumah sought a rapid expansion of secondary education, he recruited Peace Corps volunteers to meet the demand for teachers. As a result, Drake spent several summers training the volunteers for their tours in Ghana. But while U.S. officials hoped to tap into Drake's expertise and connections, Drake's loyalty remained with Nkrumah. Indeed, even after Nkrumah's government was overthrown, Drake continued to defend the deposed leader despite widespread vilification of him in the press.[9]

Drake leveraged his expertise on Africa to lobby for greater foundation support of Roosevelt University's African studies program. In addition, Drake used his status as a liaison between Nkrumah and other African nationalists and the U.S. establishment to offer assessments of the situation in Ghana that might counter unfavorable press coverage. To whoever would listen, Drake put in a good word for Ghana and its prospects while placing the government's difficulties in context. To a Ford Foundation official, Drake noted in August 1964 that the conflict in Ghana between aspirations for a higher standard of living and the government's policies of "belt-tightening in the hope of an industrial takeoff" was typical of many countries. What set Ghana apart was Nkrumah's "rigidity" and his impatience, which stemmed from his sense that death was close at hand. Drake believed that Nkrumah would steer clear of Soviet or Chinese control, but only time would tell whether he would call "the small minority on the extreme left" in the CPP to heel. While government interference in the university was regrettable, African leaders concerned above all with development and discipline could

THE COUP

not be expected to share Drake's commitment to academic freedom. Drake hoped that democratic values would take root with the spread of education and as economic problems were solved. The emergence of a more responsible kind of opposition remained critical. Drake wrote ominously, "I *know* the nature of the Ghanaian opposition and Nkrumah has a really tough problem on his hands."[10]

Drake's support for Nkrumah's Ghana had another personal aspect. Although Drake did not share the alienation from the United States of such political exiles as Mayfield or Shirley Graham Du Bois, his decision to reside in Ghana constituted a different kind of flight. At the start of his career, Drake and his wife, Elizabeth, felt that as an interracial couple with two small children, the ability to live overseas for extended periods would minimize the family's exposure to racism in the United States. Living in Ghana intermittently from the mid-1950s onward, the Drakes made lasting friendships with Ghanaians in and around the CPP and the university. Drake's daughter, Sandra, had taught French to the Young Pioneers, a CPP auxiliary organization. The Drakes' commitment to Ghana was solidified by a deep attachment to the place, its people, and the government's progressive goals and by an appreciation for the freedom Ghana afforded them from social pressures back in the States. Conditions in the United States had improved, but this development did not diminish the Drakes' affection for Ghana.[11]

Drake's commitment to Ghana led him to emphasize what he took to be mitigating factors against the barrage of dire reports about Ghana. Soviet influence in Ghana, with which anti-Nkrumah politicians and pundits in the West were obsessed, was greatly exaggerated. Drake described the Kwame Nkrumah Ideological Institute, which, depending on one's sympathies, was dedicated to either the training or the indoctrination of socialist cadres. But the library of this supposed hotbed of communist subversion contained Paul Samuelson's popular college economics text alongside works by Marx and Eastern bloc economists. In their eagerness to read a text forbidden at home, Russian personnel pored over copies of Trotsky's *History of the Russian Revolution*. While attending the Commonwealth conference, Nkrumah had ordered his ministers to the institute in Winneba to study his *Consciencism* and to meditate on the African revolution. One of Nkrumah's ministers, Krobo Edusei, ventured out one night and was in the Ambassador Hotel's nightclub when a fight broke out. "He left his two Lebanese girl friends and table full of French wines and ran to the mike, rebuking the men who were fighting: 'That's no way for you to act with Osagyefo away and us all busy building socialism here.'" Drake noted the glaring problems yet managed to shrug them off, much like other Ghanaians. Ghanaians "muddle through and the place looks pretty good despite some food shortages. The people grumble" but remain cheerful and well clothed. "Ministers continue to steal while they talk about socialism and their wives get import licenses through 'influence' and money is wasted on OAU buildings and hotels. But life goes on and change—on the whole progressive—takes place. I doubt if they'll collapse."[12]

Drake reported that his travel plans prevented him from calling on Nkrumah, adding that the Ghanaian leader "spends most of his time on Vietnam these days." Drake hardly suspected that Nkrumah's desire to mediate the deepening conflict between the United States and North Vietnamese nationalists would cause him never to see Nkrumah again. In taking up the Vietnam conflict, Nkrumah sought the prestige of global statesmanship at the expense of Ghana's thorny internal economic and political difficulties. His interest in Indochina expressed a long-held conviction that African leaders should influence global issues such as peace and nuclear disarmament. In June, at the Commonwealth conference, British Prime Minister Harold Wilson solicited Nkrumah's participation in a peace mission to Vietnam. Wary of the Commonwealth aegis, as perhaps Nkrumah should have been, the North Vietnamese personally invited Nkrumah to Hanoi. Nkrumah promptly sent a delegation there to prepare for the talks. President Ho Chi Minh, anticipating Viet Cong military gains, saw no need for negotiations, although he welcomed a visit from Nkrumah. But Ho voiced concern for Nkrumah's safety since U.S. planes were bombing targets near Hanoi. After returning to Ghana, the delegation advised against a visit by Nkrumah since Hanoi was uninterested in negotiations. Determined to mediate, Nkrumah dispatched Foreign Minister Alex Quaison-Sackey and Ambassador Miguel Ribiero to the White House to obtain U.S. support for his peace mission and President Lyndon Johnson's assurance that Nkrumah would face no danger from American bombing. LBJ, basking in that day's signing of the Voting Rights Act, laughed off the North Vietnamese suggestion that Nkrumah would be in danger, and the Ghanaians obligingly joined in the mirth. Charming his visitors all the while, Johnson rejected Nkrumah's request for support for his mission. Dei-Anang detected an ominous implication of a different peril in Johnson's written response: "If you go to Hanoi, Mr. President, you will be in no danger of American military action in Vietnam."[13]

Johnson's dealings with Nkrumah and his aides exuded a confidence born of his administration's skillful management of Ghanaian and African affairs. The same might be said for Johnson's attitude toward the civil rights movement. In LBJ's view, the passage of the Voting Rights Act had solved the

American dilemma. The government, in partnership with the movement's leadership, had at last aligned its laws and policies with its national ideals of freedom and equality. In a June 1965 speech at Howard University, Johnson endorsed compensatory measures intended to achieve "equality of result" for black Americans (laying the political groundwork for what became affirmative action) and charged his staff with translating that goal into policy. The administration hoped that this ambitious reform agenda would once and for all defuse the combustible impact of U.S. racism overseas. With domestic affairs well in hand, the administration moved to extend its dominion over foreign policy. In January 1965, following Afro-Asian criticism of U.S. involvement in Belgium's bloody suppression of Lumumbaist rebels in the Congo, the administration refused to meet with members of the American Negro Leadership Conference on Africa. A White House memorandum referred to the president's strong desire "to discourage emergence of any special Negro pressure group (a la the Zionists) which might limit his freedom of maneuver." For Johnson, the achievement of integration in the United States entailed the acquiescence of black leadership on African and foreign affairs. Maintaining African American leaders' deference toward U.S. foreign policy makers remained a crucial objective as the administration expanded its commitment to the war in Indochina.[14]

Johnson's determination to minimize African American involvement in U.S. foreign affairs contrasted starkly with Nkrumah's conception of the African personality—the assertion of an active African presence in global affairs. Ghana had provided a global platform for African American radicals critical of U.S. foreign policy who in America would have been condemned to political obscurity or outright repression. Moreover, in Ghana, African American expatriates' analyses of the global impact of U.S. power were shaped by an engagement with African politics and dialogue with African and Afro-Caribbean radicals and an international Left in ways that U.S.-based activists and publications could at best only approximate. In particular, the *African Review* provided a forum for Mayfield's sharp criticism of LBJ's domestic and foreign policy, although the emergence of the antiwar movement, the Black Panther Party and Students for a Democratic Society, and such important new journals as *First World* and the *Black Scholar* would eventually provide vital new outlets for such radical Afro-diasporic commentary.

For Mayfield, the magazine also provided somewhat of a balm for his grief at the cruelly premature deaths of Malcolm X, murdered at age thirty-nine, and the improbably successful playwright Lorraine Hansberry, who had succumbed to cancer in January 1965 at the age of thirty-five. The debut issue,

Unsigned editorials by Mayfield castigated the OAU for failing to live up to its name and warned that the Johnson administration's civil rights reforms would fail to "still the discontent seething in black communities across the nation." In his indictment of LBJ, Mayfield asserted that urban blacks increasingly identified their cause with that of "the African–Asian–Latin American revolution." Mayfield found the administration's foreign policy even more ominous for developing nations fighting their way out of colonial and neocolonial impoverishment. Mayfield criticized the government's recent interventions in Vietnam and the Dominican Republic and its hypocrisy toward Africa, professing friendship while covertly supporting South Africa's repressive Verwoerd government with investment, trade, and political support at the United Nations. After lending military assistance to Belgium in the Congo, the United States "express[ed] astonished hurt that Africans rise almost as one man to condemn it." Mayfield decried the American obsession with anticommunism and its aversion to social and economic issues and doubted that Johnson, his electoral landslide notwithstanding, could reverse the policies of what Mayfield described as a predatory military-industrial complex.[15]

The first issue of the *African Review* mostly lived up to Mayfield's independent vision. Among the magazine's contributions, including illustrations by Tom Feelings and Ollie Harrington, Mayfield penned another tribute to Malcolm X, this time speculating that his assassination had been a Central Intelligence Agency (CIA) operation employing Muslim adherents of Elijah Muhammed. (In contrast to Shirley Graham Du Bois's strangely upbeat though prescient tribute, "The Beginning, Not the End," delivered over Ghana radio, Mayfield intimated that America's best hope for revolutionary change had died with Malcolm.)[16] Mayfield's claim about the CIA, active since the early 1950s as a destabilizing factor in such nonaligned governments as Iran, Guatemala, and Guyana and soon to play a role in the bloody liquidation of the Indonesian Left with a death toll approaching five hundred thousand, was unlikely to have appeared in such rival publications as *Transition*, the *African Forum, Encounter*, or the newsletter put out by the American Society for African Culture. All of these publications, it would be disclosed in March 1967, were secretly funded by the CIA as part of the government's clandestine cultural Cold War.[17]

The centerpiece of the issue was an essay by Preston King that argued for an African integrated military force in the wake of the Stanleyville invasion. King pointed out that the illogical national boundaries inherited from colo-

"South African Striptease." This May 1965 Ollie Harrington cartoon reflects the *African Review*'s condemnation of Western financial investments in apartheid South Africa.

nialism remained a source of weakness and instability. Such boundaries
exacerbated ethnic and linguistic tensions, increasing the likelihood of fron-
tier disputes and military conflicts between adjacent states. King believed
that an integrated force would contribute to the stability of African nations
and channel national and military resources toward continental unity. He
noted that such a force might divert national armies from overthrowing
African governments. (King's acknowledgment of this problem after the recent coup in Algeria implied Ghana's vulnerability.) In retrospect, given the
army coup leaders' stated objections to political interference by Nkrumah,
King's blueprint for merging national armies into an African force would
probably have inflamed rather than defused tensions. In any case, the lack of
such a force during the Stanleyville invasion laid bare Africa's political and
military impotence, as those Africans who wished to serve alongside the
freedom fighters in the Congo lacked a mechanism for doing so. Written in a
judicious, closely reasoned style, King's essay epitomized the magazine's
project of translating Nkrumah's vision of unity into reality.[18]

In that debut issue, King also contributed a negative review of a British
author's dismissive exegesis on the concept of neocolonialism. The review
was representative of the magazine's detailed elaboration of the nature and
instances of neocolonialism. In addition, Maya Angelou, Mayfield's features
editor, contributed "Point Counterpoint," a side-by-side comparison of the
starkly divergent views of Martin Luther King Jr. and, in this instance, the
selectively read Frantz Fanon on the validity of armed struggle. Angelou and
Mayfield showed a greater interest in Fanon's reflections on the necessity of
violence against the colonizer than in his perhaps more salient critique of
bourgeois nationalism (much of which was written during Fanon's residence
in Ghana months before his death in the United States of leukemia while
receiving treatment and debriefing). Mayfield focused the magazine's scrutiny on the newly exposed Achilles heel of American indulgence for the
South African apartheid regime. The inaugural issue also featured an essay
by exiled South African writer Bessie Head, a personal reflection on the
condition of exile and the psychological dimensions of the struggle against
apartheid. Quite possibly alluding to the marginalization of African women,
Head's essay extolled individual freedom as a corrective to the inadequate
nostrums of nationalist politicians. Perhaps seeking to foster sympathy for
the author and her views, Mayfield introduced the essay with an impassioned, self-deprecating statement from Head acknowledging her bouts with
poverty and despair and her determination to resist oppression through her
writing.[19]

But, as Conor Cruise O'Brien reminded Mayfield in a letter congratulating him on the inaugural issue, the magazine was not entirely free from Nkrumahist idolatry. O'Brien pointed to the cover feature, a puff piece on Nkrumah's *Consciencism* that appeared under the title "New Horizons in Modern Philosophy." Its author, S. G. Ikoku, was a Nigerian exile who taught Marxist theory and "scientific socialism" at the Ideological Institute in Winneba and was a prolific contributor to the *Spark*, the voice of the CPP's left wing, for whom the African personality seemed to entail doctrinaire appropriations of Leninism. Back in March, O'Brien, fed up with government intervention in university affairs, had announced his resignation in protest of the government's attacks on academic freedom.[20]

As both Mayfield and O'Brien knew, maintaining the magazine's editorial independence would be a struggle. Mayfield resisted official pressure (which may or may not have come from Nkrumah—his subordinates sometimes acted at the supposed behest of the president)[21] to denounce O'Brien in its pages for his criticism of the government.

Mayfield envisioned the journal as a forum, transcontinental and beyond, for African and Third World revolution and criticism of U.S. imperialism. As evident in the contributions of King, Angelou, Feelings, Drake, and others, Mayfield relied heavily on the Afros, with Jean Carey Bond (also a member of the *Freedomways* editorial collective) and Leslie A. Lacy providing valuable editorial assistance. Mayfield continued to rely on material sent by John Henrik Clarke, who also arranged for distribution of the magazine throughout New York's Africa-conscious black communities. The success of this stateside distribution is difficult to determine, and the magazine's distribution throughout Africa was haphazard. Aside from the internal intrigues suggested by the censorship of C. L. R. James's article, Mayfield complained of insufficient support. Moreover, if its distribution system was not faulty, it may have faced censorship by rival African governments as well.

Economist Ann Seidman, who taught at the University of Ghana and served as the magazine's finance editor, recalled that she never saw any copies while she was in Nigeria. Seidman commuted to that country, where her husband, Bob, taught law after having been deported by the Ghanaian government despite a vigorous protest by O'Brien. Bob Seidman most likely became suspect when a CPP official coveted his post. Several expatriates and visitors, including Shirley Graham Du Bois, Thomas and Dorothy Hodgkin, and Basil Davidson, interceded on Seidman's behalf, eventually securing his return and reinstatement at the university. The Seidmans vividly recalled the crisis at the university as a situation tailor-made for opportunists. During her husband's exile, Ann Seidman cowrote *Unity or Poverty? The Economics of* *Pan-Africanism*, articulating the economic case for continental unity, with fellow economist Reginald Herbold Green. Both Seidman and Green contributed separately to the *Ghanaian Times* several analyses of neocolonialism and the consequent need for regional economic cooperation among impoverished African states.[22] Unlike her husband, Ann Seidman was never targeted, she believed, because no one wanted her university job.

The Seidmans had known the Du Boises through Ann's parents, who had worked with W. E. B. Du Bois in the peace movement. At the OAU summit in Cairo, to which Ghana sent a ninety-person delegation (including Mayfield and Basner), Shirley Du Bois had introduced Ann Seidman to Malcolm X. "You see, not all whites are bad," Du Bois teased the Muslim leader. Ann Seidman believed the distribution problems of the *African Review* reflected the Ghanaian government's failure to build new institutions for transformative change. "There was a lot of talk, but no change in economic structure," she recalled. By this time, according to Seidman, Mayfield had become cynical about the problem of corruption, though she, like many others, believed the situation in Ghana was not as bad as in other places in Africa and elsewhere. Returning from Nigeria, she proposed an exposé of the rampant corruption there. Mayfield advised against such an article, which he feared would make them a laughingstock given the magnitude of the problem in Ghana.[23]

Mayfield brought out four issues of the *African Review* while preparing for and attending the Commonwealth conference in London and the OAU summit in Accra in October, a hectic pace that contributed to his decision to take a leave of absence in December. As always, Mayfield corresponded while in Ghana with African American friends back in the States. From Martin Kilson, a scholar of politics in West Africa who had recently returned to the United States after teaching at Legon, Mayfield learned of an event that shattered the American nation's perception of racial progress. Less than a week after the signing of the voting rights bill, residents of Watts, a black ghetto in Los Angeles, responded to an altercation between police and a young black man with firebombing attacks, targeting property owned by whites. Heavily armed Los Angeles police descended on Watts with their customary lack of restraint. All of the thirty-four people killed in Watts were black. Watts was not the first time that blacks and whites interpreted the same events differently, nor would it be the last. But the media images of black rage and the destruction it spawned and exaggerated reports of organized black snipers dredged up in the white American psyche the age-old nightmare of black insurrection. In fact, investigations later determined that most of what was believed to be sniping was actually indiscriminate firing by police and national guardsmen. Nevertheless, President Johnson's outraged response set the tone for pervasive and misplaced white fears of black violence: "Neither old wrongs nor new fears can justify arson and murder." Johnson and the nation were unable to acknowledge, as Godfrey Hodgson wrote, "that if blacks had committed a good deal of arson in Watts, the killing had been done by white men, and by white men in uniform at that."[24]

If the violence in Watts angered and appalled many whites, as it had Johnson, African Americans in Ghana and their allies back in the States interpreted events in Los Angeles as a new phase in the struggle. Watts revealed the awakened fury of long-invisible urban black masses demanding self-respect and recognition of their plight. Where the expatriates and their allies back in the United States had privileged Africa over America as the locus of meaningful change, the Watts uprising led some to view the United States as a highly fraught yet legitimate terrain of struggle. To Kilson, the rebellion rang down the curtain on a compliant middle-class black leadership and its decorous pas de deux with the establishment. But more importantly, the siege in Los Angeles suggested the irrelevance of Nkrumah's Ghana as the vessel of black revolutionary hopes. Kilson, who strongly objected to Nkrumah's autocratic leadership, bluntly told his friends Drake and Mayfield that the party was over in Ghana: "I've written all those 'revolutionary' [folks] around Accra about the riots and told them to make it home fast; phony exile radicalism in Accra is now for the birds . . . and they are needed here in all sorts of ways, as articulators of the new stage of Negro masses' assertion." Kilson urged Drake, who was also in the States, to convince the other black militants that Ghana constituted a dead end. In Kilson's eyes, Mayfield, Cordero, and the rest of the expatriates were needed in America to provide leadership and direction for insurgent blacks lest their assertiveness fester into hopelessness and despair.[25]

By November, a fatigued and discouraged Mayfield was finalizing his leave of absence from Ghana. But his plans did not include a return to the United States. Mayfield moved to the island of Ibiza, off Spain, where he lived in a house loaned to him by Guyanese writer and activist Jan Carew. Mayfield had engaged Carew, who was visiting Africa for the first time, to take over the magazine. Mayfield's January 1966 departure also effected his separation from Cordero, who remained with their children in Ghana, where she continued to run a women's clinic. Before leaving, Mayfield had secured the services of a promising young Achimota- and Harvard-educated Ghanaian writer, Ayi Kwei Armah. With his leave of absence from Ghana, Mayfield escaped the personal and political turmoil that defined his life there. Despite his misgivings about conditions in Ghana, Mayfield hoped to defend Nkrumah against the West's criticism with a book that explained Ghana's objectives and flaws within the crucial context of Western opposition to African unity. He left Ghana fully intending to return and resume his work in the Publicity Secretariat. Ironically, Nkrumah's overthrow enabled Mayfield to pull no punches in critically approaching his subject.

Mayfield's departure coincided with the final breakdown of relations between the U.S. and Ghanaian governments. In September, the Ghanaian government rejected the recommendation of a World Bank mission to cease trading with socialist countries and adopt stringent fiscal reforms. The government's refusal to accede to the bank's terms, as much as any of Ghana's difficulties, may well have sealed Nkrumah's fate.[26] In October, Nkrumah published *Neocolonialism: The Final Stage of Imperialism*, in time for distribution at the OAU summit in Accra. Forty years later, it may be difficult to imagine that the publication of a book could roil officials in the corridors of metropolitan power. Such, however, was the impact of Nkrumah's gloss on Lenin's *Imperialism: The Final Stage of Capitalism*, in which the Ghanaian leader sought to convince reluctant African states of the necessity for continental unity. Its detailed exposé of the West's financial stranglehold on African economies sparked outrage among U.S. officials, confirming their worst suspicions regarding Nkrumah's leftist leanings. For those who had for some time contemplated Nkrumah's ouster, the book's appearance represented the last straw after many months of articles and editorials in the Ghanaian press lambasting American imperialism, neocolonialism, and CIA subversion. Well before the book's appearance, the Ghanaian press had previewed the volume's thesis of persistent American and Western corporate control over the resources and economies of small, underdeveloped African nations after they achieved political independence. The book was said to have resulted from Nkrumah's collaborations with several expatriate ghostwriters, including Shirley Graham Du Bois, Dorothy Padmore, and Hodee Edwards, a white American woman linked by marriage to the African American expatriates. The government had engaged Edwards to help build the intellectual case for scientific rather than African socialism.[27]

Nkrumah had previously disclaimed responsibility when Ghanaian press attacks on the United States elicited protests from Ambassador William Mahoney. Journalists were free to write as they pleased, Nkrumah shrugged. He studiously kept aloof from the press's more radical utterances. The highly favorable terms enjoyed by the U.S.-based Kaiser Corporation for the Volta River project and Valco aluminum smelter notwithstanding, now that Nkrumah had signed his name to the condemnation of neocolonial Western financial interests, U.S. officials responded angrily. In Washington, Assistant Secretary of State G. Mennen Williams gave Ambassador Ribiero a tongue-lashing, threatening that Nkrumah's book would be the cause of any negative consequences that might ensue. Soon thereafter, Ghana's request to the United States for $100 million worth of emergency surplus food aid was turned down. Nkrumah's book merely gave State Department officials and the Johnson administration, who were already expecting a pro-Western coup against Nkrumah in July, a pretext to deny any material assistance that might prolong Nkrumah's regime.[28]

The furor over Nkrumah's book coincided with the crisis on the African continent sparked by the announcement by Ian Smith, the prime minister of Southern Rhodesia, of his country's unilateral declaration of independence (UDI) from Britain. Coming at a time when Britain had approved full independence to the neighboring African states of Zambia and Malawi while refusing to do so for Rhodesia, Smith's UDI defied the trend of decolonization and self-determination by consolidating the dominance of his country's white minority over the Africans who constituted 95 percent of the population. Smith justified his action, claiming that Rhodesia was a bulwark against the spread of communism on the African continent. Many African governments strongly protested the UDI and criticized Britain for refusing to take more forceful measures against Smith's regime. The UN ambassador to the moderate Ivory Coast urged African military intervention in Rhodesia, citing the recent alliance of Belgians, Americans, and the British for the so-called humanitarian rescue of white hostages in the Congo. The Johnson administration, leery of jeopardizing its relationship (and the heavy investments of U.S. financial interests) with South Africa and preoccupied by its extensive commitment of ground and air forces in Vietnam, condemned the UDI and imposed mild sanctions on Smith's government.[29]

Nkrumah joined other African governments in demanding military action against the Salisbury regime but appeared willing to back up his statements with action. He requested authorization from Parliament to form a militia and planned to begin recruitment, warning the population that sacrifices would be necessary.[30] Nkrumah's threats of military intervention provided an additional grievance to those army officers already plotting a coup against him. Indeed, training maneuvers in preparation for a possible intervention in

Rhodesia provided the coup leaders with the pretext for marching their troops to Accra.

Kofi Batsa, editor of the *Spark*, the voice of the CPP's left wing, recalled a Nkrumah visibly fatigued by Ghana's deepening political and economic problems. When Ghana broke off its relations with its primary trading partner, Great Britain, over Rhodesia's UDI, the downward economic spiral worsened. Years later, Batsa recalled Ernesto "Ché" Guevara's January 1965 visit to Ghana and the Bolivian revolutionary's reflections on the necessity of transforming a mass party into an organization of disciplined cadres. Batsa quoted Guevara: "In a party of cadres, every one of its members should accept being subject to an effective control of his ideological activity, and even of his private life." The demands for such a transition were so rigorous that a very careful selection of membership was necessary before any attempt at reorganizing the party structure could be made. After military coups overthrew several African governments beginning in 1964, including the Nigerian government in January 1966, Nkrumah assented to Chinese diplomats' suggestion that a "people's militia" be formed as a bulwark against a possible military coup. Though approved, the militia was never organized because of the lack of sufficient funds in the treasury.[31]

Ironically, as U.S. officials had decided that Nkrumah's support for Congolese rebels and intelligence operations against rival African governments made him expendable, Nkrumah sought to conciliate Washington, refraining from criticism of America's involvement in Vietnam.[32] In late January, Ambassador Mahoney returned for the dedication of the Volta hydroelectric dam. Mahoney, who had departed the previous summer, was replaced by Franklin Williams, an African American civil rights attorney and former Peace Corps official. Williams was an acquaintance of Nkrumah's from their days as classmates at Lincoln University. At the Volta dedication, Williams and Mahoney watched as Nkrumah praised the United States for upholding its share of the responsibility for the development of Africa.

With the failure of attempts to smooth over tensions with the United States, Batsa advised Nkrumah not to leave for Hanoi.[33] Against the advice of several aides, on February 21, 1966, Nkrumah boarded a jet bound for Beijing and then Hanoi while guards, aides, ministers, and diplomats at the airport reportedly speculated on the likelihood and timing of a coup. Three days later, Nkrumah arrived in Beijing, where Chou En Lai informed Nkrumah that his government had been overthrown by mutinous members of the army and police forces.

Nkrumah's absence had provided his enemies the chance to strike. Early on the morning of February 23, a convoy of six hundred troops in thirty-five vehicles traveled south from Tamale. After 150 miles they were met by two officers from Kumasi, Major Ekwensi Afrifa and Colonel Emmanuel Kotoka. Afrifa, who had contemplated plots against Nkrumah after returning from the Congo in 1962 and again in November 1964, took command, and the convoy continued the remaining 250 miles to the coast. Kotoka traveled ahead to Accra to notify General A. K. Ocran and Police Commissioner John Harlley that the coup could proceed as planned for 4:00 A.M. the next day. That night, the police began arresting Nkrumah's ministers, members of Parliament, and any CPP officials it could find. By dawn on February 24, Colonel Afrifa's column had reached Accra. Detachments of troops easily gained control of the radio station, airport, and cable office. The commander of the Ghanaian army, Major General Charles Barwah, was killed when he resisted the coup. The president's guard in Flagstaff House put up a fierce though brief resistance. The coup leaders installed General Joseph Ankrah, whom Nkrumah had dismissed in June 1965, at the head of the National Liberation Council. Ankrah informed the nation of the coup, citing Nkrumah's autocratic rule and corruption, the squandering of Ghana's reserves into massive external debts by ruinous policies, the "adventurism" of a communist-leaning foreign policy, and political interference in the army and police. At 6:00 A.M., Ankrah announced over Ghanaian radio that "the myth of Kwame Nkrumah is broken."[34]

The Coup through the Eyes of the Expatriates

Before dawn on February 24, Preston King was jolted awake by an explosion, followed by the crackling of rifle and small-arms fire. He awakened his wife, Hazel, and they set out from their residence near the university to investigate. They drove their Volkswagen Beetle through darkness toward the highway leading to Accra, where the firing seemed to originate. The sound of gunfire as they approached Flagstaff House convinced them that a coup was on. They stopped behind some empty army transport trucks, hearing persistent submachine gun and rifle fire. Mustering the nerve to venture closer to the shooting, the Kings were met by a young soldier, who warned of "trouble up ahead."[35]

The Kings wisely retreated and decided to visit Ana Livia Cordero, who lived nearby. It was still dark, about five o'clock in the morning. The gunfire crackled on, and a fire illuminated the gated entrance of Flagstaff House.

Intense return fire was coming from Flagstaff and the adjacent apartments used by security forces. Forced again to retreat, the Kings reached Cordero's house in ten minutes.

Cordero was there, along with several people who had converged on the premises, including Jan Carew, who had arrived a month earlier to assume the editorship of the *African Review*. All had been awakened by the explosions, and the shooting sounded frighteningly close. Making telephone inquiries, they learned that the radio station, airport, and police headquarters were controlled by the forces initiating the coup. Several ministers had been arrested in their homes, and some were falsely rumored to have been killed. Nkrumah's elite force, the Presidential Guard, and security officers at Flagstaff were holding out. With dire rumors circulating regarding the execution of government ministers, Geoffrey Bing sought asylum in the Australian High Commission, where he surrendered two days after the shooting stopped.

Careful to avoid soldiers posted at checkpoints, Preston King decided to return to Flagstaff House to assess the situation there. By afternoon, the shooting had subsided, with no guards visible along the road from the south. Independence Avenue was littered with the wreckage of smashed vehicles and army trucks. The entrance to Flagstaff was blocked by two vehicles, a small sedan and a large sand-dumping truck. The front of the car was riddled with bullets, the windshield gone. A door hung open, with a bloodied shoe sitting outside it. The bodies of a man, a woman, and a child remained in the car, civilians caught in the cross fire. The truck's only sign of damage was a single bullet hole in the windshield. The southern-facing wall of Flagstaff House was pockmarked by bullet holes, with several gaping holes evidently made by grenade explosions. As King recalled, "Suddenly, there was a tremendous explosion behind me," at the barracks for security personnel across the road. King hit the ground. He heard doors slamming and then the ominous sound of "evenly spaced and deliberate rifle shots." Near the gate sat a riddled Ghana Airways bus. It had been raked by machine gun fire while traveling past Flagstaff House toward the airport that morning. One of the flight hostesses inside had been killed, and many of the rest had been wounded. King learned that several university workers had died in the same way.

Inside the main gate, in front of Flagstaff House, two army trucks were smoldering, hit by mortar shells. Other trucks and vehicles had been damaged in the fighting. The main gate still stood, though surrounded by signs of carnage. Abandoned rifles, submachine guns, helmets, and shoes were strewn about. Blood patches dotted the road like the painterly handiwork of death itself, the grisly scene further adorned by broken glass and a lingering haze of smoke. A solitary, overlooked corpse of a soldier lay in a trench. No one was in sight.

As King decided to rejoin his wife, a truckload of soldiers brandishing weapons raced by. The sound of gunfire resumed, this time from deeper within Flagstaff House. As King passed the car and the truck, a little boy appeared, whispering that a dead man was inside the truck. Peering in, King saw a young man, doubled over in his seat, a bullet hole in his temple. "I climbed on the running board to make sure he was dead. The boy who had seen him now was repeating in a muted voice, may he rest in peace."

Any further curiosity dampened by the sight of the dead man, King headed back to Cordero's house, where he found Hazel. Preston and Hazel King returned home to Legon, where students lost no time in persecuting the new regime's enemies. Students mobbed a Chinese student and rounded up student members of the CPP for similar beatings, ransacking their rooms for good measure. The once-mighty Willie Abraham, vice chancellor pro tem of the university and Nkrumah's court philosopher, was arrested and detained. The university hastily pledged its support to the new regime without consulting the faculty. "Everyone is assuring the new regime of everyone's support," King observed drily. Such declarations of unanimity struck him as being just as dubious as those only recently staged by the ousted regime.

In subsequent days, King gathered information about what had transpired. Only a fragment of the army had taken part in the coup. No more than seven hundred troops stationed five hundred miles north of Accra had been involved. The troops, under the command of Major Afrifa and Colonel Kotoka, were incited by rumors that Nkrumah intended to have them fight in Rhodesia and Vietnam and that Russians were taking over Ghana. The troops were divided into three groups. One seized control of the airport and then headed for the Accra garrison. Other detachments of troops took control of the castle at Osu (formerly Christianborg Castle) and the Broadcasting House before moving on to the siege at Flagstaff House. The soldiers then demolished the quarters of security officers, looting the residences, beating and raping the residents, and shooting those who resisted. The initial attack on Flagstaff House cost the rebel troops twenty men killed and many more wounded. The coup leaders expected forces loyal to Nkrumah to arrive from Ho and Sekondi-Takoradi to resist, but these troops never came. A separate attack on a government munitions facility lasted for two days, with seventeen attackers and twelve defenders killed.

Based on his investigations, King estimated the number of dead at at least

two hundred, basing that figure on a coroner's estimate. King regarded the
initial reports of a bloodless coup as "part of the old style of lying mer-
cilessly." The government had forbidden morgue workers and pathologists to
divulge casualty figures in an effort to safeguard the legitimacy of its action.
In any event, the toll was high, with many people killed inside Flagstaff
House. Others, mostly security personnel, were killed in the flats nearby
while sleeping. Many civilians, including stewards and other workers, had
been caught in the cross fire. While King's estimate was more conservative
than those of other expatriates and later Nkrumah's, it contradicted Ghanaian and U.S. press reports of a bloodless coup. That characterization was,
in fact, the official American version of events, encouraged by Ambassador Williams and the State Department in anticipation of the allegations of
slaughter by the nation's political adversaries.[36]

As best King could discern, the coup by the self-proclaimed National Liberation Council (NLC) was being handled smoothly and effectively. Nkrumah's wife and children were spirited out of the country in a jet supplied by
Egypt's President Nasser and exiled to Cairo. None of the ministers was
executed, and martial law was not imposed. But the Preventive Detention
Act, often cited as evidence of Nkrumah's dictatorial methods, proved as
useful to the NLC as it had been to the previous government. The council
freed twelve hundred prisoners imprisoned by Nkrumah, clearing the jails
for as many members of Parliament, high-ranking ministers, security men,
advisers, and journalists as could be arrested. The CPP was banned outright.
According to King and contrary to press reports, none of the mass demonstrations hailing the coup and its leaders was spontaneous. As before the
coup, they were staged, this time by the NLC. King correctly predicted that
the military regime would terminate the Nkrumah government's costly prestige, propaganda, and anticolonial liberation projects. Freedom fighters
from other parts of the continent were expelled. Frank Robertson took on
himself the responsibility and cost of arranging the safe passage to Tanzania
of more than a dozen freedom fighters.[37]

King wrote his eyewitness account of the Ghana coup within a week of the
events it recorded and mailed copies to family and friends in the States.
King's boldness and curiosity produced an account that both supplements
and contradicts aspects of official Ghanaian and U.S. versions of the coup.
While King saw the coup as very much the result of Nkrumah's excesses and
errors, he grasped that the new regime perpetuated the undemocratic practices of the deposed CPP. Overall, King's response to the coup was the mea-

sured one of a sympathizer troubled by Nkrumah's failures but convinced that the coup represented a setback for the aspirations of Ghanaians and Africans.

For anyone living near Flagstaff House, the terror of the fighting, looting, harassment, and threatened detention by troops made for a harrowing experience. On the whole, university-affiliated personnel were left alone. Those expatriates closely aligned with Nkrumah, such as Geoffrey Bing and H. M. Basner, were detained and faced mistreatment at the hands of troops. Had he been in Ghana, Julian Mayfield would have been detained. Shirley Graham Du Bois was taken into custody and deported, first to London and then to Cairo, having been prevented from securing her possessions, including her late husband's library and mementos. With the assistance of her brother and attorney Bernard Jaffe, who rushed to Ghana at news of the coup, the Du Boises' possessions were placed in storage shortly before the NLC granted a Ghanaian jurist and his wife possession of the Du Boises' home.[38]

Another expatriate, Sylvia Boone, wrote an informative and insightful account of the coup while in Ghana three months after the event and included it in a lengthy letter to Mayfield. Along with her reactions and analysis, Boone recorded the fates of members of the expatriates' circle. Somber yet attuned to the absurdities and intrigues of the situation, Boone's letter likened the coup to the day of Kennedy's assassination, a moment eternally suspended in memory. Amid speculation as to which minister would replace Nkrumah, Boone traveled with a friend to the Trans Volta region. There, market and harvest celebrations continued without interruption or even awareness of the violence in the capital. Boone and her companion found the situation "hotter" when they returned to Accra that evening. Police stationed along the road repeatedly stopped and searched their car. There was nothing to do but go home.[39]

For a couple of days, Boone recalled, a shocked silence prevailed in Accra as people waited to see what would happen. In castigating Ghanaians for what she perceived as their defeatism, Boone voiced a mordant version of pan-African solidarity expressed by other black expatriates after the coup, drawing a parallel between African American and African "Uncle Tom-ism." Boone might have noted, however, that good reasons existed for caution. Mobility was still restricted by checkpoints, and police were harassing the public with frequent searches. Hundreds of people were being arrested. Accra was abuzz with stories of escapes and near escapes and of soldiers' menace and capriciousness. An unnamed African American woman's house had been robbed by soldiers, who also threatened to rape her. In the end,

they decided to spare her that fate because she was a "civil servant." One
government minister monitored events from his veranda, unmolested by
soldiers. The next day, after the radio announcement calling for the surrender of all party officials, ministers, and political appointees, this minister
turned himself in. The minister of finance was reportedly apprehended while
disguised as a woman and attempting to board a boat in Tema.[40]

Contradicting King, Boone confirmed reports of the popular jubilation
that greeted the coup. After two days, "absolute hilarity broke out. . . .
[P]eople were genuinely delighted." Students, market women, army wives,
erstwhile Young Pioneers, and even jockeys on horseback paraded daily,
damning the old and praising the new. Bars and hotels were jammed to
capacity with revelers taking advantage of the absence of security men to
freely and loudly express their opinions. People keenly aware that a careless
statement might land them in detention undoubtedly felt liberated by the
end of Nkrumah's reign. At the same time, public demonstrations against
Nkrumah and in support of the NLC suggested that the CPP's invisible surveillance had been replaced by the openly intimidating presence of armed
soldiers. In this atmosphere, gossip and rumor flourished, encouraged by the
NLC's determination to destroy the president's image. Nkrumah's parentage
and Ghanaian citizenship were widely disputed. Each new rumor, however
outlandish, was eventually sanctioned by a serious news story printed in the
NLC-controlled *Evening News*. The carnival atmosphere even extended to the
newly incarcerated party officials, according to a friend of Boone's who had
been jailed. (While such may well have been the case for small fry, troops
and police menaced Bing and other high-ranking expatriate prisoners.)[41]
Those Ghanaians with whom Boone spoke saw the coup as having had
nothing to do with national liberation. Rather, her informants welcomed the
coup as a vehicle for their personal ambitions, which they believed had been
unfairly stifled under Nkrumah's regime.[42]

Among the expatriates' wider circle of Nkrumah loyalists, several Nige-
rians were deported to their country of origin, including S. G. Ikoku, who
was tortured and flown to Nigeria in a canvas sack. There, they languished in
detention after Nigeria's crackdown on leftist individuals and groups. William Gardner and Solange Smith returned to France weeks after the coup.
Like other expatriates whose talents made them useful to the NLC, Bill Smith
was courted by the authorities, but he declined the NLC's offer to stay on as a
newspaper editor and was allowed to leave the country with passage for the
whole family paid. Carew remained longer after a brief stint in detention.
The *African Review* was banned, and Carew eventually left, his expenses paid

by the new government. Not as fortunate was artist Tom Feelings, less prominent than the others but prominent enough in his association with Nkrumah to be persona non grata. Evicted from his house, he was forced to leave at his own expense. Troops ignored Preston and Hazel King as well as other university personnel, who benefited from the relative independence gained by the university with the change of regimes. Maryse Condé, a novelist from Guadeloupe who taught Francophone literature at the Ideological Institute in Winneba, was jailed but obtained her release with the assistance of a Ghanaian attorney friend. Condé was then expelled. Julia Wright Hervé and her husband took refuge in the Cuban embassy until friends persuaded them to leave the country, which they did at NLC expense. The skills of the African American "workers," or technicians, seemed to earn them a protected status. One nonpolitical expatriate landed a job with the Kaiser Corporation, earning U.S. dollars. Carlos Allston, the African American director of All-Afra Electric, welcomed the coup as good for business, disappointing his partner, Frank Robertson.

Boone also reported to Mayfield the fate of their Ghanaian comrades. Writer and playwright Christina (Ama Ata) Aidoo was soon to depart to begin a fellowship at Harvard. Ayi Kwei Armah refused to take a loyalty oath imposed by the NLC and was promptly sacked from his university job. He then accepted a teaching job in Navrongo in the Northern Territories. Nana Nketsia IV, a pro-Nkrumah Ashanti chief and friend of Mayfield and Maya Angelou, went into hiding. Efua Sutherland, a playwright and director of the Ghana Drama Studio, was vilified in the rampant anti-Nkrumah mudslinging. She denied allegations that she had received government money to build her home. She was fine but disgusted at the turn of events.

Boone reported that the Chinese ambassador, Huang Hua, a favorite of the Afros and future foreign minister of China, had fortunately been out of the country; he was eventually deported. The Russian and Chinese embassy staffs were decimated by deportations. Freedom fighters from throughout the African continent who were receiving training at the African Affairs Center under the guidance of T. Ras Makonnen and Chinese advisers were deported, reportedly deposited by several planeloads in Dar es Salaam. Boone added incredulously that the NLC had pledged its support to African liberation movements through the toothless OAU. Signaling their break with Nkrumah's anticolonialism as well as their pro-American orientation, the NLC also claimed that apartheid South Africa was a legally constituted government.

The coup had drastically altered the expatriates' outlook toward an African people they had once regarded as progressive. Boone reported that one

Efua Sutherland, late 1960s. (Willis E. Bell)

of their mutual friends, probably another African American expatriate, had angrily written to her in the most disparaging terms about blacks as the "unreadiest people God or whoever made." Boone agreed, despite the harsh words, claiming that Ghanaians capitulated not because they were being tortured but because "a soldier threatened to break a vase." What Boone presumed to be the failure of Ghanaians reflected badly on people of African descent across the board. She and other supporters of African unity and development had little patience for the renunciation of worldly power and modern technique they associated with Negritude. Yet her frustration at

THE COUP

Nkrumah's overthrow provoked cynical and even stereotypical musings about the psychology of oppressed black people. Even their militancy was circumscribed by what was evidently their true calling in Western culture—entertaining whites. After all, whites crowded to be insulted by LeRoi Jones, and even Malcolm, for all his virtues, provided irresistible television fare. Boone was certainly correct about the mass media's capacity to reduce black opposition to spectacle. But her sweeping assessment of African-descended people as lacking the seriousness to carry off a revolution reopened wounds created by Western culture's assault on the image of Africa. For Boone and others, Nkrumah and Ghana had been a reassuring balm. With the coup and the elimination of Ghana's revolutionary hope, a sense of historical inadequacy returned with a vengeance.

Gender played a substantial role in Boone's analysis of the self-imposed obstacles to the fulfillment of black radical aspirations. Shifting from Ghana to the United States, Boone identified a problem that would continue to plague black activism for years to come. The exclusion of black women from leadership and equal participation in activist groups and organizations demonstrated the lack of revolutionary commitment by black men—"all of them." Mayfield was not exempted from her accusation. All black men, she told him, wanted black women out of black and nationalist groups. "You use two strategies—let a black chick *head* the movement, then you all sabotage it or pull out." Here, Boone was referring to the Organization of Afro-American Unity, which historian Bill Sayles contended had been debilitated by male resentment at the prominent role played by women organizers. The situation was so poisonous that Malcolm had defended the leadership of women at a meeting of the group the night before his murder.[43] The other strategy by which black women were shunted aside referred to white women's disproportionate influence within interracial organizations such as the Congress of Racial Equality, the Student Nonviolent Coordinating Committee, and the National Association for the Advancement of Colored People. Malcolm X, she believed, understood this well enough to insist on the inclusion of black women, "knowing that all other groups had planned them out."[44]

Boone doubted that the expatriates had contributed anything toward building socialism or African unity. "For all I know our roles were highly parasitic." Although she understood the quixotic nature of Nkrumah's pan-Africanism, she chose not to dwell on it. Although Nkrumah had failed, Boone praised him for managing the feat of getting black people to build and work together. Boone could forgive Nkrumah's deficiencies given his serious bid for authentic power as evidenced by his plans for a munitions factory complex and his unprecedented willingness to use state and military power in the service of African liberation. Whatever personal corruption Nkrumah may have engaged in paled before the fact that African liberation parties and movements numbered among the main beneficiaries of Ghana's largesse.

Boone described the coup's dampening effect on Accra society. Depression was endemic among the people she knew, a postcoup hangover brought on by personal and political dreams yet again unfulfilled. Office seekers did not advance as they had anticipated, and journalists were dismayed to learn that they labored under conditions of censorship as stringent as those of the old regime. Boone ended ominously, acknowledging the disorder and brutality entirely absent from press accounts of the coup. According to Boone, a friend of Nkrumah, Genoveva Marais, a South African who worked in Ghanaian television, had been raped "continually and brutally," as were the "girl friends" and companions of government ministers. The wife of a prominent minister was forced to submit to gain her husband's release from jail and prevent the destruction of property.

In stark contrast to the accounts of Boone and other eyewitnesses, the version of the coup advanced by U.S. officials was echoed by the major Western news organizations, which portrayed the action as the humanitarian rescue of the Ghanaian people from Nkrumah's tyranny. In the coup's immediate aftermath, Ambassador Williams, the State Department, and Johnson administration aides were concerned with managing the worldwide perception of events in Ghana. Williams's version of events from Ghana provides a fascinating contrast with the expatriates' accounts. Washington replied tellingly to Williams's reports of the situation and his relaying of the NLC's appeal for economic assistance. The first move was the NLC's in channeling its requests for assistance through the same international lending agencies—that is, the International Monetary Fund and the World Bank—whose conditions Nkrumah had refused to accept.[45] Without naming his sources, Williams wrote a note to Johnson aide Bill Moyers celebrating the "extremely fortunate" occurrence and noting that "all the personalities involved are strong friends of ours." Also noteworthy to Williams was the lack of violence and bloodshed, save for the death of Major General Barwah, which Williams inaccurately suggested might have been a suicide. He praised the coup leaders for their restraint in allowing security officers three hours to surrender before attacking.[46] Whatever his methods of obtaining information, his reports on the coup to State Department officials and colleagues in the foreign service were shaped by U.S. national security imperatives and accordingly sought to cast events in the most favorable light. The note contained the first of Williams's several personal appeals to Moyers for economic assistance for the new regime: "Bill, this is the kind of change people like you and I hope for. It must succeed—it can succeed—but we're going to have to be responsive and vigorous in that response."[47]

But assistance of the magnitude Williams sought as well as an official recognition of the NLC would have to wait. Responding to the NLC's pressure for U.S. recognition too quickly might lend credence to charges that the U.S. had masterminded the takeover. The State Department thus deemed it prudent to wait until other African states recognized the new regime. A White House memorandum agreed that caution was warranted yet acknowledged that "privately, we think Nkrumah's demise is great."[48] Ambassador Williams assured State of Ankrah's anticommunism and his total compliance with U.S. objectives. Williams sent another exultant missive to Moyers about "our local coup," reiterating quid pro quo requests for support. Williams would have been dismayed by the cynical response of the administration's national security team. Assessing the coup as a "fortuitous windfall" and the ousted Nkrumah as having done "more to undermine our interests than any other black African," Johnson's national security affairs adviser described the NLC as "almost pathetically pro-Western." Only a little support would be required to keep the new government in the U.S. camp. A modest gift to the NLC (and the pro-American military regime that had recently toppled Indonesia's Sukarno) of a "few thousand tons of surplus wheat or rice" would suffice. Anticipating the State Department's reluctance to provide even minimal assistance, the aide insisted that lavish aid was unnecessary—"indeed giving them a little only whets their appetites, and enables us to use the prospect of more as leverage." Days later, Williams again wrote to Moyers, imploring him to help break the "log jam" stalling an Agency for International Development package for Ghana and citing the threat of famine in the north and the prospect of Nkrumah's return.[49]

In an account of the coup written from exile in Guinea, where Sekou Touré had given Nkrumah asylum, the deposed leader accused Williams and the CIA of complicity in the action. This perception of Williams's involvement would persist among advocates of African liberation throughout the black world.[50] Williams strongly denied any involvement in the coup and enlisted an intermediary to convey his denial to Nkrumah.[51] Such suspicions of CIA involvement and Williams's complicity in the Ghana coup are supported by a sanitized letter CIA Director Richard Helms wrote to Williams. Helms acknowledged Williams's letter praising the recent work of the station chief in Accra and informed Williams that the unnamed official had been rewarded with a promotion within the agency.[52] Williams's conduct after the coup did little to dispel such suspicions. The ambassador responded to a defense of Nkrumah by Elizabeth Drake published in the *Palo Alto Times* (her husband, St. Clair Drake, had recently been a visiting professor at Stanford). Elizabeth Drake noted the "indecent haste" with which U.S. officials recognized the "government" established by the military coup. That official recognition came just a week after the coup "can only serve to deepen the widespread conviction among Africans and others, that the coup was accomplished with the active connivance of the U.S. and certain Western allies." For Drake, the lesson was that governments of small, underdeveloped countries were defenseless against the alliance of U.S. officialdom and military dictators.

Williams responded by claiming in a letter to the *Times* that Elizabeth Drake had failed to understand conditions in Ghana and the significance of diplomatic recognition. The NLC "exercised complete control of the country and enjoyed the overwhelming support of the people." Williams asserted that the people of Ghana did not share Drake's favorable assessment of Nkrumah's rule. In support of this claim, Williams invoked Robert Gardiner, the Ghanaian executive secretary of the United Nations Economic Commission for Africa. According to Williams, Gardiner returned after the coup to proclaim at a press conference that Ghanaians "perhaps did not realize how close they came to starvation"—they would have run out of food in two months if Nkrumah had not been overthrown. Neglecting to mention the enmity between Gardiner and Nkrumah,[53] Williams cited Nkrumah's betrayal by most of his senior ministers and officials as proof of the deposed leader's lack of popularity in Ghana and the NLC government's support of the people.[54]

Elizabeth Drake and other expatriate sympathizers saw the coup as a grossly undemocratic action sanctioned by U.S. officialdom. Drake forcefully contested the official story that Ghanaians had hailed the NLC as saviors. Demonstrations to that effect were staged, if not compelled at gunpoint. In such a climate, few people risked public support for Nkrumah. One of the chief methods employed by the NLC and its troops to destroy Nkrumah's image and charisma was the destruction of the many portraits of the president. Many Ghanaians, including one of the black American expatriates, had preemptively burned their pictures and paintings of the "Old Man."[55] According to Nkrumah, a woman in the Makola market in Accra had been executed after refusing to remove his picture over her stall.[56] The NLC raided the offices of Flagstaff House, destroying many of the records of Nkrumah's government, and bonfires of books, pamphlets, and records associated with

240   the CPP and its expatriate supporters were a common sight.[57] According to his biographer, E. Franklin Frazier's library, donated to Ghana in an act of pan-African idealism, was reportedly destroyed during this rampage.[58] Numerous ministers obtained their release from detention by testifying to Nkrumah's corruption before NLC commissions of inquiry whose purpose was to discredit the president before Ghanaians and world opinion. Like Boone, several African American expatriates marveled at the sorry spectacle of some of the most venal ministers securing their own fortunes by fabricating tales of Nkrumah's personal corruption, his dependency on juju priests, and so on, slanders gleefully detailed in the Ghanaian and Western press. Although Nkrumah had tolerated unacceptable levels of corruption to secure the mercenary allegiance of Ghanaian chiefs, professionals, and nouveau riche elements within the CPP, accusations of his personal corruption were exaggerated.[59] Their propagandistic intent was to undermine the source of Nkrumah's popularity among Africans and African-descended peoples in the West: Nkrumah's use of Ghana's resources for its diplomatic and foreign policy objectives of anticolonialism, material and military aid to nationalist parties, and continental unity. The widespread violence, rapes, beatings, vandalism, looting, and detentions that had occurred in the aftermath of the coup suggested that Ambassador Williams's claim, to a colleague at the United Nations, that the coup was carried out in a "sensitive, civilized fashion" was at best premature.[60]

From Ibiza, Mayfield corresponded with fellow expatriates in and out of Ghana and with Clarke in Harlem, trying to sort out actual conditions in Ghana from press accounts of the coup and news and rumors emanating from throughout Africa. The coup had enhanced the timeliness of Mayfield's study of Nkrumah and Ghana for a New York publisher. Events had also strengthened Mayfield's determination to understand what had gone wrong in Ghana. Choosing critical analysis over apologetics, Mayfield argued that the glee throughout the West at Nkrumah's overthrow had not erupted because he was a dictator or corrupt or because he had wrecked Ghana's economy; rather, the true source of the widespread scorn for Nkrumah was the ideological threat he posed to Western interests. Mayfield sought to draw out for posterity the lessons of Nkrumah's mistakes. Clarke shared with Mayfield a lengthy account from Ghana by Hodee Edwards, whom John Tettegah had recently fired as a writer and researcher. Mayfield agreed with Edwards's analysis that Nkrumah had been brought down by the corrupt bargain between neocolonial expatriate firms and self-seeking CPP ministers and by his failure to smash the colonial machinery inherited from the British, particularly the army and police. Surrounded by rascals, Nkrumah became isolated from ordinary Ghanaians, who refused to lift a finger when a fraction of the army moved against him.[61] Months after the coup, Mayfield implored Clarke not to commit *Freedomways* to the glorification of Nkrumah's image.[62] In late March Ana Livia Cordero had been held incommunicado for ten days before being released. The NLC detained her after learning that Mayfield had communicated with Nkrumah in Conakry for his book. (Mayfield had forwarded to the exiled leader a list of pointed questions, which went unanswered.) Cordero was expelled from Ghana in June, and she and Mayfield publicized the incident in the United States, exposing the falsity of General Ankrah's claim that the NLC had restored freedom and individual rights.[63]

By late 1966, Mayfield was sending his manuscript, "The Lonely Warrior," to friends, including Preston King, St. Clair Drake, and Clarke. Mayfield argued that Nkrumah was a great albeit flawed man who, in retrospect, had little chance of succeeding against the West. Nkrumah was a statesman whose valiant fight for African liberation would outlive the petty charges of corruption. When Mayfield started working in the former president's office, "I sneered like all the rest about the impossibility of realizing African unity." Before long, however, "I understood its absolute necessity." So did Africa's enemies, who were determined to prevent it and to eliminate any leaders bent on achieving it, as seen by the fates of Malcolm, Lumumba, and Felix Moumie, the Cameroonian nationalist mysteriously poisoned in 1960.

Clarke balked at Mayfield's request to forward the manuscript to Conor Cruise O'Brien because of his public criticisms of Nkrumah. O'Brien, in Clarke's view, had joined the chorus of Western damnation, and Clarke would now have nothing to do with O'Brien. Having set forth the premises for his book, Mayfield defended O'Brien. Mayfield had witnessed the government's attack on O'Brien. For people who had not been there, the best analogy of "what it was like in government circles during certain ridiculous periods is to refer back to the McCarthy days in America." Once a person had been declared suspect, "you were not supposed to even say hello to him." As a journalist, Mayfield was offended by the pettiness of the calumnies directed at O'Brien in the Ghanaian press, which ill served the nation and should have been stopped by Nkrumah. If Mayfield had been subjected to attack without the means to fight back, as O'Brien had, Mayfield would have felt entitled to expose Nkrumah in the world press.[64]

For Mayfield, as with so many of Nkrumah's expatriate supporters, a sense of the necessity of African unity, however elusive, in combination with the extensive and growing record of U.S. intervention in global affairs, provided the proper context for discussing Nkrumah's errors without necessarily condoning them. From Cairo, Mayfield's friend David Du Bois and his mother, Shirley Graham Du Bois, maintained close contact with Nkrumah in Conakry. They, along with Alice Windom, now employed on the secretarial staff of the Economic Commission for Africa in Addis Ababa, and journalist Charles Howard, hoped to aid Nkrumah's restoration. Howard flooded the African American press with rebuttals and refutations of the anti-Nkrumah onslaught in the Western press and the official U.S. version of the coup. The indefatigable Howard even confronted Ambassador Williams and voiced objections to members of the NLC at press gatherings. Mayfield heard frequently from Du Bois and Windom but seemed less hopeful than they were of Nkrumah's return to power. Overcoming his reluctance to return to the States, Mayfield accepted a fellowship at Cornell University for the new academic year, planning to lecture on African American literature and politics.[65]

The destruction of his vision offers a glimpse of Nkrumah's appeal for the expatriates and for many people of African descent. But inescapably, with so much at stake for some of the expatriates, their disappointment included in some measure a personal sense of betrayal by Nkrumah and an equally personal sense of their own failure. Windom, who had produced accounts of the demonstration at the U.S. embassy and later of Malcolm's visit, expressed these mixed feelings in her reports to Mayfield from Ethiopia on the intolerable levels of crime, poverty, and brutal repression under the pro-American regime of Haile Selassie, fueling her nostalgia for Ghana. Although he might have differed with parts of it, Mayfield would have agreed with her general assessment: "I did fail Ghana and of course [so did] all the expatriates including you." Why had they failed to challenge the sycophants surrounding Nkrumah? Although Nkrumah was a proud African who demanded a place for peoples of African descent in world affairs, "he failed us. He starved us. . . . Kwame has let you all down." For Windom's part, as she marked time in Addis, she read Malcolm's autobiography and Fanon's *Wretched of the Earth*, trying to wring inspiration from these posthumous texts.[66]

Although he had his defenders, Nkrumah's many detractors in the United States came from both the left and on the right. Nkrumah dismissed his leftist critics as naive purists who would discard the revolutionary baby with its bathwater.[67] While maintaining an active correspondence with supporters and working in vain to orchestrate his return to power in Ghana, Nkrumah attended to writing his account of the coup, published as *Dark Days in*

Ghana, in which he defended himself against accusations of corruption. He sought to refute Western news organizations' indulgent treatment of the NLC, breaking the silence on the troops' acts of murder, rape, torture, and looting. The closest Nkrumah came to self-criticism was in acknowledging the contradiction created by his having prioritized Ghana's external policy of African liberation and unity at the expense of the nation's internal affairs. Nkrumah believed that the urgent pursuit of continental unity precluded his ability to address the inadequacies of the CPP structure. Then, too, he had tried to make a socialist revolution peacefully, with foreign capital investment and without convinced socialists to carry out his vision. Beyond this, Nkrumah admitted of little second-guessing or soul-searching. Nkrumah was a brilliant organizer and politician, and his subsequent emphasis on neocolonialism as the root of Africa's ills had much validity; nevertheless, that analysis remained a barrier to sustained self-criticism. As the inevitable confrontation with the West loomed, his acquiescence to widespread corruption and his intolerance of dissent undermined his popular support. It is ironic, then, that Nkrumah's analysis of the coup would invoke Richard Wright's open letter from *Black Power,* which called for Nkrumah to militarize Ghanaian society. As Nkrumah saw it, Wright had provided a justification for the deposed leader's undemocratic measures.[68] In retrospect, however, Nkrumah's reliance on expatriates and ultimately the Ghanaian people required greater rather than less democratic freedom. While a less repressive atmosphere would not have deterred Nkrumah's adversaries from plotting his removal, it might have enabled the survival of his regime, sparing the people of Ghana the trauma and tragedy of the coup whose ultimate purpose was never to liberate them.

8

AFTER GHANA

Ways of Seeing, Ways of Being

After the coup, few African American expatriates remained in Africa. Although Tanzania under the leadership of Julius Nyerere replaced Ghana as the leading exponent of African liberation and continental unity, only Bill Sutherland among the Ghanaian expatriates emigrated there. The Huntons ended up in Zambia, where Alphaeus died in 1970; Alice Windom worked at the United Nations Economic Commission for Africa in Addis Ababa. Shirley Graham Du Bois and her son, David, resided in Cairo until she moved on to China. Preston King took a teaching job in Kenya, continuing a distinguished if nomadic career as a political philosopher that carried him to far-flung positions throughout the British commonwealth until a pardon by President Bill Clinton ended almost forty years of exile and enforced separation from his family in Albany, Georgia. Victoria Garvin settled in Beijing, working as a government translator and polishing the English syntax of official communiqués.

Dispersed by the coup, most of the African American expatriates returned to the United States to pursue careers or to confront anew the challenge of making a living. With the ouster of Nkrumah's government and as black movement activism was weakened by a combination of assassinations, government repression, and internecine conflict, many of the expatriate "Afros" turned inward. Those involved with *Freedomways* continued the struggle over black politics and collective memory. Sharing a unique bond, the former expatriates corresponded among themselves, encouraging each others' efforts, reflecting on events in the United States and Africa, offering congratulations or consolation as needed, and apprising comrades of recent news from third parties. They discussed current events, but in some cases, the present paled in comparison to the Ghana they had known. Windom served for many years as a corresponding secretary for the group, linking the scattered former expatriates with those who remained in Ghana, including dentists Robert and Sarah Lee and technicians Frank Robertson and Carlos Allston. A year after the coup, Windom wrote to Julian Mayfield of her sense of isolation and lack of stimulating company. "The Ghana experience was so important, and the collapse of the dream so devastating that I don't think I can get anything of value from someone who didn't live through that."[1]

Time and distance enabled the expatriates to overcome the trauma and disruption of the coup. With varying degrees of success, they pursued intellectual and cultural projects that sought to cultivate a politically conscious black public sphere. Though separated by distance, this tight-knit community enacted the vision that their singular experience in Ghana had instilled in them through their various literary, intellectual, and artistic projects. As witnesses to a momentous yet misunderstood period in the history of the black world, some endeavored to tell their story in memoirs or worked to publicly commemorate black history. As a Yale professor, Sylvia Boone led historic-preservation efforts commemorating New Haven's role in the insurrection by African captives aboard the slave ship *Amistad* on the 150th anniversary of that event. During the early 1990s, Dr. Robert Lee became involved in efforts to refurbish the slave castles on the coast of Ghana as monuments to the slave trade, traveling to the United States to enlist African American support for the endeavor. Those who had known Malcolm X viewed the commodification of his legacy, including the 1992 film biography by Spike Lee, with proprietary uneasiness. Among those who remained politically active, Jean Carey Bond continued her involvement with *Freedomways* and became a founding member during the early 1990s of the Black Radical Congress, a revival of the 1930s-era National Negro Congress in which St. Clair Drake had participated.

Nkrumah's Ghana had changed the lives of these men and women and had endowed them with a unique perspective on the politics of the African diaspora. The vision of an expansive, interconnected black world informed by traditions of black nationalism and radicalism and epitomized by Ghana informed their assessments of the continuing struggles of Africans and African Americans. That way of seeing the connections between Africa and its diaspora informed their conception of being in the world as peoples of African descent. Most of all, they were active members of that segment of committed, conscious, and progressive people for whom blackness, otherwise a malleable if not vacuous concept, entailed a specific historical, spiritual, and ethical commitment to democracy and social justice. In one sense, through their commitment to the preservation of an African American cultural heritage and collective memory, including the legacies of such mentors and colleagues as Paul Robeson, W. E. B. Du Bois, Malcolm X, and Lorraine Hansberry, they had assumed the cultural leadership that E. Franklin Frazier had found so sorely lacking among the African American intelligentsia during the late 1950s. But in another sense, even after their return, they became exiles within an America defined by conservative backlash and the deferred dreams of social and economic freedom and citizenship. They became exiles from their own past within an America also defined by the erasure of the memory of Nkrumah's Ghana and all it meant for African American consciousness.

The Ghana Coup Contested

For the former expatriates and others committed to African liberation, the overthrow of Nkrumah's government sparked angry controversy throughout Africa and its diaspora. Guinea, Mali, Egypt, and Tanzania registered their protests by refusing to recognize the military tribunal of the National Liberation Council (NLC). In a gesture of solidarity, Sekou Touré granted asylum to Nkrumah, declared him copresident of Guinea, and installed him in a modest seaside villa. Touré showed his disdain for the NLC by closing down Ghana's embassy and placing its resources at Nkrumah's disposal. Tanzanian Prime Minister Julius Nyerere denounced the coup and defended Nkrumah against the torrent of vilification unleashed by the metropolitan press. "The enemies of Africa are now jubilant," Nyerere told a press conference. He was certain that the white minority governments of Rhodesia and South Africa rejoiced at Nkrumah's demise. Nkrumah's overthrow and the previous month's coup in Nigeria were comprehensible only within a neocolonial framework. Anyone could see that this coup would not help Africa. "Kwame was absolutely committed to true independence. . . . Divided as we are, we shall be weak. Kwame was completely uncompromising on African unity. Whom was he angering? Not Africa."[2]

Tanzania under Nyerere's leadership was a natural successor to Ghana as a leading advocate, along with Touré's Guinea, of continental unity and pan-Africanism. Tanzania challenged the West through a commitment to nonalignment and pan-African ideals, becoming the headquarters of the Organization of African Unity's liberation committee. Like Nkrumah, Nyerere supported nationalist movements throughout southern Africa, including the African National Congress, the Zimbabwe African National Union, the Zimbabwe African People's Union, and the Popular Movement for the Liberation of Angola. In 1965, Tanzania, like Ghana, had broken off diplomatic relations with Britain after it refused to intervene against Rhodesia's unilateral declaration of independence. Perhaps learning from Ghana's mistakes, Nyerere forged pragmatic diplomatic ties to socialist countries, with China providing aid and technical assistance for the training of a new army and the building of an infrastructure. Tanzania became even more of a beacon for progressive hopes in February 1967, when Nyerere announced the Arusha declaration, a socialist economic initiative that involved land reform, nationalized foreign industries, and established a state-controlled bank and insurance company. Nyerere also used the occasion to fight corruption by enacting a stringent code of conduct for political leaders, prohibiting ministers and leaders from the ruling party from receiving more than one salary and owning more than one residence. Although its ambitious agenda eventually fell victim to poor management and the nation's chronic underdevelopment, the Arusha declaration convinced a hopeful C. L. R. James that "once again, something new had come out of Africa," a way of life that would lead to the reconstruction of modern humankind. As Ghana had once been, Tanzania became a major destination for exiled African freedom fighters and black diaspora expatriates, including Bill Sutherland and Robert Moses, the former director of the Student Nonviolent Coordinating Committee. A brilliant young Guyanese historian, Walter Rodney, helped make the University of Dar es Salaam a haven for expatriate intellectuals and students.[3]

In the months following the coup, many people, including Charles Howard, an African American United Nations correspondent and friend of Nkrumah, shared Nyerere's perspective. Howard, a civil rights attorney penalized for his progressive affiliations during the McCarthy period, flooded the black American press with dispatches that challenged U.S. and Western press reports of a bloodless coup and popular Ghanaian support for the takeover. Howard attributed criticism of Nkrumah to the West's implacable opposition to African unity.[4] Howard sent Nkrumah press clippings on NLC missions in the United States and recounted combative exchanges with Ghanaian opposition leaders and NLC officials during their visits to New York. At a press conference, Howard told the Ghanaians that the coup was the worst thing that had ever happened to Africa; it would take generations to repair the NLC's damage. Howard was one of the exiled Nkrumah's many correspondents, providing encouragement and information. The latter was vital because opportunists, possibly inspired by press allegations of riches salted away by Nkrumah, sometimes approached the exiled leader and appealed for cash while claiming to share his goal of African liberation. Howard was asked to investigate such inquiries: in one instance, he advised Nkrumah that an African American group calling itself the Blackman's Volunteer Army of Liberation fell into this dubious category.[5]

Nkrumah also heard from another friend, Cheddi Jagan, the former prime minister of Guyana, a South American nation of eight hundred thousand adjacent to Venezuela that had gained its independence from Britain in 1966. Jagan, then leader of the opposition People's Progressive Party, commiserated with Nkrumah and hoped for his prompt return to power. Jagan noted that recent exposés of clandestine Central Intelligence Agency (CIA) activities had implicated U.S. intelligence in toppling his government in 1963. In 1992, after Jagan was elected president in Guyana's first free elections in thirty years, the painful memory of his defeat at the hands of undercover U.S. forces was revived when the Clinton administration nominated as ambassador the American official instrumental in destabilizing Jagan's government. That official, William Doherty, led the operation after President John F. Kennedy, believing Jagan a communist, ordered the CIA to oust him. Doherty exploited the colony's racial tensions—its population was divided between a slight majority of Indians, descended from migrant workers from the South Asian subcontinent, and the descendants of enslaved Africans. Jagan's party was predominantly Indian, and most of the supporters of Afro-Guyanese Prime Minister Forbes Burnham's ruling Progressive National Congress were of African descent. In his letter to Nkrumah, Jagan denounced the policies of his U.S.-backed rival, Burnham, claiming that they had been dictated by Washington. Jagan may have mildly reproached Nkrumah by criticizing Burnham's use of preventive detention and antistrike legislation to curb mass discontent over economic chaos, unemployment, and inflation. As discussed later in this chapter, Julian Mayfield joined the Burnham government in 1971 in a sad reprise of his role as a journalist for Nkrumah's Ghana.[6]

From exile in Conakry, Nkrumah followed events in Ghana, initially confident of his imminent return. His last and only chance was an April 1967 countercoup against the NLC by military officers, but it was quickly defeated. Two coup leaders were executed by firing squad, the first state executions in Ghana's history. From Guinea, Nkrumah wrote prolifically on African affairs, becoming an elder statesman of the armed struggle phase of the African revolution. In articles penned for Western leftist and anti-imperialist publications, Nkrumah hailed the U.S. black power movement as part of the

global armed struggle against imperialism and capitalism. He also criticized
the idea of a "third world," which had acquired common currency as a
temporal designation for the bloc of formerly colonized nations that had
emerged sequentially following the First and Second Worlds—that is, the
global historical formations of Western capitalism and Eastern socialism.
Nkrumah saw this understanding of global order as a diversion from the
fundamental global struggle of anti-imperialist forces throughout Africa,
Asia, and Latin America against Western capitalism and neocolonialism.
Violent white resistance to national liberation movements in southern Africa
led him to repudiate the concept of a diplomatic nonaligned Third Force
that Ghana, the United Arab Republic, and other anticolonial nations had
previously espoused. Until his illness, Nkrumah frequently received visitors
at his villa in Guinea, including such African freedom fighters as Amilcar
Cabral, an Angolan revolutionary whom Portuguese agents assassinated in
Guinea in 1974.[7] Nkrumah never returned to Ghana; he died in exile in 1972
while being treated for cancer in Romania.

In the politically charged aftermath of the coup, Nkrumah's supporters bitterly disputed claims regarding the coup's popularity among Ghanaians, a
staple of Western press accounts. Against this view, supporters emphasized
the violence, intimidation, and censorship employed by the NLC regime. But
a campaign in the Western press to demonize Nkrumah drowned out the
dissenting voices of Nyerere, Howard, British radical scholar Thomas Hodgkin, and others. Of course, Nkrumah, as an avowed Marxian socialist, had
long been subject to anticommunist attacks, as syndicated columnists, politicians, and other journalists registered their disapproval shortly after Ghana
gained independence. Indeed, Nkrumah and Touré's nonaligned stance had
skillfully exploited this suspicion, gaining for their countries substantial aid
from a United States fearful of "losing" them to the Soviets. Postcoup allegations of Nkrumah's corruption reflected U.S. officials' hopes that his exile
would become permanent. The NLC provided fodder for such exposés with
public hearings at which notoriously corrupt Convention People's Party ministers furnished lurid accounts of Nkrumah's personal malfeasance. While
charges of Nkrumah's personal corruption were exaggerated, allegations of
economic mismanagement and autocratic rule contained enough truth to
make the accusations, no matter how outlandish, credible.[8]

The campaign to discredit Nkrumah had manifestly clear objectives. Such
personal attacks obscured the political goals of liberation that Nyerere had
emphasized. Moreover, the NLC's anti-Nkrumah propaganda lent the coup a

humanitarian veneer and sought to prevent Nkrumah's return to power by destroying his popularity. In Ghana, the NLC's strong-arm tactics sought to ensure this outcome. Outside Ghana, African Americans constituted a vital audience for anti-Nkrumah propaganda. Not surprisingly, given civil rights leaders' establishment leanings—indeed, their view of the U.S. government as a vital partner in racial reform—those leaders who had once helped Nkrumah celebrate Ghana's independence maintained a discreet silence on his ouster. In an equally striking departure from its once proud and favorable coverage of Nkrumah and Ghana dating from before independence, the African American–owned, Chicago-based *Ebony* magazine joined the chorus of Western condemnation. In a damning exposé whose title, "Fall of a Messiah," signaled its intended ideological effect, a correspondent reproduced the version of the coup propagated by U.S. authorities and reported the NLC's hyperbolic rumormongering and accusations of corruption designed to destroy Nkrumah's image.[9]

Although it is difficult to measure the impact of such attacks on Nkrumah's image among people of African descent, an anecdote about Nkrumah's enduring appeal to black people in the West sheds some light on the question. An African American taxi driver in New York City ordered the NLC's commissioner for foreign affairs out of the vehicle when the passenger stated that he was from Ghana. The Ghanaian official hesitated, flabbergasted, until the driver insisted, "After what you people did to Kwame Nkrumah, I don't want anything to do with you." This Ghanaian official learned that not only in America but also in places such as Jamaica, pro-Nkrumah sentiment remained so strong that it was prudent for him to claim that he was from somewhere other than Ghana.[10]

Two widely noticed critical appraisals of Nkrumah written after the coup that appeared in *Transition*, published from Uganda, suggested to some observers that the magazine, known for its irreverent coverage of African affairs, was retreating from its independent stance. One was an essay by Kenyan political scientist Ali Mazrui that claimed that Nkrumah's admiration of Leninist theory and practice was at odds with the atavistic cult of personality that he encouraged. The other was a hostile appraisal by a British-born, naturalized American journalist, Russell Warren Howe, charging that Nkrumah's opposition to regional African federations and his disputes with rival African governments made him an enemy of pan-Africanism. Mazrui's essay combined measured criticism of Nkrumah's autocratic policies with serious engagement with his writings. But Mazrui's comparison of Nkrumah to Lenin, despite the obvious parallels, struck some as redolent of the West's disingenuous reading of African affairs through a Cold War lens. Howe, who had been expelled from Ghana in 1959 and was already notorious in some circles for having characterized African Americans as "strangers in Africa," lacked Mazrui's restraint. Ghana under Nkrumah represented "a fairly typical fascist state." Howe equated Nkrumah's autocratic methods with those of late South African Prime Minister Hendrik Verwoerd. Ghana's strained relations with pro-Western African states suggested to Howe that Nkrumah had, contrary to his rhetoric, rejected pan-Africanism. History would view Nkrumah as a "colorful scoundrel" and a "consummate headline hunter" whose talents were better suited to the stage than to politics. Despite their considerable differences in tone, many readers found it difficult to separate the Mazrui and Howe articles from the general tendency to discredit Nkrumah and his anti-imperialist politics.[11]

Both Mazrui's measured critique and Howe's venom generated indignant responses, including a scathing, sarcastic letter from a Ghanaian writer and associate of the Afro-American expatriates, Ama Ata Aidoo. Aidoo thanked "our big white father" Howe "[o]n behalf of Africans dead, alive, and un-born, 'free' and enslaved" for his analysis of Kwame Nkrumah. "Our ignorance was extreme," she confessed. While Africans knew that "Nkrumah was squeamish at the kind of unabashed licking of pale Western feet that some of our leaders find attractive" and that he opposed the sale of the future of Africa and its people, "we did not know he was against pan-Africanism. . . . [W]e register our appreciation of [Howe's] obvious concern for the success of pan-Africanism and, therefore, our well being." As a parting shot, Aidoo thanked Mazrui "and all the other objective and non-partisan African intellectuals" whose writings, in her view, made possible statements such as Howe's. In a lengthy response to his many critics, Mazrui defended his right to dispassionate analysis and observed that his most strident detractors were African students abroad whose ability to romanticize Nkrumah would have been sorely tested had they lived in Ghana. Distancing himself from Howe, Mazrui stood by his assessment of Nkrumah as a flawed visionary, a great African, but a failure as a Ghanaian leader.[12]

Negritude versus the African Personality: The Dakar Festival

Just as the *Transition* articles on Nkrumah elicited few indifferent responses in the aftermath of the coup, events planned long before the takeover were inevitably perceived through a lens of suspicion and controversy. Thus, the Ghana coup shadowed the long-planned First World Festival of Negro Art, conceived by President Léopold Senghor of Senegal as a showcase not only for the writers and performing artists of Africa and the diaspora but for his version of Negritude. To some observers, implicit in the celebration of Negritude was a declaration of its triumph over Ghana's rival pan-African ideology of the African personality. Senghor and a friend, Afro-American scholar and U.S. ambassador Mercer Cook, shared the patronizing official U.S. view of Nkrumah as unstable. Shortly after Nkrumah's ouster, Senghor told Cook, "That was one coup that I do not regret," although Senghor also emphasized that the economic difficulties of all African countries threatened their stability unless the rich countries came to their aid.[13]

In its inception during the 1930s, Negritude had been a defiant anti-colonial statement of pride in African origins. During the 1950s, such critics as Frantz Fanon had viewed Negritude as an understandable yet limited response to the alienation of blacks in and by Western culture. By the mid-1960s, however, Senghor's moderate policies shaped black and African radicals' perceptions of Negritude. As president of Senegal, Senghor pursued a pro-Western policy and maintained his country's close political and economic relationship with France. Senegal's foreign relations diverged sharply from the militant pan-Africanism of Ghana and Guinea. Relations between Senegal and Guinea reflected the strained coexistence of Senghor and Sekou Touré. During Senghor's early 1965 visit to Guinea, the two leaders quarreled over the protracted unrest in the Congo. Touré taunted Senghor, reminding him that Guinea received more U.S. aid than Senegal. Cook monitored their testy exchanges, sharing Senghor's frustration at the low level of U.S. support despite Senegal's pro-American stance. Cook hoped that Touré's insouciance would not be lost on Washington. To drive home his point, Cook reported that Touré led Senghor and the visiting Cuban minister of industry, Ernesto "Che" Guevara, on a tour of the site of the Kinkom Dam being built by Chinese engineers and workers. Touré's advocacy of socialism had no place for Senghor's pet theory of Negritude, which Touré and other Guinean diplomats openly belittled.

The ongoing rivalry with Touré, along with the disparagement of Negritude that often accompanied Ghanaian officials' explications of the "African personality," provided the context for Senghor's organization of the Dakar festival.[14] Senghor viewed the festival as a means of strengthening Senegal's relationship with the United States. For its part, Washington hoped that the festival would not only provide a platform for the artistry of the black world but also celebrate the American nation's triumphant dismantling of legal segregation, represented by the signing of the Voting Rights

Act. Senegal organized the festival in partnership with the State Department; the United Nations Educational, Scientific, and Cultural Organization; the French-based Society of African Culture; and its U.S. counterpart, the American Society of African Culture (AMSAC). The festival's announcement the preceding July had sparked a clamor for invitations among black American Africanists and the founding eminences of Negritude. Funded with public and private contributions (the six hundred thousand dollars raised by a U.S. committee fell considerably short of the millions initially sought), the festival and its organizers could not accommodate many of those with a legitimate claim for attendance, including such pioneers of Negritude as Paulette Nardal. Some African Americans perceived in their inability to wangle an invitation evidence of the U.S. government's exclusionary criteria. The February 1966 AMSAC newsletter, which went to press before the Ghanaian coup, reported that the association had chartered a plane that would bring 180 people to the festival. It also advertised that the next issue of its journal, *African Forum*, would feature a debate between Nkrumah and Senghor on "African socialism." Nkrumah's position asserted the primacy of "scientific socialism" and an anticapitalist emphasis on class conflict over less confrontational notions of classless, indigenous African socialism espoused at various times by Senghor and other African leaders, including Nyerere and Jomo Kenyatta.[15] AMSAC's preference for African socialism over avowedly Marxian formulations was apparent in its framing of the debate. For its part, the State Department hoped that a demonstration of African and Negro artistic and cultural excellence would be free of political controversy if not completely devoid of politics.[16]

The Dakar festival represented a triumph for the U.S. State Department. As Penny Von Eschen has argued, State Department officials could finally exhale, relieved that their projection of the image of American democracy as embodied by the nation's preeminent black writers and artists had roots in the political realization of formal equality.[17] African American cultural luminaries Langston Hughes, Duke Ellington and his orchestra, the Alvin Ailey Dance Company, and gospel singer Marion Williams lent their artistry to U.S. officials' long-standing claim of an American society defined by steady racial progress. In Dakar, with Nkrumah out of the picture, it was now safe to confine assertions of the compatibility of African and African American peoples to the realm of culture rather than politics. But coming so soon after Nkrumah's ouster, Senghor's assertion of African cultural unity proved controversial. Wole Soyinka, whose play, *Kongi's Harvest*, a thinly veiled attack on Nkrumah, was performed at the festival, found the timing of this staging unsettling: "It's like kicking a man when he's down." Although some observers saw Soyinka's play as an unseemly celebration of Nkrumah's demise, Robert July further suggests that the work may also have rankled its audience of distinguished African leaders, none of whom was immune from its no-holds-barred satire of autocratic leadership, a phenomenon that probably explained the play's tepid reception.[18] Soyinka and others in attendance notably dissociated themselves from Negritude, somewhat marring Senghor's celebratory view of the cultural unity of the black world. Katherine Dunham, an African American choreographer and early exponent of Afro-diasporic modern dance, described Negritude as "meaningless."

Dismissing the role of Senghor's government and AMSAC, Hoyt Fuller, the Afro-American editor of *Negro Digest*, noted the controversy over Negritude. Fuller found even more disturbing what he viewed as the white-controlled State Department's inordinate influence on the festival. Fuller reported that Senegalese writers and artists had expressed disappointment at the absence of younger militant black writers and such musicians as Miles Davis and Thelonious Monk, and many lamented singer-activist Harry Belafonte's absence. Though refraining from any mention of the Ghana coup, Fuller expressed misgivings about AMSAC's role in the festival.[19]

Fuller's suspicions would be borne out by the disclosure in 1967 that AMSAC had received covert CIA funding, as had many other Cold War–era cultural institutions and publications, including the Congress for Cultural Freedom, as part of an official strategy to subsidize and thus co-opt the noncommunist Left. Later, aware of the CIA involvement, Fuller recalled the disturbing candor of an American official at the festival: "Yes . . . we are keeping black radicals away from the Africans, and we will succeed." Acknowledging his and Fuller's participation in AMSAC conferences, Julian Mayfield recalled that playwright Alice Childress had from the start suspected covert government support and had refused to have anything to do with the organization.[20] AMSAC members suspicious or even knowledgeable about the source of its funding previously had quietly gone along, convincing themselves that the organization might achieve its worthy goals despite the government's clandestine role. Coming at the moment of a swelling tide of black militancy, the revelation that the CIA controlled the purse strings destroyed AMSAC's credibility among African American and African intellectuals who had been associated with it. Despite desperate efforts by John A. Davis to secure new sources of support, the organization collapsed, its utility to the U.S. government having passed.[21]

Mayfield had returned to an American society at a paradoxical moment. As political repression had escalated apace with the growing urgency of the black movement's rhetoric and demands, American cultural industries, particularly book publishing, sought to cash in on the so-called black revolution. Mayfield pursued success on his own terms, hoping to storm the gates of mainstream culture with his outsider's perspective. His unpublished manuscripts, "The Lonely Warrior" and a revised version, "When Ghana Was Ghana," offered insightful and critical assessments of Nkrumah's failures. But both were flawed by Mayfield's failure to reconcile disparate narrative registers. Mayfield felt bound to a journalistic model of empirically grounded discourse. But this empiricism came at the expense of his true talent—the telling personal anecdote, rendered with his mordant sense of the absurd. Had he found his voice, Mayfield would likely have produced an original work of lasting significance. As it was, his motives and approach were too instrumental. Still animated by revolutionary ideals, Mayfield believed that an analysis of Ghana's successes and failures would provide crucial lessons for posterity. His vision thus constrained by his preoccupation with Nkrumah's image and by his desire to analyze what had gone wrong in Ghana, Mayfield neglected the opportunity to reflect deeply on his personal experiences. Unable to the satisfaction of publishers to distinguish his criticisms of Nkrumah from the spate of denunciations that followed the coup, Mayfield also did not discern that posterity would exhibit far greater interest in Malcolm X than in the deeply flawed Nkrumah. While several of Malcolm's associates planned biographies of their martyred leader, Mayfield, who had spent much time with Malcolm during his diplomatic sojourning throughout Africa, refused to write about him, seeming to regard such a project as exploiting the dead. Mayfield's final manuscript on Ghana, "Tales of the Lido," was written during the early 1980s. In its surviving fragments, this memoir of the Ghanaian expatriates abandons the journalistic demeanor of the previous manuscripts, interspersing historical and political analysis with a more informal, gossipy, and sexualized remembrance of Ghana. His tough-minded facade yielding in this instance to masculinist nostalgia, Mayfield fell considerably short of his serious objectives in his writings on Nkrumah's Ghana. After strong initial interest, publishers rejected these efforts.[22]

In 1967, Mayfield returned to the States to accept a teaching fellowship at Cornell University. Since leaving Ghana, Mayfield had also written *Fount of the Nation,* a play about the charismatic leader of a small African country. He corresponded with a circle of friends and comrades, many of them former expatriates and associates of Malcolm X. Together they contemplated some sort of engagement with black power activism. With these colleagues, including Sylvia Boone, Mayfield planned a new journal, *Black Directions,* intended as a revolutionary think tank directed at leaders and decision makers in the freedom movement. The project was necessitated not only by the perception that the movement lacked strategic and ideological vision but also by a "concern for the survival of our people as a people." The perceived need for an ideology was heightened by the hysteria and violence that followed the assassination of Martin Luther King Jr. and a student protest at Cornell that included a theatrical display of firearms. But time had passed Mayfield by. He failed to regain the prominence he held as a social critic before his exile. A major difficulty was that Mayfield was inconsistent during those volatile times. He abhorred nonviolence yet feared that the Black Panthers' stance of armed confrontation was suicidal. Indeed, his rigid opposition to nonviolence bespoke a man who had run out of ideas if not hope. Before King's death made Mayfield's antipathy to nonviolence a moot point, he had continued to disparage the civil rights leader despite King's evolution toward a radical democratic antiwar stance. Fellow expatriates and *Freedomways* colleagues Calvin and Elinor Sinnette, who helped organize a memorial service for King at Ibadan University in Nigeria, did not share Mayfield's hostility toward the reverend. For whatever reasons—perhaps because Mayfield gravitated toward other projects—*Black Directions* never got off the ground.[23]

Mayfield saw himself as engaged in a battle for the minds of black students. An inkling that he was on the losing side may have led him to review Harold Cruse's best-selling manifesto *The Crisis of the Negro Intellectual* (1967) for *Negro Digest,* a journal that served as the Johnson Publishing Company's concession to progressive black consciousness. Written during the spring of 1968, Mayfield's review sparked a debate that resonated among black leftist intellectuals in Harlem and beyond. Cruse's influential book was part of a newly ascendant vogue of the black revolution in commercial publishing. Its rhetorical onslaught against black leadership crystallized black militants' demands for grassroots control of black communities and for cultural and economic nationalism. But in *Crisis,* Cruse, who had accompanied Mayfield, Robert Williams, and other black American progressives to Cuba in 1960 and had penned influential left-wing journal articles on the salience of world revolutions and anticolonialism for African American nationalism,

denounced the black Left as mired in bourgeois integrationism. Cruse carica-
tured such figures as Paul Robeson and Lorraine Hansberry as too dependent
on paternalistic communist ideologues to address the black community's
cultural needs. Cruse's book achieved mass appeal and the endorsement of
white liberal reviewers with a formula synthesizing black nationalism and
Cold War anticommunism. Cruse's anticommunism had a decidedly nativist
strain, expressed in attacks on Jewish and black West Indian leftists as sinister influences on African American politics. By conflating the internationalism of Harlem's black Left with the suspect category of integration, Cruse
rewrote the history of black radicalism, including his own. Not only had
Cruse himself previously espoused the internationalism and the critique of
the limits of integration of those he disparaged, but he had also been a
member of the Communist Party during the late 1940s and early 1950s.[24]

The acrimony between Mayfield and Cruse existed well before their ran-
corous exchange over *Crisis*. Cruse's earlier assessment of "the dilemma of
the Negro intellectual" appeared to have Mayfield as its unnamed target. In
his political writings of the early 1960s, Mayfield had forcefully advocated
the approach taken by such militant leaders as Robert Williams as well as a
black radicalism aligned with the Cuban Revolution and the emergent anticolonial bloc.[25] Forced to monitor subsequent developments in the United
States (and political scuttlebutt from Harlem) from Ghana, Mayfield could
not be faulted for perceiving Cruse's analysis as a personal attack. According
to Cruse, the Negro leftist intellectual, unable to integrate into the mainstream status quo, had resorted to "talking like a revolutionary [and] flirting
with the revolutionary nationalism of the non-West." The Negro intellectual
of this sort was merely "floating in ideological space," unable to connect with
radical elements in the black working class.[26] The harrowing circumstances
of Mayfield's flight from Monroe and into exile (which, in fairness to Cruse,
perhaps had not occurred when he penned his words) must have made
Cruse's assertions all the more galling for Mayfield. From Ghana, Mayfield
spoke disparagingly of Cruse but refused to be drawn into an open conflict.[27]

After the appearance of Cruse's best-selling polemic targeting Mayfield's
generation of black leftist writers and activists, a work that he feared would
mislead militant black students and youth, Mayfield faulted Cruse for what
Mayfield viewed as a self-serving account motivated by personal vendettas.
Cruse had exaggerated the black Left's ties to the Communist Party, reinforcing myths of black dependency and white paternalism. Although he
remained highly skeptical of the party's interracialism ("Black and white
unite and fight!"), Mayfield praised the organized Left for its campaigns

against Jim Crow injustice during the 1950s and viewed with pride his participation in some of them. Noting that Cruse had said practically nothing of W. E. B. Du Bois, Mayfield indicated that the militant black Left was far too complex a phenomenon to be so easily dismissed as "integrationist." Cruse answered Mayfield's fierce though measured critique with an attack that suggested more than a passing acquaintance with Mayfield's personal foibles and his publishing travails. Cruse urged Mayfield to be more forthcoming about his romantic escapades in Harlem, Puerto Rico, and Ghana, his taunts reducing the politics of exile to sexual adventurism. Mayfield's was not the only critique of Cruse's work: *Freedomways* entered the fray by publishing Ernest Kaiser's scathing dissection of the book. Despite such criticism, Cruse's interpretation carried the day, arguably dividing younger nationalists from the legacy of the black radicals of the 1940s and 1950s. In 1979, Mayfield was asked to contribute to a *Freedomways* issue edited by Jean Carey Bond and dedicated to the memory of Lorraine Hansberry, in part to counter continuing accusations of bourgeois integrationism against her patterned after the example set by Cruse.[28] Winston James, Alan Wald, Nikhil Pal Singh, Jerry Watts, and others have recently pointed out *Crisis*'s numerous flaws, including its distorted portrayal of an independent black Left and its gratuitous attacks on West Indian and Jewish leftists. The influence that Cruse's text enjoyed suggests the enormous cost of exile for Mayfield. Cut off from the United States, his ability to help elucidate an African American culture of opposition was severely limited. Mayfield's departure had effectively abandoned the field to Cruse.[29]

Cruse's jibes had struck a nerve, for Mayfield's revolutionary aspirations competed with equally powerful ambitions for personal success. Necessity forced him to accept temporary teaching appointments at Cornell and New York University, the latter in the Albert Schweitzer Program in the Humanities from 1968 to 1970. During the summer of 1968, it looked as though Mayfield's prospects were finally catching fire through his involvement with the Paramount Pictures film *Uptight*, directed by a radical American auteur, Jules Dassin. Dassin, Mayfield, and his costar, Ruby Dee, shared the screenwriting credit for the film, a remake of the 1935 Victor McLaglen classic *The Informer*. Mayfield portrays Tank, a drunken, down-and-out antihero who is killed in retribution for having betrayed the black movement. Although *Uptight* received mixed reviews and failed to find an audience, it revived Mayfield's hopes for a film career. During his brief taste of success, he purchased property in upstate New York and established a production company for treatment of Haitian postrevolutionary leader Henri Christophe.[30]

Mayfield's abortive film career illustrates the struggles of African American dramatic actors of his generation. Beyond the short list of black film stars whose careers were launched or boosted by Hansberry's *Raisin in the Sun* (including Sidney Poitier, Ossie Davis, Ruby Dee, and Diana Sands, whose promise was tragically cut short by cancer), many more African American performers schooled in the theater vainly struggled to launch independent film projects equal to their talents. Reflecting a condition common to actors of all backgrounds but perhaps more trying for African Americans, many were compelled to accept film and television roles that were considerably beneath their abilities. Mayfield's partner in the Christophe project, William Marshall, had played De Lawd in the 1951 Broadway revival of *Green Pastures* but is best known for a blaxploitation horror film, *Blacula*. Mayfield's socially conscious aesthetics were at a disadvantage within a film industry that employed former professional athletes in "superstud" roles at the expense of veteran stage actors, including Ivan Dixon, Frank Silvera (whose numerous film and television roles as Mexicans and other swarthy types subsidized such ventures as his lead role in a Joseph Papp production of *King Lear*), and many others. As black writers and critics assayed definitions of the "black aesthetic," Mayfield continued to juggle various projects, writing screenplays, an autobiography, novels, literary criticism, and reviews.[31] He edited a collection of short stories, *Ten Times Black*, that contained his only published writing based on his Ghanaian experience, the autobiographical short story "Black on Black: A Political Love Story," which Mayfield's friend Hoyt Fuller had originally published in *Black World*.[32]

Despite his best efforts, Mayfield could not benefit from the commercial vogue of blackness in literary and popular culture. His production company collapsed, leaving him deeply in debt and forcing him to sell his upstate New York property. Lacking the stability and resources enjoyed by his associates in academia—a group that included St. Clair Drake, Martin Kilson, Preston King, and Conor Cruise O'Brien—or his friend, playwright, television writer, and documentary producer (and sometime academic) William Branch, Mayfield frequently lived at the edge of poverty. During the late 1960s and early 1970s, as federal and local counterintelligence programs jailed, murdered, or drove underground members of the Black Panthers and other activists, Mayfield withdrew from activism and became increasingly cynical about the prospects for change.[33] Brief anecdotal reflections on his time in Ghana in his lectures and reviews from this period illustrated his belief in American power's intractable opposition to the political autonomy and freedom of black and African peoples. Mayfield believed that African Americans faced nothing less than a battle for their survival. Years later, for a special issue of *Freedomways* edited by Jean Carey Bond honoring Hansberry, Mayfield penned a moving remembrance of the playwright. Unlike other black actors who, Mayfield claimed, allowed success to erode their political commitment, Hansberry used her celebrity as a platform for her radical outspokenness. But, perhaps bearing in mind recent disclosures during Senate investigative hearings of covert U.S. assassination plots, Mayfield intimated a conspiratorial aspect to the early deaths of Hansberry, Frantz Fanon, and black American novelist Frank London Brown, who had succumbed to leukemia. Mayfield dreamed of emulating Hansberry's refusal to let success compromise her politics; his disappointments magnified his pessimism at the condition of blacks in America and may also have fueled his admittedly "paranoid" refusal to be resigned to Hansberry's death.[34]

Reliving Ghana: Mayfield's Sojourn in Guyana

In 1971, Mayfield rejected the relative security of a teaching position to emigrate to Guyana. He had been recruited by the government of Prime Minister Forbes Burnham to work as a journalist. Mayfield's friend and fellow Ghanaian expatriate, artist Tom Feelings, was already there, producing educational children's books for the Ministry of Information intended to mitigate the nation's racial tensions by describing the genesis of Guyana's African and East Indian populations.[35] *Black World* had recently published an open letter to Mayfield in which Feelings promoted Guyana as a New World counterpart to Tanzania and thus a more proximate haven for black diaspora expatriates. While in Ghana, Sidney King, who was in Accra seeking diplomatic support for Burnham's government, had briefed Mayfield on the former British colony's political history. King had described the antiblack sentiments of the nation's East Indian majority, persuading Mayfield of the necessity of defending black power there. Mayfield had published in *African Review* King's indictment of East Indian racialism in Guyana. After an exploratory visit, Mayfield leapt at the opportunity, drawn to Guyana because he viewed it as the only country in the Western hemisphere completely controlled by blacks.

Mayfield's brief sojourn in Guyana represented an idealistic attempt to relive the promise of Ghana. This time, escapism rather than the need to get away from political repression formed the basis for Mayfield's departure. He

cited African Americans' powerlessness and lack of a coherent movement.
Mayfield was probably unaware that Burnham had vanquished Jagan with
covert CIA assistance. Mayfield was impressed by Burnham's progressive
credentials, which included cordial relations with Castro's Cuba. Burnham
avowed socialism and had nationalized bauxite interests in the country, but
the United States nevertheless considered him the lesser of two evils, preferable to Jagan.[36] In Guyana, Mayfield regained what had been lost after
Ghana—that is, institutional support for his political activism. Most of all,
Guyana provided refuge from his various setbacks in the States. Won over by
Burnham's knack for exploiting pan-African symbolism, Mayfield attacked
Jagan for his supposed pro-Soviet leanings. Mayfield found Burnham's pragmatism and lack of the sort of mystique that Nkrumah projected to be a
refreshing change. It was sufficient that Burnham wanted to settle Guyana
with more people of African descent and to develop the land. Then, too, the
country's natural beauty and Georgetown's bustling urban life, so reminiscent of Accra, constituted irresistible attractions for Mayfield.

In Ghana, Mayfield had voiced his misgivings about the government's
lapses; he was much more indulgent toward Guyana, which became for him
a more fitting locale for his pursuit of the American dream. There, expressing
a quintessentially African American yearning for deliverance from rural tyranny and urban deprivation, Mayfield hoped to purchase land and support
himself by livestock farming while he tried to keep his Hollywood irons in the
fire and pursued his writing. One of Mayfield's tasks, besides helping keep
Burnham in power, was trying to stem the tide of outmigration by inculcat-
ing a sense of national pride in Guyanese youth. When Nkrumah died in
1972, Mayfield published a critical remembrance of the Ghanaian leader in
the newspaper he edited, finally getting his didactic reflections into print for
posterity.[37]

Although he met his second wife, Afro-Guyanese writer Joan Cambridge,
while in Guyana and dreamed of permanently settling there, Mayfield did
not last in South America. Mayfield and Feelings became embroiled in bitter
sectarian conflict among African American expatriates. They clashed with
African American followers of Eusi Kwayana (the former Sidney King), who
by this time had broken with Burnham. In addition, Mayfield's efforts were
often hampered by Guyanese officials who blocked his proposed initiatives
for the nation's development. Unable to realize his dreams of landownership
after some four years, Mayfield returned to the States, accompanied by Cambridge. Health issues may also have been a factor in Mayfield's departure.[38]
From Frankfurt, where he spent a year on a Fulbright fellowship, Mayfield

scorned efforts by black Guyanese intellectual Walter Rodney to build a progressive multiracial working-class party in opposition to Burnham.[39] Subsequent events betrayed Mayfield's support of Burnham.[40] Rodney was killed in 1980 by a bomb concealed in a walkie-talkie provided to him by Gregory Smith, an undercover member of the Guyanese defense forces. Burnham responded with a cover-up of accusations in Guyana and beyond that his government had been responsible for the killing. In 1985, Burnham died suddenly in office. When the case was finally reopened in 1996, charges were brought against Smith in absentia for Rodney's murder. It is unclear whether Mayfield revised his assessment of Burnham in light of the controversy surrounding Rodney's death.[41]

Feelings returned to the United States, where he enjoyed modest success as an author and illustrator of children's books and with acclaimed exhibitions and publications of visual narratives, or series, inspired by African American history. After the urban revolts of the late 1960s, the federal government had provided school libraries with funding to purchase books on minorities, and Feelings concentrated on illustrating children's books that provided positive images of Africans, combating the onslaught of widespread images of savagery and backwardness.[42] Mayfield struggled to establish an academic career, having taken the Fulbright as a means of boosting his credentials. Driven into bankruptcy by a disastrous film venture, Mayfield returned home to Washington, D.C., where he taught at the University of Maryland and Howard University. As his bond with Feelings suggested, Mayfield remained at the center of correspondence among the expatriates who shared the indelible memory of Ghana. As a friend and as a teacher (though he disliked teaching), Mayfield had much to offer; he was great company in person or over the telephone, gregarious and funny, ruthlessly honest about the pariah status of black and African peoples, and possessed of a hard-won skepticism for the rhetoric of the political Left. Mayfield was a devoted correspondent, generous whenever he was able, and his friends forgave his alcoholism, in part because of his candid acknowledgment of the problem. Though Mayfield was beloved by those who knew him best, university academics and administrators regarded him as an uncredentialed maverick. At what was still very much the Howard University of Frazier's *Black Bourgeoisie*, Mayfield's unsparing assessment of the condition of black people routinely met with impatience if not outright derision, though the institution had no qualms about burdening him with onerous teaching and administrative obligations. As writer in residence in the English department, Mayfield participated in the groundbreaking African diaspora studies conference,

Julian Mayfield and Joan Cambridge, Georgetown, Guyana, 1973.
(Julian Mayfield Collection, Schomburg Center for Research in
Black Culture, New York Public Library, New York)

presenting a paper that revisited his earlier arguments about the necessity of an independent African American cultural identity, without which black people were "defenseless" in a racist society. Howard terminated Mayfield's contract shortly before his final illness. Mayfield died of congestive heart failure in Washington in 1984, at the age of fifty-six. Maya Angelou and Ossie Davis delivered eulogies at Mayfield's memorial service at Howard's Rankin Chapel. Feelings paid tribute to his friend with a prose depiction of an imagined abstract painting inspired by Mayfield's life: the painting would have been "a bittersweet duality . . . balancing pain and joy" that told an old and agonizing story yet remained "a beautiful saga, and the insight gained is profound . . . for this painting, and this man, have made you see it . . . in a new way."[43]

The Expatriate Experience as a Setting for Reflections on Gender Politics

What Feelings described as the new insight afforded by Mayfield's life and work can also be said of the community of Ghanaian expatriates, who brought a unique perspective to the challenges facing black people. Even as debates over militancy, internationalism, and transnational black solidarity continued to enliven the pages of such periodicals and journals as *Black World* and the *Black Scholar*, the Ghanaian expatriates drew on their experience to probe matters of gender politics with a depth and immediacy seldom on view in these publications. With whom else but a sharer of those years in Ghana could one discuss the sensitive yet increasingly vital question of gender politics in distinguishing mere militants from true revolutionaries? Although Mayfield and his associates spoke of the need for black activists to renounce interracial sexual relationships for the sake of community harmony and condemned the sexual hedonism and patriarchal power plays rampant within such groups as the Black Panthers, their detachment limited the broader impact of their analyses of gender politics.[44]

Such discussions represented an outgrowth of the gulf between expectations of gender egalitarianism of the community of expatriate Afros in Ghana and the realities of male dominance among advocates of black and African liberation. On the one hand, as seen in Ghana's hosting the 1960 Conference on Women of Africa and of African Descent, women regarded themselves as equal contributors to African nationalism. Nigerian nationalist leader F. Ransome-Kuti (perhaps best known as the mother of legendary Afro-beat musician Fela) articulated a commitment to gender equality as essential to freedom and modernity: "Now the old orders have changed; our women have rapidly been taking their proper places in the role of Nigeria. Our men are now learning that their women are no longer their slaves but their immediate associates."[45] On the other hand, the belief that African freedom would bring women's equality collided with the patriarchal politics of postindependence African leaders. Such inequality amid the Ghanaian revolution epitomized the gendered nature of the expatriate experience in Africa, with contrasting experiences of male sexual license and obstacles raised by African custom to Western women's expectations of independence.

This contradictory experience contributed to several female expatriates' early formulations of black feminist critique by the late 1960s. That, along with the intensifying gender tensions among black activists besieged by federal and local crackdowns and the Moynihan report, which interpreted poverty among blacks as the product of a pathological matriarchal culture, made black women's engagement with these issues all the more urgent. *Freedomways* published a 1966 symposium on "The Negro Woman in American Literature." Contributors Alice Childress, Paule Marshall, and Sarah Wright criticized pervasive stereotypes of black women in U.S. popular culture, denounced black male militants' use of myths of matriarchal domination to justify the subordination of women, and viewed such misrepresentations as a stimulus to literary production by and for black women.[46] The importance of gender politics among the expatriates stemmed from the internationalist black cultural Left that Cruse had disparaged. Apart from the presence in Ghana of several strong-willed women intellectuals and activists, the differently gendered experiences of male and female expatriates had made a strong impression on Mayfield. He recalled that African American women had a greater access to the higher echelons of politics in Ghana, a proximity unavailable to most African American men. He confessed that when he visited the residence shared by Angelou, Garvin, and Windom, their home cooking would be served with scathing criticism of the sexual exploitation of Ghanaian women in which he and other men engaged.[47]

Boone, who after the coup had told Mayfield that sexism was the Achilles heel of black movement organizations, facilitated the articulation of black women's plight and perspectives during the late 1960s. Having returned to the United States after completing extensive field research in West Africa, Boone helped to organize the 1970 Chubb Conference on the Black Woman at Yale, cosponsored by the Afro-American studies program. Speakers included former Ghanaian expatriates Angelou and Shirley Graham Du Bois along with John Henrik Clarke and poet Gwendolyn Brooks. The conference included declarations of support for the radical intellectual-activist Angela Davis, then imprisoned on conspiracy charges of which she would later be acquitted.[48]

Against Racialism: St. Clair Drake, Black Studies, and the Legacy of Pan-Africanism

When his pan-African activism and research in Ghana were cut short by Nkrumah's ouster, Drake, who had returned with his family to the United States months before the coup, served informally as an adviser to the Student Nonviolent Coordinating Committee during its short-lived black power and anti–Vietnam War internationalist phase. As had been the case with Nkrumah, the committee existed on borrowed time, its indictment of U.S. foreign policy drawing the aggressive scrutiny of U.S. counterintelligence. Drake continued to pursue his academic interest in the black diaspora and the historical relationships among African Americans, Caribbean peoples, and Africans. In 1968, Drake left Roosevelt for a position at Stanford University, where, as founding director of that institution's African American Studies Department, he became a sought-after lecturer and guiding spirit of black studies as an intellectual movement. Drake continued to defend Nkrumah against his many detractors.[49]

From the States, Drake maintained his involvement in pan-African affairs. During the mid-1970s he joined the chorus of outrage among black activists at U.S. military support for right-wing paramilitaries against the new Marxist government in Angola. Not unlike Mayfield and others, Drake wrote extensively, though seldom for publication, on the history of pan-Africanism and on Nkrumah's Ghana. Perhaps his analysis of Nkrumah's political philosophy was intended as part of his autobiography, which Drake never completed, an unfortunate outcome given his firsthand acquaintance with the leading personalities of the era and his flair for storytelling. But these unpublished reflections, including fragmentary personal memories and recollections of Ghana, contain valuable insights.

In 1969, Drake sketched a preliminary vision of the black studies project. Hoping to discourage anti-intellectualism among student activists, Drake cautioned that the struggle demanded a clear distinction between propaganda and sound research. Drake also envisioned black studies as devoted to the demystification of putatively objective yet Eurocentric scholarship, which he termed white studies, adding that white racism and the impact of changing race relations on white identities merited academic scrutiny in their own right.[50]

Central to his vision of black studies, Drake pursued an analysis of black radicalism through his participation in a symposium organized by black law students at Stanford in tribute to Walter Rodney. An engagement with Rodney's career was in keeping with Drake's increased post-Ghana interest in exploring his Caribbean background. Rodney had earned Drake's admiration for keeping alive the tradition of pan-Africanism through scholarship and activism that carried him from England, where he completed his doctoral training, to Jamaica, from which he was expelled for his political activities, to Tanzania and back to his native Guyana. Toward the end of his life, after the Guyanese government rescinded his university appointment, Rodney lectured frequently in the United States and worked under the auspices of the Institute of the Black World in Atlanta. Drake recalled that during Rodney's previous visits to Stanford, black students gave him a mixed reception. Rodney was a formidable intellect and a committed pan-Africanist, but, as Drake recalled, students balked at his racially inclusive working-class politics, typified by his view that the identification "black" should be extended to all the nonwhite oppressed people of the Caribbean, including East Indians and Chinese as well as those of African descent. Rodney's advocacy of a coalition between Guyanese workers of African and South Asian descent rankled separatist students. Rodney's belief in transracial alliances made the formation of his working-class opposition party possible, a course that led to his assassination. Drake enlarged on Rodney's significance. "The message that Rodney, Fanon, Malcolm, and Stokely [Carmichael] had was that some form of Third World coalitions must be formed. Fanon thought it desirable that coalitions with whites would lead to some form of cultural assimilation and structural integration after the stage of negritude was passed." In his discussion of Rodney's significance, Drake revisited the perennial issue of the fraught relationship between race and class. "Rodney made it impossible for us to discuss black liberation solely in terms of race and racism. He forced us to think about how class relations within the race, outside of it, and in the interactions with others played a role, too."[51]

Drake recalled Rodney's historical analysis of pan-Africanism, an account explaining his refusal to participate in the Sixth Pan-African Congress, held in Dar es Salaam, because African and Caribbean governments, including Guyana, had banned radical and opposition political parties and organizations from the gathering. For Rodney, that conflict was symptomatic of the limitations of black and African national independence movements. New African states had inherited the boundaries and economies of imperialism, their bourgeois leaders all too willing to settle for neocolonial sovereignty rather than demand economic democracy and continental unity. African mini-states existed to protect imperialism by guaranteeing the existence of an African petit bourgeoisie devoted to the subordination of the African masses. Pan-Africanism was dead, and the Organization of African Unity had betrayed its original intentions by upholding the exploitation of African peoples. Nkrumah and Padmore were to be commended for their visionary commitment to pan-African unity, but they too had succumbed to petit bourgeois thought and, in Nkrumah's case, had failed to champion the aspirations of the Ghanaian masses, workers, and peasants. Despite admitting that Nkrumah had employed nationalism to sidestep the demands of organized labor, Drake believed that Rodney had been too hard on Nkrumah and Padmore in claiming they misunderstood the class dynamics of the African liberation movement. "I knew both men and was convinced that once they had power in their hands they should hang onto it at all cost and try to use Ghana as a base for extending the concept of continental government and eventual socialism." Their base was continually weakened by compromises with those who did not share their ideals, high levels of illiteracy, and the authority of reactionary chiefs. "When the price of cocoa began to fall and the neocolonialist squeeze began it was all over."[52]

Drake's final book, published posthumously, *Black Folk Here and There*, was a work of engaged black studies scholarship that stemmed from his deepest intellectual and political concerns. His study of Nile Valley antiquity, partly an intervention against the persistent erasure of the African presence in classical antiquity, was part of his planned and unfinished multivolume history of the black diaspora. In *Black Folk Here and There*, Drake advanced an antiracist agenda similar to that promulgated by himself and other advocates of pan-Africanism, especially Senegalese scholar Cheikh Anta Diop. Just as racism had underwritten the erasure of Africa from the origins of Western civilization, Drake's survey of social science research on race relations found that racialist thinking remained a persistent feature of scholarship. Not only was Drake's study a rebuttal of academic racism, it also criticized the excesses of black nationalist cultural common sense. As a member of AMSAC, Drake had frequently worked to demonstrate and solidify cooperation between African Americans and Africans. By this time, however, Drake viewed Afrocentrism as a problematic African American reinvention of Africa. Drake's dual emphasis on black solidarity and nonracialism constituted an outgrowth of both his Quaker education and his background as the son of a Barbadian Garveyite minister.

Drake viewed black studies scholarship as an antidote to the increased racial polarization of the 1980s, from national electoral politics and conservative attacks on the welfare state to heightened racial tensions on college campuses, including culture wars over Afrocentric and multicultural canons and curricula. But he emphasized the double-edged significance of what he called black studies' vindicationist dimension. On the one hand, wholly detached scholarship was not an option for black scholars confronted by segregation and its legacy. Vindicationism, or what Drake called a "black perspective," thus represented a necessary corrective to academic cant about objectivity and universalism. The urban environmental emphasis of black studies social science scholarship built on such pioneering scholars as Franz Boas, Carter G. Woodson, and W. E. B. Du Bois in discrediting theories of biological racism within the academy.[53] On the other hand, Drake realized that the desire of some vindicationist writers to counter the historical erasure of an African presence and contribution in antiquity had sometimes resulted in factual errors and in assertions of myth and folklore as fact.

The primary objective of Drake's study of Nile Valley antiquity in the fields of Egyptology, anthropology, and African American history was to challenge a specific problem in U.S.-based race relations theory. Drake opposed the argument advanced by social scientists and historians during the 1970s that "dark skin-color in general, and black skin-color in particular, are universally considered undesirable." These "Modern Manichaeans," as Drake termed them, claimed that the word "black" had derogatory connotations and referents that contrasted with the positive symbolic associations accorded to the word "white." They asserted that the negative associations of blackness and their relevance for invidious distinctions between light and dark people were universal (even shared by persons of African descent). Drake identified the work of historian Carl Degler (who, in turn, drew on the work of Kenneth Gergen, a social psychologist) as a representative example of the position claiming the universality of prejudice against black as a color and, in effect, an innate aversion to black people. As Degler wrote in his work on race relations in Brazil,

If the culture of peoples with pigmented skin as well as that of white Europeans is permeated with a preference for white as a color and in skin, then perhaps we are in the presence of an attitude that is universal and not simply the consequence of mere history. It is surely more than a coincidence that in Africa and Asia as well as in Europe, black is associated with unpleasantness, disaster or evil. . . . White, on the other hand, is the color of light. . . . Is it any wonder that white is seen everywhere as the symbol of success, virtue, purity, goodness. . . . For our purposes the conclusion to be drawn from this brief excursion into color symbolism is that perceptions of dark color are not only universally made, but that dark color is generally denigrated. It would seem that color prejudice is a universal phenomenon, not simply North American or Brazilian.[54]

Drake took exception to the Modern Manichaeans' disregard for historical explanations for the prejudices groups may harbor toward those darker than themselves. He argued that racist attitudes based on perceptions of moral or intellectual deficiencies and even romantic racialism, with its belief in a group's mystical or spiritual attributes, were not the province of human nature but instead "operate within social systems that are, in turn, articulated to specific modes of production that reflect ecological and demographic particularities." Social institutions and structures were decisive in shaping the meanings of interactions between racialized groups, an analysis confirmed by the fact that racialization was not restricted to those of darker hue but also targeted lighter-skinned persons in accord with the "one-drop rule." For Drake, Africa, inhabited by people of many colors, languages, and ethnicities—most of whom could be classified as "black" in the American sense—provided an ideal setting for testing the Modern Manichaean thesis that the color black was always contrasted negatively with white, that such evaluations shaped social interactions, and that all people, including blacks, exhibited an innate prejudice against dark skin color.[55]

Drake's analysis of archaeological and written evidence covering several millennia of contact between Negroid and Caucasoid peoples in the Nile Valley did not support the theory of a universal aversion to black skin color. Much social and cultural contact had occurred between Africans, Europeans, Semitic peoples, and Asians within the ancient Nile Valley empires of Egypt and later Kush, or Ethiopia. He found little evidence that such contacts were structured by antiblack prejudice or dominance. Noting the dispute over the racial identity of certain Egyptian pharaohs between racist Egyptologists and others, including such vindicationist black scholars of antiquity as Du Bois and Diop, Drake found abundant visual evidence to support the vindicationist position. Drake's primary concern, however, was not the documentation of a black presence in Egypt. But this was a necessary precondition to his more salient argument that no derogatory significance was attached to dark skin color and that social hierarchies were not shaped by antiblack racism. Nor were Egyptian identities derived from the racial denigration of Nubians from the south; instead, Egyptians marked their foreign political rivals chiefly in terms of geographical rather than racial difference. Drake delighted in puncturing the racial perspectives of Egyptologists. He cited the laudatory accounts of the political and intellectual achievements of some pharaohs (identified by other scholars as Negroid) by biased Egyptologists who refrained from disclosing the black African identity of those they held in such high esteem. Explicitly following in the footsteps of Du Bois—Drake's title echoed Du Bois's study of race in antiquity, *Black Folk Then and Now*—Drake's appropriation of antiblack scholarship for revisionist purposes was reminiscent of Du Bois's use of the factual data provided in antiblack Reconstruction historiography for the revisionist interpretation of his *Black Reconstruction* (1935).

Drake's primary objective in *Black Folk Here and There* was to challenge the racial assumptions propounded by social science academics. However, within several bibliographic essays, Drake also addressed the equally dubious theories of some black scholars seeking to explain antiblack racism. Drake commented that exponents of "melanin theory" were "noteworthy for their decisive rejection of the environmentalist orientation that has prevailed in the study of race relations since the 1930s, and for turning back toward pre-Boasian biological determinism."[56]

Drake challenged a presentist black nationalist approach to the study of race in antiquity that echoed the Manichaean theory's naturalizing of antiblack prejudice. He cited Chancellor Williams's *The Destruction of Black Civilization*, which claimed that racially motivated "white" barbarians conquered the "black" civilizations of Egypt and Kush. While Drake made it clear that he shared the vindicationist aims of such otherwise flawed approaches, he took exception not only to the anachronistic imposition of modern racism but also to a central tenet of black nationalist discourse—that is, the black cultural commonplace that a connection necessarily existed between the derogatory connotations of the word "black" and negative attitudes toward and mistreatment of black people. Citing mitigating circumstances, including the fact that blackness as a socially constructed racial classification in the United States is not confined to dark skin color, Drake rejected such generalizations as unproven and untenable. Given Drake's background and experiences and his reflections on Walter Rodney, the relevance of Drake's debunking of this popular black nationalist myth for his belief in transracial alliances becomes clearly evident.[57]

In *Black Folk Here and There*, Drake noted the resurgence of academic racism in the form of genetic theories of racial inferiority measured by intelligence tests. During the conservative Reagan years, Drake noted a convergence of (white) social science and black nationalist theories naturalizing racial difference and prejudice. Drake's account of the racial diversity of the world of Nile Valley antiquity, while vindicationist, was more intent on challenging the peculiar cross-racial consensus around the belief in universal and transhistorical racial prejudice, making unlikely bedfellows of white liberal academics and black nationalists.

As a product of the postwar culture of black freedom and modernity, Drake's *Black Folk Here and There*, like other classic black studies texts, is dedicated to advancing a transformative consciousness. It challenges its readers to question racialist myths and to move beyond unproductive debates and narrow identities that inhibit the ability to function effectively and cooperatively in a rapidly changing world. In the work, Drake implied that a preoccupation with Afrocentrism as the panacea for social disenfranchisement and pariah status diminished African Americans' capacity to imagine a more inclusive political community, as Rodney had so compellingly done. Largely overlooked except by specialists, Drake's *Black Folk Here and There* contains a valuable and lucid review of the evolution of scholarship on race relations. Drake's text is a fitting and highly instructive tribute to its author's lifelong commitment to intellectual activism.

In Ghana, Drake, Mayfield, Feelings, Boone, and others confronted, for better or worse, the limitations of their transnational political vision. Yet while their vision of black diasporic citizenship and African social emancipation did not prevail in that time and place, it made a powerful resurgence during the 1980s in the Free South Africa movement led by Mary Frances Berry, Randall Robinson, and TransAfrica, the African American foreign policy lobby that worked with members of the Congressional Black Caucus to orchestrate a series of antiapartheid demonstrations at the South African embassy in Washington, D.C. The protests galvanized a U.S. antiapartheid movement, joining criticism by South African Bishop Desmond Tutu of the Reagan administration's policy of "constructive engagement" with the apartheid regime.[58] Visiting the United States on the way to receiving the Nobel Peace Prize, Tutu denounced Reagan's policy and called the demonstrations "superb." High-level black appointees in the Reagan administration, including Clarence Thomas and Clarence Pendleton, opposed the demonstrations. Pendleton claimed a mere "pigment attachment" as the motivation for the protests and wondered whether a black person at the top of the military would defend U.S. interests in South Africa. "Are they going to be just blacks, or go beyond that?"[59]

Pendleton's question struck at the heart of the politics of the Ghanaian expatriates, who, along with other African American dissenters, posed vital and enduring questions about what sort of American citizenship African Americans might claim and how they might enact that vision of citizenship against the grain of U.S. domestic and foreign policies. Pendleton posed for African Americans the unenviable and false choice between either affiliation with a United States embarked on an unjust and unconscionable alliance with white minority rule or what he viewed pejoratively as a narrow racial identity. That characterization trivialized the historical memory of the postwar anticolonial alliance between African American leaders and African nationalists, binding black Americans and African peoples together in their respective struggles for freedom, a worldview that had led numerous African American elected officials and activists—and their nonblack allies—to engage in direct-action protests against apartheid. Then, as at other times, the expatriates' way of seeing, of imagining a more just world, could not be so easily reduced to race or confined to the policy imperatives of the American nation. Even as it issued from a deep historical memory of racial oppression, that way of seeing and being in the world also rallied others outside that background, as Drake, Rodney, and other advocates of a politics of alliance would have noted, to join African Americans on the picket lines and to be handcuffed together as American participants in a global antiapartheid movement.

EPILOGUE

*Memory and the Transnational Dimensions
of African American Citizenship*

During the summer of 1994, the Reverend Desmond Tutu, Archbishop of South Africa, visited Ghana to participate in a service marking the centenary of Accra's Cathedral Church of the Most Holy Trinity. In his sermon, Archbishop Tutu noted that Ghana would always have a special place in the heart of South Africans for the inspiration and support it provided during that nation's struggle against apartheid. Recalling the leadership of Kwame Nkrumah and Ghana's leading role as the Black Star of Africa, Tutu declared that Africa would have been better off if it had more leaders like Nkrumah, committed to African unity and the welfare of its peoples. The timing of Tutu's praise of Nkrumah's Ghana was telling, coming months after the Rwandan genocide and as Nigerian labor unions and prodemocracy activists staged a nationwide general strike against Sani Abacha's brutal military dictatorship.[1]

Tutu's favorable assessment was in keeping with the rehabilitation of Nkrumah within Ghanaian political culture, a process that began with Nkrumah's death in 1972 and the return of his remains for a state reinterment in his home village of Nkroful.[2] After a series of military and civilian governments proved unable to curb endemic corruption and lift the country out of its economic morass, many Ghanaians made their peace with Nkrumah's memory, acknowledging his historic achievement as a founder of Ghanaian nationhood. In that tumultuous summer of 1994, some observers saw the tribute to Nkrumah by such a prominent African as an implicit criticism of Ghana's current president, Jerry Rawlings, whose victory in a civilian election held in 1992 was contested by opponents from both the left and the right. As a flight lieutenant in Ghana's Air Force, Rawlings had seized power in a bloody 1981 military coup, espousing a populist agenda against corruption but also cracking down on critics in the courts and the press. But if

Rawlings had exercised a chilling effect on Ghanaian civil society, by 1994 he presided over a Ghana widely touted in the West as the showcase for the World Bank and International Monetary Fund Structural Adjustment Programs, which involved the privatization of state-owned industries, the retrenchment of state employees, and the reduction of such vital social services as education and public health.[3]

I happened to be in Ghana during Tutu's 1994 visit. I watched Wole Soyinka, interviewed on CNN International, identified as a spokesman for the African Democratic League instead of by his more familiar incarnation as Nobel laureate author, condemn the crimes of the Abacha regime. A year later, Abacha further demonstrated his defiance of the world community by executing several dissenters, including renowned Nigerian writer and activist Ken Saro-Wiwa. Beginning my research on this book in Ghana, I was surprised to find Ghanaians still buzzing about the previous year's government-sanctioned visit by Louis Farrakhan of the Nation of Islam (NOI). According to those Ghanaians with whom I spoke, Farrakhan's exhortations in speeches broadcast over state television to support Rawlings and not to begrudge their leaders the amenities of power, prestige, and wealth flew in the face of Ghanaians' long-standing resentment of corruption. Some Ghanaians read Farrakhan's warnings that whites were using religion to recolonize Africa as an open appeal for support for Islam in the face of the growing popularity of Christian evangelism in Ghana and throughout Africa. While I cannot claim that those Ghanaians with whom I spoke constituted a consensus, their skepticism suggested that although many Ghanaians speak the same language as Farrakhan, much remains to be desired in the translation of the NOI leader's statements within Ghanaian political culture.[4]

At the time, I was struck by Rawlings's official welcome to Farrakhan. Both parties clearly hoped to capitalize on the historical symbolism of pan-Africanism. Although he would have been loathe to acknowledge it, Farrakhan seemed obsessed with retracing the footsteps of Malcolm X, whose image and memory were ubiquitous within African American popular culture at that time. Farrakhan's warm reception in Ghana enabled him to reprise Malcolm's role as militant world statesman. For his part, Rawlings hoped to bask in the aura of Farrakhan's image as pan-Africanist firebrand and, through his association with the NOI leader, to appeal for the support of Ghana's Islamic minority in the Northern Territories as well as in the Accra suburb of Nima. The partnership with Farrakhan also furthered Rawlings's agenda of promoting tourism, a major growth industry, by attracting African American visitors. That October, the NOI held its annual Savior's Day convention in Accra, bringing approximately two thousand African Americans to the country.

Louis Farrakhan's 1993 visit to Ghana provides a fascinating contrast with that of his mentor, Malcolm X, almost thirty years earlier. In 1964, the pan-Africanism represented by Malcolm X posed a direct challenge to American legitimacy, as Malcolm was poised to mobilize global opposition to an American military-industrial liberalism subsidized in part by lucrative investments in repressive southern African white minority regimes and maintained by covert operations and military interventions in Africa, Southeast Asia, and Latin America. Indeed, Malcolm's eloquent exposure of the American nation's contradictory domestic liberalism and organized violence abroad was potentially explosive enough for Nkrumah to keep Malcolm at arm's length for fear of further incurring the wrath of U.S. officials. The NOI newspaper that Malcolm founded, *Muhammed Speaks*, printed no coverage of his diplomatic errand in Ghana and throughout Africa. Instead, its pages were filled with inflammatory death threats against Malcolm, a campaign in which Farrakhan had actively participated. In 1993, Farrakhan devoted much coverage in the NOI newspaper, *The Final Call*, to his triumphant reception in Ghana. Farrakhan reciprocated Rawlings's generosity in permitting unlimited access to the Ghanaian media by granting Rawlings an exclusive interview in *Final Call*.

While the pan-African unity shared by Farrakhan and Rawlings barely concealed an underlying bourgeois nationalism, when Farrakhan visited Cape Coast Castle, a Danish-built seventeenth-century slave-trading fort taken over by the British to mark the establishment of the Gold Coast colony, he could not help voicing the tensions that have often defined the diasporic encounter between African Americans and Africans and that Richard Wright articulated in *Black Power*. Reproach seemed to prevail over forgiveness in Farrakhan's remarks addressed to Ghanaians, as he toured the site where African captives were held before the calamitous Middle Passage across the Atlantic to enslavement in the Americas: "Any of us who sees this should be so moved that you will never sell out the future of your people for any advantage."[5] If that occasion did not spur in Farrakhan a chastening awareness of how in his lifetime the worst of black and African leaders have repeatedly murdered the best at the behest of even more powerful others, then perhaps while in Cape Coast Castle he received the epiphany that African American men must atone for their transgressions, a view he articulated at the 1995 Million Man March in Washington, D.C. Farrakhan's diversionary mass mobilization as the Republican Party readied its "Contract with Amer-

ican citizenship informed by a transnational solidarity with the wretched of
the earth.

Like those crowds of NOI pilgrims that fall, I visited the Cape Coast Castle
during my monthlong stay in Ghana. As it surely did for the NOI members,
the visit to the site where African captives began their tragic journey to the
Americas underscored for me what it meant to be an African American as
well as the transnational dimensions of American citizenship. I had already
seen images of the castle in Ethiopian-born filmmaker Haile Gerima's *Sankofa*, a candid and graphic meditation on the history of enslavement and
resistance that explodes the romantic and paternalistic depictions of slavery
so common in Hollywood cinema. The film's opening and closing sequences,
set in and around the castle, enact the centrality of the history of the slave
trade for the making of African American, African Caribbean, and Afro–
Latin American peoples. At the start of the film in present-day Ghana, the
castle's grounds are haunted by a Ghanaian drummer, a shaman-like figure
dressed in white robes with his face and bare skin covered in white chalk
who is engaged in intense drumming and chanting. He bears witness to
visitors that the castle's grounds have been consecrated by the souls of the
many ancestors who departed through its "door of no return," whether to
bondage in slave societies in the Americas or to death at sea, where many
perished of disease and others lost their lives in defiant acts of suicide or
insurrection. The drummer-priest, played by musician-activist Kofi Ghanaba,
is a committed, perhaps overzealous, keeper of memory who clashes with
the imperatives of the Ghanaian state and its vested interest in tourism, as is
evidenced by his hostile confrontation with a group of tourists. An armed
soldier chases the priest away from the tourist group, identifying him to its
frightened members as Sankofa, a self-appointed guardian of the castle.

Through Ghanaba's presence, the film's subtext evokes the history of pan-
Africanism, in which politics and culture were inextricably interwoven. Ghanaba was formerly known as Guy Warren, a renowned Ghanaian percussionist and Afro-jazz fusion innovator. Warren emigrated to New York City
during the early 1950s, attracted by the Afro-diasporic bebop revolution of
Charlie Parker, Dizzy Gillespie, and others. In Chicago, Warren recorded two
influential albums (one of them titled *Africa Speaks, America Answers*) that
contained his arrangements blending traditional Ghanaian percussion styles
and West African highlife, with music performed by American jazz musicians. Returning to his birthplace, Ghana, after independence, Warren resumed his busy performance schedule and became a strong advocate in the

Ghanaian press of Nkrumah's agenda as well as an exponent of the cultural dimension of the African personality through his synthesis of Ghanaian traditional and modern Afro-diasporic musical styles.[6]

The film's narrative begins with the abduction of a contemporary African American woman into slavery through a supernatural suspension of historical time. She is a model on a photo shoot at the unlikely setting of Cape Coast Castle. She had earlier incurred the drummer-priest's wrath for her conduct while being photographed, writhing on the nearby beach clad in a tiger-striped swimsuit in response to her white photographer's exhortations to look sexy. She is later a member of the tour group confronted by the Sankofa figure. She wanders from the group, exploring the tunnels leading down to the dungeons where male and female captives were kept separately. She is suddenly confronted by a vision of male captives, chained and crowded together in the darkness of the dungeon, illuminated by torchlight. When she tries to escape, she is seized by white men, whose dress, demeanor, and drawn weapons mark them as slave traders from the past. As the chained male captives watch silently and as she screams in protest that she is African American, implying that the men are making a mistake, she is restrained, stripped to the waist, and branded with a hot iron on the back, as was customary for African captives. At the moment of her branding, her screams give way in the soundtrack to a live recording of Aretha Franklin singing the gospel hymn "Precious Lord, Take My Hand." In the recording, Franklin (who appeared on the cover of her early 1970s gospel album *Amazing Grace* in full African regalia) has reached a climactic point in the performance in which she briefly departs from the lyrics with a repeated wordless melismatic scream, a vocal expression suspended somewhere between speech and music. In that particular pairing of image and sound, Franklin's gospel-inflected scream figures an ancestral memory of the agonies and rage of enslavement. Yet the music also imparts a retrospective sense of grace and resiliency to the scene's depiction of the collective trauma of enslavement, as suggested by the lyrics sung by Franklin: "At the river, here I stand, take my hand, Precious Lord, and lead your child on home."

The film's action, situated in the indistinct past of plantation slavery and maroon resistance, centers on the gradual transformation of the woman, named Shola, from fearful and compliant house slave subjected to sexual abuse by the master to a rebellious stance and her eventual initiation into a group of resisters among a pan-African community of slaves of African, Caribbean, and North American origin. *Sankofa* concludes with a symbolic reunion of peoples of African descent scattered by multiple histories of slavery, all wearing colorful neo-African dress when they return to one of the sites of the dispersal of their ancestors. They congregate on the grounds of Cape Coast Castle and seat themselves, symbolizing the return of the ancestral spirits uprooted from the African continent. As Ghanaba's Sankofa character accompanies the film soundtrack, playing his Ghanaian drums with curved wooden sticks, these multihued black people, including the actress who plays Shola, take their places among a symbolically reconstituted African diasporic world.

I had seen *Sankofa* before visiting Cape Coast. The film is a powerful, wrenching depiction of the horrors of slavery and the daily dilemma of slaves, which, in its essence, amounted to what manner of death they might choose under the regimen of the slave system. But seeing Cape Coast Castle on film was no preparation for the experience of being there. The castle, a massive whitewashed structure pocked by wind and weather, rises from the rocks on the shoreline, its mounted cannons aimed toward the Atlantic Ocean. Elmina Castle, constructed by the Portuguese in 1482 as the first West African slave-trading fort, was just visible on the coast ten kilometers to the north. Our Ghanaian guide led a group composed of two Ghanaians, tourists from Nigeria and the Netherlands, and me across the open courtyard in the midday sun, passing pyramids of stacked cannonballs and the grave sites of colonial governors and other notables. Looking past the cannons out onto the shoreline, we could see local fishermen plying their trade. The guide led us down into the darkening passageways leading to the dungeons, one for men and one for women, each holding around two hundred captives. As our eyes adjusted to the darkness, we could make out large, dark rooms with high ceilings, lacking ventilation save two tiny openings at the top of one of the walls that permitted the entry of a small shaft of sunlight or windblown sprays of rain and surf. It must have been fearfully dark at night and suffocating from the lack of ventilation. The air in the dungeons was thick with the lingering stench of centuries of excreta compressed into the floor, an awful remnant of the inhuman conditions the captives endured. The dungeon reserved for men had trenches for the drainage of human wastes. No such trenches were visible in the dungeon for female captives; I wondered if they had ever existed. When enough captives had been gathered to fill the slave ships, the men and women were marched from their separate dungeons through tunnels that converged, leading to the "door of no return." Inhabiting that momentous yet obscure place, I readily imagined the abject horror felt by the captives, not knowing what awaited them as their captors forced them onto the ships. When I was there, the door was blocked—walled off, we were told, since the end of the slave trade. Stunned into silence, shading our eyes, we emerged into the bright sunshine of the courtyard.

From the cobblestoned courtyard, we ascended the stairs leading to the colonial governor's residence, a spacious room overlooking the Atlantic, buffeted that day by a steady ocean breeze. The governor's sitting room was located two floors directly above the dungeon for male captives. Sandwiched on the floor in between, directly below the governor's sitting room and directly above the dungeon, was an Anglican church, the first established in West Africa. How fitting, I thought, that the church should provide a physical if not moral buffer, as the castle's architects perhaps hoped, between colonial officialdom and the captives whose sale enriched the Crown colony.

Taking in the colonial architecture of Cape Coast castle makes tangible to all visitors, regardless of their background, the meaning of *sankofa*, an Akan word that tells us that "to move forward, you must know where you came from." The visit impressed on me the inescapable reality that New World blacks in the United States, the Caribbean, and Latin America owe their existence to the primal scenes of capture, imprisonment, and enslavement that transpired in places such as Cape Coast Castle. No wonder that Shola's pleas to her captors that as an African American she was immune to such mistreatment fell on deaf ears. The ancestral bond of indebtedness to those many millions gone, those captive and enslaved forebears to whom African Americans owe their existence as a people, cannot be so easily willed away. From the vantage point of Cape Coast, the indebtedness of citizens of the Western world to the generations of slaves whose unpaid labor built the wealth of the United States and that of the Western industrial nations cannot be so easily denied. Indeed, as Richard Wright observed during the early 1950s, such places of darkness and dire suffering actually constitute quintessential sites of Western modernity, enlightenment, and even rationality by virtue of the planned efficiency of their commodification of human flesh.

That this history is far too powerful to be eradicated by the sanitized version of history that accompanied Nkrumah's ouster and the dispersal of the black expatriates had also been apparent in a much earlier film. Made only four years after the 1966 coup, the documentary *Soul to Soul*, a concert film record of the visit of African American R & B and soul musicians to Ghana, contained a sequence filmed at Cape Coast. The film intersperses footage of concert performances on a stage underneath the Independence Arch in Accra's Black Star Square by Wilson Pickett, Roberta Flack, Les McCann, Ike and Tina Turner, Santana, the Staples Singers, and others with

The front wall of Cape Coast Castle, facing the Atlantic Ocean.
(Time Life Pictures/Getty Images)

cinema verité sequences of the artists' offstage activities. We see the black R
& B stars as they are treated to performances by Ghanaian music and dance
troupes and engage in such commonplace tourist activities as shopping in
Ghana's open-air markets. The African American celebrities' encounters with
Ghanaians and their culture, Ghanaian audiences' reception of the Afro-
American musicians' performances, and the performers' engagement with
the history of the slave trade record the ongoing diasporic dialogue over the
meaning of the shared past of peoples of African descent. Midway through
the film, Flack and her mentor, McCann, are seen walking through Cape
Coast Castle after several external shots of the castle, its oceanside setting,
and local children playing nearby on the shore as fishermen haul in their
nets. Voice-overs by McCann and Flack testify to the emotional experience of
touring the castle. In one of the dungeons, Flack performs an impromptu a
cappella rendition of the spiritual "Oh Freedom" (Before I'll be a slave, I'll
be buried in my grave / And go home to my Lord and be free). When I was
in Ghana, Mike Eghan, a Ghanaian media celebrity and businessman who
served as master of ceremonies for the concert, told me that Flack was so
shaken by her visit to Cape Coast that she was almost unable to perform that
evening. I first learned of the film from Eghan. I spent several years locating
the soundtrack recording of the film on a vinyl album and several more years

finding a copy of the film. Nothing, it seems, is rarer than such visual documentation of African American encounters with Ghana and its history of the slave trade.

The sequence with Flack and McCann at Cape Coast immediately precedes a concert performance by the Staples Singers gospel group. They performed a song whose refrain is "When will we be paid for the work we've done?" The song's lyrics discuss black people's pariah status within American society despite enslaved and free African Americans' substantial economic and military contributions to the nation. Although the reception of the song's message among the Ghanaian audience is difficult to discern, the two sequences constitute a compelling articulation of an Afro-diasporic memory of unrequited toil and service to the American nation reminiscent of the freedpeople's postemancipation demands for landownership as compensation for their unpaid slave labor.

Not surprisingly, coming only four years after Nkrumah's ouster, *Soul to Soul* makes no reference to the political history of pan-Africanism and Nkrumah's Ghana. However, it provides a detailed record of cultural pan-Africanism in practice, with both the misunderstandings and affirmations that characterized cross-cultural interchanges between Ghanaians and African Americans.

Four decades later, Ghana remains home to only a handful of the initial wave of African American expatriates who relocated there in response to Nkrumah's appeal to the African diaspora. Yet the continued African American presence in Ghana informs an ongoing dialogue sparked by the legacies of slavery, colonialism, and pan-Africanism. When I met Dr. Robert Lee, who remains in Ghana after being part of the first wave of African Americans to relocate there before independence, he noted that African Americans and Caribbean Americans had immigrated to Ghana during the 1990s. Many were retirees, some were entrepreneurs, and a handful were celebrities who had established homes in Ghana, including Rita Marley, Stevie Wonder, and Isaac Hayes. Then well into his seventies, Lee continued his dental practice and set an energetic pace as I accompanied him on several errands around Accra. It bothered him that no one seemed to talk about pan-Africanism anymore. Instead, people use the term "diaspora," which to Lee connotes separateness rather than solidarity. On another occasion, Lee shared with a journalist his regret that more young Africans were not committed to the development of Ghana. "A young African gets trained in something, and immediately he's off to England or Chicago, so you see it all gets confused. The African goes to America, and the American wants to come here." While it is understandable that Lee finds this trend worrisome, this remaking of the African diaspora may well revitalize links between African Americans and Africans.[7]

By any measure, the Accra of the 1990s was a far cry from Ghana's heyday of freedom and modernity. Declarations of impressive economic growth by Western economists were belied by the frequent electricity blackouts and the widespread poverty in Accra, the latter exacerbated by structural adjustment programs that diverted much of state's resources to the servicing of foreign debt. The "informal sector" of Ghana's economy, which some observers held up as an engine of growth, in fact comprised countless Ghanaian youth and adults in Accra's streets hawking castaway items of little use to anyone. To Lee and Ghanaians of his generation, such stagnation must have seemed a disappointment compared with Ghana's halcyon days as the Black Star of Africa. Despite such deprivation, Ghana and its people have maintained the country's reputation for hospitality to visitors and tourists. As the memory of the political pan-Africanism led by Nkrumah fades among both Ghanaians and black expatriates from the diaspora, the memory of the slave trade continues to shape the transnational diasporic discussion. That discussion is inescapably informed by similar yet distinct racial and colonial legacies of underdevelopment that plague its participants. African American emigrants' and visitors' encounters with Ghanaians are mediated by several factors, including the persistence of racial inequality in the United States, Ghana's chronic poverty, the quite different experiences of racism of both groups, and the perception among many Ghanaians—an unsettling one for many African Americans—of the comparative wealth and privilege of black emigrants and visitors from the diaspora. A cosmopolitan Ghanaian man who had insisted that I visit Cape Coast Castle pointed out matter-of-factly that many Ghanaians considered African Americans much better off for their enslaved ancestors' travails and misfortune.

Nowhere were such different perceptions of the past more controversial than those surrounding official Ghanaian historic-preservation efforts to transform Cape Coast and Elmina Castles into museum sites as part of the state's promotion of the tourist industry. African American expatriates and visitors bitterly opposed some of the renovations by Ghanaians, particularly plans to paint and install lighting in the dungeons and build a restaurant and bar within the Cape Coast structure. Efforts to remove the stench from the dungeons also met with vehement objections from concerned African Americans. Such changes struck them as dubious acts of whitewashing history by depriving visitors of the opportunity to experience the brutal and inhuman conditions of captivity. Such attempts to cater to the tourist trade constituted a desecration of a place that African Americans felt had been hallowed by their ancestors' suffering. In the face of these objections to the handling of the slave-trading castles, Ghanaian authorities scrapped plans for some of the more unpopular changes. Through their protest at what they viewed as the Disneyfication of the slave trading forts, African Americans asserted not only a distinct memory of the slave trade but also a strong claim to the ownership of that historical memory. They engaged in a painful yet fruitful dialogue with Ghanaian authorities that transformed distinct perceptions of the past into something approaching a shared memory.[8]

The cultural interactions between Ghanaian officials and concerned African Americans over the historical commemoration of the slave-trading forts as well as the interactions between the black American performers of the Soul to Soul revue and Ghanaians may lack a direct link to the African American expatriates attracted to Ghana during the early days of independence, as Ghanaians of a certain age refer to that era. Moreover, these encounters bear little resemblance to the activist initiatives of TransAfrica and the Congressional Black Caucus. Yet the engagement with the history of the making of Africa and its diaspora in the conflict over the slave castles and as depicted in *Sankofa* and *Soul to Soul* suggests that despite latter-day attempts by Farrakhan and Rawlings to manipulate the political history of pan-Africanism and despite U.S. officialdom's wariness toward an African American citizenship informed by solidarity with African peoples, these articulations of cultural pan-Africanism draw on indelible historical traditions of solidarity and alliance that bind African American and African peoples. The continuing plight and challenges facing black people in the diaspora ensure the persistence of this cultural orientation toward Africa. That orientation can be the path to civic engagement and demands for human rights, including equal protection and due process, as seen in the antiapartheid mobilizations of the Congressional Black Caucus and TransAfrica or more recently in the protests by black elected officials in New York State against the police killing of Amadou Diallo, an unarmed immigrant from Guinea. As long as African Americans face discrimination, racism, and cultural denigration in U.S. society, they will search for better or worse beyond the boundaries of the American nation for an affirming cultural identity and for an American citizenship informed by past and present affiliations with Africa and its diaspora. As was the case during the momentous convergence of the U.S. civil rights movement and the movements for national liberation in Africa, a major challenge for the African American intelligentsia and leadership class is to help articulate a political and cultural relationship to both the American nation and the African continent on behalf of a diverse African American population that includes both native-born members and African and Caribbean immigrants and their children.

While many African American expatriates looked to Ghana and Africa for the fulfillment of their deferred dreams of freedom in a segregated American society, their engagement with the world represented the leading edge of African Americans' articulations of not so much a dual but a transnational U.S. citizenship. Today, the identification with Africa among increasing numbers of African Americans can be regarded not as a rejection of America but instead as a crucial foundation for expressions of American citizenship. The resources of hope articulated by Nkrumah and the expatriates linked the fate of Africans not only to people of African descent in the diaspora but to Asian and Middle Eastern peoples' articulations of anti-imperialism, democracy, nonalignment, and nonracialism. This global emancipatory vision was grounded in the shared histories of racialized groups yet broke the boundaries of race. As articulated by African American expatriates and their allies, including W. E. B. Du Bois, George Padmore, Bill Sutherland, Richard Wright, E. Franklin Frazier, George Lamming, Lorraine Hansberry, Julian Mayfield, St. Clair Drake, Malcolm X, and others, this vision in the U.S. setting represented a path not taken in African American politics, a radical democratic path between the Scylla of integration and the Charybdis of separatism.

That vision was informed by the postwar anticolonial nonaligned movement of Afro-Asian nations. Not only had that movement joined nations in foreign policy and international arenas, it recognized and wrestled with ethnic pluralism, acknowledging that Asian and Middle Eastern peoples had for some time been integral parts of African and U.S. societies and polities. Today, the importance of that pluralistic vision of Africa and America is heightened by the political violence and ethnic and religious conflict that menaces the stability of African states, including the Congo, Nigeria, and the Sudan. While several commentators have questioned the validity of the nation-state as the mechanism for political change in Africa,[9] such conflicts remind us that the collapse of viable nation-states poses a dire threat to regional and global security. In addition to the recent slaughter of millions in the Congo and the killing and displacement of thousands currently taking place in the western Sudan, failed and lawless regimes such as Liberia under recently deposed President Charles Taylor become sites of illicit arms trafficking and money laundering for the likes of al-Qaida.[10] Well before the rise of fundamentalist terror and the 1996 al-Qaida bombings of U.S. embassies in Kenya and Tanzania, Julius Nyerere had insisted on the importance of strong African states. In Nyerere's view, postindependence states were not inherently flawed but were prevented by external interference from achieving their objectives of social development. Not only had the military governments that had overthrown leaders such as Nkrumah failed to articulate the interests of African people, but even worse, the Cold War had deprived African states of the opportunity to develop unfettered. Said Nyerere, "[T]he Cold War took over and we had these externally supported dictatorships everywhere over the continent. . . . We were never allowed a chance."[11] While valid criticisms have been made about the detrimental effect of African states on indigenous institutions and civil society,[12] in the current global order it seems utopian at best to reject the framework of African nation-states, particularly as the African Union struggles to resolve conflicts through peacekeeping and diplomacy.

As Nyerere made clear, U.S. policies, past and present, remain crucial for an understanding of the continuing challenges facing the African continent. Today, as the American nation's racial demographics are becoming dramatically transformed by the immigration of Africans, Asians, and Latin American and Caribbean peoples, the challenges and obligations of an interdependent world require fresh and unsparing accounts of the role of American power in that world. The African American expatriates in Nkrumah's Ghana were more prescient about the international dimensions of American citizenship than the majority of their fellow citizens. Their story demonstrates that at the start of the twenty-first century, the question of how U.S. citizens shall define their relationship to the rest of the world is no small matter. The expatriates insisted on global demands for a more equitable distribution of wealth and resources, demands that far too many U.S. citizens have wished and willed away, to no avail. Moreover, we dismiss at our own peril their passionate conviction that these constitute life-and-death matters for humanity.

NOTES

Abbreviations

Bond Papers	Horace Mann Bond Papers, University of Massachusetts at Amherst, Special Collections, Amherst, Mass.
Clarke Papers	John Henrik Clarke Papers, Schomburg Center for Research in Black Culture, New York Public Library, New York
Drake Papers	St. Clair Drake Papers, Schomburg Center for Research in Black Culture, New York Public Library, New York
FRUS	U.S. Department of State, *Foreign Relations of the United States, 1964–1968*, vol. 24, *Africa* (Washington, D.C.: U.S. Government Printing Office, 1999)
Mayfield Papers	Julian Mayfield Papers, Schomburg Center for Research in Black Culture, New York Public Library, New York
MLK Papers	Clayborne Carson, ed., *The Papers of Martin Luther King, Jr.*, vol. 4 (Berkeley: University of California Press, 2000)
Murray Papers	Pauli Murray Papers, Radcliffe College Archives, Schlesinger Library, Harvard University, Cambridge, Mass.
Nkrumah Papers	Kwame Nkrumah Papers, Moorland-Spingarn Research Center, Howard University, Washington, D.C.
State Department Records	U.S. State Department Records, RG 59, National Archives, College Park, Md.
Williams Papers	Franklin Williams Papers, Lyndon Baines Johnson Presidential Library, Austin, Tex.
Wright Papers	Richard Wright Papers, Beinecke Rare Book Library, Yale University, New Haven, Conn.

1. Gbedemah and Nkrumah quotations taken from *The People's Century—Freedom Now: Colonial Rule Is Overthrown in Asia and Africa, 1947–1990*, documentary coproduced by WGBH-Boston and the BBC, 1997; see also Kwame Nkrumah, "Extract from the Midnight Pronouncement of Independence," in *Revolutionary Path* (New York: International Publishers, 1973), 121–22.

2. St. Clair Drake, "Birth of Ghana a Tribute to Africans, British," *Toward Freedom* 6, no. 3 (March 1957): 1, 3.

3. Lawrence Reddick, *Crusader without Violence: A Biography of Martin Luther King, Jr.* (New York: Harper, 1959).

4. Nixon's encounter is described in Erica Powell, *Private Secretary (Female)/Gold Coast* (London: Hurst, 1984), 106.

5. Martha Biondi, *To Stand and Fight: The Struggle for Civil Rights in Postwar New York City* (Cambridge: Harvard University Press, 2003); Robert Korstad, *Civil Rights Unionism* (Chapel Hill: University of North Carolina Press, 2004); see also Penny M. Von Eschen, *Race against Empire: Black Americans and Anticolonialism, 1937–1957* (Ithaca: Cornell University Press, 1997). On the federal government's repression of the Communist Party, liberals, and progressives, see Ellen Schrecker, *Many Are the Crimes: McCarthyism in America* (Boston: Little, Brown, 1998).

6. Nikhil Pal Singh, *Black Is a Country* (Cambridge: Harvard University Press, 2004).

7. Anthony Platt, *E. Franklin Frazier Reconsidered* (New Brunswick, N.J.: Rutgers University Press, 1991), 208–12.

8. Kenneth O'Reilly, *Racial Matters: The FBI's Secret File on Black America* (New York: Free Press, 1989); Clayborne Carson, *Malcolm X: The FBI File* (New York: Carroll and Graf, 1991).

9. Gerald Horne, *Black and Red: W. E. B. Du Bois and the Afro-American Response to the Cold War, 1944–1963* (Albany: State University of New York Press, 1985); Brenda Gayle Plummer, *Rising Wind: Black Americans and U.S. Foreign Affairs, 1935–1960* (Chapel Hill: University of North Carolina Press, 1996); Von Eschen, *Race against Empire*; Mary L. Dudziak, *Cold War Civil Rights: Race and the Image of American Democracy* (Princeton: Princeton University Press, 2000); Azza Salama Layton, *International Politics and Civil Rights Politics in the United States* (New York: Cambridge University Press, 2000); Thomas Borstelmann, *The Cold War and the Color Line: American Race Relations in the Global Arena* (Cambridge: Harvard University Press, 2002).

10. George Padmore, *How Britain Rules Africa* (London: Wishart, 1936); C. L. R. James, *Black Jacobins: Toussaint L'Ouverture and the Haitian Revolution* (London: Secker and Warburg, 1938); Amy Jacques Garvey, *Memorandum Correlative of Africa, the West Indies, and the Americas* (Kingston, Jamaica: n.p., 1944); Richard Wright, *Black Power: A Record of Reactions in a Land of Pathos* (New York: Harper, 1954);

Richard Wright, *The Color Curtain: A Report on the Bandung Conference* (New York: 289
World, 1956); Learie N. Constantine, *Colour Bar* (London: Anchor, 1954); Frantz
Fanon, *Black Skin, White Masks* (1952; New York: Grove, 1967); George Padmore,
Pan-Africanism or Communism? (1956; Garden City, N.Y.: Anchor, 1972); James Bald-
win, *Notes of a Native Son* (Boston: Beacon, 1955); Aimé Césaire, *Discourse on Colo-
nialism* (Paris: Présence Africaine, 1955).

11. Bill Schwarz, ed., *West Indian Intellectuals in Britain* (Manchester: Manchester
University Press, 2003).

12. David Birmingham, *Kwame Nkrumah: Father of African Nationalism* (Athens:
Ohio University Press, 1998), 63–69.

13. Ayi Kwei Armah, *The Beautyful Ones Are Not Yet Born* (Oxford: Heinemann,
1988); Ama Ata Aidoo, *No Sweetness Here* (London: Longman, 1970); Maryse Condé,
A Season in Rihata (Oxford: Heinemann, 1988); Chinua Achebe, *A Man of the People*
(Garden City, N.Y.: Anchor, 1967).

14. Tariq Ali criticizes the moral failings of such anticolonial leaders as Indonesia's
President Sukarno in his memoir, *Street Fighting Years* (New York: Citadel, 1987),
62–64.

15. Curtis J. "Kojo" Morrow, *Return of the Afro-American* (Huntington, N.Y.:
Kroshka, 2000); Leslie Alexander Lacy, *The Rise and Fall of a Proper Negro: An Autobiography* (New York: Macmillan, 1970); Maya Angelou, *All God's Children Need Traveling Shoes* (New York: Vintage, 1984); Aidoo, *No Sweetness Here*; Julian Mayfield,
"Black on Black: A Love Story," in *Ten Times Black*, ed. Julian Mayfield (New York:
Bantam, 1972); Julian Mayfield, "Tales of the Lido," unpublished manuscript, Mayfield Papers, box 14, folders 8–12.

16. Singh, *Black Is a Country*; Brent Hayes Edwards, *The Practice of Diaspora*
(Cambridge: Harvard University Press, 2003); Robin D. G. Kelley, *Freedom Dreams*
(Boston: Beacon, 2001); Cedric Robinson, *Black Marxism: The Making of the Black
Radical Tradition* (Chapel Hill: University of North Carolina Press, 1998); Paul Gilroy,
The Black Atlantic: Modernity and Double Consciousness (Cambridge: Harvard Univer-
sity Press, 1993); Manthia Diawara, *In Search of Africa* (Cambridge: Harvard Univer-
sity Press, 1998).

17. Frederick Cooper, "Conditions Analogous to Slavery," in Frederick Cooper,
Thomas C. Holt, and Rebecca J. Scott, *Beyond Slavery: Explorations of Race, Labor, and
Citizenship in Postemancipation Societies* (Chapel Hill: University of North Carolina
Press, 2000), 147; Leti Volpp, " 'Obnoxious to Their Very Nature': Asian Americans and
Constitutional Citizenship," *Citizenship Studies* 5, no. 1 (2001): 57–71; Danielle Allen,
Talking to Strangers: Anxieties of Citizenship since Brown v. Board of Education (Chi-
cago: University of Chicago Press, 2004).

18. Ntozake Shange, *Ellington Was Not a Street* (New York: Simon and Schuster
Books for Young Readers, 2004).

19. Mahmood Mamdani, *Good Muslim, Bad Muslim: America, the Cold War, and the
Roots of Terror* (New York: Pantheon, 2004).

20. George Ball, *The Past Has Another Pattern* (New York: Norton, 1983), 185.

21. Arthur Schlesinger Jr., *The Disuniting of America* (New York: Norton, 1992); Gary Gerstle, *American Crucible* (Princeton: Princeton University Press, 2000).

Chapter One

1. L. H. A. Scotland, "W.I. Colonial Expert to Tour West Africa," *Beacon* (Trinidad), July 14, 1951, 3. I am indebted to Michael Hanchard for sharing with me a copy of this source.

2. Brenda Gayle Plummer, *Rising Wind: Black Americans and U.S. Foreign Affairs, 1935–1960* (Chapel Hill: University of North Carolina Press, 1996); Penny M. Von Eschen, *Race against Empire: Black Americans and Anticolonialism, 1937–1957* (Ithaca: Cornell University Press, 1997); Winston James, *Holding Aloft the Banner of Ethiopia* (London: Verso, 1998); James H. Meriwether, *Proudly We Can Be Africans: Black Americans and Africa, 1935–1961* (Chapel Hill: University of North Carolina Press, 2002).

3. Michael Hanchard, "Afro-Modernity: Temporality, Politics, and the African Diaspora," *Public Culture* 11, no. 1 (Winter 1999): 245–68.

4. Mark Naison, *Communists in Harlem during the Depression* (New York: Grove, 1983); James A. Miller, Susan Pennybacker, and Eve Rosenhaft, "Mother Ada Wright and the International Campaign to Free the Scottsboro Boys, 1931–1934," *American Historical Review* 106, no. 2 (April 2001): 387–430.

5. Thomas Holt, *The Problem of Race in the Twenty-first Century* (Cambridge: Harvard University Press, 2000), 69–71.

6. Martha Biondi, *To Stand and Fight: The Struggle for Civil Rights in Postwar New York City* (Cambridge: Harvard University Press, 2003), 28–29.

7. Bill Schwarz, ed., *West Indian Intellectuals in Britain* (Manchester: Manchester University Press, 2003).

8. Hakim Adi, *West Africans in Britain, 1900–1960* (London: Lawrence and Wishart, 1998), 45–82.

9. Beth Bates, *Pullman Porters and the Rise of Protest Politics in Black America, 1925–1945* (Chapel Hill: University of North Carolina Press, 2001); Nikhil Pal Singh, *Black Is a Country* (Cambridge: Harvard University Press, 2004), 9.

10. *London Is the Place for Me: Trinidadian Calypso in London, 1950–1956*, compact disc, Honest Jon's Records, 2002.

11. Wolfgang Bender, "Independence, Highlife, Liberation Wars: Lagos 1950s and 1960s," in Okwui Enwezor, *The Short Century: Independence and Liberation Movements in Africa, 1945–1994* (Munich: Prestel, 2001), 279–80.

12. Paul Gilroy, *The Black Atlantic: Modernity and Double Consciousness* (Cambridge: Harvard University Press, 1993); Manthia Diawara, *In Search of Africa* (Cambridge: Harvard University Press, 1998).

13. I am indebted to Abiola Irele for this insight, which he provided in a talk as part

of a conference in honor of Sierra Leonean literary scholar and poet Lemuel Johnson sponsored by the Center for Afroamerican and African Studies, University of Michigan, March 12, 2004.

14. Brent Hayes Edwards, *The Practice of Diaspora* (Cambridge: Harvard University Press, 2003), 242–43.

15. Cedric Robinson, *Black Marxism: The Making of the Black Radical Tradition* (Chapel Hill: University of North Carolina Press, 1998), 248–49.

16. James Hooker, *Black Revolutionary: The Life of George Padmore* (New York: Praeger, 1970), 6.

17. "Information Obtained from Dr. Legrand Coleman," George Padmore materials, Nkrumah Papers, box 154-41, folder 16. After Padmore's death, his widow, Dorothy, planned to write her husband's biography and solicited the recollections of many of Padmore's associates. One of the most vivid of these is Coleman's account.

18. Hooker, *Black Revolutionary*, 7.

19. Ibid.

20. "Information Obtained from Dr. Legrand Coleman."

21. Raymond Wolters, *The New Negro on Campus: Black College Rebellions of the 1920s* (Princeton: Princeton University Press, 1975).

22. Robin D. G. Kelley, *Hammer and Hoe: Black Communists in Alabama* (Chapel Hill: University of North Carolina Press, 1989).

23. Ras Makonnen, *Pan-Africanism from Within* (New York: Oxford University Press, 1973), 102; Hooker, *Black Revolutionary*, 31–32.

24. "Three Dillard Professors Who Protested Parade of Italians Threatened," *Norfolk Journal and Guide*, May 30, 1936, n.p., Drake Papers, box 2, folder 19.

25. "American Notes," *International African Opinion* 1, no. 2 (August 1938): 12; Langston Hughes, "August 19th: Scottsboro Death Date (A Poem for Clarence Norris)," *International African Opinion* 1, no. 2 (August 1938): 6–7; "Brief History of the Case," *International African Opinion* 1, no. 2 (August 1938): 7.

26. W.H., "Negro Life and Letters," *International African Opinion* 1, no. 4 (October 1938): 11.

27. Marika Sherwood, *Kwame Nkrumah: The Years Abroad, 1935–1947* (Legon: Freedom, 1996), 15–16.

28. Dennis Austin, *Politics in Ghana, 1946–1960* (London: Oxford University Press, 1964), 16–17.

29. Sherwood, *Kwame Nkrumah*, 17–20.

30. Ibid., 22.

31. L. D. Reddick, "What the 'Brothers' Need to Know," *African Interpreter* 1, no. 4 (Summer 1943): 11.

32. Sherwood, *Kwame Nkrumah*, 42. I am indebted to Abdul Alkalimat for sharing a photograph of this outdoor rally in Harlem.

33. Ibid., 50–51.

34. Ibid., 52–53.

35. Ibid., 70–71.

36. "Nkrumah Pays Tribute to Lincoln," *Lincoln University Bulletin*, Summer 1951, 12.

37. St. Clair Drake, "The Politics of Kwame Nkrumah: A Pan-African Interpretation," unpublished manuscript, Drake Papers, box 23, folder 38.

38. St. Clair Drake to Richard Wright, March 31, 1948?, Wright Papers, box 96, folder 1302.

39. Drake cautioned Walter White against blaming communists for white mob violence and assaults against African American homeowners in Chicago. See St. Clair Drake to Walter White, July 14, 1951, Drake Papers, box 10, folder 15.

40. "Britain Faces the Race Problem," *Ebony*, November 1951, 90–96. Drake's authorship of this article is confirmed in Drake to John Johnson, October 4, 1951, Drake Papers, box 10, folder 15; "Africa's Quiet Revolution," *Ebony*, June 1952, 94–98.

41. St. Clair Drake to Charles Johnson, March 12, 1953, Drake Papers, box 4, folder 2.

42. David Brokensha, "St. Clair Drake: The African Years," 1–2, Drake Papers, box 52, folder 7.

43. St. Clair Drake to Horace Mann Bond, January 29, 1956, Bond Papers, ser. 2, box 12, folder 30A.

Chapter Two

1. Richard Wright, *Black Power: A Record of Reactions in a Land of Pathos* (New York: Harper, 1954), xiii–iv.

2. Constance Webb, *Richard Wright* (New York: Putnam, 1968), 251.

3. Paul Gilroy, *The Black Atlantic: Modernity and Double Consciousness* (Cambridge: Harvard University Press, 1993), 155–57, 173.

4. Richard Wright, *The Outsider* (New York: Harper-Perennial, 1993), 33–35.

5. George Lamming, *The Pleasures of Exile* (1960; Ann Arbor: University of Michigan Press, 1995); Edward R. Braithwaite, *A Kind of Homecoming* (Englewood Cliffs, N.J.: Prentice-Hall, 1962).

6. Examples include W. E. B. Du Bois, *Black Reconstruction* (New York: Harcourt, Brace, 1935); C. L. R. James, *Black Jacobins: Toussaint L'Ouverture and the Haitian Revolution* (London: Secker and Warburg, 1938); C. L. R. James, *A History of Pan-African Revolt* (Chicago: Kerr, 1995); Frantz Fanon, *The Wretched of the Earth* (New York: Grove, 1963); Cedric Robinson, *Black Marxism: The Making of the Black Radical Tradition* (Chapel Hill: University of North Carolina Press, 2000).

7. My discussion of Wright expands on Stuart Hall's contention that diaspora should not be defined in relation to a "sacred homeland" as the source of authentic identity posed as the solution to alienation and dispersion. Rather, Hall sees diaspora in terms of hybridity and internal diversity. Thus, diaspora identities are constantly made and remade and lived through an acceptance of difference; see Stuart Hall,

"Cultural Identity and Diaspora," in *Identity: Community, Culture, Difference*, ed. Jonathan Rutherford (London: Lawrence and Wishart, 1990). For discussions of the origins and history of the concept of the African diaspora and its significance within pan-Africanism, see Elliott P. Skinner, "The Dialectic between Diasporas and Homelands," in *Global Dimensions of the African Diaspora*, ed. Joseph E. Harris (Washington, D.C.: Howard University Press, 1993), 11–40; George Shepperson, "African Diaspora: Concept and Context," in *Global Dimensions*, ed. Harris, 41–49.

8. A copious literature explores the tensions of pan-Africanism mapped along the opposition between the diaspora and the African continent; see Wilson Moses, *Alexander Crummell: A Study of Civilization and Discontent* (New York: Oxford University Press, 1989); James T. Campbell, *Songs of Zion: The African Methodist Episcopal Church in the United States and South Africa* (Chapel Hill: University of North Carolina Press, 1998).

9. Michel Fabre, *The Unfinished Quest of Richard Wright* (New York: Morrow, 1973), 310, 312.

10. Ibid., 529.

11. Wright praised Padmore for his selfless work as the "ideological father of many of the nationalist movements in Black Africa" and, like Padmore, insisted on the independence of African liberation movements from communist influence. See George Padmore, *Pan-Africanism or Communism?* (1956; Garden City, N.Y.: Anchor, 1972), xxi–xxiv. Padmore's December 10, 1954, letter to W. E. B. Du Bois is quoted in James R. Hooker, *Black Revolutionary: George Padmore's Path from Communism to Pan-Africanism* (New York: Praeger, 1970), 123–24.

12. Chester Himes, *My Life of Absurdity* (New York: Doubleday, 1976), 8.

13. Diawara, *In Search of Africa*, rehearses the varieties of criticism leveled at *Black Power*. Margaret Walker writes of the "terrible ambivalence" of the text and characterizes Wright's response to Africa as "disappointment, distaste, and . . . downright disgust" (*Richard Wright: Daemonic Genius* [New York: Warner, 1988], 240–41). For criticism of Wright's use of modernization theory, see Nina Kressner Cobb, "Richard Wright and the Third World," in *Critical Essays on Richard Wright*, ed. Yoshinobu Hakutani (Boston: Hall, 1982). For an account based on interviews with some of the individuals Wright spoke with in the Gold Coast, see Jack B. Moore, "Black Power Revisited: In Search of Richard Wright," *Mississippi Quarterly* 41 (Spring 1988): 161–86. For the claim that *Black Power* exhibits Western ethnographic excess and crypto-fascism, see K. Anthony Appiah, "A Long Way from Home: Wright in the Gold Coast," in *Richard Wright: Modern Critical Views*, ed. Harold Bloom (New York: Chelsea House, 1987), 173–90.

14. See, for example, Wright's description of being confounded by what he thinks is a cultural practice of spitting among Akan peoples in the northern territories. This impression, he wrote, prompted an experiment in the privacy of his hotel room in which he expectorated before a mirror, with predictably messy results (Wright, *Black Power*, 283).

15. Diawara, *In Search of Africa*, 74.

16. Frederick Cooper and Mamadou Diouf have argued that discourses of development (and by implication and extension modernization) cannot be reductively cast as Western impositions. Rather, they were marked by contestation as African governments struggled to define development in the image of local interests and employed the concept to make oppositional claims. See Frederick Cooper, "Africa in a Capitalist World," in *Crossing Boundaries: Comparative History of Black People in Diaspora*, ed. Darlene Clark Hine and Jacqueline McLeod (Bloomington: Indiana University Press, 1999), 404–6; Mamadou Diouf, "Senegalese Development: From Mass Mobilization to Technocratic Elitism," in *International Development and the Social Sciences: Essays in the History and Politics of Knowledge*, ed. Frederick Cooper and Randall Packard (Berkeley: University of California Press, 1997), 291–319.

17. This phenomenon of military service as instrumental for the formation of black political subjects is discussed in Tyler Stovall, *Paris Noir* (Boston: Houghton Mifflin, 1996), 1–24, 118–29; Robin D. G. Kelley, " 'This Ain't Ethiopia, but It'll Do': African Americans and the Spanish Civil War," in *Race Rebels* (New York: Free Press, 1994), 123–58; see also Michael Hanchard, "Afro-Modernity: Temporality, Politics, and the African Diaspora," *Public Culture* 11, no. 1 (Winter 1999): 245–68.

18. For the impact of Cold War politics on Wright, see Fabre, *Unfinished Quest*; Addison Gayle, *Ordeal of a Native Son* (Garden City, N.Y.: Anchor, 1980); Faith Berry, "On Richard Wright in Exile: Portrait of a Man as Outsider," *Negro Digest*, December 1968, 26–37.

19. Wright, *Black Power*, 118–19. Wright's position on anthropology in the service of colonialism is similar to that of Frantz Fanon, *Black Skin, White Masks* (1952; New York: Grove, 1967).

20. Wright, *Black Power*, 9, 11.

21. Ibid., 7.

22. Ibid., 37, 40.

23. Ibid., 339, 341–42.

24. Ibid., 53–54.

25. Marika Sherwood, *Kwame Nkrumah, The Years Abroad, 1935–1947* (Legon: Freedom, 1996).

26. Wright, *Black Power*, 91.

27. Ibid., 60–61, 64–66.

28. Ibid., 117, 153, 247.

29. Ibid., 66, 168–29.

30. Ibid., 157.

31. Richard Wright, "Tradition and Industrialization: The Tragic Plight of the African Elite," *Présence Africaine*, June–November 1956, 347–60, reprinted in *White Man Listen!* (New York: Harper, 1956), 45–69.

32. Wright, *Black Power*, 63.

33. Dorothy Padmore to Richard and Ellen Wright, March 14, 1959, Wright Papers, box 103, folder 1521.

34. Dorothy Padmore to Richard Wright, October 17, 1960, Wright Papers, box 103, folder 1521.

35. Ibid.

36. Richard Wright, "The Negro Intellectual and Artist in the U.S. Today," speech at the American Library in Paris, November 1960, transcript in the Constance Webb/ Richard Wright Papers, Schomburg Center for Research in Black Culture, New York Public Library, New York.

37. Penny M. Von Eschen, *Race against Empire: Black Americans and Anticolonialism, 1937–1957* (Ithaca: Cornell University Press, 1997); Timothy B. Tyson, *Radio Free Dixie: Robert F. Williams and the Roots of Black Power* (Chapel Hill: University of North Carolina Press, 1999).

38. I am indebted to Mauricio Tenorio for this insight.

39. E. Franklin Frazier, "Potential American Negro Contributions to African Social Development," in Présence Africaine, *Africa Seen by American Negro Scholars* (New York: American Society of African Culture, 1963), 263–78.

40. E. Franklin Frazier, "The Failure of the Negro Intellectual," in *The Death of White Sociology*, ed. Joyce Ladner (New York: Random House, 1973), 56; James Ivy, "The NAACP as an Instrument of Social Change," *Présence Africaine*, June–November 1956, 330–35.

41. Langston Hughes, *Ask Your Mama: Twelve Moods for Jazz* (New York: Knopf, 1961) 4–5. Frazier was referring to the lines "There forbid us to remember / Comes an African in mid-December / Sent by the State Department / Among the shacks to meet the blacks: / Leontyne Sammy Harry Poitier / Lovely Lena Marian Louis Pearlie Mae . . . / Pushcarts fold and unfold in a supermarket sea. . . . / Come what may the signs point: Ghana Guinea."

42. Frazier, "Failure," 62–66.

43. Mary L. Dudziak, *Cold War Civil Rights: Race and the Image of American Democracy* (Princeton: Princeton University Press, 2000); Brenda Gayle Plummer, *Rising Wind: Black Americans and U.S. Foreign Affairs, 1935–1960* (Chapel Hill: University of North Carolina Press, 1996).

44. Lamming, *Pleasures of Exile*, 161, 163.

45. Ibid., 173.

46. Rob Nixon, "Caribbean and African Appropriations of 'The Tempest,'" *Critical Inquiry* 13, no. 3 (Spring 1987): 557–78.

47. Lamming, *Pleasures of Exile*, 181.

48. Ibid., 183.

49. Ibid., 188.

50. Ibid., 195, 201–3.

51. Anthony Platt, *E. Franklin Frazier Reconsidered* (New Brunswick, N.J.: Rutgers University Press, 1991), 153–55.

1. George and Dorothy Padmore to W. E. B. and Shirley Graham Du Bois, March 18, 1957, Shirley Graham–Du Bois Papers, box 17, folder 19, Schlesinger Library, Radcliffe College Archives, Harvard University, Cambridge, Mass.

2. For a contemporary discussion of the Third Force movement in global politics, see Colin Legum, *Bandung, Cairo, and Accra: A Report on the First Conference of Independent African States* (London: Africa Bureau, 1958).

3. George Padmore, *Pan-Africanism or Communism?* (1956; Garden City, N.Y.: Anchor, 1972), 356.

4. Legum, *Bandung, Cairo, Accra*, 23.

5. Kwame Nkrumah to June Milne, April 6, 1968, in *Kwame Nkrumah: The Conakry Years, His Life and Letters,* comp. June Milne (London: PANAF, 1990), 231.

6. Stuart Burns, ed., *Daybreak of Freedom: The Montgomery Bus Boycott* (Chapel Hill: University of North Carolina Press, 1997), 341.

7. Lawrence D. Reddick, *Crusader without Violence: A Biography of Martin Luther King, Jr.* (New York: Harper, 1958), 179–81.

8. Burns, *Daybreak*, 317.

9. Thomas Borstelmann, *The Cold War and the Color Line: American Race Relations in the Global Arena* (Cambridge: Harvard University Press, 2001), 226–28.

10. *MLK Papers*, 146–47.

11. Ibid., 145.

12. Reddick, *Crusader*, 182; *MLK Papers*, 7–9, 145; Bill Sutherland with Matt Meyer, *Guns and Gandhi in Africa: Pan-African Insights on Nonviolence, Armed Struggle, and Liberation in Africa* (Trenton, N.J.: Africa World, 2000), 34.

13. *MLK Papers*, 149–50.

14. "The Birth of a New Nation," sermon at Dexter Avenue Baptist Church, in *MLK Papers*, 151–53.

15. Ibid., 160–61.

16. Ibid., 164–66.

17. W. H. Lawrence, "Nixon Proposes Broad Program of Aid to Africa," *New York Times,* April 7, 1957, 1-A; Borstelmann, *Cold War and the Color Line,* 111.

18. Penny M. Von Eschen, *Race against Empire: Black Americans and Anticolonialism* (Ithaca: Cornell University Press, 1997).

19. "A Realistic Look at the Question of Progress in the Area of Race Relations," address at St. Louis Freedom Rally, April 10, 1957, in *MLK Papers*, 173, 175–76; Mary L. Dudziak, *Cold War Civil Rights: Race and the Image of American Democracy* (Princeton: Princeton University Press, 2000); Borstelmann, *Cold War and the Color Line.*

20. Sutherland with Meyer, *Guns and Gandhi*, 44–45.

21. Accra, Embtel 145, October 10, 1957, State Department Records.

22. John D'Emilio, *Lost Prophet: The Life and Times of Bayard Rustin* (New York: Free Press, 2003), 298.

23. James H. Meriwether, *Proudly We Can Be Africans: Black Americans and Africa, 1935–1961* (Chapel Hill: University of North Carolina Press, 2002), 172–73.

24. St. Clair Drake to Claude and Etta Barnett, n.d., Claude Barnett Papers, Chicago Historical Society, box 238-1; *Accra Daily Graphic*, October 24, 1958, 1; "Professor Drake Honour PM," *Evening News*, October 23, 1958, 8.

25. Adu Boahen, *Ghana: Evolution and Change in the Nineteenth and Twentieth Centuries* (London: Longman, 1975), 203.

26. Ezekiel Mphahlele, "Accra Conference Diary," in *An African Treasury: Articles, Essays, Stories, Poems by Black Africans*, ed. Langston Hughes (New York: Crown, 1960), 45–49; David Macey, *Frantz Fanon: A Biography* (New York: Picador USA, 2000), 367–70.

27. Peter Benson, *"Black Orpheus," "Transition," and Modern Cultural Awakening in Africa* (Berkeley: University of California Press, 1986), 168.

28. Hughes, *African Treasury*, 67.

29. Mercer Cook, "The New Africa Charts Its Course . . . but the 'Strategy' of the Africans Remains Unclear," *AMSAC Newsletter*, supp. 2 (1959), reprinted from Forum-Service, Congress for Cultural Freedom, Paris, n.d.

30. "Observations on the All African Peoples Conference at Accra, Ghana, Dec. 8–13, 1958 by George McCray, Lecturer, ICFTU. American Labour College, Kampala, Uganda," RG 18-001, International Affairs Department, Country Files, 1945–71, George Meany Memorial Archives, Silver Spring, Md., ser. 3, subser. 2, box 14, folder 14. See also George McCray to St. Clair Drake, November 22, 1957, Drake Papers, box 7, folder 43. On the Wilson case, see John Tettegah to George Meany, September 16, 1958, RG 18-001, International Affairs Department, Country Files, 1945–71, Meany Archives, box 9, folder 23.

31. George Houser, "A Report on the All-African People's Conference Held in Accra, Ghana, December 8–13, 1958," RG 18-004, International Affairs Department, Irving Brown Files, 1943–89, Meany Archives, box 25, folder 18.

32. Summary Report, Second Annual Conference, American Society of African Culture, June 26–29, 1959, Bond Papers, ser. 3, box 30, folder 80C; American Society of African Culture, June 30, 1959, in Records of Component Offices of the Bureau of Intelligence and Research, 1947–1963, State Department Records, lot 65D 350, box 13, folder "AFB Outgoing Memos, 1959."

33. D'Emilio, *Lost Prophet*, 279–88; Sutherland with Meyer, *Guns and Gandhi*, 36–40.

34. Bill Sutherland, untitled autobiographical essay, in Muriel Snowden Papers, M 17, box 1/9, folder 5, Northeastern University Special Collections, Boston, Mass.

35. Sutherland with Meyer, *Guns and Gandhi*, 6–7; D'Emilio, *Lost Prophet*, 183; George Houser, *No One Can Stop the Rain: Glimpses of Africa's Liberation Struggle* (New York: Pilgrim, 1984), 10–15; "Matchet's Diary," *West Africa*, August 20, 1960, 937.

36. Bill Sutherland, "Awudome-Tsito Calling," unpublished manuscript, Drake Papers, box 70, folder "Awudome Residential Adult College."

37. Sutherland with Meyer, *Guns and Gandhi*, 39–40.

38. D'Emilio, *Lost Prophet*, 288.

39. Dorothy Padmore to Ellen Wright, April 9, 1957, Wright Papers, box 103, folder 1521.

40. Dorothy Padmore to Richard Wright, October 31, 1959, Wright Papers, box 103, folder 1521.

41. "His Soul Was Linked with Africa," *Ghanaian Times*, October 5, 1959, 8.

42. St. Clair Drake, "The Politics of Kwame Nkrumah: A Pan-African Interpretation," 9, unpublished manuscript, Drake Papers, box 23, folder 38.

Chapter Four

1. The republication of Murray's autobiography was a catalyst for renewed scholarly interest in various aspects of her life and career. See Pauli Murray, *Pauli Murray: The Autobiography of a Black Activist, Feminist, Lawyer, Priest, and Poet* (Knoxville: University of Tennessee Press, 1989); Pauli Murray, *Song in a Weary Throat: An American Pilgrimage* (New York: Harper and Row, 1987); roundtable in *Journal of Women's History* 14, no. 2 (June 2002): Patricia Bell-Scott, "'To Write Like Never Before': Pauli Murray's Enduring Yearning," 58–62; Susan Ware, "Pauli Murray's Notable Connections," 54; Glenda E. Gilmore, "Admitting Pauli Murray," 62; Rosalind Rosenberg, "The Conjunction of Race and Gender," 68.

2. Barbara Ransby, *Ella Baker and the Black Freedom Movement: A Radical Democratic Vision* (Chapel Hill: University of North Carolina Press, 2002), 72.

3. Yevette Richards, *Maida Springer, Pan-Africanist and International Labor Leader* (Pittsburgh: University of Pittsburgh Press, 2000), 75–76.

4. Pauli Murray, *Proud Shoes: The Story of an American Family* (New York: Harper, 1956).

5. Pauli Murray, *States' Laws on Race and Color* (n.p.: Woman's Division of Christian Service, 1951).

6. On Williams and Murray's association with his defense, see Timothy B. Tyson, *Radio Free Dixie: Robert F. Williams and the Roots of Black Power* (Chapel Hill: University of North Carolina Press, 1999), 159–60.

7. Doreen Drury, "'Experimentation on the Male Side': Race, Class, Gender, and Sexuality in Pauli Murray's Quest for Love and Identity, 1910–1960" (Ph.D. diss., Boston College, 2000), 69, 79–80; Rosenberg, "Conjunction of Race and Gender."

8. Geoffrey Bing, *Reap the Whirlwind: An Account of Kwame Nkrumah's Ghana from 1950 to 1966* (London: MacGibbon and Kee, 1968), 321; Richards, *Maida Springer*, 206–7.

9. Richards, *Maida Springer*, 204.

10. See, for example, "Ghanaian Embassy Distributes Anti-American Propaganda," Department of State Instruction, CW-1136, August 7, 1961, Bureau of African Affairs, Records of G. Mennen Williams, Subject File, 1961–66, State Department

Records, box 15. This document discusses attacks on U.S. Congolese policy that appeared in the Ghanaian publication *Voice of Africa*. 299

11. Bill Sutherland with Matt Meyer, *Guns and Gandhi in Africa: Pan-African Insights on Nonviolence, Armed Struggle, and Liberation in Africa* (Trenton, N.J.: Africa World, 2000), 45.

12. Kwame Nkrumah, *I Speak of Freedom: A Statement of African Ideology* (New York: Praeger, 1962), 262–81.

13. Pauli Murray to John Tettegah, October 25, November 1, 1960, Tettegah to Murray, October 27, 1960, Murray Papers, box 41, folder 714.

14. "Dr. Nkrumah Re-States His Policy," *West Africa*, October 15, 1960, 1179; Dorothy Padmore to Richard Wright, October 17, 1960, Wright Papers, box 103, folder 1521.

15. Personal Secretary to Pauli Murray, November 28, 1960, Murray Papers, box 41, folder 714.

16. David Roediger, *Colored White: Transcending the Racial Past* (Berkeley: University of California Press, 2002).

17. Julian Mayfield, "Black First or American First?: Sorting Us Out," *Washington Post*, April 20, 1984, 32.

18. Penny M. Von Eschen, *Race against Empire: Black Americans and Anticolonialism, 1937–1957* (Ithaca: Cornell University Press, 1997); Anthony Platt, *E. Franklin Frazier Reconsidered* (New Brunswick, N.J.: Rutgers University Press, 1991).

19. See Pauli Murray to Edith Sampson, April 26, 1952, Sampson to Murray, April 28, 1952, Murray Papers, box 100, folder 1787. Murray protested the publication of Worthy's attack in the *Crisis* to its editor, James Ivy; see Pauli Murray to James Ivy, May 5, 1952, Murray Papers, box 100, folder 1787. For another attack on Sampson's Denmark speech, see Eslanda G. Robeson, "Mrs. Edith Sampson Tells Europeans Negroes Are Happy, Almost Free," *Freedom*, June 1952, 2.

20. Richards, *Maida Springer*, 207; Pauli Murray to Immanuel Wallerstein, February 4, 1961, Wallerstein to Murray, February 16, 1961, Murray Papers, box 41, folder 714.

21. See Pauli Murray diary, June 5, 1960, Murray Papers, box 41, folder 710.

22. David N. Gibbs, *The Political Economy of Third World Intervention: Mines, Money, and U.S. Policy in the Congo Crisis* (Chicago: University of Chicago Press, 1991), 77–86.

23. Thomas Borstelmann, *The Cold War and the Color Line: American Race Relations in the Global Arena* (Cambridge: Harvard University Press, 2002), 129–31.

24. Gibbs, *Political Economy*, 94–95.

25. Madeline Kalb, *The Congo Cables: The Cold War in Africa from Eisenhower to Kennedy* (New York: Macmillan, 1982).

26. Gibbs, *Political Economy*, 98–99.

27. "Death of Patrice Lumumba," Accra, February 14, 1961, in *Selected Speeches of Kwame Nkrumah*, comp. Samuel Obeng (Accra: Afram, 1997), 15.

300   28. Anna Arnold Hedgeman, *The Trumpet Sounds: A Memoir of Negro Leadership* (New York: Holt, Rinehart, and Winston, 1964).

29. Ibid., 137.

30. Ibid., 138–39.

31. Pauli Murray diary (typescript), July 22, 1960, Murray Papers, box 41, folder 723.

32. Pauli Murray to Robert F. Kennedy, May 25, 1961, Murray Papers, box 103, folder 1866.

33. Adelaide Cromwell, interview by author, September 21, 1998.

34. Pauli Murray, "A Question of Identity," unpublished manuscript, Murray Papers, box 85, folder 1478.

35. Carol Polsgrove, *Divided Minds: Intellectuals and the Civil Rights Movement* (New York: Norton, 2001), 137; Murray, "Question of Identity."

36. Von Eschen, *Race against Empire*.

37. Mary L. Dudziak, *Cold War Civil Rights: Race and the Image of American Democracy* (Princeton: Princeton University Press, 2000), 152–202.

38. "Surprise," *Newsweek*, October 31, 1960, 45; "Artist Sues Newsweek," *Mr. Muhammed Speaks* (special ed.), n.d., 23.

39. Brenda Gayle Plummer, *Rising Wind: Black Americans and U.S. Foreign Affairs, 1935–1960* (Chapel Hill: University of North Carolina Press, 1996), 303–4.

40. Pauli Murray diary, September 18, 1960, Murray Papers, box 41, folder 710.

41. Ludo de Witte, *The Assassination of Lumumba* (London: Verso, 2001), 163–64.

42. For example, see "Lumumba's Legacy: Troubles All Over," *Life*, February 24, 1961, 18. On the prosecession, anti-Lumumba bias at the United Nations and in the Belgian and Western press, see de Witte, *Assassination*, 9–26.

43. Obeng, *Selected Speeches*, 24. De Witte, *Assassination*, 97–124, 140–43, provides details regarding Lumumba's execution by Belgian officials and military personnel and the destruction of his remains.

44. A visual record of the demonstration in the UN gallery, with footage of Lumumba and his aides in custody of Congolese troops and scenes from other demonstrations around the world, appears in a 1961 Pathé Studios newsreel in possession of author. I am indebted to Ron Gregg for this extraordinary footage.

45. James Baldwin, "A Negro Assays the Negro Mood," *New York Times Sunday Magazine*, March 12, 1961, 25, 103–4.

46. James Baldwin, "Princes and Powers," in *Nobody Knows My Name* (New York: Dell, 1962), 13–55.

47. Era Bell Thompson, "Africa, Land of My Fathers," in *Apropos of Africa: Sentiments of American Negro Leaders on Africa from the 1880s to the 1950s*, ed. Adelaide Cromwell Hill and Martin Kilson (London: Cass, 1969), 272–77.

48. Russell Howe, "Strangers in Africa," *Reporter*, June 22, 1961, 34–35; Harold Isaacs, "A Reporter at Large—Back to Africa," *New Yorker*, May 13, 1961, 105–42. For perspectives linking the articles to the UN demonstration, see St. Clair Drake, "The

Negro's Stake in Africa," *Negro Digest*, June 1964, 42–43; Julian Mayfield, "Ghanaian
Sketches," in *Young Americans Abroad*, ed. Roger H. Klein (New York: Harper and
Row, 1962), 185.

49. Horace Mann Bond, "Howe and Isaacs in the Bush: The Ram in the Thicket,"
Negro History Bulletin (1962), reprinted in *Apropos of Africa*, ed. Hill and Kilson,
278–88.

50. Drake believed the articles were "inevitable," recalling that soon after the UN
demonstration, he received a call from an editor for *Reporter* who solicited an article
from him showing "the American Negroes once and for all that these Africans don't
care . . . about them and that there is really no kind of tie between them." According
to Drake, the editor claimed to be acting on the suggestion of a couple of American
Negro leaders who wished to emphasize that the American Negro identified with
America rather than with Africa. Drake begged off and claimed that his "paranoic
suspicions" had been sparked by Isaacs's article (Drake, "Negro's Stake," 43–45).

51. Hedgeman, *Trumpet Sounds*, 145; Horace Mann Bond, "Howe and Isaacs in the
Bush: The Ram in the Thicket," *Negro History Bulletin* (1962), 67–70. On the difficulty
of publishing rebuttals to the new discourse on American Negroes and Africans, see
Adelaide Cromwell to St. Clair Drake, February 7, 1962, Drake Papers, box 5, folder
50. For African American objections to Howe's article, see Claude Barnett to Drake,
July 22, 1961, Drake Papers, box 6, folder 12.

52. Hedgeman, *Trumpet Sounds*, 149.

53. See Murray's memorandum to the American Women's Association of Accra,
"Pilot Project—What Can We Do for Our Country?," Murray Papers, box 41, folder 712.

54. Archie Lang, political affairs officer at the U.S. embassy in Accra from 1957 to
1959, confirms that Murray's acquaintance in the U.S. embassy, Earl Link (deceased),
was a CIA agent (Lang to author, [August 2001], in possession of author). Garrison
informed Williams that Murray was in constant touch with Link, "an American Negro
on the staff of the Embassy in Accra (and who I think reports to the CIA)" (Lloyd K.
Garrison to G. Mennen Williams, January 23, 1961, Murray Papers, box 96, folder
1686).

55. Murray kept in touch with U.S. government personnel after her departure from
Ghana as part of her effort to raise funds for a Ghanaian student's travel for study in
the United States. The opposition activities of this student as a courier for Murray's
legal briefs written for opposition leader J. B. Danquah had placed the student at risk
of detention. One U.S. Information Agency official wrote to Murray of "the hushed
conferences we had on your correspondence with Nkrumah and Tettegah" (David J.
Du Bois to Pauli Murray, July 30, 1962, Murray Papers, box 93, folder 1615).

56. Under Lovestone's guidance, Springer assisted African nationalist trade unions
and attended pan-African conferences as an observer, sending her reports to Lovestone. Ted Morgan ambiguously refers to Springer as one of Lovestone's "agents."
Yevette Richards disputes such allegations of Springer's involvement with covert
attempts to influence African trade unions; see Ted Morgan, *A Covert Life: Jay Love-*

302   *stone: Communist, Anti-Communist, Spymaster* (New York: Random House, 1999), 304–9; Richards, *Maida Springer*; Jay Lovestone to Pauli Murray, September 26, 1960, Murray Papers, box 41, folder 714.

57. A report to the State Department Bureau of African Affairs on American specialists stationed in Ghana under U.S. auspices had high praise for Murray, referring to her as "a continual embarrassment to the Government party. She is good. . . . [A]fter she quits . . . she would be excellent for other English-speaking countries in Africa. She has never taught before but is obviously a brain. . . . Her line [on race] is that it doesn't exist, or rather, that you pay no attention to it" ("Report by Frederick A. Colwell, American Specialist Branch, Accra—March 4–7," Bureau of African Affairs Records, box 1, folder 17.0, State Department Records).

58. Murray was undoubtedly aware of the controversy among blacks regarding Isaacs's article. A manuscript copy of Bond's rebuttal, "Howe and Isaacs in the Bush: The Ram in the Thicket," is contained in the Murray Papers, box 97, folder 1708.

59. Pauli Murray, "American in Ghana," March 20, 1960, Murray Papers, box 41, folder 722.

60. Carl Rowan, *Breaking Barriers: A Memoir* (New York: HarperCollins, 1991). On Rowan's dismay at U.S. military participation along with Belgian forces and white South African mercenaries in their campaign against Congolese rebels, see his memorandum to President Lyndon Baines Johnson, "Propaganda Problems Relating to the Congo," August 14, 1964, White House Central Files, Confidential File, Lyndon Baines Johnson Presidential Library, Austin, Tex., box 8, folder "CO 52 Congo."

Chapter Five

1. John Henrik Clarke, "The New Afro-American Nationalism," *Freedomways* 1, no. 3 (Fall 1961): 283–95.

2. Julian Mayfield, "Into the Mainstream and Oblivion," in *The American Negro and His Roots*, Proceedings of Conference of American Negro Writers (New York: American Society of African Culture, 1959), 29–34.

3. See "Negro Leadership Blasted," *Muhammed Speaks* (January 1962), 24. The article is an unsigned report on a Los Angeles speech by Malcolm X probably authored by the Muslim leader. See also E. U. Essien-Udom, *Black Nationalism: The Search for Identity* (Chicago: University of Chicago Press, 1962); John Pepper Clark, *America, Their America* (New York: Africana, 1971).

4. E. Franklin Frazier, *Black Bourgeoisie* (Glencoe, Ill.: Free Press, 1957); Lorraine Hansberry, "The Negro Writer and His Roots: Toward a New Romanticism," in *Speech and Power: The African-American Essay and Its Cultural Content, from Polemics to Pulpit*, ed. Gerald Early (Hopewell, N.J.: Ecco, 1993), 2:129–41.

5. Ronald Walters, *Pan-Africanism in the African Diaspora: An Analysis of Modern Afrocentric Political Movements* (Detroit: Wayne State University Press, 1993), 89–126.

6. William Branch, "Julian Mayfield," *Dictionary of Literary Biography Yearbook* 303 (Detroit: Gale, 1984), 181–85.

7. Federal Bureau of Investigation, San Juan, December 14, 1955, Julian Mayfield FBI file 100-412872, in possession of author.

8. Conrad Lynn, *There Is a Fountain* (Brooklyn, N.Y.: Hill, 1993), 162; Ora Mobley-Sweeting with Ezekiel Mobley, *Nobody Gave Me Permission: Memoirs of a Harlem Activist* (Philadelphia: Xlibris, 2000).

9. Julian Mayfield, "Challenge to Negro Leadership," *Commentary*, April 1961, 297–305; Van Gosse, *Where the Boys Are: Cuba, Cold War America, and the Making of a New Left* (New York: Verso, 1993); Timothy B. Tyson, *Radio Free Dixie: Robert F. Williams and the Roots of Black Power* (Chapel Hill: University of North Carolina Press, 1999).

10. Julian Mayfield, "A Love Affair with the United States," *New Republic*, August 7, 1961, 25; Julian Mayfield, "The Cuban Challenge," *Freedomways* 1, no. 2 (Summer 1961): 185–89.

11. Mayfield, "Cuban Challenge"; Mayfield, "Love Affair," 25.

12. Julian Mayfield, autobiographical fragment, 29, Mayfield Papers, box 15, folder 9.

13. Ibid.

14. John Hope Franklin, "W. E. B. Du Bois: A Personal Memoir," *Massachusetts Review*, Autumn 1990, 409–28.

15. David L. Lewis, *W. E. B. Du Bois: The Fight for Equality and the American Century, 1919–1963* (New York: Holt, 2000), 556–68.

16. W. E. B. Du Bois to George Padmore, December 10, 1954, Padmore to Du Bois, January 12, 1955, W. E. B. Du Bois Papers, reel 70, frame 959, reel 71, frame 640, University of Massachusetts at Amherst, Special Collections, Amherst, Mass.

17. See manuscript of keynote address by W. E. B. Du Bois to Sixth Annual Conference, the All-African Student Union of the Americas, University of Chicago, June 18–22, 1958, Dabu Gizenga Collection on Kwame Nkrumah, Moorland-Spingarn Research Center, Howard University, Washington, D.C., box 128-19, folder 405. The text of Du Bois's statement to the All African People's Conference is reprinted in W. E. B. Du Bois, *The Autobiography of W. E. B. Du Bois* (New York: International Publishers, 1983), 402–4.

18. W. E. B. Du Bois to Kwame Nkrumah, October 10, 1960, in *The Correspondence of W. E. B. Du Bois*, vol. 3, *Selections, 1944–1963*, ed. Herbert Aptheker (Amherst: University of Massachusetts Press, 1978), 443–44; Julian Mayfield, "The Great Disturber of the Peace: Was Du Bois a Progenitor of Negritude?," *Sagala: A Journal of Art and Ideas*, Summer 1980, 29.

19. David L. Lewis, *W. E. B. Du Bois*, 567.

20. W. E. B. Du Bois, "Queen and President," *National Guardian*, December 12, 1961, 2; W. E. B. Du Bois, "Opening Speech, Conference of Encyclopedia Africana,"

304   *Freedomways*, Winter 1963, 28–30. On the Black Flame Trilogy, see Arnold Rampersad, *The Art and Imagination of W. E. B. Du Bois* (New York: Schocken, 1989), 266–87.

21. O'Brien quoted in *Conor: A Biography of Conor Cruise O'Brien: Anthology*, ed. Donald H. Akenson (Ithaca: Cornell University Press, 1994), 246–47.

22. Ronald Segal, *African Profiles* (Harmondsworth: Penguin, 1963), 265–72; "Egypt Paces Rise of African Power," *Muhammed Speaks*, October 15, 1962, 17–18.

23. Segal, *African Profiles*, 261–63.

24. Julian Mayfield to John Henrik Clarke, December 17, 1961, Clarke Papers, folder "Julian Mayfield Correspondence."

25. C. L. R. James, *Nkrumah and the Ghana Revolution* (London: Allison and Busby, 1982). Manning Marable's account of the strike (*African and Caribbean Politics: From Kwame Nkrumah to Maurice Bishop* [London: Verso, 1987], 127–32) is unsympathetic to the Ghanaian government, regarding the CPP as a state capitalist entity hostile to the legitimate claims of organized labor. A more sympathetic account of the government's role that foregrounds the political dimension of the strike is St. Clair Drake and Leslie Alexander Lacy, "Government versus the Unions: The Sekondi-Takoradi Strike, 1961," in *Politics in Africa: 7 Cases*, ed. Gwendolyn M. Carter (New York: Harcourt, Brace, and World, 1966), 67–118.

26. Julian Mayfield to John Henrik Clarke, March 9, 1962, Clarke Papers, folder "Julian Mayfield Correspondence."

27. On U.S. government monitoring of Mayfield's activities in Ghana, see Foreign Service Dispatch 623, U.S. embassy in Accra, June 9, 1962 (incomplete document), from Mayfield's FBI file, in possession of author.

28. On U.S. and Soviet officials in Ghana, see Julian Mayfield to John Henrik Clarke, March 29, 1962, Clarke Papers, folder "Julian Mayfield Correspondence"; Julian Mayfield, "Why They Want to Kill Mae Mallory," *Ghana Evening News*, April 6, 1962, 5; Julian Mayfield to John Henrik Clarke, April 1, May 22, 1962, Clarke Papers, folder "Julian Mayfield Correspondence."

29. *Nationalism, Colonialism, and the United States: One Minute to Twelve* (New York: Liberation Committee for Africa, 1961); Kwame Nkrumah, "African Liberation and Unity," *Freedomways*, Fall 1962, 409–35.

30. Julian Mayfield to John Henrik Clarke, March 9, 1962, Clarke Papers, folder "Julian Mayfield Correspondence"; Julian Mayfield, "Ghanaian Sketches," in *Young Americans Abroad*, ed. Roger H. Klein (New York: Harper and Row, 1962), 186–87.

31. William Gardner Smith, *Return to Black America* (Englewood Cliffs, N.J.: Prentice-Hall, 1970), 95–96.

32. Randall Kenan, *Walking on Water: Black American Lives at the Turn of the Twenty-first Century* (New York: Knopf, 1999), 331–34.

33. Curtis J. "Kojo" Morrow, *Return of the Afro-American* (Huntington, N.Y.: Kroshka, 2000), 9; Leslie Alexander Lacy to Martin Kilson, April 20, 1966, in possession of author; Leslie Alexander Lacy, *The Rise and Fall of a Proper Negro: An Auto-*

biography (New York: Macmillan, 1970); Julian Mayfield to Tom Feelings, January 29, 1977, in possession of author.

34. Sylvia Ardyn Boone, *Radiance from the Waters: Ideals of Feminine Beauty in Mende Art* (New Haven: Yale University Press, 1986).

35. Tom Feelings, interview by author, April 27, 1997; Tom Feelings, *Tommy Traveler in the World of Black History* (New York: Black Butterfly, 1991).

36. Julian Mayfield, "When Ghana Was Ghana," Mayfield Papers, box 14; statement for program for Herman Bailey, "Ghana: An Exhibition of Drawings and Paintings," Spelman College, n.d., Mayfield Papers, box 4, folder 5.

37. Max Bond and Jean Carey Bond, interview by author, July 31, 1997; Maryse Condé to author, November 19, 2001, in possession of author.

38. Mary Helen Washington, "Alice Childress, Lorraine Hansberry, and Claudia Jones: Black Women Write the Popular Front," in *Left of the Color Line: Race, Radicalism, and Twentieth-Century Literature of the United States*, ed. Bill V. Mullen and James Smethurst (Chapel Hill: University of North Carolina Press, 2003), 183–204; Kevin Gaines, "From Center to Margin: Internationalism and the Origins of Black Feminism," in *Materializing Democracy: Toward a Revitalized Cultural Politics*, ed. Russ Castronovo and Dana D. Nelson (Durham: Duke University Press, 2002), 294–313; Maya Angelou, *The Heart of a Woman* (New York: Vintage, 1986).

39. Bill Sutherland to St. Clair Drake, Drake Papers, box 1, folder 4; St. Clair Drake, "Nkrumah's 'Ban-the-Bomb' Conference," unpublished fragment, Drake Papers, box 70, Ghana ser.; Bill Sutherland with Matt Meyer, *Guns and Gandhi in Africa: Pan-African Insights on Nonviolence, Armed Struggle, and Liberation in Africa* (Trenton, N.J.: Africa World, 2000), 46.

40. St. Clair Drake to William Gardner Smith, May 15, 1963, Drake Papers, box 13.

41. St. Clair Drake to Nana Nketsia, June 13, 1962, Drake Papers, box 8, folder 30.

42. St. Clair Drake, "Where Nkrumah Stands," *New York Times*, July 30, 1963, 28.

43. Julian Mayfield to John Henrik Clarke, May 22, 1962, Clarke Papers, folder "Julian Mayfield Correspondence." On the Accra Assembly, see also "55 Nation Peace Assembly Spurred by Nkrumah Crusade for International Justice," *Muhammed Speaks*, August 31, 1962, 11–12; *Ghanaian Times*, June 21, 1963, 1 (for a picture of Mayfield among a group presenting a volume of the conference proceedings to Nkrumah).

44. Julian Mayfield to John Henrik Clarke, March 9, 1962, Clarke Papers, box 6, folder "Julian Mayfield Correspondence."

45. David Rooney, *Kwame Nkrumah: The Political Kingdom in the Third World* (New York: St. Martin's, 1988), 219–20.

46. Maya Angelou, *All God's Children Need Traveling Shoes* (New York: Vintage, 1984), 78–80; Hugh and Mabel Smythe to St. Clair Drake, January 2, 196[3], Drake Papers, box 12, folder 11.

47. Richard Mahoney, *JFK: Ordeal in Africa* (New York: Oxford University Press, 1983), 181–86.

48. Julian Mayfield, seminar paper, Africana Studies and Research Center, Mayfield Papers, box 26, folder 9.

49. Julian Mayfield, "And Then Came Baldwin," *Freedomways*, Spring 1963, 143–55.

50. Julian Mayfield to John Henrik Clarke, June 11, 1963, Clarke Papers, folder "Julian Mayfield Correspondence."

51. Julian Mayfield to John Henrik Clarke, March 14, June 11, 1963, folder "Julian Mayfield Correspondence."

52. Julian Mayfield, "Horror in the Deep South," *Ghana Drum*, August 1963, 11–19.

53. "Africa, Help Us Civilise Barbaric Racists Here," *Ghanaian Times*, August 16, 1963, 2; incoming telegram, Department of State (Accra), June 11, 1963, State Department Records, box 3260.

54. Julian Mayfield, "Uncle Tom Abroad," *Negro Digest*, June 1963, 37–39; Julian Mayfield to John Henrik Clarke, June 28, 1963, Clarke Papers, folder "Julian Mayfield Correspondence."

55. This discussion of the demonstration and its organization and Du Bois's final illness is taken from an unsigned account by Alice Windom, September 11, 1963, Mayfield Papers, box 6, folder 21.

56. David L. Lewis, *W. E. B. Du Bois*, 569.

57. See, for example, W. Alphaeus Hunton, "Africa and Neocolonialism," *Political Affairs* 40 (February 1961), 88–97.

58. Department of State Airgram A-125, U.S. embassy in Accra, September 1, 1963, State Department Records, box 3916; "Kennedy, Where Is the Civil Rights Bill?," *Ghanaian Times*, August 28, 1963, 2.

59. Department of State Airgram A-125, U.S. embassy in Accra, September 1, 1963, State Department Records, box 3916; "Give Afro-Americans Civil Rights," *Ghanaian Times*, August 29, 1963, 2.

60. ". . . And His Soul Goes Marching On," *Ghana Drum*, November 1963, 22–25.

61. O'Brien's review, "White Gods and Black Americans," is reprinted in *Conor*, ed. Akenson, 59–64.

62. Julian Mayfield, "Ghanaian Sketches," in *Young Americans Abroad*, ed. Roger H. Klein (New York: Harper and Row, 1962), 176–204.

63. John Henrik Clarke to Julian Mayfield, September 30, 1963, Clarke Papers, folder "Julian Mayfield Correspondence."

64. Leslie Alexander Lacy, *Rise and Fall*, 180–85. Drake believed that Afro-Americans had accused Jean Pierre of CIA ties; see St. Clair Drake, "Black Power: Dilemmas and Contradictions, 1945–1966," 98, unpublished manuscript, Drake Papers, box 22, folder 29.

65. Conor Cruise O'Brien, *Writers and Politics* (New York: Pantheon, 1965), 251–590.

66. David Lewis, "Ghana 1963," *American Scholar* 68, no. 1 (Winter 1999): 39–60; Rooney, *Kwame Nkrumah*, 242.

67. C. L. R. James, *Nkrumah and the Ghana Revolution*, 179–81.

68. "George Padmore Lives On," *Ghanaian Times*, September 24, 1963, 2.

69. Julian Mayfield, autobiographical fragment, Mayfield Papers, box 1, folder 12.

Chapter Six

1. Malcolm X, *The Autobiography of Malcolm X* (New York: Ballantine, 1973), 287, 291–92.

2. Karl Evanzz, *The Judas Factor: The Plot to Kill Malcolm X* (New York: Thunder's Mouth, 1992), 147–54.

3. Kenneth O'Reilly, *Racial Matters: The FBI's Secret File on Black America, 1960–1972* (New York: Free Press, 1989), 111–14.

4. Leon Forrest, "Elijah," in *The Furious Voice for Freedom: Essays* (Wakefield, R.I.: Asphodel, 1995), 88–89.

5. Alex Haley, "Epilogue," in Malcolm X, *Autobiography*, 404–5.

6. Grace Lee Boggs, *Living for Change: An Autobiography* (Minneapolis: University of Minnesota Press, 1998), 128–29; Rosemary Mealy, *Fidel and Malcolm X: Memories of a Meeting* (Melbourne, Aus.: Ocean, 1993); Brenda Gayle Plummer, *Rising Wind: Black Americans and U.S. Foreign Affairs, 1935–1960* (Chapel Hill: University of North Carolina Press, 1996), 288–92.

7. Claude A. Clegg, *An Original Man: The Life and Times of Elijah Muhammed* (New York: St. Martin's, 1997), 199–204.

8. Ibid., 203–12.

9. Ibid.

10. E. U. Essien-Udom, *Black Nationalism: The Search for Identity* (Chicago: University of Chicago Press, 1962), 364.

11. Manthia Diawara, *In Search of Africa* (Cambridge: Harvard University Press, 1998), 120–33; Robin Kelley, "The Riddle of the Zoot," in *Malcolm X: In Our Image*, ed. Joe Wood (New York: St. Martin's, 1992), 155–82; Ferrucio Gambino, "The Transgression of a Laborer: Malcolm X in the Wilderness of America," *Radical History Review* 55 (Winter 1993): 7–32.

12. William Sayles, *From Civil Rights to Black Liberation: Malcolm X and the Organization of Afro-American Unity* (Boston: South End, 1994), 158.

13. Taylor Branch, *Pillar of Fire: America in the King Years, 1963–65* (New York: Simon and Schuster, 1998), 267–69.

14. Patricia Sullivan, *Days of Hope: Race and Democracy in the New Deal Era* (Chapel Hill: University of North Carolina Press, 1996).

15. For efforts by Hoover's FBI to expose communist influence on Martin Luther King Jr. and the civil rights movement, see Taylor Branch, *Pillar of Fire*; see also O'Reilly, *Racial Matters*; David Garrow, *The FBI and Martin Luther King, Jr.* (New York: Penguin, 1983).

308   16. Testimony of Rev. James H. Robinson, Hearing before the Committee on Un-American Activities, House of Representatives, 88th Cong., 2d sess., May 5, 1964.

17. Gerald Horne, *Race Woman: The Lives of Shirley Graham Du Bois* (New York: New York University Press, 2000), 188.

18. Incoming telegram, Department of State, Accra, February 4, 1964, State Department Records, box 2235.

19. "Rumours—Govt Will Take Firmest Action against Enemies," *Ghanaian Times*, February 6, 1964, 1; "Big Anti-US Protest in Accra," *Ghanaian Times*, February 6, 1964, 1; "6 Subversionists Bundled Out," *Ghanaian Times*, February 10, 1964, 1; "Ghana Says That Africa Is Nobody's Plantation!," *Muhammed Speaks*, February 28, 1964, 11–14.

20. See the documents on Ghana reproduced in *FRUS*, 411–40; for Mahoney's discussion with Reitsch, see Department of State Airgram A-480, March 19, 1964, State Department Records, box 2234. For Accra embassy commentary on Nkrumah's *Consciencism*, see Department of State Airgram A-503, March 26, 1964, State Department Records, box 2234. For the discussion between Williams and Ribiero over the demonstrations and the Player incident, see Department of State Memorandum of Conversation, February 14, 1964, State Department Records, box 2233.

21. Archie Epps, "Malcolm X at the Leverett House Forum," *Journal of Blacks in Higher Education* 1 (Autumn 1993): 35–37.

22. Department of State, telegram from Accra, April 15, 1964, State Department Records, box 2234. For Mahoney's briefing on Malcolm, see Department of State, telegram from Accra, April 18, 1964, in box 89, National Security File, Ghana, Cables, March 1964 to February 1966, Lyndon Baines Johnson Presidential Library, Austin, Tex.

23. Leslie Alexander Lacy, *The Rise and Fall of a Proper Negro: An Autobiography* (New York: Macmillan, 1970), 202.

24. Maya Angelou, *All God's Children Need Traveling Shoes* (New York: Vintage, 1984), 131.

25. Leslie Alexander Lacy, *Rise and Fall*, 203.

26. Alice Windom, unpublished account of Malcolm's visit, 2–3, Mayfield Papers, box 6, folder 21.

27. Malcolm X, *Autobiography*.

28. Leslie Alexander Lacy, *Rise and Fall*, 204–6.

29. Malcolm X, *Malcolm X Talks to Young People* (New York: Pathfinder, 1991), 10–18.

30. Angelou, *All God's Children*, 138–42; Jim Lacy, interview by author, February 2002.

31. Windom account, 3; Julian Mayfield, "When Ghana Was Ghana, 28–29, Mayfield Papers, box 14.

32. June Milne, comp., *Kwame Nkrumah: The Conakry Years, His Life and Letters* (London: PANAF, 1990), 184.

33. Leslie Alexander Lacy, *Rise and Fall*, 212–13.

34. Jim Lacy interview.

35. Alice Windom to Julian Mayfield, October 4, 1969, Mayfield Papers, box 6, folder 21.

36. Preston King to author, March 16, 2002, in possession of author.

37. Windom account, 6.

38. David Remnick, *King of the World* (New York: Random House, 1998), 303.

39. Malcolm X, *Autobiography*, 359; Taylor Branch, *Pillar of Fire*, 314; "Unite to Win True Freedom," *Muhammed Speaks*, June 5, 1964, 1, 8; Charles P. Howard, "How Africa Greets Champ!," *Muhammed Speaks*, June 5, 1964, 1, 3, 9.

40. *Ghanaian Times*, May 19, 1964. For Nkrumah's invitation to Floyd Patterson, see *West Africa*, July 30, 1960, 859.

41. H. M. Basner, "Malcolm X and the Martyrdom of Rev. Clayton Hewett," *Ghanaian Times*, May 18, 1964, 2.

42. Julian Mayfield, "Basner Misses Malcolm X's Point," *Ghanaian Times*, May 19, 1964, 2.

43. H. M. Basner, "Four Years in Kwame's Court" (unpublished manuscript), 19, in possession of author.

44. Leslie Alexander Lacy, "African Responses to Malcolm X," in *Black Fire: An Anthology of Afro-American Writing*, ed. LeRoi Jones and Larry Neal (New York: Morrow, 1968), 19–38.

45. Malcolm X, "We Are All Blood Brothers," *Liberator*, July 1964.

46. "Organization of Afro-American Unity: A Statement of Basic Aims and Objectives," in *Malcolm X: The Man and His Times*, ed. John Henrik Clarke (Trenton, N.J.: Africa World, 1990), 335–42.

47. "Afro-American Troops for Congo—Malcolm X," OAAU Press Release, n.d., Clarke Papers, *Freedomways* box, folder "Julian Mayfield."

48. "Speech to African Summit Conference, Cairo, Egypt," in *Malcolm X*, ed. Clarke, 288–93.

49. Taylor Branch, *Pillar of Fire*, 482.

50. Clayborne Carson, *Malcolm X: The FBI File* (New York: Carroll and Graf, 1991).

51. Cameron Duodu, "Malcolm X: Prophet of Harlem," *Ghana Drum*, October 1964.

52. Julian Mayfield, "What Has Driven the Blacks into Rebellion," *Ghanaian Times*, August 13, 1964, 5.

53. Arnold H. Lubasch, "Malcolm Favors a Mau Mau in U.S.," *New York Times*, December 21, 1964, 20.

54. Taylor Branch, *Pillar of Fire*, 401–6.

55. I. F. Stone, *In a Time of Torment* (New York: Random House, 1967), 162–63; "Six Negro Leaders Ask Shift on Africa," *New York Times*, November 29, 1964, 5.

56. John W. Finney, "Africans' Charge Rejected by U.S.," *New York Times*, November 29, 1964, 5.

57. Audio recording of Malcolm's Oxford debate speech, December 3, 1964, in possession of author.

58. Ibid.

59. Derrick Bell, *And We Are Not Saved: The Elusive Quest for Racial Justice* (New York: Basic Books, 1989); Patricia Williams, *The Alchemy of Race and Rights* (Cambridge: Harvard University Press, 1991); J. Morgan Kousser, *Colorblind Injustice: Minority Voting Rights and the Undoing of the Second Reconstruction* (Chapel Hill: University of North Carolina Press, 1999); John Hope Franklin, *The Color Line: Legacy for the Twenty-first Century* (Columbia: University of Missouri Press, 1993); Lani Guinier and Gerald Torres, *The Miner's Canary: Enlisting Race, Resisting Power, Transforming Democracy* (Cambridge: Harvard University Press, 2002).

60. *New York Times*, August 13, 1964, quoted in Ruby M. Essien-Udom and E. U. Essien-Udom, "Malcolm X: An International Man," in *Malcolm X*, ed. Clarke, 257.

61. Thomas Borstelmann, *The Cold War and the Color Line: American Race Relations in the Global Arena* (Cambridge: Harvard University Press, 2002); Paul L. Montgomery, "Malcolm X Exhorts Negroes to Look to African Culture," *New York Times*, December 13, 1964, 80; on the prominence of Malcolm's political vision in the *Muhammed Speaks*, see Charles P. Howard, "Africans: No Back Down on Congo," *Muhammed Speaks*, January 1, 1965, 1–2; "White Mercenary Talks! Hired Killer Tells of Slaughter in the Congo," *Muhammed Speaks*, January 1, 1965, 5; "Students Say FBI Part of Negroes' Dixie Oppression," *Muhammed Speaks*, January 1, 1965, 10; Sylvester Leaks, "Mississippi Women Spur Black Revolt," *Muhammed Speaks*, January 15, 1965, 2.

62. Ossie Davis, eulogy for Malcolm X, in *Malcolm X*, ed. Clarke.

63. Julian Mayfield, "Malcolm X: A Tragic Loss," *Ghanaian Times*, February 24, 1965, 6.

64. "The Tragic End of Malcolm X," *Ghanaian Times*, February 27, 1965, 7.

65. "Malcolm's Assassination Will Not End the Struggle," *Ghanaian Times*, February 26, 1965, 3.

66. See "The Violent End of the Man Called Malcolm X," *Life*, March 1965, 26–27. This article was accompanied by more sympathetic personal remembrance by Gordon Parks, "I Was a Zombie Then—Like All Muslims, I Was Hypnotized," *Life*, March 1965, 28–30. See also Julian Mayfield to John Henrik Clarke, March 22, 1965, Clarke Papers, *Freedomways* box, "Mayfield" folder.

67. Theodore Kornweibel, *Seeing Red: Federal Campaigns against Black Militancy, 1919–1925* (Bloomington: Indiana University Press, 1998); Carson, *Malcolm X*; Peter Goldman, *The Death and Life of Malcolm X* (Urbana: University of Illinois Press, 1979), 256–62.

68. Ossie Davis, "On Malcolm X," in Malcolm X, *Autobiography*, 457–60; Miriam Makeba, *Live from Paris and Conakry*, compact disk, DRG Records LC 5866, n.d.; Julia Wright, "To Malcolm X," *Présence Africaine*, Second Quarter 1965, 239.

69. John Henrik Clarke to Julian Mayfield, June 1, 1965, Clarke Papers, *Freedom-*

see Goldman, *Death and Life*, 243; on the FBI campaign to destroy the OAAU, see Sayles, *From Civil Rights to Black Liberation*, 152–61.

70. Goldman, *Death and Life*, 239–56.

Chapter Seven

1. Erica Powell, *Private Secretary (Female)/Gold Coast* (London: Hurst, 1984), 192.

2. Michael Dei-Anang, *The Administration of Ghana's Foreign Relations, 1957–1965: A Personal Memoir* (London: Athlone, 1975), 9.

3. Ibid., 45–46.

4. W. Scott Thompson, *Ghana's Foreign Policy, 1957–1966* (Princeton: Princeton University Press, 1969), 395–96.

5. Reginald Herbold Green, "The Triple Challenge before Ghana: Austerity, Participation, and Dialogue," *New African*, May 1966, 93–96.

6. Martin Kilson, interview by author, May 16, 2003.

7. Incoming telegram, Department of State, Accra, February 4, 15, 1965, State Department Records, box 2232.

8. Julian Mayfield to John Henrik Clarke, June 23, 1965, Clarke Papers, *Freedomways* box, "1965–66" folder.

9. St. Clair Drake, "Ghana's Young Pioneers" (letter to the editor), *Chicago Tribune*, n.d., Drake Papers, box 70.

10. St. Clair Drake to Melvin Fox, May 12, 1964, Drake Papers, box 13, folder 6.

11. St. Clair Drake to Frank Untermayer, August 9, 1965, Drake Papers, box 52, folder 4.

12. Ibid.

13. Dei-Anang, *Administration*, 53; W. Scott Thompson, *Ghana's Foreign Policy*, 409–11; *FRUS*, 447–49.

14. "Memorandum from Robert W. Komer of the National Security Council Staff to the President's Special Assistant for National Security Affairs (Bundy)," January 6, 1965, in *FRUS*, 294; Michael Krenn, *Black Diplomacy: African Americans and the State Department, 1945–1969* (Armonk, N.Y.: Sharpe, 1999), 133–35.

15. "Crisis for the O.A.U.," *African Review*, May 1965, 6.

16. Julian Mayfield, "Malcolm X: 1925–1965," *African Review*, May 1965, 8–9; Shirley Graham Du Bois, "The Beginning, Not the End," in *Malcolm X: The Man and His Times*, ed. John Henrik Clarke (Trenton, N.J.: Africa World, 1990), 125–27.

17. On political controversies surrounding the American Society for African Culture, including the disclosure of its covert CIA funding, see Wayne J. Urban, *Black Scholar: Horace Mann Bond, 1904–1972* (Athens: University of Georgia Press, 1992), 160–64. On covert CIA funding of the Uganda-based periodical *Transition*, see Peter Benson, *"Black Orpheus," "Transition," and Modern Cultural Awakening in Africa* (Berkeley: University of California Press, 1986), 160–76; *Transition 75–76: The Anni-*

versary Issue (Durham: Duke University Press, n.d.); see also Frances Stonor Saunders, *The Cultural Cold War: The CIA and the World of Arts and Letters* (New York: New Press, 1999).

18. Preston King, "Wanted: An African Integrated Force," *African Review*, May 1965, 22–25, 90–94.

19. Bessie Head, "The Human Condition: On the Edge of Everything," *African Review*, May 1965, 26–27.

20. Conor Cruise O'Brien to Julian Mayfield, June 5, 1965, Mayfield Papers, box 6, folder 12; "Critic of Ghana," *New York Times*, March 29, 1965, 12.

21. Powell, *Private Secretary*, 212–13.

22. Reginald H. Green and Ann Seidman, *Unity or Poverty? The Economics of Pan-Africanism* (Harmondsworth: Penguin, 1968); Ann Seidman, "Economics of Neo-Colonialism," *Ghanaian Times*, June 18, 1964, 2.

23. Ann and Bob Seidman, telephone interview by author, October 30, 2000.

24. Godfrey Hodgson, *America in Our Time* (New York: Vintage, 1976), 265–67.

25. Martin Kilson to St. Clair Drake, n.d., Drake Papers, box 7, folder 22; Martin Kilson to ". . . Julian and Ana Livia," n.d., in possession of author.

26. Eboe Hutchful, *The IMF and Ghana: The Confidential Record* (London: Institute for African Alternatives/Zed Books, 1987).

27. Kwame Nkrumah, *Neocolonialism: The Last Stage of Imperialism* (London: Nelson, 1965).

28. "Circular Telegram from the Department of State to Embassies in Africa," November 23, 1965, in *FRUS*, 451–52.

29. Thomas Borstelmann, *The Cold War and the Color Line: American Race Relations in the Global Arena* (Cambridge: Harvard University Press, 2002), 195–97.

30. W. Scott Thompson, *Ghana's Foreign Policy*, 393–94, 401.

31. Kofi Batsa, *The Spark: Times behind Me* (London: Collings, 1985), 22, 41–42.

32. W. Scott Thompson, *Ghana's Foreign Policy*, 396–97.

33. Batsa, *Spark*, 41.

34. Dennis Austin, *Ghana Observed* (Manchester: Manchester University Press, 1976), 102–6.

35. The following account is based on Preston King's account of the coup, a copy of which can be found in the August Meier Papers, box 2, folder "Preston King, 1953–1967, 1 of 2," Schomburg Center for Research in Black Culture, New York Public Library, New York.

36. Franklin Williams to Bill Moyers, February 25, 1966, Williams Papers, box 8, folder "CO 93 Ghana."

37. Frank Robertson, telephone interview by author, February 2001.

38. Geoffrey Bing, *Reap the Whirlwind: An Account of Kwame Nkrumah's Ghana from 1950 to 1966* (London: MacGibbon and Kee, 1968), 372–73; Paul Davis to Bernard Jaffe, June 19, 1966, Shirley Graham–Du Bois Papers, box 19, folder 4.

39. Sylvia Boone to Julian Mayfield, May 29, [1966], Mayfield Papers, box 4, folder 8.

40. Ibid.

41. Bing, *Reap the Whirlwind*, 372–73.

42. Sylvia Boone to Julian Mayfield, May 29, [1966], Mayfield Papers, box 4, folder 8. All subsequent references to Boone's account are to this letter.

43. William Sayles, *From Civil Rights to Black Liberation: Malcolm X and the Organization of Afro-American Unity* (Boston: South End, 1994), 151–52.

44. Sylvia Boone to Julian Mayfield, May 29, [1966], 14, Mayfield Papers, box 4, folder 8.

45. Outgoing telegram, Department of State, February 25, 1966, State Department Records, box 2235, folder Pol 23-9 Ghana. A copy was sent to the U.S. embassy in London.

46. Franklin Williams to Bill Moyers, February 25, 1966, Williams Papers, box 1, folder "White House, 1966–67." Barwah's murder is confirmed in the account of the coup by one of its leaders, Col. A. A. Afrifa, *The Ghana Coup: 24th February 1966* (London: Cass, 1966), 33.

47. Williams's preliminary observations on the coup were sent from Accra to Washington as well as to African embassies and those in Bonn, London, Paris, and Moscow (incoming telegram, Department of State, February 25, 1966, State Department Records, box 2235, folder Pol 23-9 Ghana).

48. Robert Komer to Lyndon Baines Johnson, March 4, 1966, Williams Papers, box 8, folder "CO 93 Ghana."

49. Robert Komer to Lyndon Baines Johnson, March 12, 1966, in *FRUS*, 457–58; Franklin Williams to Bill Moyers, March 17, 1966, Williams Papers, box 1, "White House Files, 1966–67."

50. Kwame Nkrumah, *Dark Days in Ghana* (London: PANAF, 1968), 49; "Did Not Aid in Nkrumah's Ouster," *Jet*, August 20, 1970, 20–22.

51. The president of Nkrumah's alma mater, Lincoln University, Dr. Marvin Wachman, informed Nkrumah of Williams's assurance that he had not been a party to the Ghanaian coup. In an otherwise cordial letter to Wachman, Nkrumah wrote, "I have noted what you say about Franklin Williams" (Wachman to Nkrumah, July 21, 1969, Nkrumah to Wachman, August 10, 1969, in *Kwame Nkrumah: The Conakry Years, His Life and Letters*, comp. June Milne [London: PANAF, 1990], 321, 325).

52. "Helms to the ambassador," n.d., Williams Papers, box 1, "Personal Correspondence."

53. Ambassador Mahoney reported a testy exchange between Nkrumah and Gardiner over the issue of African unity; see Department of State Airgram A-631, May 28, 1964, State Department Records, box 2234.

54. Elizabeth Drake, "American Woman Who Lived in Ghana Deplores U.S. Recognition of Coup Regime," *Palo Alto Times*, March 16, 1966, 37; Franklin Williams, letter

to the editor, *Palo Alto Times*, April 15, 1966, n.p., Drake Papers, box "Ghana: Politics and Government," folder "Elizabeth Drake/Franklin Williams on Coup."

55. Tom Feelings to Julian Mayfield, March 10, 1966, Mayfield Papers, box 5, folder 1.

56. Nkrumah, *Dark Days*, 31.

57. K. A. B. Jones-Quartey to Martin Kilson, April 4, 1966, in possession of author.

58. Anthony Platt, *E. Franklin Frazier Reconsidered* (New Brunswick, N.J.: Rutgers University Press, 1991).

59. "Dictator Leaves His Cash to Kind June," *Evening News*, January 4, 1973, n.p., Dabu Gizenga Collection on Kwame Nkrumah, Moorland-Spingarn Research Center, Howard University, Washington, D.C.; "Nkrumah Left £6,250 to Woman," *London Daily Telegraph*, May 1, 1973, n.p., Gizenga Collection.

60. Franklin Williams to Charles Delgado, March 4, 1966, Williams Papers, container 1, folder "Official General 1966."

61. Hodee Edwards to John Henrik Clarke, April 4, 1966, Clarke Papers, *Freedomways* box, "Correspondence—1966" folder.

62. Julian Mayfield to John Henrik Clarke, January 24, 1966, Clarke Papers, *Freedomways* box, "Correspondence—1966" folder.

63. Julian Mayfield to John Henrik Clarke, March 29, 1966, Clarke Papers, *Freedomways* box, "Correspondence—1966" folder; "For Immediate Release: Puerto Rican Doctor Jailed and Expelled from Ghana, 6-11-66," Clarke Papers, *Freedomways* box, "Julian Mayfield" folder.

64. John Henrik Clarke to Julian Mayfield, January 27, 1966 [1967?], Julian Mayfield to John Henrik Clarke, February 1, 1967, Mayfield Papers, box 4, folder 10.

65. Julian Mayfield to John Henrik Clarke, February 1, 1967, Mayfield Papers, box 4, folder 10.

66. Alice Windom to Julian Mayfield, May 16, November 28, 1966, March 25, 1967, Mayfield Papers, box 6, folder 21.

67. Bob Fitch and Mary Oppenheimer, *Ghana: End of an Illusion* (New York: Monthly Review Press, 1967); Milne, comp., *Kwame Nkrumah*, 59.

68. Nkrumah, *Dark Days*.

Chapter Eight

1. Alice Windom to Julian Mayfield, March 25, 1967, Mayfield Papers, box 6, folder 21.

2. Nyerere's remarks are quoted in Shirley Graham Du Bois, "What Happened in Ghana? The Inside Story," *Freedomways* 6, no. 3 (Summer 1966): 201–23.

3. Rupert Charles Lewis, *Walter Rodney's Intellectual and Political Thought* (Detroit: Wayne State University Press, 1998), 124–29; C. L. R. James, *Nkrumah and the Ghana Revolution* (London: Alison and Busby, 1982), 26.

4. Charles P. Howard, "Ghanaians Stooging for West Are Enemies of All Africa," 315
Los Angeles Herald-Dispatch, May 5, 1966, 4.

5. Charles P. Howard to Kwame Nkrumah, November 10, 1966, Nkrumah Papers; Charles P. Howard, "Charles P. Howard Refutes U.S.'s Anti-Nkrumah Lies," *Los Angeles Herald-Dispatch*, April 7, 1966, 3.

6. Cheddi Jagan to Kwame Nkrumah, April 25, 1967, Nkrumah Papers, box 154-4, folder 76; Tim Weiner, "A Kennedy-C.I.A. Plot Returns to Haunt Clinton," *New York Times*, October 30, 1994, A-10.

7. Kwame Nkrumah, "The Spectre of Black Power," in *Revolutionary Path* (New York: International Publishers, 1973), 421–28; Kwame Nkrumah, "The Myth of the Third World," in *Revolutionary Path*, 435–38 (originally published in *Labour Monthly*, October 1968).

8. "Nkrumah Left £6,250 to Woman," *London Daily Telegraph*, May 1, 1973, n.p.; "Kwame Nkrumah's Estate in Britain," *London Times*, May 1, 1973, n.p.; Joe Hall, "London Woman in Nkrumah Will," *London Evening Standard*, April 1, 1973, n.p.

9. Charles L. Sanders, "Kwame Nkrumah: The Fall of a Messiah," *Ebony*, September 1966, 138–46.

10. William Raspberry, "A Shift on Nkrumah," *Washington Post*, July 28, 1972, A-15.

11. Ali Mazrui, "Nkrumah: The Leninist Czar" (1966), in *Transition 75/76: The Anniversary Issue* (Durham: Duke University Press, n.d.), 106–26; Russell Warren Howe, "Did Nkrumah Favor Pan-Africanism?," (1966), in *Transition 75/76*, 128–34.

12. Ama Ata Aidoo, "Thank You, Mr. Howe," in *Transition 75/76*, 136–37; Ali Mazrui, "A Reply to Critics," in *Transition 75/76*, 147–54.

13. Department of State Telegram, Dakar, February 28, 1966, State Department Records, box 2235.

14. Department of State Airgram, January 17, 1965, State Department Records, box 2648; Alex Quaison-Sackey, *Africa Unbound: Reflections of an African Statesman* (New York: Praeger, 1965), 43–58.

15. Kwame Nkrumah, "'African Socialism' Revisited," in *Revolutionary Path*, 438–45.

16. *AMSAC Newsletter* 8, no. 1 (February 1966): 1; David Osborn (Department of State, Bureau of Educational and Cultural Affairs) to St. Clair Drake, July 30, 1965, Drake Papers, box 13, folder 9.

17. Penny M. Von Eschen, *Satchmo Blows Up the World: Jazz Ambassadors Play the Cold War* (Cambridge: Harvard University Press, 2004), 151.

18. Robert July, *An African Voice: The Role of the Humanities in African Independence* (Durham: Duke University Press, 1987), 72–73.

19. Von Eschen, *Satchmo Blows Up the World*, 158; Hoyt W. Fuller, "World Festival of Negro Arts," *Ebony*, July 1966, 96–106; Hoyt W. Fuller, "An Editorial," *Negro Digest*, June 1966, 97–98.

20. Julian Mayfield, manuscript review of Hoyt Fuller, *Journey to Africa*, n.d., 5, Mayfield Papers, box 22, folder 3.

316   21. Frances Stonor Saunders, *The Cultural Cold War: The CIA and the World of Arts and Letters* (New York: New Press, 1999), provides a general account, though it is generally silent on AMSAC and African American politics. See also Hoyt Fuller, *Journey to Africa* (Chicago: Third World, 1971), 92–93. On the view that AMSAC's secret funding by the government might facilitate the organization's goals, see Adelaide Cromwell Hill to "Members of the Board of AMSAC," February 24, 1967, Drake Papers, box 14, folder 7. On Davis's attempts to revive AMSAC, see the memorandum of his conference with the State Department's assistant secretary for cultural affairs, Charles Frankel, June 12, 1967, Bond Papers, ser. 3, box 32, folder 90F; John A. Davis to Averell Harriman, April 1, 1968, Bond Papers, ser. 3, box 33, folder 91A.

22. All three of Mayfield's Ghana manuscripts, "The Lonely Warrior," "When Ghana Was Ghana," and "Tales of the Lido" are in Mayfield Papers, box 14, "Ghana manuscripts." See also Arnold C. Tovell to Julian Mayfield, May 17, 1968, Mayfield Papers, box 9, folder 8. On Mayfield's refusal to write about Malcolm X, see Julian Mayfield to Alice Windom, May 20, 1978, Mayfield Papers, box 6, folder 21.

23. "Black Directions," n.d., Mayfield Papers, box 4, folder 8; Julian Mayfield to James Forman, September 3, 1968, Mayfield Papers, box 5, folder 2. For Mayfield's views on Martin Luther King Jr., see Julian Mayfield to Preston King, March 6, 1968, Mayfield Papers, box 6, folder 2; Elinor and Calvin Sinnette to "Dear Friends," April 16, 1968, Mayfield Papers, box 6, folder 17.

24. Harold Cruse, *Crisis of the Negro Intellectual* (New York: Quill, 1984); Harold Cruse, "Revolutionary Nationalism and the Afro-American" (1962), in *Rebellion or Revolution?* (New York: Morrow, 1968), 74–96.

25. Julian Mayfield, "Challenge to Negro Leadership: The Case of Robert Williams," *Commentary*, April 1961, 207–305.

26. Cruse, "Revolutionary Nationalism," 90–91.

27. Julian Mayfield to John Henrik Clarke, March 14, 1963, Clarke Papers, folder "Julian Mayfield Correspondence."

28. Julian Mayfield, "A Challenge to a Bestseller: Crisis or Crusade?," *Negro Digest*, June 1968, 10–24; Harold Cruse, "Replay on a Black Crisis: Harold Cruse Looks Back on Black Art and Politics in Harlem," *Negro Digest*, November 1968, 25; Robert Nemiroff to Julian Mayfield, August 24, 1979, Mayfield Papers, box 21, folder 12.

29. Ernest Kaiser, "The Crisis of the Negro Intellectual" (1969), reprinted in *The Freedomways Reader*, ed. Esther Cooper Jackson (Boulder, Colo.: Westview, 2000), 284–88. For recent critiques of Cruse's book, see Winston James, *Holding Aloft the Banner of Ethiopia* (London: Verso, 1998); Alan Wald, "Narrating Nationalisms: Black Marxism and Jewish Communists through the Eyes of Harold Cruse," in *Left of the Color Line: Race Radicalism and Twentieth-Century Literature of the United States*, ed. Bill V. Mullen and James Smethurst (Chapel Hill: University of North Carolina Press, 2003), 141–61; Nikhil Pal Singh, *Black Is a Country* (Cambridge: Harvard University Press, 2004), 181–83. A wide-ranging variety of critical perspectives on Cruse's text

sidered (New York: Routledge, 2004).

30. John Agard, "We're All United in the Struggle," *Georgetown Sunday Chronicle*, December 17, 1972, 6; on *Uptight*'s reception, see Julian Mayfield to Jules Dassin, n.d., Mayfield Papers, box 4, folder 11.

31. Joan Cambridge to Paul Mann, November 20, 1984, Mayfield Papers, box 1, folder 7.

32. Addison Gayle, *The Black Aesthetic* (Garden City, N.Y.: Doubleday, 1971); LeRoi Jones and Larry Neal, eds., *Black Fire: An Anthology of Afro-American Writing* (New York: Morrow, 1968); Julian Mayfield, "Frank Silvera, 1914–1970," *New York Times*, June 21, 1970, 83; Hollie I. West, "The Goal of Julian Mayfield: Fusing Art and Politics," *Washington Post*, July 7, 1975, B-1; Julian Mayfield, "Black on Black: A Political Love Story," in *Ten Times Black*, ed. Julian Mayfield (New York: Bantam, 1972), 125–49.

33. See, for example, Julian Mayfield, "Explore Black Experience," *New York Times*, February 2, 1969, D-9.

34. Mayfield, review of Fuller, *Return to Africa*; Robert Nemiroff to Julian Mayfield, August 24, 1979, Mayfield Papers, box 21, folder 12; Julian Mayfield, "Lorraine Hansberry: A Woman for All Seasons," *Freedomways* 19, no. 4 (Fourth Quarter 1979): 263–68.

35. Tom Feelings, interview by author, April 27, 1997.

36. On CIA subversion of Jagan's government, see Weiner, "Kennedy-C.I.A. Plot," A-10; Hollie I. West, "Goal of Julian Mayfield," B-1.

37. Julian Mayfield, "Kwame Nkrumah: 'Don't Mourn for Me; Learn from Me,'" *Georgetown Sunday Chronicle*, April 30, 1972, 9.

38. Joan Cambridge to Paul Mann, November 20, 1984, Mayfield Papers, box 1, folder 7.

39. For Mayfield's negative assessment of Rodney, see Julian Mayfield to Tom Feelings, August 1, 1977, Mayfield Papers, box 5, folder 1. For background to the disputes among African American expatriates in Guyana, see Julian Mayfield, "Political Refugees and the Politics of Guyana," *Black Scholar*, July–August 1973, 33–35; Julian Mayfield to John Henrik Clarke, January 15, 1972, Clarke Papers, folder "Julian Mayfield Correspondence."

40. See, for example, Julian Mayfield, "If Forbes Burnham Fails—Blacks Everywhere Lose!," *Black X-Press*, July 21, 1973, 14–15.

41. Mayfield's friend, Hoyt Fuller, contended that Burnham lied in asserting that Rodney and his brother, who survived the blast, had been engaged in an act of sabotage; see Hoyt W. Fuller, "Conspiracy in the Caribbean," *First World* 2, no. 4 (1980): 35.

42. Feelings interview; Tom Feelings, *The Middle Passage: White Ships, Black Cargo* (New York: Dial, 1995).

43. On Mayfield's political views and their reception at Howard as well as his precarious financial situation, see Julian Mayfield to David Du Bois, June 24, 1978, Mayfield Papers, box 4, folder 15; Julian Mayfield, "The Foolish Consistency of Saunders Redding and Others," 1979, Mayfield Papers, box 21, folder 11. For Mayfield's treatment by Howard University, see Eugenia Collier to Tom Feelings, July 1, 1985, in possession of author; Tom Feelings, "Julian Mayfield: A Written Depiction of the Man as an Abstract Painting . . . In MY Mind," 1985, n.p., in possession of author. I am indebted to Tom Feelings for sharing copies of these documents with me.

44. Alice Windom to Julian Mayfield, July 30, 1968, Mayfield Papers, box 6, folder 21.

45. F. Ransome-Kuti, "The Status of Women in Nigeria," *Journal of Human Relations*, Autumn 1961, 67–72.

46. Alice Childress, Paule Marshall, and Sarah E. Wright, "The Negro Woman in American Literature" (1966), reprinted in *Freedomways Reader*, ed. Jackson, 291–98.

47. Julian Mayfield, "Tales of the Lido," unpublished manuscript, n.d., Mayfield Papers, box 14, folders 8–12.

48. Thomas A. Johnson, "Yale Conference Studies Role of Black Woman," *New York Times*, December 14, 1970, 45.

49. St. Clair Drake, "The Politics of Kwame Nkrumah: A Pan-African Interpretation," unpublished manuscript, Drake Papers, box 23, folder 38.

50. St. Clair Drake, "Toward an Intellectual Framework," Drake Papers, box 25, folder "various articles."

51. St. Clair Drake, "Remarks at Walter Rodney symposium," n.d., Stanford University, Drake Papers, box 24, folder 2. On Rodney, see Rupert Charles Lewis, *Walter Rodney's Intellectual and Political Thought*.

52. St. Clair Drake, seminar presentation on Walter Rodney and Pan-Africanism, n.p., n.d., Drake Papers, box 24, folder 3.

53. For an important critique of liberal academic social science grounded in the social movements of the 1960s, see Joyce Ladner, ed., *The Death of White Sociology* (New York: Random House, 1973).

54. Carl Degler, *Neither Black nor White: Slavery and Race Relations in Brazil and the United States* (New York: Macmillan, 1971), quoted in St. Clair Drake, *Black Folk Here and There: An Essay in History and Anthropology* (Los Angeles: Center for Afro-American Studies: University of California, Los Angeles, 1991), 1:68.

55. Drake, *Black Folk*, 1:115.

56. Ibid., 1:99–101. Drake cited the writings of Dr. Frances Cress Welsing, noting that while adherents of melanin theory had been invited by black student groups to lecture on college campuses, none had subjected their theories to controlled research experimentation.

57. Ibid., 1:102–9.

58. Gerald M. Boyd, "Committee to Steer South Africa Protests Is Named," *New*

York Times, December 7, 1984, A-15; Juan Williams, "Black Leaders Find a Hot New 319 Issue," Washington Post, December 12, 1984, A-2.

59. Marjorie Hyer, "Tutu Urges U.S. Action: Says Hard-Line Policy Could End Apartheid," Washington Post, December 24, 1984, C-1; Juan Williams, "Three Administration Blacks Oppose South Africa Protests," Washington Post, December 7, 1984, A-4.

Epilogue

1. Gillian Heathcote, "Tutu Warns African Leaders against Greed," Ghanaian Times, August 15, 1994, 1.

2. William Raspberry, "A Shift on Nkrumah," Washington Post, July 28, 1972, A-15.

3. Lareef Zubair, "Ghana I.M.F. Program Drains the Country," New York Times, November 11, 1994, A-22.

4. A. K. Afful, "A Leader's Followers Must Be Apostles of His Vision—Farrakhan," Ghanaian Times, June 1, 1993, 1.

5. "Farrakhan Calls on the Colonialists to Pay Africa," Ghanaian Times, June 2, 1993, 1.

6. Guy Warren, I Have a Story to Tell (Accra: Guinea, 1983).

7. Jennifer Ludden, "Black American Couple Finds Home in Ghana," Christian Science Monitor, August 7, 1997.

8. Edward M. Bruner, "Tourism in Ghana: The Representation of Slavery and the Return of the Black Diaspora," American Anthropologist 98, no. 2 (June 1996): 290–304.

9. Michael Crowder, "Whose Dream Was It Anyway? Twenty-five Years of African Independence," African Affairs 86, no. 9 (January 1987): 7–24; Cedric Robinson, "In Search of a Pan-African Commonwealth," Social Identities 2, no. 1 (February 1996): 161–68; Basil Davidson, The Black Man's Burden: Africa and the Curse of the Nation-State (New York: Times Books, 1992).

10. Edward Harris, "Al-Qaida Dealt in Diamonds: Funds Laundered in Africa, Witnesses Say," Ann Arbor News, August 8, 2004, A-9.

11. Julius Nyerere's views on the importance of African nation-states appear in Bill Sutherland with Matt Meyer, Guns and Gandhi in Africa: Pan-African Insights on Nonviolence, Armed Struggle, and Liberation in Africa (Trenton, N.J.: Africa World, 2000), 70–89.

12. Manthia Diawara, In Search of Africa (Cambridge: Harvard University Press, 1994).

SELECTED BIBLIOGRAPHY

Manuscript Collections

Horace Mann Bond Papers, University of Massachusetts at Amherst, Special Collections, Amherst, Mass.

John Henrik Clarke Papers, Schomburg Center for Research in Black Culture, New York Public Library, New York.

St. Clair Drake Papers, Schomburg Center for Research in Black Culture, New York Public Library, New York.

W. E. B. Du Bois Papers, University of Massachusetts at Amherst, Special Collections, Amherst, Mass.

Lloyd Garrison Papers, Harvard Law School, Cambridge, Mass.

Dabu Gizenga Collection, Moorland-Spingarn Research Center, Howard University, Washington, D.C.

Shirley Graham–Du Bois Papers, Schlesinger Library, Radcliffe College Archives, Harvard University, Cambridge, Mass.

Langston Hughes Papers, Beinecke Rare Book Library, Yale University, New Haven, Conn.

W. Arthur Lewis Papers, Seeley Mudd Manuscripts Library, Princeton University, Princeton, N.J.

Julian Mayfield Papers, Schomburg Center for Research in Black Culture, New York Public Library, New York.

August Meier Papers, Schomburg Center for Research in Black Culture, New York Public Library, New York.

Pauli Murray Papers, Radcliffe College Archives, Schlesinger Library, Harvard University, Cambridge, Mass.

Kwame Nkrumah Papers, Moorland-Spingarn Research Center, Howard University, Washington, D.C.

Muriel Snowden Papers, Northeastern University, Special Collections, Boston.

Richard Wright Papers, Beinecke Rare Book Library, Yale University, New Haven, Conn.

Newspapers and Magazines

African Review

AMSAC Newsletter

Amsterdam News

Black World

Daily Graphic

Ebony

Freedom

Freedomways

Ghana Drum

Ghanaian Evening News

Ghanaian Times

International African Opinion

Liberator

Muhammed Speaks

National Guardian

Negro Digest

Newsweek

New York Times

Présence Africaine

Transition

Washington Post

West Africa

Published Sources

Adamafio, Tawia. *By Nkrumah's Side: The Labour and the Wounds*. London: Collings, 1982.

Adi, Hakim. *West Africans in Britain, 1900–1960*. London: Lawrence and Wishart, 1998.

Aidoo, Ama Ata. *The Dilemma of a Ghost and Anowa*. New York: Longman, 1998.

Akenson, Donald Harmon. *Conor: A Biography of Conor Cruise O'Brien: Anthology*. Ithaca: Cornell University Press, 1994.

Ali, Tariq. *Street Fighting Years*. New York: Citadel, 1987.

Allen, Danielle. *Talking to Strangers: Anxieties of Citizenship since* Brown v. Board of Education. Chicago: University of Chicago Press, 2004.

Allman, Jean. *The Quills of the Porcupine*. Madison: University of Wisconsin Press, 1993.

American Society of African Culture. *The American Negro and His Roots*. Proceedings of Conference of American Negro Writers. New York: American Society of African Culture, 1959.

Angelou, Maya. *All God's Children Need Traveling Shoes*. New York: Vintage, 1984.

——. *The Heart of a Woman*. New York: Bantam, 1993.

Appiah, Kwame Anthony. *In My Father's House: Africa in the Philosophy of Culture*. New York: Oxford University Press, 1992.

Aptheker, Herbert, ed. *The Correspondence of W. E. B. Du Bois*. Vol. 3, *Selections, 1944–1963*. Amherst: University of Massachusetts Press, 1978.

Armah, Ayi Kwei. *The Beautyful Ones Are Not Yet Born*. Oxford: Heinemann, 1988.

Armah, Kwesi. *Africa's Golden Road*. London: Heinemann, 1965.

Austin, Dennis. *Ghana Observed*. Manchester: Manchester University Press, 1976.

——. *Politics in Ghana, 1946–1960*. London: Oxford University Press, 1964.

Baldwin, James. *The Fire Next Time*. New York: Dial, 1963.

——. *No Name in the Street*. New York: Dell, 1972.

——. *Notes of a Native Son*. Boston: Beacon, 1955.

Ball, George. *The Past Has Another Pattern*. New York: Norton, 1983.

Bates, Beth. *Pullman Porters and the Rise of Protest Politics in Black America, 1925–1945*. Chapel Hill: University of North Carolina Press, 2001.

Batsa, Kofi. *The Spark: Times behind Me*. London: Collings, 1985.

Benson, Peter. *Black Orpheus, Transition, and Modern Cultural Awakening in Africa*. Berkeley: University of California Press, 1986.

Bing, Geoffrey. *Reap the Whirlwind: An Account of Kwame Nkrumah's Ghana from 1950 to 1966*. London: MacGibbon and Kee, 1968.

Biondi, Martha. *To Stand and Fight: The Struggle for Civil Rights in Postwar New York City*. Cambridge: Harvard University Press, 2003.

Birmingham, David. *Kwame Nkrumah: Father of African Nationalism*. Athens: Ohio University Press, 1998.

Boahen, Adu. *Ghana: Evolution and Change in the Nineteenth and Twentieth Centuries*. London: Longman, 1975.

Boggs, Grace Lee. *Living for Change: An Autobiography*. Minneapolis: University of Minnesota Press, 1998.

Boone, Sylvia Ardyn. *Radiance from the Waters: Ideals of Feminine Beauty in Mende Art*. New Haven: Yale University Press, 1986.

Borstelmann, Thomas. *The Cold War and the Color Line: American Race Relations in the Global Arena*. Cambridge: Harvard University Press, 2002.

Braithwaite, Edward R. *A Kind of Homecoming*. Englewood Cliffs, N.J.: Prentice-Hall, 1962.

Branch, Taylor. *Pillar of Fire: America in the King Years, 1963–65*. New York: Simon and Schuster, 1998.

Breitman, George. *The Last Year of Malcolm X*. New York: Pathfinder, 1967.

Bruner, Edward M. "Tourism in Ghana: The Representation of Slavery and the Return of the Black Diaspora." *American Anthropologist* 98, no. 2 (June 1996): 290–304.

Burns, Stuart, ed. *Daybreak of Freedom: The Montgomery Bus Boycott*. Chapel Hill: University of North Carolina Press, 1997.

324   Carew, Jan. *Ghosts in Our Blood: With Malcolm X in Africa, England, and the Caribbean*. Chicago: Hill, 1994.

Carson, Clayborne. *Malcolm X: The FBI File*. New York: Carroll and Graf, 1991.

——, ed. *The Papers of Martin Luther King, Jr.* Vol. 4. Berkeley: University of California Press, 2000.

Clark, John Pepper. *America, Their America*. New York: Africana, 1971.

Clarke, John Henrik, ed. *Malcolm X: The Man and His Times*. Trenton, N.J.: Africa World, 1990.

Clegg, Claude A. *An Original Man: The Life and Times of Elijah Muhammed*. New York: St. Martin's, 1997.

Cooper, Frederick, Thomas C. Holt, and Rebecca J. Scott. *Beyond Slavery: Explorations of Race, Labor, and Citizenship in Postemancipation Societies*. Chapel Hill: University of North Carolina Press, 2000.

Cooper, Frederick, and Randall Packard, eds. *International Development and the Social Sciences: Essays in the History and Politics of Knowledge*. Berkeley: University of California Press, 1997.

Cruse, Harold. *Crisis of the Negro Intellectual*. New York: Quill, 1984.

Dei-Anang, Michael. *The Administration of Ghana's Foreign Relations, 1957–1965: A Personal Memoir*. London: Athlone, 1975.

D'Emilio, John. *Lost Prophet: The Life and Times of Bayard Rustin*. New York: Free Press, 2003.

De Witte, Ludo. *The Assassination of Lumumba*. London: Verso, 2001.

Diawara, Manthia. *In Search of Africa*. Cambridge: Harvard University Press, 1998.

Drake, St. Clair. *Black Folk Here and There: An Essay in History and Anthropology*. Vol. 1. Los Angeles: Center for Afro-American Studies, University of California, Los Angeles, 1991.

Drake, St. Clair, and Leslie Alexander Lacy. "Government versus the Unions: The Sekondi-Takoradi Strike, 1961." In *Politics in Africa: 7 Cases*, ed. Gwendolyn M. Carter, 67–118. New York: Harcourt, Brace, and World, 1966.

Du Bois, W. E. B. *The Autobiography of W. E. B. Du Bois*. New York: International Publishers, 1983.

——. *The World and Africa*. New York: International Publishers, 1987.

Dudziak, Mary. *Cold War Civil Rights: Race and the Image of American Democracy*. Princeton: Princeton University Press, 2000.

Dunbar, Ernest. *The Black Expatriates*. New York: Pocket Books, 1970.

Edwards, Brent Hayes. *The Practice of Diaspora*. Cambridge: Harvard University Press, 2003.

Ellison, Ralph. *Shadow and Act*. New York: Vintage, 1972.

Enwezor, Okwui. *The Short Century: Independence and Liberation Movements in Africa, 1945–1994*. Munich: Prestel, 2001.

Essien-Udom, E. U. *Black Nationalism: The Search for Identity*. Chicago: University of Chicago Press, 1962.

Evanzz, Karl. *The Judas Factor: The Plot to Kill Malcolm X*. New York: Thunder's Mouth, 1992.

Fabre, Michel. *The Unfinished Quest of Richard Wright*. New York: Morrow, 1973.

———. *The World of Richard Wright*. Jackson: University Press of Mississippi, 1985.

Fanon, Frantz. *The Wretched of the Earth*. New York: Grove Weidenfeld, 1968.

Fitch, Bob, and Mary Oppenheimer. *Ghana: End of an Illusion*. New York: Monthly Review Press, 1967.

Forrest, Leon. *The Furious Voice for Freedom: Essays*. Wakefield, R.I.: Asphodel, 1995.

Franklin, John Hope. *The Color Line: Legacy for the Twenty-first Century*. Columbia: University of Missouri Press, 1993.

Frazier, E. Franklin. *Black Bourgeoisie*. Glencoe, Ill.: Free Press, 1957.

———. "The Failure of the Negro Intellectual." In *E. Franklin Frazier on Race Relations*, ed. G. Franklin Edwards, 267–79. Chicago: University of Chicago Press, 1968.

French, Howard. *A Continent for the Taking: The Tragedy and Hope of Africa*. New York: Knopf, 2004.

Fuller, Hoyt. *Journey to Africa*. Chicago: Third World, 1971.

Gallen, David, ed. *Malcolm as They Knew Him*. New York: Carroll and Graf, 1992.

Gibbs, David N. *The Political Economy of Third World Intervention: Mines, Money, and U.S. Policy in the Congo Crisis*. Chicago: University of Chicago Press, 1991.

Gilroy, Paul. *The Black Atlantic: Modernity and Double Consciousness*. Cambridge: Harvard University Press, 1993.

Goldman, Peter. *The Death and Life of Malcolm X*. Urbana: University of Illinois Press, 1979.

Gosse, Van. *Where the Boys Are: Cuba, Cold War America, and the Making of a New Left*. New York: Verso, 1993.

Guinier, Lani, and Gerald Torres. *The Miner's Canary: Enlisting Race, Resisting Power, Transforming Democracy*. Cambridge: Harvard University Press, 2002.

Hadjor, Kofi Buenor. *Nkrumah and Ghana: The Dilemma of Post-Colonial Power*. London: Kegan Paul International, 1988.

Hanchard, Michael. "Afro-Modernity: Temporality, Politics, and the African Diaspora." *Public Culture* 11, no. 1 (Winter 1999): 245–68.

Hedgeman, Anna Arnold. *The Trumpet Sounds: A Memoir of Negro Leadership*. New York: Holt, Rinehart, and Winston, 1964.

Hill, Adelaide Cromwell, and Martin Kilson, eds. *Apropos of Africa: Sentiments of American Negro Leaders on Africa from the 1880s to the 1950s*. London: Cass, 1969.

Hine, Darlene Clark, and Jacqueline McLeod, eds. *Crossing Boundaries: Comparative History of Black People in Diaspora*. Bloomington: Indiana University Press, 1999.

Hodgson, Godfrey. *America in Our Time*. New York: Vintage, 1976.

Hoffman, Elizabeth Cobbs. *All You Need Is Love: The Peace Corps and the Spirit of the 1960s*. Cambridge: Harvard University Press, 1998.

Holt, Thomas. *The Problem of Race in the Twenty-first Century*. Cambridge: Harvard University Press, 2000.

326   Hooker, James. *Black Revolutionary: The Life of George Padmore*. New York: Praeger, 1970.

Horne, Gerald. *Black and Red: W. E. B. Du Bois and the Afro-American Response to the Cold War, 1944–1963*. Albany: State University of New York Press, 1985.

——. *Race Woman: The Lives of Shirley Graham Du Bois*. New York: New York University Press, 2000.

Houser, George. *No One Can Stop the Rain: Glimpses of Africa's Liberation Struggle*. New York: Pilgrim, 1984.

Hunton, Dorothy. *Alphaeus Hunton: The Unsung Valiant*. Richmond Hill, N.Y.: Hunton, 1986.

Hutchful, Eboe. *The IMF and Ghana: The Confidential Record*. London: Institute for African Alternatives/Zed Books, 1987.

James, C. L. R. *Nkrumah and the Ghana Revolution*. London: Allison and Busby, 1982.

James, Winston. *Holding Aloft the Banner of Ethiopia*. London: Verso, 1998.

July, Robert. *An African Voice: The Role of the Humanities in African Independence*. Durham, N.C.: Duke University Press, 1987.

Kalb, Madeline. *The Congo Cables: The Cold War in Africa from Eisenhower to Kennedy*. New York: Macmillan, 1982.

Kapuscinski, Ryszard. *The Shadow of the Sun*. New York: Knopf, 2001.

Kelley, Robin D. G. *Freedom Dreams: The Black Radical Imagination*. Boston: Beacon, 2001.

——. *Hammer and Hoe: Black Communists in Alabama*. Chapel Hill: University of North Carolina Press, 1989.

——. *Race Rebels*. New York: Free Press, 1994.

Kenan, Randall. *Walking on Water: Black American Lives at the Turn of the Twenty-first Century*. New York: Knopf, 1999.

Kilson, Marion. *African Urban Kinsmen: The Ga of Central Accra*. New York: St. Martin's, 1974.

King, Preston. *An African Winter*. London: Penguin, 1986.

Korstad, Robert. *Civil Rights Unionism*. Chapel Hill: University of North Carolina Press, 2004.

Krenn, Michael L. *Black Diplomacy: African Americans and the State Department, 1945–1969*. Armonk, N.Y.: Sharpe, 1999.

Lacy, Leslie Alexander. *The Rise and Fall of a Proper Negro: An Autobiography*. New York: Macmillan, 1970.

Ladner, Joyce, ed. *The Death of White Sociology*. New York: Random House, 1973.

Lamming, George. *The Pleasures of Exile*. 1960; Ann Arbor: University of Michigan Press, 1995.

Layton, Azza Salama. *International Politics and Civil Rights Politics in the United States*. New York: Cambridge University Press, 2000.

Legum, Colin. *Bandung, Cairo, and Accra: A Report on the First Conference of Independent African States*. London: Africa Bureau, 1958.

Lewis, David Levering. "Ghana 1963." *American Scholar* 68, no. 1 (Winter 1999): 39–60.

———. *W. E. B. Du Bois: The Fight for Equality and the American Century, 1919–1963*. New York: Holt, 2000.

Lewis, Rupert Charles. *Walter Rodney's Intellectual and Political Thought*. Detroit: Wayne State University Press, 1998.

Macey, David. *Frantz Fanon: A Biography*. New York: Picador USA, 2000.

Mahoney, Richard. *JFK: Ordeal in Africa*. New York: Oxford University Press, 1983.

Makonnen, Ras. *Pan-Africanism from Within*. New York: Oxford University Press, 1973.

Malcolm X. *The Autobiography of Malcolm X*. New York: Ballantine, 1973.

———. *Malcolm X Talks to Young People*. New York: Pathfinder, 1991.

Mamdani, Mahmood. *Good Muslim, Bad Muslim: America, the Cold War, and the Roots of Terror*. New York: Pantheon, 2004.

Marable, Manning. *African and Caribbean Politics: From Kwame Nkrumah to Maurice Bishop*. London: Verso, 1987.

Mayfield, Julian. *The Hit and the Long Night*. Boston: Northeastern University Press, 1989.

Mealy, Rosemary. *Fidel and Malcolm X: Memories of a Meeting*. Melbourne, Aus.: Ocean Press, 1993.

Meriwether, James H. *Proudly We Can Be Africans: Black Americans and Africa, 1935–1961*. Chapel Hill: University of North Carolina Press, 2002.

Mikell, Gwendolyn. *Cocoa and Chaos in Ghana*. Washington, D.C.: Howard University Press, 1982.

Miller, James A., Susan Pennybacker, and Eve Rosenhaft. "Mother Ada Wright and the International Campaign to Free the Scottsboro Boys, 1931–1934." *American Historical Review* 106, no. 2 (April 2001): 387–430.

Milne, June, comp. *Kwame Nkrumah: The Conakry Years, His Life and Letters*. London: PANAF, 1990.

Mobley-Sweeting, Ora, with Ezekiel Mobley. *Nobody Gave Me Permission: Memoirs of a Harlem Activist*. Philadelphia: Xlibris, 2000.

Morrow, Curtis J. "Kojo." In *Return of the Afro-American*. Huntington, N.Y.: Kroshka, 2000.

Moses, Wilson. *Afrotopia: The Roots of African American Popular History*. Cambridge: Cambridge University Press, 1998.

———. *Alexander Crummell: A Study of Civilization and Discontent*. New York: Oxford University Press, 1989.

Mphalele, Ezekiel. *The African Image*. London: Faber and Faber, 1960.

Murray, Pauli. *Pauli Murray: The Autobiography of a Black Activist, Feminist, Lawyer, Priest, and Poet*. Knoxville: University of Tennessee Press, 1989.

328   Naison, Mark. *Communists in Harlem during the Depression*. New York: Grove, 1983.

Nichols, Charles, ed. *Arna Bontemps–Langston Hughes Letters, 1925–1967*. New York: Paragon House, 1980.

Ninsin, Kwame A. *The Informal Sector in Ghana's Political Economy*. Accra: Freedom, 1991.

Nixon, Rob. "Caribbean and African Appropriations of 'The Tempest.'" *Critical Inquiry* 13, no. 3 (Spring 1987): 557–78.

Nkrumah, Kwame. *Dark Days in Ghana*. London: PANAF, 1968.

——. *Ghana: The Autobiography of Kwame Nkrumah*. New York: Nelson, 1957.

——. *I Speak of Freedom: A Statement of African Ideology*. New York: Praeger, 1962.

——. *Neocolonialism: The Last Stage of Imperialism*. London: Nelson, 1965.

——. *Revolutionary Path*. New York: International Publishers, 1973.

O'Brien, Conor Cruise. *To Katanga and Back: A UN Case History*. New York: Simon and Schuster, 1962.

O'Reilly, Kenneth. *Racial Matters: The FBI's Secret File on Black America*. New York: Free Press, 1989.

Padmore, George. *How Britain Rules Africa*. London: Wishart, 1936.

——. *Pan-Africanism or Communism?* 1956; Garden City, N.Y.: Anchor, 1972.

Platt, Anthony. *E. Franklin Frazier Reconsidered*. New Brunswick, N.J.: Rutgers University Press, 1991.

Plummer, Brenda Gayle. *Rising Wind: Black Americans and U.S. Foreign Affairs, 1935–1960*. Chapel Hill: University of North Carolina Press, 1996.

Polsgrove, Carol. *Divided Minds: Intellectuals and the Civil Rights Movement*. New York: Norton, 2001.

Powell, Erica. *Private Secretary (Female)/Gold Coast*. London: Hurst, 1984.

Prah, Kwesi. *Beyond the Color Line*. Trenton, N.J.: Africa World, 1998.

Présence Africaine. *Africa Seen by American Negro Scholars*. New York: American Society of African Culture, 1963.

Quaison-Sackey, Alex. *Africa Unbound: Reflections of an African Statesman*. New York: Praeger, 1965.

Rampersad, Arnold. *The Art and Imagination of W. E. B. Du Bois*. New York: Schocken, 1990.

Ransby, Barbara. *Ella Baker and the Black Freedom Movement: A Radical Democratic Vision*. Chapel Hill: University of North Carolina Press, 2002.

Raymond, Robert. *Black Star in the Wind*. London: MacGibbon and Kee, 1960.

Reddick, Lawrence. *Crusader without Violence: A Biography of Martin Luther King, Jr.* New York: Harper, 1959.

Richards, Yevette. *Maida Springer, Pan-Africanist and International Labor Leader*. Pittsburgh: University of Pittsburgh Press, 2000.

Robinson, Cedric. *Black Marxism: The Making of the Black Radical Tradition*. Chapel Hill: University of North Carolina Press, 1998.

Rooney, David. *Kwame Nkrumah: The Political Kingdom in the Third World*. New York: St. Martin's, 1988.

Rowley, Hazel. *Richard Wright: The Life and Times*. New York: Holt, 2001.

Saunders, Frances Stonor. *The Cultural Cold War: The CIA and the World of Arts and Letters*. New York: New Press, 1999.

Sayles, William. *From Civil Rights to Black Liberation: Malcolm X and the Organization of Afro-American Unity*. Boston: South End, 1994.

Schwarz, Bill, ed. *West Indian Intellectuals in Britain*. Manchester: Manchester University Press, 2003.

Sherwood, Marika. *Kwame Nkrumah: The Years Abroad, 1935–1947*. Legon: Freedom, 1996.

Singh, Nikhil Pal. *Black Is a Country*. Cambridge: Harvard University Press, 2004.

Smith, Ed. *Where to, Black Man? An American Negro's Travel Diary*. Chicago: Quadrangle, 1968.

Smith, William Gardner. *Return to Black America*. Englewood Cliffs, N.J.: Prentice-Hall, 1970.

Stone, I. F. *In a Time of Torment*. New York: Random House, 1967.

Stovall, Tyler. *Paris Noir*. Boston: Houghton Mifflin, 1996.

Sutherland, Bill, with Matt Meyer. *Guns and Gandhi in Africa: Pan-African Insights on Nonviolence, Armed Struggle, and Liberation in Africa*. Trenton, N.J.: Africa World, 2000.

Thompson, W. Scott. *Ghana's Foreign Policy, 1957–1966*. Princeton: Princeton University Press, 1969.

Tyson, Timothy B. *Radio Free Dixie: Robert F. Williams and the Roots of Black Power*. Chapel Hill: University of North Carolina Press, 1999.

Urban, Wayne J. *Black Scholar: Horace Mann Bond, 1904–1972*. Athens: University of Georgia Press, 1992.

Von Eschen, Penny. *Race against Empire: Black Americans and Anticolonialism, 1937–1957*. Ithaca: Cornell University Press, 1997.

——. *Satchmo Blows Up the World: Jazz Ambassadors Play the Cold War*. Cambridge: Harvard University Press, 2004.

Walters, Ronald. *Pan Africanism in the African Diaspora: An Analysis of Modern Afrocentric Political Movements*. Detroit: Wayne State University Press, 1993.

Warren, Guy. *I Have a Story to Tell*. Accra: Guinea, 1963.

Watts, Jerry, ed. *Harold Cruse's "The Crisis of the Negro Intellectual" Reconsidered*. New York: Routledge, 2004.

Webb, Constance. *Richard Wright*. New York: Putnam, 1968.

Werner, Craig. *A Change Is Gonna Come: Music, Race, and the Soul of America*. New York: Plume, 1999.

Williams, John A. *The Man Who Cried I Am*. New York: Signet, 1967.

330   Wolters, Raymond. *The New Negro on Campus: Black College Rebellions of the 1920s*.
         Princeton: Princeton University Press, 1975.
      Wood, Joe, ed. *Malcolm X: In Our Image*. New York: St. Martin's, 1992.
      Wright, Richard. *Black Power: A Record of Reactions in a Land of Pathos*. New York:
         Harper, 1954.
      ——. *The Outsider*. New York: Harper Perennial, 1993.

INDEX